NATION BUILDING

Princeton Studies in Global and Comparative Sociology
Andreas Wimmer, *Series Editor*

Nation Building

Why Some Countries Come Together While Others Fall Apart

Andreas Wimmer

PRINCETON UNIVERSITY PRESS

PRINCETON AND OXFORD

Copyright © 2018 by Princeton University Press

Published by Princeton University Press,
41 William Street, Princeton, New Jersey 08540

In the United Kingdom: Princeton University Press,
6 Oxford Street, Woodstock, Oxfordshire OX20 1TR

press.princeton.edu

Jacket design by Amanda Weiss

All Rights Reserved

ISBN 978-0-691-17738-0

Library of Congress Cataloging-in-Publication Data

Names: Wimmer, Andreas, author.
Title: Nation building : why some countries come together while others fall
apart / Andreas Wimmer.
Description: Princeton, NJ : Princeton University Press, 2018. | Series:
Princeton studies in global and comparative sociology | Includes
bibliographical references and index.
Identifiers: LCCN 2017009584 | ISBN 9780691177380 (hardback)
Subjects: LCSH: Political development. | BISAC: SOCIAL SCIENCE / Sociology / General. |
POLITICAL SCIENCE / Political Ideologies / Nationalism. | POLITICAL SCIENCE / Peace. |
SOCIAL SCIENCE / Research. | PHILOSOPHY / Political. | SOCIAL SCIENCE / Statistics.
Classification: LCC JC336 .W56 2018 | DDC 320.1—dc23 LC record available
at https://LCCN.loc.gov/2017009584

British Library Cataloging-in-Publication Data is available

This book has been composed in Adobe Text Pro

Printed on acid-free paper. ∞

Printed in the United States of America

10 9 8 7 6 5 4 3 2

To my father, finally

CONTENTS

FIGURES

TABLES

A NOTE TO THE READER ON
THE ONLINE APPENDIX

The two online appendix figures show, for each country, how the two main aspects of nation building have evolved over time: the population share of ethnic groups not represented in national government (measuring the political integration aspect of nation building) and the degree to which citizens are proud of their nation (referring to the identification aspect). The online material can be found at http://press.princeton.edu/titles/11197.html

PREFACE

I grew up in a small town on the river Rhine in Northern Switzerland, just south of the border with Germany. This border sometimes follows the river, sometimes trails off north of it, and sometimes circles around small enclaves of German territory surrounded by Swiss lands. The medieval patchwork of small principalities and ecclesiastical domains dissolved, from the 16th to the 19th centuries, into two nation-states without the wars that produced more clear-cut frontiers elsewhere in Europe. Hence the zigzag pattern of today's border.

As adolescents, we would pole wooden punts up the Rhine, looking for a riverfront clear of trees to make a fire, where we would roast a chicken or pork shoulder steaks, play Bob Dylan or bossa nova songs on the guitar, and drink cheap Chianti from a carboy. Sometimes we heard someone breaking through the woods making his way toward the shore; unsure on which side of the border we were, we would have to wait to see the guard's uniform to discover whether he was Swiss or German. The guards often came for a little chat and never asked for papers. While the World War II bunkers on the Swiss side of the river reminded us of a different and not so distant past, the national boundaries along which we grew up seemed to be rather irrelevant.

In many ways, this was also true of the ethnic boundaries within Switzerland. When politics entered the adolescent mind, it was never about the relationship between French, German, and Italian speakers who populate the different parts of the country. Had we been raised in Belgium, Canada, or Spain, it would certainly have been different. In middle school, we debated feminist, social-democratic, and conservative views, often quite vehemently. Later on, various Trotskyist, Maoist, Protestant Fundamentalist, and Hippie Christian groups appeared on the high school terrain—nobody cared much about ethnic identities, and certainly no one thought that any major political issue was related to our shared ethnic background as German-speaking Swiss.

The newspapers were full of stories about the results of the latest ballot votes—Switzerland is a direct democracy. But there was not much to report in terms of ethnic politics: not a single political party claims to represent one of the three ethnolinguistic groups, no political movements were in sight that would rally French or German speakers around a common cause, and everybody took it for granted that when a minister in the central government would have to be replaced, the overall balance between language groups would be maintained. Occasionally, there would be concerns raised and complaints voiced when national votes on ballot initiatives would coalesce along linguistic divides—French speakers usually voting in more government-friendly, less anti-immigrant, more Europe-oriented ways than the Alemannic- or Italian-speaking cantons. But the next vote would usually diffuse the situation with a different pattern of alignment. In short, ethnic difference simply didn't matter all that much in the political arena.

So much did I take this state of affairs for granted that it appeared puzzling, once becoming more aware of the outside world, that so much political conflict around the globe was fought along ethnic divides. What was wrong with Flemish and Walloon speakers in Belgium that they seemed to get at each other's throats all the time? How could Protestants in Northern Ireland think of Catholics as second-class citizens to be kept in check with the police baton? Why did Serbs in Bosnia fight a brutal war to join their ethnic brethren east of the Drina river that separates Bosnia from Serbia proper? Who in their right mind would ever think that a system such as apartheid, where the white minority ruled over the black majority like an internal colony, could be justified or work? Why didn't others simply deal with ethnic difference in a normal, that is Swiss, way?

Later on, this rather naïve puzzlement gave way to a more systematic search for answers. As a student of anthropology and later sociology, I wanted to understand why certain countries came together across ethnic divides, granting political representation in national government to groups small and large. Why did others not arrive at a similarly inclusive arrangement but resembled, in the extreme, the racial ethnocracy of South Africa? Why were others, like Belgium, at the brink of falling apart along ethnic fault lines? Why had still others, such as Iraq, already descended into conflict and war? Was this a matter of history—whether a country's diverse groups joined together voluntarily to form a common state, as in Switzerland, or whether one group had historically dominated the others after conquest, as in South Africa? Was it a matter of democracy—Switzerland's or India's long record of peaceful elections explaining why minorities have a say in national-level politics there? This intellectual challenge has kept me busy for two decades, and I have pursued it across the disciplinary terrains of anthropology, sociology, and political science, and with a variety of methods, from large-N statistics to fine-grained historical case studies.

A series of books have resulted from this endeavor, and this is—I hope—the last one in what has now become a quadrilogy. It addresses some of the puzzles left unsolved in the previous three books. In *Nationalist Exclusion and*

Ethnic Conflicts (2002), I argued that nationalist principles of political legitimacy—the idea that government should rule in the name of a nationally defined people rather than God or dynasty—radically changed the meaning of ethnic, racial, or national boundaries. New political hierarchies between such groups emerged to replace older forms of stratification such as estates. To show that this was the case everywhere around the world, I discussed a set of countries that had as little in common as possible: Switzerland, Iraq, and Mexico.

To be sure, the new lines of ethnic and racial exclusion differed dramatically, depending on whether political integration across ethnic divides succeeded: immigrants were excluded from basic citizenship rights where national boundaries hardened in the process of nation building, as in Switzerland; domestic ethnic minorities suffered a similar fate where less encompassing networks of political alliances emerged and nation building failed, as in Iraq and prerevolutionary Mexico. Modernity, I argued, has its shadow side: ethnopolitical hierarchies between nationals and foreigners or between ethnic majorities and minorities. These shadows were largely overlooked by classic and contemporary theories of the modern age that emphasized the universalistic and open nature of contemporary societies. The book also outlined some hypotheses of why nation building succeeded in countries such as Switzerland and failed in others, such as in Iraq. *Nation Building* follows up on this charcoal sketch with a fully colored painting.

The second book moved away from the macro-political concerns of the first and zoomed in on the drawing of national, ethnic, or racial boundaries in everyday life. *Ethnic Boundary Making* (2014) analyzed how individuals in pursuit of recognition and power negotiate with each other which ethnic, racial, or national categories should be considered relevant and legitimate. Depending on how much these individuals differ in terms of the power and resources they command and whether or not they can agree on who should be classified as what, different kinds of boundaries will emerge. They can be more or less politically salient, involve more or less discrimination, separate more or less similar cultures, and last for generations or dissolve quickly.

Rather than continuing to debate whether ethnicity is, as a matter of ontological principle, a primordial or a "constructed" phenomenon, the book argued, researchers should explore and understand this variation more systematically. A series of chapters showed how this can be done in empirical research, focusing on a variety of topics and deploying a series of different methodological strategies. The book did not, however, explain why some boundaries are marked by stark power hierarchies while others are not and why boundaries are therefore more or less stable over time.[1] *Nation Building* fills this lacuna by identifying the conditions under which ethnopolitical hierarchies emerge that stabilize ethnic differences over time, while in other contexts flat hierarchies encourage individuals to dissolve these boundaries during the process of nation building.

The third book, *Waves of War* (2013), returned to some of the macro-political arguments that the first had already outlined in broad strokes. Introducing the principle of national self-rule led to wave after wave of wars sweeping over different parts of the world at different times as empire after empire dissolved. Largely overlooked by mainstream research on conflict and war, nationalism is the main driving force of this process. Nationalism delegitimizes the ethnopolitical hierarchies of empire by portraying them as instances of "foreign rule." New states, now ruled in the name of the nation, emerged wherever the balance of power allowed nationalists to overthrow the ancien régime, often in violent wars of national independence.

Where postcolonial nation building failed, the leaders of politically excluded groups mobilized against the dominant groups in power, leading to secessionist wars or ethnic conflicts over who controls the national government. Newly established nation-states also competed with each other over ethnically mixed territories or over the fate of conationals across the border, sometimes leading to wars between neighboring states. *Waves of War* showed in detail, using newly assembled datasets that cover the entire world over long stretches of time, that transitioning to the nation-state is indeed a war-prone process and that the struggle against ethnopolitical inequality explains why. However, it again didn't ask why some newly founded nation-states were more unequal than others and thus more war-prone. This is the puzzle that *Nation Building* solves.

This book joins others in trying to understand modern society in its full historical complexity and its manifold manifestations around the globe. We authors often argue with each other, as is perhaps unavoidable in the rather acidic world of academia, where we most passionately disagree with those who speak the same theoretical and methodological language. But we nevertheless form part of a collective endeavor: to detach ourselves from our own struggles, visions, and hopes to gain a broader and perhaps more complete understanding of the historical forces that move humanity in different directions. Over the past two decades, social science research has begun to focus on smaller and smaller questions for which rock-solid empirical answers can be found, fleeing from the complexity of historical reality into the secure settings of a laboratory or toward the rare occurrences of quasi-experiments that the social world has to offer. Scholars concerned with macro-historical processes who dare to compare across a wide range of contexts find it increasingly difficult to justify their endeavor. I hope that this book helps to reinvigorate this intellectual tradition by showing a younger generation of scholars that its promise has not yet been exhausted.

ACKNOWLEDGMENTS

I began to work on these pages seven years ago. My thinking on the topic has been influenced by conversations with colleagues in the departments of sociology and political science at UCLA and Princeton University, most importantly Mark Beissinger, Rogers Brubaker, Miguel Centeno, Mitch Duneier, Miriam Golden, Evan Lieberman, Michael Mann, Michael Ross, Edward Telles, and Deborah Yashar. I also maintain long-distance conversations—occasionally crystallizing in lunch or dinner—with Laia Balcells, Nitsan Chorev, Dalton Conley, Yuval Feinstein, John Hall, Stathis Kalyvas, Matthias König, Michèle Lamont, Harris Mylonas, Violaine Roussel, Nicholas Sambanis, Gisèle Sapiro, Patrick Simon, Thomas Soehl, and Loïc Wacquant. I am grateful to all these friends and colleagues for their wise advice, frank critiques—often animated by what Ingeborg Bachmann once called "bravery before a friend"—and the intellectual companionship without which no work can flourish.

Most of the chapters were presented at departmental talks or conferences and profited from questions and suggestions from the audience. I would also like to acknowledge the research assistants I have had the privilege to work with over these years. The introductory chapter was discussed by a cohort of fellows at Princeton's Institute for Advanced Study under the leadership of Didier Fassin. Mitch Duneier and Andrea Puente offered helpful suggestions on how to make the introduction easier to read. Chapter 2 received valuable feedback from sociologists at New York University, especially Thomas Ertman. Sharon Cornelisson (Princeton) summarized and translated sources written in Dutch. Parts of Chapter 2 have been previously published in "A Swiss anomaly? A relational account of national boundary making," *Nations and Nationalism* 17, no. 4 (2011): 718–737. David Laitin (Stanford) was kind enough to point out some factual errors in the Somalia section of Chapter 3.

Chapter 4 could not have been written without the reading suggestions offered by Benjamin Elman (Princeton), Sonying Fang (Rice), King-To Yeung (California State University, San Bernardino), Han Zhang (Princeton), Stephen Kotkin (Princeton), and Henry Hale (George Washington). Sonying Fang and Han Zhang also offered helpful comments on the China section of the chapter, and Georgi Derluguian (NYU Abu Dhabi) read and richly commented on the entire chapter. Anna Kuismin (University of Helsinki) was kind enough to answer my questions about Finnish and Baltic literacy in the early 19th century. The China part of the chapter was presented at a seminar of the Ecole des hautes études en sciences sociales in Paris organized by the anthropologist Enric Porqueres and the historian Jean-Paul Zuniga.

As far as I can remember, Chapter 5 has been presented to the sociology departments of Brown, Harvard, Princeton, Stanford, Wisconsin, and British Columbia, the political science departments of UCLA, Yale, UC Irvine, and George Washington, the annual meetings of the Social Science History Association and the Analytical Sociology Network, and the Wissenschaftszentrum Berlin, the Hertie School of Government in Berlin, and the California Center for Population Research at UCLA. Stelios Michalopoulos (Brown) offered written comments on a first draft of that chapter, and Evan Schofer (University of California Irvine) and Wesley Longhofer (Emory) generously provided advance access to their data on associations around the world. I am grateful to Yuval Feinstein (Haifa University) for superb research assistance in assembling the literacy and railways data that we used for a previous project. Nicholas Pang (Columbia) worked on the dataset that records the wars fought around the world since 1400. Philip Ender from UCLA's Statistical Consulting Group patiently gave advice regarding the modeling approach. Dalton Conley (Princeton), Chris Winship (Harvard), and Nicholas Sambanis (University of Pennsylvania) helped me understand the logic of instrumental variable regressions. None of these colleagues are responsible for any possible flaw in the analyses. A previous version of the chapter was published as "Nation building: A long-term perspective and global analysis," *European Sociological Review* 30, no. 6 (2014): 1–28. I am grateful to the anonymous reviewers of this and a whole series of other journals where I unsuccessfully tried to publish the article before it found a happy home at *ESR*.

Aaron Gottlieb (Princeton) assembled the various datasets analyzed in Chapter 6. Sharon Cornelisson as well as the indefatigable Alexander Wang and Charlotte Wang (both Oxford) matched the ethnic groups listed in the EPR to the various survey group lists. Thomas Soehl (McGill) and Joerg Luedicke (StataCorp) provided advice on how to solve statistical problems. Andrew Gelman and Jonah Sol Gabry organized the production of the STAN versions of the models and Rayleigh Lei (all at Columbia) executed them. The chapter profited from audience comments and criticism at the Hertie School of Government (Berlin), the departments of sociology of Washington University, Tel Aviv University, Princeton University, and NYU Abu Dhabi, as well as the International Relations Program of the Université de Montréal. A previous version of this chapter was published as "Power and pride: National identity and ethno-political inequality around the world," *World Politics* 69, no. 4

(2017): 605-639. I am grateful for five very helpful reviews from the journal and the editors' guidance in how to address them.

Chapter 7 was presented at two conferences, one at Harvard and one in Barcelona, both organized by Prerna Singh and Matthias vom Hau, as well as the Ecole des hautes études en sciences sociales in Paris, where I stayed in the spring of 2015 as a visiting professor at the invitation of Gisèle Sapiro. It was published as "Is diversity detrimental? Ethnic fractionalization, public goods provision, and the historical legacies of stateness," *Comparative Political Studies* 28 (2015): 1407–1445. Daniel Karell (NYU Abu Dhabi) and Christoph Zürcher (University of Ottawa) directed me toward the relevant literature as well as the data on Afghanistan analyzed in Chapter 8. Daniel Karell generously commented on the relevant sections.

Finally, I would like to thank the team at Princeton University Press for taking such good care of the manuscript: my editor Meagan Levison for welcoming it to the press and for helpful suggestions on how to structure the chapters; Jennifer Backer and Joseph Dahm for precise and patient copyediting; Carrie Hudak for keeping the production process together and on track; and last but not least, three anonymous reviewers for their serious and engaging critiques.

NATION BUILDING

Introduction

Why Nation Building?

Why did some countries fall apart, often along ethnic fault lines, while others held together over decades and centuries, despite hosting a diverse population? Why is it, in other words, that nation building succeeded in some places and failed in others? This book shows how slow-moving processes unfolding over generations influence the prospects of nation building around the world. In places where centralized states had emerged long ago, citizens speak the same language today and can thus more easily forge political alliances across ethnic, racial, and regional divides. If governments have inherited a tradition of bureaucratic centralization they are also more capable of providing public goods and can therefore encourage their citizens to support the state politically and develop a sense of loyalty toward the nation. Finally, the early rise of civil society organizations enables politicians to knit different regions of a country into a quilt of political networks. Ties that bridge divides reduce the salience of ethnicity in politics, undermine support for separatism, make violent conflict and war less likely, and eventually lead citizens to identify with the nation and perceive it as a community of lived solidarity and shared political destiny.

Political integration and national identification thus form the two sides of the nation-building coin. To achieve both, it is crucial to forge political ties between citizens and the state that reach across ethnic divides and integrate ethnic majorities and minorities into an inclusive power arrangement. If citizens are connected to government through relationships of authority and support, an inclusive national community emerges and nation building can be said to have succeeded. Whether such ties emerge from democratic elections or through other political institutions is not of primary concern, I will argue. Conversely, not all democracies have succeeded at forging an integrated nation. The United States, for example, maintained slavery during the first 70 years of its democratic existence and politically excluded African Americans for another century after slavery ended, creating a lasting legacy of subordination and segregation.

This understanding of nation building diverges from that of most contemporary policymakers. After the US-led wars in Afghanistan and Iraq, experts in Western think tanks, governments, and militaries sought to craft programs that would foster national cohesion in a handful of years. They often used the term "nation building" synonymously with democratization (Dobbins 2003–2004) or even more generally with rebuilding states after the governments of faraway lands had been toppled by Western troops (see summary in Osler Hampson and Mendeloff 2007). The underlying assumption of much of this debate in the United States was that its government is entitled to overthrow threatening regimes around the world as it sees fit as long as it then "rebuilds" these nations in its own capitalist and democratic image and "teach[es] these peoples to govern themselves," as a well-known public intellectual put it (Fukuyama 2004: 162).

This book joins others (Mylonas 2012; Sambanis et al. 2015) in an effort to rescue the meaning of nation building from these debates and assumptions. It also arrives at a different set of policy prescriptions. As discussed in the concluding chapter, nation building from the outside, such as attempted in Afghanistan, Iraq, and Bosnia, is likely to fail if domestic conditions don't already favor political integration across ethnic divides. More to the point, public goods need to be provided by local governments, rather than foreigners, if the goal is to foster the political cohesion of struggling nations. Furthermore, the tectonic theory of nation building introduced here suggests that fixing failed states or building nations cannot be done within the time span of an American presidency or two. It is a matter of generations rather than years.

MODERNIZING THE MODERNIZATION LITERATURE

My understanding of nation building directly follows up on an earlier, now largely forgotten literature in the social sciences. Such eminent scholars as Karl Deutsch (1953), Reinhard Bendix (1964), Clifford Geertz (1963), and Edward Shils (1972) sought to understand the challenges of political integration faced by the newly independent countries of Africa and Asia. As I do in this book, they distinguished between the formation of nation-states and nation building. Creating an independent nation-state with a flag, an army, an anthem, newly minted money, and freshly printed passports did not guarantee that citizens identified with the nation or that they accepted the authority of the state. These scholars also distinguished between political stability and nation building. Not every new nation-state that remained peaceful did so because nation building had succeeded. In many newly independent states, autocratic regimes lasted for decades thanks to the ruthless repression of political opposition, rather than because they were able to integrate their countries politically.

The first generation of nation-building scholars also identified the conflicts that nation building often entailed and the obstacles it faced. Locals might resist a national government that intruded more into their daily lives than did its colonial predecessor. Political elites competed over who controlled the new center of power. Economic poverty, artificially drawn boundaries, the legacies of colonial divide-and-rule policies, and the weakness of postcolonial states made national political integration difficult. In order to understand how these obstacles could be overcome, this first generation of scholars dared to compare—in line with the classic tradition of historical sociology since Max Weber: lessons learned from 18th- and 19th-century Europe were swiftly applied to the developing countries of Asia and Africa, mostly in the form of broad historical analogies.

In justifying these comparisons, most authors relied on modernization theory. They thought that the introduction of modern bureaucracies, technological changes that increased communication and information flows across regions, and granting citizenship rights to the lower classes all transformed the way states related to their subjects, whether in Meiji Japan, Bismarck's Germany, or contemporary India. In other words, they saw nation building as a challenge that arose wherever modernity brought previously smaller and self-contained social units into closer contact with each other.

From the 1970s onward, Marxists faulted this school of thought for overlooking class exploitation within newly independent countries and their continued dependency on the centers of the capitalist world system. Proponents of the emerging rational choice school criticized nation-building scholars for not asking why self-interested individuals would engage in something as idealistic and lofty as "nation building." Advocates of multiculturalism accused nation builders of violating the rights of minorities and annihilating their cultures through forced assimilation (e.g., Connor 1972). Methodologists deplored the habitus of "armchair theorizing" and the tendency to cherry-pick examples that suited the argument, eschewing a more systematic and disciplined analysis of negative and positive cases. Soon, the topic was abandoned or subsumed under other strands of research, such as on civil war, economic development, or democratization.

This book revitalizes the earlier interest in the topic. Like the works of the first-generation scholars, it pursues a broad comparative agenda, taking us around the world and across centuries to wherever the model of the modern nation-state was introduced: the ideal that a country should be ruled in the name of a nation of equal citizens rather than in the name of God or a royal dynasty. This was the case in 19th-century Switzerland and Belgium, early 20th-century Russia and China after the end of empire, and Botswana and Somalia during the 1960s—the six examples discussed in detail in the following chapters.

Unlike the earlier generation of scholarship, however, this book precisely identifies the processes and mechanisms of political integration, rather than pointing at the abstract forces of modernization. And rather than collecting illustrative examples to support broad theoretical claims, it pursues the old questions with more analytical precision and methodological rigor. It uses three carefully chosen pairs of country cases to show how a particular mechanism fostering nation building operates in the details of the historical process. It then demonstrates, through the statistical analysis of large datasets, that these mechanisms are at work in the rest of the world as well. The book thus deploys a "nested methods" design, in which different research strategies combine to support the same theoretical argument (cf. Lieberman 2005; Humphreys and Jacobs 2015). If these different routes of empirical investigation lead to the same points of conclusion, this should increase our confidence that the hypothesized causal forces are indeed at work "out there" in the world (for a more detailed discussion of methodological principles, see Chapter 1).

THE IMPORTANCE OF NATION BUILDING

But isn't the idea of nation building rooted in the Cold War ideology? Indeed, the term was meant to suggest that the newly independent countries of the Global South could modernize to become as democratic, capitalist, and individualist as Western societies, rather than turn to the communist nemesis (see Latham 2000). More important, who needs a book on nation building now that we have entered the postnational age when more and more individuals hold multiple citizenships, migrate back and forth between continents, organize in transnational social movements, and create new, postnational identities fed by free-flowing streams of digital information and communication? In other words, isn't studying nation building passé? I see three major reasons why revisiting the question is necessary.

First, nation building brings peace and fosters economic development. In previous research my colleagues and I showed that a lack of political integration across ethnic divides often leads to civil war (Wimmer et al. 2009): armed rebellions spread in countries where a large proportion of the population is not represented and has no say in national-level politics and government. If the elites of marginalized groups can escape surveillance and recruit followers and if the state reacts to such initial mobilization with indiscriminate violence, armed conflict becomes very likely indeed (Lindemann and Wimmer 2017). Failed nation building, in short, is a recipe for civil war.

Ethnopolitical exclusion also inhibits economic growth, as shown by Birnir and Waguespack (2011; see also Alesina et al. 2016). Ethnocratic rulers favor businesses, economic sectors, and occupations that are dominated by citizens of their own ethnic background. They therefore choose policies that don't benefit the entire economy. Conversely, the success of the East Asian developmental states has shown that national political integration—rather than freewheeling markets uninhibited by government intervention, as the so-called Washington consensus once had it—is a key precondition for economic development (see also Rodrik et al. 2004).

Second, the topic of nation building is important because many societies around the world struggle with ethnopolitical inequalities inherited from the past—and not just in the Global South. Many successor states of the Soviet Union face the same challenges as the newly formed states that emerged from the colonial empires in the 1960s: regional disintegration, separatism, escalating political competition between ethnic elites, and so on. Recent developments in Ukraine illustrate the point. In many much older countries the question of national political integration now dominates politics more than ever, including in Belgium, Bolivia, Ethiopia, Spain, and the United Kingdom.

One should also note that few alternatives to national political integration are in sight. The European Union, once the crown witness of those who saw the coming of a postnational age, seems to have failed, as the Greek financial troubles and the subsequent refugee crisis showed, at "nation building" at a higher, European level. A sense of pan-European solidarity is hard to instill in populations whose visions of the world remain shaped by the nation-building projects of the 19th and 20th centuries. On a global level, the Internet has certainly created unprecedented flows of information and allowed new, postnational forms of identity and solidarity to flourish. Furthermore, national boundaries have become increasingly porous for elite migrants with multiple passports and marketable skills sought by global companies. But only 3% of the world's population lives outside their country of birth. More generally, politics remains tied to democratic legitimacy, which continues to be organized within national states. And so does the provision of roads and health clinics, the organization of military defense, and social security—even within supranational political units such as the European Union. The recent resurgence of nationalist political movements in the West therefore doesn't come as a surprise. The postnational age has yet to arrive.

Third, one can easily strip the term "nation building" of the ideological connotations that some may associate with it. Nation building does not mean modernist "progress" along a continuum "from tribe to nation" (Cohen and

Middleton 1970). It can be understood in less evolutionary and less teleological terms as extending networks of political alliances, whatever their nature, across a territory. A nation can be built on a "tribal" basis, as the example of Botswana will show. When studying nation building we also don't have to assume the perspective of nationalists who see history as a one-way road toward the fulfillment of the national project (see the "methodological nationalism" discussed by Wimmer and Glick Schiller [2002]). To avoid this trap, I will consider the counterfactual possibility that a nation-building project could have failed (or succeeded) or that other projects—perhaps focused on differently defined national communities—could have won out in the historical struggle. I will discuss at length, for example, that China could have fallen apart along its deep linguistic divides, similar to Romanov Russia, and so could have Switzerland. Nation building can be studied, in other words, without assuming that historically stable "nations" are the relevant units of observation or that success or failure is somehow predetermined by political destiny.

Nation building, as defined here, is also not synonymous with the forced assimilation of minorities by nationalist governments (as argued by Connor 1972), let alone with the scapegoating of minorities by chauvinist movements seeking to rally conationals around the flag. Quite to the contrary, political equality between ethnic groups is a key defining element of nation building, as we will see in a moment. Oppressing or even physically harming minority individuals shows that a nation-building project has failed—not that it is on the road to success.

One example may suffice to illustrate the point. In Ukraine, the rise of an independent, if short-lived, state after the fall of the Romanov empire was accompanied by signs of popular identification with the Ukrainian nation—propagated by the newly established nationalist government and army. This army funded the production and distribution of a postcard that shows a united Ukrainian nation, defended by heroic Cossack troops fighting both the Bolshevik and anti-Bolshevik armies during the Russian Civil War. During these years, the Jewish population of Ukraine suffered some of the worst pogroms of its history, many committed by these very same armed forces. In cases of successful nation building, such as in Switzerland and Botswana, there was certainly plenty of nationalist rhetoric and xenophobia as well, especially in the early moments of nation building. These were never directed against domestic minorities, however, and never reached deadly dimensions.

Maybe this is the moment to pause and briefly discuss nation building from a normative point of view. Given its role in preventing war and poverty, many observers see nation building in a positive light, and so do I. However, it is open to debate whether this means that we should embrace the political philosophy of "liberal nationalism" (Miller 1995; Tamir 1995), according to which nationalism is morally superior to other, more cosmopolitan political ideologies because it facilitates providing public goods such as peace, welfare, and a sense of cultural dignity. As I have argued previously, even where nation building succeeds and domestic minorities are integrated into the ruling coalition, we observe new boundaries of exclusion that are normatively problematic: non-national others remain outside this integrative realm of the nation and are systematically discriminated against (Wimmer 2002; Shachar 2009). Normatively speaking, nations remain as problematic as other political communities with strong membership rights.

I am also agnostic as to what the appropriate units should be within which to foster political integration. Should we advocate nation building in large and heterogenous states, or is it normatively preferable to have smaller and more homogeneous units? I haven't heard any convincing arguments why homogeneous states such as Korea, Poland, and Iceland should be preferred over heterogeneous states such as India, Tanzania, and Switzerland, even though nation building in polyglot countries is more difficult to achieve, as we will see. Studying nation building thus means neither to argue against secession nor to advocate for it. This normative agnosticism is supported by research showing that secession and the creation of more homogeneous states is not a recipe for future peace (Sambanis 2000; Sambanis and Schulhofer-Wohl 2009); nor are ethnically homogeneous countries more peaceful (Fearon and Laitin 2003; Wimmer et al. 2009). Similarly, large economies can foster growth as much as smaller ones more open to trade (Alesina et al. 2005). Small and large, heterogeneous and homogeneous—all states face the same task of political integration. This book seeks to understand under which conditions it *can* succeed rather than to argue how it *should* proceed in an ideal world.

The Argument

CHAPTER 1

To understand why nation building fails or succeeds, I assume what is called a "relational" perspective and combine it with elements of exchange theory. Seen from a relational perspective, ties between individuals and organizations form the core of a society. We therefore don't focus on the institutional rules that govern behavior, on market mechanisms that coordinate decisions, or on individual motives that drive actions, as in alternative theoretical perspectives. Instead, we seek to understand how political alliances form between national government on the one hand and individuals and political organizations—voluntary associations, parties, professional organizations—on the other hand.

I distinguish between three aspects of these relationships: how they are organized, what kind of resources are exchanged, and how partners negotiate and communicate with each other. For each of these, I identify a crucial factor that enables alliances to reach across regional and ethnic divides, generating an inclusive configuration of political power and therefore fostering nation building. Chapter 1 elaborates this theory in more detail. Chapters 2–4 show how these factors shape the historical process by analyzing three pairs of countries, each pair and each chapter illustrating one of the three mechanisms.

CHAPTER 2

The organizational aspect concerns the institutional form that political alliances assume. They can be weakly institutionalized, as when a vote is exchanged against the promise to implement a specific policy or when the political loyalty of a client is exchanged against the patron's support in the event of an emergency. Or they can be fully institutionalized, as in countries with strong, independent parties or with many voluntary organizations such as local political clubs, reading circles, trade unions, professional associations, and the like.

Such voluntary organizations facilitate building alliances across ethnic communities and regions, I will argue. They bundle individual interests, as it were, such that politicians or state agencies can respond to them more easily. In patronage systems, by contrast, each alliance needs to be managed separately: a patron needs to provide political protection or government favors to each of his clients on an individual basis. On average, access to government therefore tends to be more limited. Furthermore, voluntary organizations can build horizontal alliances with each other—such as a coalition of all local nursing associations of California—and alliance networks can therefore proliferate across the territory and across ethnic divides, generating a nationwide umbrella organization that can then be linked into a governing alliance. Patronage systems, by contrast, tend to spread vertically between more and less powerful actors and thus within, rather than across, ethnic communities.

How far such voluntary organizations have developed matters especially in the early years after a country transitions to the nation-state—when an absolutist monarchy is overthrown or when a former colony becomes independent. If a dense web of such organizations has already emerged, the new power holders can tap into these networks to extend relationships of authority and support across the country. Under these circumstances, it is less likely that ethnic minorities or even majorities remain without representation in national level government because voluntary organizations, from whose ranks the new political elite will be recruited, will already have developed branches in various parts of the country inhabited by different ethnic communities.

This is shown empirically by comparing Switzerland and Belgium in Chapter 2. In Switzerland, voluntary organizations—shooting clubs, reading circles, choral societies, and so on—had spread throughout the territory during the late 18th century and first half of the 19th century thanks to an even economic development across all major regions and thanks to the decentralized and comparatively democratic character of the political system. In Belgium, by contrast, Napoleon, as well as the authoritarian Dutch king who was crowned after Napoleon's demise, suppressed these associations. More importantly, Belgian associations remained confined to the more affluent and more educated French-speaking regions and segments of the population.

When Belgium became independent of the Kingdom of the Netherlands in 1831, the new rulers of the country were linked into these French-speaking associational networks. They declared French the official language of the administration, army, and judiciary. Flemish speakers were not part of these networks and were ruled, despite forming a slight demographic minority, as an internal colony until the end of the century. Early nation building failed; and the language issue became heavily politicized later on. The country is now close to breaking apart along the linguistic divide.

In Switzerland, the transition to the nation-state occurred after a brief civil war in 1848. The liberal elites who won the war and dominated the country for generations relied on the already existing cross-regional, multiethnic civil society organizations to recruit followers and leaders. The ruling elites were therefore as multiethnic as the population at large. Language diversity never became a serious political issue during most of the subsequent history of the country—and to this day.

CHAPTER 3

The political economy aspect concerns the resources that the state exchanges with its citizens. Citizens are more likely to politically support a government that provides public goods in exchange for the taxes, dues, and fees collected from them. The relationship between rulers and ruled is then no longer based on extraction under the threat of force—as was typically the case for the more coercive regimes that preceded the nation-state. The more a government is capable of providing public goods across all regions of a country, the more attractive it will be as an exchange partner and the more citizens will attempt to establish an alliance with the political center. The ethnic composition of governing elites will reflect such encompassing alliance structures and thus the ethnic diversity of the population.

This second mechanism is illustrated in Chapter 3 with a comparison of Somalia and Botswana. When Botswana became an independent country in 1966, its government efficiently expanded export opportunities for cattle breeders, extended roads across the country, constructed schools as well as health and sanitation facilities, and provided emergency relief during the periods of drought that periodically devastated the cattle economy. These initiatives profited all regions equally, and there was little evidence of ethnic favoritism in the distribution of public goods. Correspondingly, the ruling party gained support across regions and ethnic constituencies, which in turn translated into a parliament and cabinet that largely mirrored the ethnic composition of the population. This inclusionary power configuration then produced, over time, a strong identification with the state and the Tswana majority, into which more and more minorities assimilated over time.

In Somalia, conditions for nation building were less favorable. After the British and Italian colonies were unified into an independent country, there was little capacity to provide public goods to the population overall. The rapidly expanding bureaucracy was nourished by foreign aid, marked by clan and lineage clientelism, and endemically corrupt. Siad Barre's military coup changed this dynamic only temporarily. Given the lack of institutional capacity, his regime tried to provide public goods through military-style campaigns, such as when it sent all middle and high school students to the countryside to teach the nomad population how to read and write—rather than through a nationwide system of elementary schools. The government could not build durable political alliances across Somalia's various clans in this way. Barre based his rule increasingly on loyal followers from his own (and his mother's) clan coalition. Those who lost out in the power game resented this ethnic tilting of the power structure. Civil war, pitting changing alliances of clans and warlords against each other, soon broke out.

CHAPTER 4

The third aspect concerns how actors communicate with each other when negotiating political alliances. Establishing ties across regions and across ethnic divides is easier, I argue, if individuals can converse with each other in a shared language. This decreases "transaction costs," meaning the effort needed to understand each other's intentions, to resolve disagreements and negotiate compromise, and thus to build durable relationships of trust. In line with Deutsch's early theory of nation building, linguistic divides therefore tend to slow down the spread of political networks across a territory.

Chapter 4 illustrates how the communication mechanism operates by comparing China and Russia from the early 19th century to the end of the 20th. China's population speaks many different tongues, which should make nation building more difficult. But letters, newspapers, books, and political pamphlets are written in a uniform script. The very nature of this script allows speakers of different languages to understand each other with ease. Scriptural homogeneity also enabled the Chinese court, throughout the imperial period, to recruit its administrators and army officers through a system of written examinations which did not privilege any of the spoken languages of the empire. This in turn ensured that this elite was as polyglot as the population at large. Political factions among this literati class also contained members from all language groups, and the same was true for the anti-imperial, nationalist associations that formed in the late 19th century. After the nationalist forces rose to power under the Kuomintang and overthrew the imperial dynasty in 1911, the power structure therefore remained multiregional and showed few signs of a linguistic tilt. The same can be said of the Communist Party that took control of the state in 1949. Correspondingly, no linguistic nationalism ever emerged among the non-Mandarin-speaking groups of the Han majority. The Han were imagined as an ethnically homogenous and linguistically diverse nation. The dogs of linguistic nationalism never barked among the Han Chinese.

They did throughout the modern history of Russia, however, and the empire twice fell apart along ethnolinguistic lines: after the Bolshevik Revolution in October 1917 and again in the thaw of Gorbachev's reforms around 1989. In no small measure, I will argue, this was because it is difficult to form political alliances across a population that speaks and writes a great many languages of entirely different linguistic stock, from Finnish to German, from Russian to Turkish, from Korean to Romanian, and written in different scripts, including Latin, Arabic, Cyrillic, and Mongolian. When the age of mass politics arrived during the late 19th century, political networks clustered along linguistic lines because recruiting followers in a foreign language and script proved to be rather difficult. The mobilization of the Jewish population through Yiddish propaganda pamphlets will illustrate this most clearly. The popular parties that emerged during the late 19th and early 20th centuries therefore catered exclusively to specific linguistic communities, or they resembled patchworks of linguistically confined alliance networks. National consciousness became cast in dozens of separate, linguistically defined molds rather than in an overarching identity comparable to that of the Han Chinese. Soviet nationalities policy after the revolution of 1917 cemented this state of affairs by alphabetizing and educating minorities in their own language and giving them privileged access to newly formed, linguistically defined provinces and districts. This ensured that clientelist networks would form within these separate ethnic compartments. The integrated, multiethnic nation—the "Soviet people" that leaders of the Soviet Union dreamed of—could not be built.

STATE FORMATION AND NATION BUILDING

Looking further back into history, one wonders where a government's capacity to provide public goods and the linguistic homogeneity of a population come from. I will argue that they are both legacies of states already built before the age of mass politics arrived in the late 19th century and with it the challenge of national political integration. Where indigenous elites were able to monopolize and centralize political power, bureaucratic administrations emerged that learned how to organizationally integrate and politically control the various regions of the country. In the 20th century or after independence had been achieved, subsequent governments could rely on this know-how and bureaucratic infrastructure to provide public goods equitably across regions. Over the very long run, political centralization also encouraged subordinate elites and their followers to adopt the language (or in the Chinese case, the script) of the central elites, both to promote their own career and to lay claim to the prestigious "high" culture of the political center.

This is illustrated by the Botswana case, where the Tswana kingdoms had developed, in the precolonial and colonial periods, into half a dozen highly centralized and tightly integrated polities. After independence, these kingdoms were subsumed and subdued under a national government, which greatly facilitated public goods provision by the postcolonial bureaucracy. The centralized mini-states also promoted, throughout the precolonial, colonial, and postcolonial periods, the assimilation of non-Tswana populations into the dominant Tswana culture and language, thus creating a linguistically more homogeneous society. In Somalia's history, no centralized polity governing over the interior lands and its nomadic majority ever emerged. This represented a major impediment, as Chapter 3 will show, to postcolonial public goods provision. Centralized indigenous states, on which colonial rule often rested, therefore provided an important background condition for successful nation building because they left a legacy of bureaucratic capacity and a uniform language that helped establish ties across the territory of a country.

FROM PAIRED CASE STUDIES TO LARGE *N*

The three pairs of cases were chosen because they illustrate the three mechanisms in the clearest and most effective way. Switzerland and Belgium are similar in terms of geographic location, population size, and linguistic diversity but diverge when it comes to how far voluntary organizations had spread in the first half of the 19th century. Somalia and Botswana share the African colonial experience, are characterized by similar levels of ethnic diversity, and their economies were both based on cattle breeding. But the postcolonial government of Botswana was much more capable in providing public goods. China and Russia form their own centers of civilizational gravity, contain enormous, polyglot populations, and were never subjected to Western colonial rule. China's elites communicated in a shared script across linguistic divisions, however, while Russia's communicative space was fragmented by linguistic and scriptural diversity.

Quite obviously, these case studies don't allow us to see which of the three mechanisms is more important. This becomes evident as soon as we compare cases across pairs, rather than within them. Somali all speak the same language, while the Swiss are linguistically more diverse—and yet the two histories of nation building diverge in opposite ways. In Switzerland, the organizational mechanism seems to have "overpowered," as it were, the linguistic diversity mechanism. Does this mean that the organizational mechanism always trumps? Another cross-pair comparison shows that this is not necessarily the case. Compared to Switzerland, China lacked much civil society development up to 1911 and yet a similarly transethnic alliance structure emerged thanks to the integrated communicative space established by the shared script. In other words, the *ceteris* refuse to be *paribus* when we compare across a handful of cases only, a problem comparative social scientists have always struggled with.

Perhaps more importantly, other factors could be crucial for nation building but were not considered in the country case studies in any systematic way. Doesn't the colonial experience itself make a difference? Countries like Somalia and Botswana were subjugated to European colonial powers and shaped by their divide-and-rule policies, which could make the task of national political integration more difficult than in Switzerland, Russia, or China.

Alternatively, don't political institutions determine the prospects of nation building? Forging political alliances across regions and ethnic groups could be easier in democracies such as Switzerland, Belgium, and Botswana because their elites need to win the votes of a majority of the population. By contrast, the authoritarian regimes of Romanov or Soviet Russia, China, or Somalia under Siad Barre relied on narrower coalitions. Or perhaps we should focus on global processes and argue that governments are more inclusive if they are exposed to global ideas of multicultural justice and therefore seek to recruit elites from diverse backgrounds.

Or else, isn't nation building mainly a matter of economic development? Perhaps Botswana would not have been able to provide public goods so effectively without the discovery of diamonds in its sandy soils—while Somalia remained dependent on shipping camels and sheep to Saudi Arabia. Or is it easier to build nations in countries like Switzerland, where religious and language boundaries do not overlap? In Romanov Russia, by contrast, most linguistic minorities also adhered to a different religion than the Russian-speaking and Russian Orthodox majority. If that is the case, ethnic divides could become more politically divisive and nation building more difficult. Or perhaps we should take a more bellicist perspective and argue that nation building succeeds where countries have fought many wars with other countries, gluing their populations together through total mobilization for war. Similarly, it could be that European states had an easier time building nations because centuries of boundary adjustments and ethnic cleansings have led to more homogeneous populations that could then be integrated into a coherent national polity.

To answer these kinds of questions, the next three chapters shift to a different mode of analysis. They pursue the same arguments but analyze large datasets with information on almost all countries of the world, thus mobilizing the comparative power of large-N research. This will allow us to see whether some of these other factors indeed shape trajectories of nation building around the world. It will also allow us to determine whether the three mechanisms highlighted by my theory are at work in countries beyond Switzerland, Belgium, Somalia, Botswana, China, and Russia.

CHAPTER 5

Chapter 5 focuses on the political integration aspect of nation building. For a quantitative analysis, we first need to measure how far political integration has succeeded, how inclusionary the configuration of power in a specific country is. The Ethnic Power Relations dataset, assembled previously with a team of coauthors (Wimmer et al. 2009), offers such a measurement. It enables us to identify ethnic communities that are not represented at the national levels of government and to calculate the population share of these excluded groups.[1] These data are available from 1946 to 2005 for 155 countries—almost the entire world except some mini-states in the Caribbean, Europe, and the Pacific Ocean.

In the first step of the statistical analysis, I show that political integration is more likely where there are many voluntary organizations per capita, where governments offer many public goods, and where the population is linguistically homogeneous. To make the results of this analysis accessible to readers not accustomed to statistical research, I calculate how much the percentage of the excluded population would change, in an average country, if we reduced public goods provision by a certain amount, leaving everything else the same. We can then do the same for the number of voluntary organizations and linguistic homogeneity. Public goods provision will be measured by the density of railroad tracks and by the percentage of the adult population that is literate, which is strongly influenced by the public school system. The development of voluntary organizations is measured by a simple count of nongovernmental associations per capita. To measure linguistic homogeneity, we can calculate the chances that two randomly chosen citizens of a country speak the same language.

Figure 0.1 shows the results, which should be easy to interpret. Each independent variable is represented by its own column indicating how much political exclusion is reduced if we increased that independent variable by one

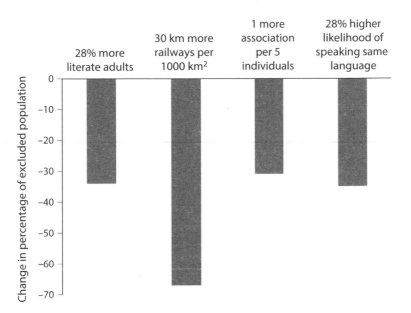

FIGURE 0.1. Determinants of nation building

Note: These figures are based on Models 1 and 10 in Table 5.2 and represent *z*-standardized coefficients.

standard deviation. A standard deviation measures how much two-thirds of the data differ from the mean value.[2] For example, increasing the literacy rate by a standard deviation of 28% is associated, on average, with a 30% lower share of the excluded population. As the figure makes clear, the associations between ethnopolitical exclusion and the three main factors facilitating nation building are quite strong.

I do not find much support for the other possible explanations of nation building briefly discussed above. While democracies are indeed more inclusive than nondemocracies, this is not because democracy leads to the political inclusion of minorities. Rather, exclusionary regimes, such as Syria under Assad, are less likely to transition to democracy and thus remain authoritarian. There is also little support for the idea that countries will fail at nation building if they look back on a long colonial experience; if they were subject to particularly divisive imperial policies; if they inherited a racial divide from slavery or settler colonialism; if they are economically poor; if they remained sheltered from global ideals of minority representation; if religious and language cleavages overlap; or if they look back on a long history of interstate wars or ethnic conflicts.

In a second step, I show that linguistically more homogeneous societies as well as governments capable of providing public goods were shaped by strongly centralized states that had emerged in previous centuries and, in the case of Africa and Asia, before Western colonization—another crucial element of the tectonic theory of nation building introduced in this book. To measure levels of state centralization I rely on two datasets. The first is available for 74 countries of Asia and Africa whose precolonial political structures are documented in the *Atlas of World Cultures*, assembled by anthropologists in the mid-1950s. This measurement does not make much sense for the settler societies in the New World, where existing indigenous states were dismantled centuries ago, or for Europe, whose states either remained independent or were incorporated into the Romanov, Hapsburg, or Ottoman empires many generations ago. The second dataset, collected by economists, covers 141 countries and measures the extent to which indigenous states controlled the territory of today's countries in the second half of the 19th century. This measurement is also meaningful for the settler societies of the Americas and the Pacific as well as for Europe. Statistical analysis then shows that countries that were governed by centralized states in the late 19th century provide more public goods and are less linguistically diverse after World War II.

A third step pursues history further into the past by asking where such highly centralized indigenous states came from. I will evaluate, in a somewhat more tentative way, some classical arguments about the rise of the territorial state, from Tilly's famed assertion that "states made war and wars made states" to more recent demographic and geographic theories of state formation. I find that the Tillyean view might very well hold for the history of Western state formation but not the rest of the world. Outside the West, countries with high mountain ranges and deep valleys seem to have developed centralized states perhaps because state builders were more successful where peasants could not escape them by simply moving away. Around the world, where population density was high enough to sustain a nonproductive political elite at the end of the Middle Ages, centralized territorial states emerged later on. With this analysis, we have arrived at causal forces such as topography and historical antecedents that cannot possibly be influenced by contemporary nation building. Put into social science jargon, they could be considered "exogenous." We can thus stop kicking the can down the historical road and avoid entering the dark domains of infinite regress.

CHAPTER 6

Chapter 6 focuses on the second aspect of nation building: the degree to which the population identifies with and feels loyal to the state and the nation. Nationalism should be more popular in states with an inclusive ruling coalition comprising majorities and minorities alike. Those tied into networks of exchange with the central government should find the idea of the nation as a family of lived solidarity and shared political destiny more plausible than those who are treated as second-class citizens without any meaningful representation in national-level government.

To explore this hypothesis, I have assembled, with a team of research assistants, a dataset based on representative surveys from 123 countries comprising roughly 92% of the world population. All surveys contain the same question: "How proud are you to be a citizen of your country?" I take this question as a rough indicator of how far an individual has internalized a nationalist view of the social world. By linking the ethnic background questions in these surveys with the list of ethnic groups in the Ethnic Power Relations dataset, we can ask whether excluded groups are less identified with their country, thus substantiating the overall argument with an analysis at the group level. This is possible for 223 ethnic groups within 64 countries.

In line with the exchange theoretic argument, citizens of more exclusionary states are less proud of their nation. At the ethnic group level, members of discriminated-against groups feel far less proud of their country and nation than do groups represented in national government. On average, discriminated-against individuals score 1.5 points lower than included individuals on a pride scale from 1 (not at all proud) to 4 (very proud). In a more dynamic analysis, I also show that groups that lost power recently are less proud than others because their exchange relationships with central government turned less favorable.

CHAPTER 7

Chapter 7 takes a side step with regard to the central line of inquiry of this book. It focuses on public goods provision as one of the three crucial factors enhancing nation building. A large literature in economics and political science maintains that ethnic diversity impedes the provision of public goods. Some authors think that this is because individuals can't cooperate easily across group boundaries, while others believe that they have a hard time agreeing on what public goods the state should provide. Seen from the long-term, historical point of view advocated in this book, however, the statistical association between linguistic diversity and low public goods provision is not brought about by a causal process.

Rather, *both* high diversity and low capacity to provide public goods emerge in societies without a historical legacy of centralized states, as argued throughout the preceding chapters. Chapter 7 shows this through a statistical analysis. Once we include a measurement of past levels of state centralization in the equations, the statistical correlation between diversity and public goods provision disappears. This is demonstrated with a series of different measures of public goods provision and a range of different measurements of diversity.

The chapter thus calls for revisiting the link between diversity and public goods provision and embedding its study into a longer-term, historically informed perspective. Overall, the book argues that a polyglot population is indeed less likely to succeed at nation building—but not because diversity is detrimental to public goods provision, as shown in Chapter 7, but because establishing political networks across a territory is more difficult if citizens speak many different languages (Chapters 4 and 5). Diversity, however, is not an "exogenous" variable outside the domain of human interactions, similar to topography, as many economists would have it. Diversity is not destiny, but a product of history. It is endogenously transformed and modified in long-term processes of state formation and nation building.

CHAPTER 8

The concluding chapter teases out the policy implications of the preceding analysis. If democracy is not an ideal recipe for nation building, what else can outsiders do to help bring a country's population together? Not that much, must be the answer from the long-term historical perspective established by this book. After all, historical legacies such as inheriting a tradition of centralized statehood cannot be manipulated after the fact. Furthermore, nation building takes time, if it is indeed driven by the three slow-moving forces identified here. In the postcolonial age, no outside force has the legitimacy or necessary stamina to wait long enough for political alliance networks to spread across a diverse territory. And finally, providing public goods from the outside doesn't help build such alliances nearly as effectively as when the national government offers security, education, basic infrastructure, health care facilities, and so on.

Chapter 8 shows this empirically on the basis of survey data from Afghanistan. Over the past decade, public goods projects by the Afghan government did indeed foster its legitimacy, led citizens to accept its authority for resolving local disputes, and encouraged them to identify as members of the Afghan nation rather than as members of an ethnic group or as Muslims. This offers some direct evidence for how public goods provision enhances nation building. Public goods projects undertaken by international NGOs or the American military, by contrast, were not nearly as effective as tools of nation building. Foreign-sponsored projects even increased support for the Taliban rather than reducing it as intended by the strategy of "winning hearts and minds."

These cautionary notes shouldn't lead us to conclude that nothing at all can be done. First, outside actors can channel resources through national governments, even though that might mean first investing in their capacity to provide public goods. International development agencies such as the World Bank have long focused on such capacity building and have become much better at it, not the least because in contrast to many Western governments, they don't follow a direct political agenda. Support for such organizations might therefore be one of the most promising ways to promote nation building in the Global South. Outside actors can also continue to support voluntary organizations that provide an alternative to ethnic patronage networks; and they can help finance strong public school systems that teach children to master a national language.

Second, political craftsmanship can help integrate a country's population, even if historical circumstances are not favorable. A statistical analysis in Chapter 8 shows that some states are doing quite well in politically integrating a diverse population even though they lack a history of political centralization, provide few public goods, govern over a polyglot population, or count only few voluntary organizations. Many of these exceptional countries were governed over long periods of time by skilled national leaders committed to an inclusionary nation-building project.

Third, outside actors can identify such leaders and support them politically. In some countries, political movements committed to the goal of nation building may already be fighting against an exclusionary, ethnocratic regime. Outside support for such political movements and leaders might eventually lead to a more inclusionary power configuration and thus foster peace and prosperity in the future. In most contemporary conflicts, *hélas*, it is very hard indeed to identify such political forces. Outside support or even military intervention, while perhaps expedient from a short-term foreign policy or security point of view, might not help nation building in the long run if local politicians are not already committed to the goal and capable of assembling a broad and inclusive coalition.

Situating the Argument

I conclude this introduction by comparing the overall argument to others that have figured prominently in recent social science research. The theory and empirical findings of this book can easily be represented in a figure (see Figure 0.2). The first half of the book illustrates how the main mechanisms shape historical developments in three pairs of country cases. The second half of the book uses statistical techniques and global datasets to identify the average effects of these mechanisms on countries around the world.

When comparing this work to others within the same broadly defined field, some differences in topical focus become apparent. Charles Tilly (1975) and a range of authors in his wake (Vu 2009) were interested in the rise of centralized states in the early modern period. Here I focus on its consequences for the prospect of national integration in the 19th and 20th centuries and on the mechanisms through which state centralization in the past influences

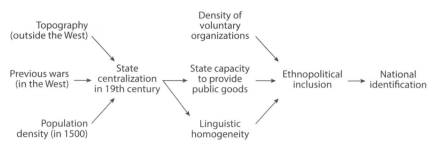

FIGURE 0.2. The argument in a nutshell

nation building in the present. Much of the literature on nationalism asks why it emerged in the first place and has identified major structural forces such as print capitalism (Anderson 1991), industrialization (Gellner 1983), the shift from indirect to direct rule during political modernization (Hechter 2000), or the role of intellectuals who recast ancient ethnic traditions into nationalist narratives (Smith 1986). In this book I don't ask why nationalist visions of the world emerge but how far they are subsequently realized and adopted by the population at large.

Other approaches to nation building focus on faster-moving, contemporary processes, such as the logic of coalition building between elites and their constituencies (Slater 2010; Roessler 2011) or the role of international actors such as rival states (Mylonas 2012). The theory of nation building proposed here highlights tectonic shifts rather than changing seasons. Relational networks evolve over the long run and relatively independent of global conjectures, international interventions, or coalitional politics, all of which reshape rather than fundamentally alter the course of political developments, as we will see in the case studies.

Some prominent theorists have examined how contingent events (Sewell 1996), transnational connections between political movements and states (Subrahmanyam 1997), or political leadership (Read and Shapiro 2014) shape historical trajectories. The six case studies certainly contain plenty of material to support such a view of history: Switzerland and Belgium were profoundly influenced by the French Revolution; Somalia's Siad Barre established deep ties to communist Russia; China's nationalists were inspired by European ideas that they received via Japan; Belgium's history would perhaps have taken a different path without Napoleon; and Botswana might not look the same today without its talented first president. But this book puts other, structural forces into relief that limit the range within which events, transnational influences, and strong-willed individuals can move historical trajectories. Political craftsmanship can enhance the prospect of nation building somewhat when these structural forces don't favor it, as mentioned above, but it does so within limits established by these forces. To put this into another metaphorical image, I am mostly interested in why certain parts of the world are covered with a certain kind of vegetation rather than with explaining the (contingent) movement of a particular group of deer through a forest.

Contingency also plays a crucial role in two popular books that seek to explain the "success and failure" of societies over long stretches of time. They merit a more extended discussion. Their empirical focus is again slightly different. Acemoglu and Robinson's *Why Nations Fail* (2012) is mostly interested in economic growth, while Fukuyama's *Political Order and Political Decay* (2014) seeks to understand why some states remain stable over centuries while others descend into anarchy. According to Acemoglu and Robinson, economies grow in favorable institutional environments: where individual property rights are secured and political institutions are broadly based and inclusionary. Capitalist democracies offer incentives to innovate and generate, through creative destruction à la Schumpeter, the economic dynamism necessary to sustain high growth rates.

Similarly, Fukuyama identifies three characteristics of stable states. They need to have political power and capable administrations: states that don't have bureaucrats can't do much, nor can states that haven't established a monopoly of violence throughout their territory. Governments should also be responsive to the changing views and interests of the population at large, not necessarily but preferably through regular multiparty elections. Finally, a stable state is based on the rule of law: disinterested bureaucrats impartially follow legal provisions without favoring their family, kin, or tribe.

Both oeuvres don't offer much of a causal argument but argue like recipe books: to have a successful society, they suggest, you need ingredients X, Y, and Z. But there is little analysis of why history, that grand master chef, puts certain ingredients into the pot of this society and other ingredients into that of another. Acemoglu and Robinson's views are more explicit in that regard: there can be no such analysis, they argue, because grand master History combines ingredients randomly, a view for which they received applause from fellow economists (Boldrin et al. 2015). To illustrate what a theory of history as pure contingency means, imagine a group of laboratory rats, each representing a different nation, running around in a labyrinth with scarce food. By sheer coincidence, some rats will eventually hit a door, squeeze through it, and find themselves in a good institutional environment with lots of food. The less lucky rats continue to starve.

This view only amounts to a true theory, however, if combined with a strong notion of path dependency: the openings through which the lucky rats squeezed would have to be one-way doors. But history is full of reversals, as Acemoglu and Robinson show. Early modern Venice had good institutions, but then bad ones emerged. Rome was on the right track until Caesar killed its proto-democracy. In historical reality, therefore, the doors in the labyrinth open both ways. Some rats are lucky enough to run through the door to institutional paradise, others never hit it, and still others find it but return through another door to the realm of scarcity. Nations "succeed" or "fail" at random, and we don't quite know why.

This book offers a more deterministic view of history. Not all rats in the lab are the same; some are fatter than others—to remain in the metaphor at the risk of overstretching it. The likelihood that the fat rats will run through the door leading to nation building is consistently lower than the likelihood that the slim rats will end up there. In more substantial terms, the chances that a society such as Somalia that was stateless in the late 19th century will end up with a politically integrated nation 150 years later are lower than in the case of China, which looks back on two millennia of state centralization. The next chapter outlines this theory in more detail.

1

A Relational Theory
and Nested Methods

Defining Nation Building

As with most other concepts in the social sciences, there is no consensus about the definition of "nation building." Most scholars agree, however, that nation building entails national identification: citizens begin to see themselves as members of a national community and feel loyal to conationals, above and beyond their attachment to an ethnic group, a tribe, a village community, or a religion. But here the consensus ends.

One strand of thinking emerged from Stein Rokkan's influential work (see Flora et al. 1999). In this view, democracy and the welfare state are important tools, but also important consequences, of nation building. This broad understanding can still be found today, for example, among American foreign policy-makers who focus on the democratization aspect (Dobbins 2003–2004; Fukuyama 2004) or among political economists who highlight the education, welfare, and infrastructure policies that support nation building (Miguel 2004).

Another strand of thinking sees nation building as a matter of power relations between citizens and the state. This is the perspective I assume in this book. It emerged first in the writings of Reinhard Bendix, for whom "the central fact of nation-building is the orderly exercise of a nationwide, public authority. . . . Some subordination of private to public interests and private to public decision," he continues, "is therefore sine qua non of a political community. Implicitly more often than explicitly, the members of a political community consent to that subordination in an exchange for certain public rights" (1964: 18–19)—hence the title of his often cited book, *Nation-Building and*

Citizenship. René Lemarchand pursued this exchange theoretic argument more explicitly. He suggested

> new perspectives from which to look at processes of nation-building in Africa: Viewed from the micropolitical perspective of traditional patterns of interaction among groups and individuals, nation-building becomes not so much an architectonic, voluntaristic model divorced from the environmental materials available; it becomes, rather, a matter of how best to extend to the national level the discrete vertical solidarities in existence at the local or regional levels. (1972: 68)

Similar to this book, in other words, Lemarchand understood nation building as a process of political inclusion through establishing encompassing exchange relationships between the state and its citizenry. National identification, in turn, will follow from such relationships as citizens will no longer define themselves primarily as members of a guild, a city, a village, a tribe, or an ethnic group and more as members of the imagined community of the nation, to cite Anderson's (1991) proverbial formula.

On both sides of the coin of nation building—political integration and identification—countries differ considerably from each other. In some places such as France, individuals have ceased paying much attention to their regional, local, guild, or ethnic identities and think of themselves primarily as nationals. Belgians, by contrast, think of themselves foremost as Walloons or Flemish, rather than Belgian. The same goes for the political integration aspect of nation building, as Figure 1.2 will illustrate. In some countries, large ethnic groups remain outside the alliance and support networks stretching from the seats of government down to the villages of the hinterland. In Syria, the Assad clan and their fellow Alawi have held a firm grip on all high-level government and military positions over the past several decades. Alawi are also dramatically overrepresented in lower-level government positions compared to Sunni or Kurds (Mazur 2015). In other societies, more inclusive configurations of power have emerged and most citizens are integrated into the web of alliances and support centered on the national government. Examples include Switzerland, Malaysia, and Burkina Faso—all ethnically heterogeneous countries.

To illustrate, Figure 1.1 shows an inclusionary and an exclusionary configuration of power. Nodes represent political actors (organizations or individuals), lines describe exchange relationships, and actors higher up in the graph wield more political power, with those at the top representing national government. Two clarifications follow from that. First, the same ethnic demographics characterize both countries represented in Figure 1.1: they are composed of an ethnic majority (the gray dots) and a minority (the white dots). This illustrates that ethnic diversity and ethnic inclusion are different concepts. Figure 1.2 shows, with data that will be more fully explained and

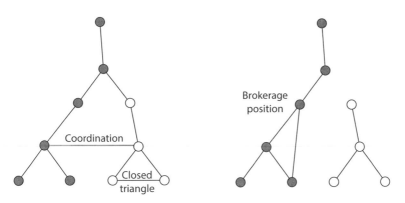

FIGURE 1.1. An inclusionary (left panel) and exclusionary (right panel) configuration of power

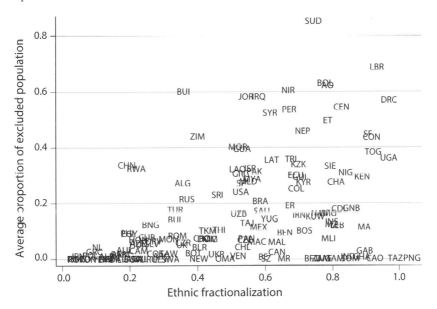

FIGURE 1.2. Nation building and ethnic diversity around the world, 1945–2010
Source: The data on ethnic fractionalization include religious and linguistic groups and are from Fearon 2003.

explored in subsequent chapters, that they also need to be distinguished from each other empirically. The y-axis reports the population share of the ethnic communities not represented at central-level government. It is a rough measurement of the extent to which nation building has succeeded (when the share is low) or failed (if it is high). The x-axis represents the ethnic diversity of a country—measured as the likelihood that two randomly chosen individuals share the same ethnic background: 1 in perfectly homogeneous countries and 0 if every individual belongs to a different ethnic group. As is clear from the figure, nation building and ethnic diversity might

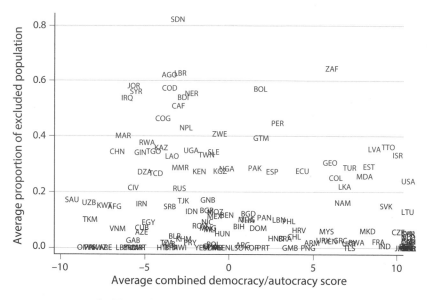

FIGURE 1.3. Nation building and democracy around the world, 1945–2010
Note: The data are from the Polity IV project.

be related to each other—as will be argued in detail—but they are conceptually distinct.

Second, political inclusion and nation building also need to be distinguished from democratization, in contrast, for example, to Dobbins (2003–2004) and much of the policymaking literature. Access to state power can also be organized, for example, through ethnic patronage networks within a one-party regime (as in Burkina Faso; Rothchild 1986). Fully democratic countries can be exclusionary (e.g., the United States until the civil rights reforms) and very undemocratic countries more inclusive (such as the Ivory Coast during the presidency of Houphouët-Boigny; see Rothchild 1986). This is shown in Figure 1.3, where the x-axis now depicts the degree to which the state is governed as a democracy. The scale ranges from –10 for total autocracies to +10 for perfect democracies. Countries that are equally democratic (or undemocratic) may have succeeded at nation building to very different degrees, as the figure illustrates. I will empirically analyze the possible relationship between democracy and nation building in Chapter 5. Here, I want to make the much simpler point that nation building and democratization need to be treated as distinct phenomena.

A RELATIONAL THEORY OF NATION BUILDING

How do we explain why societies differ so substantially in the degree to which they have politically integrated a diverse population and in how far that population identifies with the nation? Many political scientists (e.g., Diamond

[1995]) believe that democracy or particular democratic institutions, most famously proportional representation and parliamentarianism (Lijphart 1977), offer incentives for politicians to build large, multiethnic coalitions to win elections. Overall, this should lead to a more diverse governing elite that includes representatives of minorities as well. Others have pointed at the legacy of colonialism: colonial governments often recruited, as part of their divide-and-rule strategy, members of ethnic minorities into the bureaucracy, police force, or army. Examples are the Tutsi in Rwanda and the Tamils in Ceylon (Horowitz 1985: chaps. 11–13). These minorities then dominate postcolonial government as well, thus leading to starkly unequal configurations of ethnopolitical power (Chandra and Wilkinson 2008).

Other scholars think that globalization plays an important role. International organizations such as the UN, globally operating advocacy groups such as Survival International, and supranational bodies such as the European Union have set new standards for how to give minorities a political voice (Kymlicka 2007). Governments more exposed to this new global regime come under pressure to reform their house, grant minority representation in parliaments, reserve seats in cabinets for underrepresented populations, and so on. Exposure to the global minority rights regime should over time lead to more equitable representation and to a more inclusionary configuration of power.

Still other authors have looked at the calculations of government leaders who are interested in their own political survival. If they have good reason to fear that a coalition partner will drive them from the seats of power in a future coup or by calling elections, they may choose to preemptively push their competitors out of government. Exclusion thus emerges in environments where commitment problems within coalitions of ruling elites are endemic (see Roessler 2011; for other elite bargaining arguments, see Slater 2010; North et al. 2009; Acemoglu and Robinson 2006).

With the exception of the colonial legacy approach, these various theories all highlight relatively short-term factors and processes. Autocracies can be transformed into democracies, democracies overthrown in coups. Proportional rules of electing a parliament can replace majoritarian ones or the other way around. Elite bargains come and go. Countries might embrace a global minority rights discourse or, when a new government comes to power, reject it. The globally hegemonic culture itself changes as well, as the recent abandonment of multiculturalism and the rise of neo-assimilationism show (Brubaker 2002; see also Loveman 2015a).

By contrast, this book argues that long-term, slower-moving processes of political development are crucial for explaining ethnopolitical inclusion and national identification. Adopting a relational perspective,[1] it focuses on the conditions under which alliance and support relationships between state elites and citizens are more likely to stretch across a country's entire territory—and thus across ethnic divides. These far-reaching alliances, once institutionalized and taken for granted, will encourage individuals to identify primarily as members of the national community, and nationalist frames of thinking and feeling will sink into popular consciousness. The following pages explain how.

Nation Building and Political Development

I first lay the theoretical foundations of the argument, relying on exchange theoretic principles (cf. Blau 1986 [1964]). We can distinguish three basic and irreducible aspects of an exchange relationship between the state and the citizenry. The political economy aspect refers to the resources that they trade. The organizational aspect describes whether and how their relationship is institutionalized. The exchange of meaning and information between them represents the communication aspect. For each aspect, we can formulate a hypothesis that specifies the conditions under which we expect exchange relationships to cross ethnic divides, thus leading to nation building in the aggregate.

Public Goods Provision. Representatives of national government offer public goods and influence over political decisions, while nonelite individuals and organizations in return can politically support a government (including through voting), offer military services (such as in systems of universal conscription), and lessen their resistance to being taxed.[2] If states are capable to provide public goods, ruling elites represent more attractive exchange partners. More and more nonelite individuals and organizations (from whatever ethnic background) will want to establish ties with state elites, offering military, political, and fiscal support. In other words, nation building is easier in states capable of providing public goods (for a formal model of these exchange relationships, see Kroneberg and Wimmer 2012; for a related analysis, see Levi 1988).

Conversely, the rulers of less capable states will have to limit the circle of citizens whom they can provide with public goods—not every village can get a primary school if the ministry of education lacks the resources to pay teachers. Since in modern nation-states governing elites are supposed to care for "their own people," they will privilege individuals and communities of their own ethnic background. Public goods then become ethnic pork (cf. Fearon 1999; or "excludable club goods" in the terminology of Congleton 1995). Alliance networks will compartmentalize along ethnic divides, and parts of the population will remain disconnected from the exchange networks centered on governing elites.

Other explanations for the association between ethnicity and patronage have been proposed. Fearon (1999) maintains that ethnic markers are more "sticky" than signs of class membership—the color of one's skin or the language one speaks fluently can't be changed as easily as one's dress or car. This allows coalition builders to prevent too many individuals from joining a patronage network and diluting its benefits.[3] Thus patrons and clients rationally choose to build their relationship on an ethnic basis. Similarly, Chandra (2004) has argued that the ethnic background of individuals is more readily discernible from facial features, last names, or modes of speech compared to other types of social categories such as region, profession, or class. This enables voters to form a clientelist alliance when information on politicians' future behavior is limited and a vote based on a political program is therefore problematic.

Both arguments are plausible but cannot easily be generalized. To begin with, many systems of ethnic classification have a segmentally nested structure (a Hmong is a Vietnamese, is an Asian American, is an American; cf. Wimmer 2008; see Figure D.1). This is especially the case in Africa (Scarritt and Mozaffar 1999) where patronage politics is widespread (Bratton and van de Walle 1994). Under these circumstances, ethnicity cannot offer firm boundaries to limit a patronage coalition. Furthermore, in many contexts ethnic membership is not easily read off the faces or the names of politicians, and many ethnic patronage systems are not based on voting (see Rothchild 1986).

Voluntary Organizations. The organizational aspect concerns the different channels through which resources are exchanged. They can be of an informal nature (such as in patronage networks) or formalized into relationships between organizations (such as in coalitions between parties). Exchange relationships are more likely to cut across ethnic divides if they are built on networks of voluntary associations—clubs, trade unions, party youth organizations, choral societies, and so on. Ethnicity will be less politicized and governing elites more diverse. Why should this be the case?

Associational networks contain many horizontal "co-ordination" positions (Hillmann 2008) and many closed triangles (Baldassari and Diani 2007), as illustrated in Figure 1.1. Patronage structures, by contrast, are built on vertical brokerage structures (Gould and Fernandez 1989) and open triangles (the locus classicus is Scott 1972): clients connect with their respective patron, not with each other. Political alliances tend to spread horizontally across an ethnic divide when there are many voluntary organizations because it is easy to link coordinators of different ethnic backgrounds with each other. Conversely, patronage relationships spread from the bottom to the top, rather than connecting individuals of the same political standing. They therefore often form along rather than bridge ethnic divisions, making nation building more difficult.

This represents, quite obviously, a tendency rather than a law. In some cases, other organizational channels are used to build ties across ethnic divides. In Senegal, the religious leaders of Muslim Sufi orders (the *marabout*) established local patronage networks long before independence. These offered a grid of alliances that transcended the major ethnic divides of the country. The main parties of postindependence Senegal relied upon these grids to mobilize voters and form multiethnic coalitions (Koter 2013). In other cases, clientelism bridges, rather than reinforces, ethnic boundaries. In India, party clientelism sometimes trumps ethnic favoritism and leads to encompassing, transethnic networks of political alliances even though ethnic quota systems provide strong incentives to mobilize followers among particular ethnic constituencies (Dunning and Nilekani 2013; more generally, see Scott 1972).

But Senegal and India are rather special cases. In Senegal, the Sufi orders preconfigured political alliances in a durable way long before the advent of the modern nation-state. Such well-institutionalized and far-reaching networks are rare. India's caste groups are too small to effectively aggregate political interests at the national level. This encourages politicians to form multiethnic alliances within national, clientelist parties. The same could be said for other very heterogeneous countries such as Tanzania and Papua New Guinea.

Linguistic Homogeneity. The communication aspect concerns how actors exchange information about the resources they offer and demand from each other. Communication can be more or less costly. When individuals speak and write different languages, initiating and stabilizing exchange relationships is more difficult because it is harder to figure out what the other's resources are, what she demands, and what her intentions really are. This, in turn, makes it more difficult to trust each other (for empirical evidence, see Knack and Keefer 1997: 1281). When establishing ties and trusting others are more difficult, alliance networks tend to be less far-reaching and thus less likely to crisscross the entire territory of a country. Linguistic diversity, in other words, slows down nation building.

Deutsch (1966) already made this point more than half a century ago. He argued that successful nation building depends on an even "social mobilization" of the population and that such mobilization is hampered by communication barriers such as language differences. The chapter on China demonstrates, however, that a common script read in different languages may compensate for the fact that individuals can't understand each other when they talk. In the rare cases where such a writing system emerged, scriptural homogeneity can overcome the problems of linguistic heterogeneity. The same could be said of multilingual societies where every individual is also fully fluent in a lingua franca. Communicative barriers therefore don't always assume the form of language boundaries, but they most often do.

Maybe this is a good moment to pause and compare this argument with other, related approaches to how linguistic diversity relates to national integration. In Benedict Anderson's famed account of the emergence of nations as imagined communities, mass literacy in vernacular languages plays a crucial role. The emerging reading public shared a narrative cosmos, established by newspapers, books, and pamphlets written in a popular idiom, and soon imagined itself as a community of common origin and future political destiny (Anderson 1991: chap. 3). By implication, language heterogeneity will make it more difficult to create a uniform nation—quite in line with my own argument.

Anderson also foresees a second mechanism to explain why there is no single Spanish-speaking state in Latin America and why the attempt to create a single French-speaking state in Western Africa failed even though literacy in Spanish or French should have made imagining these two mega-communities easy. But the political horizon of indigenous, low-level bureaucrats was limited to a particular province of the Spanish or French empire. Their careers were confined to the colonial territory that later became Mexico, for example, and they never met colleagues from Buenos Aires or La Paz. They therefore imagined provinces as nations, rather than the entire realms of Spanish America or French West Africa.

Compared to Anderson's, my political network approach offers a more parsimonious explanation of why national identities sometimes align with language boundaries and sometimes not. The reach of political alliance networks—rather than communication in a shared language per se—turns out to be crucial. Where these networks were confined by political boundaries such as imperial provinces, nationalists divided the space of a shared language, as in Latin America. Where language barriers within imperial domains hampered the establishment of such ties, linguistic communities were imagined as nations. This is what happened in Romanov Russia. Where civil societies flourished early, as in Switzerland, or where states were exceptionally capable at providing public goods, political networks stretched across ethnic divides and the nation was imagined as polyglot. In other words, the contours of political alliance networks determine which communities will emerge as nations.

Keith Darden's book (2013) deserves a brief discussion here as well. He also relates mass literacy to nationalism but in a different way than Anderson. Focusing on Eastern Europe and Russia, he argues that a population will stick to the national identity inculcated in its collective consciousness when it was first alphabetized. Mass schooling and literacy are not devoid of political content, he argues, but carry a particular nationalist vision of the world. This nationalist narrative is then handed down within families from generation to generation and cannot be changed subsequently by school curricula written in a different nationalist spirit. Ukrainians first schooled by Ukrainian nationalists in the Austro-Hungarian Empire, he shows, developed and maintained a Ukrainian national consciousness, while Ukrainians indoctrinated with pan-Russian nationalism became Russians. The implication, then, is that nation building will be more successful if the entire population is schooled in the same curriculum with the same underlying nationalist message, irrespective of the actual languages spoken by the population.

I would like to give this argument a different twist, relating it back to the first mechanism of nation building discussed above. Alphabetizing an illiterate and polyglot population demands considerable state capacity, as the literacy campaigns undertaken in the Soviet Union, China, and other communist states have shown. It may well be that individuals are loyal to such states and identify with their nationalist projects because they received public goods—rather than because of the nationalist indoctrination.

In line with Darden's argument—and against overly constructivist theories of national identity—once a population has identified with a modern nation-state and its nationalist project, their identities will indeed be difficult to change subsequently. I would submit, however, that assimilating into another nation is not impossible, as Darden sees it. Successor states that are even more successful at delivering public goods might very well gain, over the long run, the loyalty of a population that previously had identified with another national community. Yugoslavs became Serbs or Croats; Germans educated in the German-speaking schools of Pennsylvania or Wisconsin assimilated into the American mainstream after World War I.

State Centralization before Nation Building

To sum up the argument made so far: high state capacity to deliver public goods, well-developed voluntary organizations, and low communicative barriers allow networks of political alliances between rulers and ruled to spread across a territory. In Chapter 5, I will evaluate empirically whether the causal arrow might point in the other direction as well: that nation building provides a fertile ground for the flourishing of voluntary organizations and enhances public goods provision as well as assimilation into a shared language. For now, I leave this complication on the side and instead push the analysis further back into history.

How can we explain why different societies, once they achieve national independence, are already more or less linguistically homogeneous, harbor many or few voluntary organizations, and diverge in their state's capacity to provide public goods? I argue that both linguistic homogeneity and the capacity to provide public goods are influenced by whether or not a centralized state has already emerged before nation building is attempted. For the postcolonial world, this refers to the indigenous states that ruled many of these lands before they were conquered by Western powers or Japan (in line with Englebert 2000; Bockstette et al. 2002; Gennaioli and Rainer 2007). For Europe, the settler colonies of the New World, the Ottoman domains, as well as Japan and China, this refers to how centralized states were around 1875, shortly before the masses of citizens were brought into the political arena and nation building became the order of the day. Historical levels of state building have not influenced, however, the third condition facilitating nation building: the development of voluntary organizations. On the one hand, voluntary organizations often mushroomed as a reaction to an ever more intrusive, expanding state, as was the case in many absolutist regimes in western Europe during the 18th century (Mann 1993). In many other cases, however, strongly centralized states effectively suppressed such organizations. This was the case in imperial China and Russia as well as Belgium under French and Dutch rule, as we will see. The two historical tendencies thus cancel each other out, in the aggregate and on average. Therefore, no clear association between previous state centralization and contemporary civil society emerges.

Why did the centralized states of the 19th century leave a legacy of linguistic homogeneity after World War II? They disempowered and integrated local political elites and encouraged them to adopt the language of the dominant groups and to eventually assimilate into the *Staatsvolk*. Ordinary citizens also learned the dominant language in order to communicate more easily with state officials, to demand services, participation, and recognition more effectively, or to become civil servants themselves. The stronger the capacity of the state to interfere in the daily lives of its citizens, the more likely a uniform linguistic landscape will eventually emerge.[4]

From a long-term historical perspective, therefore, linguistic diversity is not exogenously given but results from slow-moving, generation-spanning processes of assimilation and dissimilation. Following recent arguments in sociology, we expect that religious or racial differences are more resistant to such assimilation. Religion is more closely associated with specific cultural norms and practices and thus more costly to change than a language or a script (Brubaker 2013). Racial appearance cannot be changed at the individual level. For racial minorities to become incorporated into the dominant groups, therefore, the racial classification system itself has to change by reinterpreting which phenotypical features are seen as prototypical for which racial group (see Loveman and Muniz 2006). We thus expect state building to erode language diversity more so than religious or racial diversity (a point to which I briefly return in Chapter 7).

In France, to give an example of the process I have in mind, the king had started to extend a uniform and integrated bureaucracy, personified by the royal intendant, in the 17th century. Under the Third Republic during the last quarter of the 19th century, the state took over many tasks previously assumed by the church or local communities. Paris now mandated and financed public schooling for the entire population, new hospitals for the poor and sick, policing in every commune of the country, and so on (for details, see the online appendix to Kroneberg and Wimmer 2012). As a result of this increased centralization and bureaucratization of the state, as Eugen Weber (1979) has shown in a seminal historical study, fewer and fewer speakers of minority languages identified primarily as Provençale, Aquitaine, Occidental, and so forth rather than as French. And fewer and fewer were able to speak these languages after having been schooled in French and conscripted into an army commanded in standard French.[5]

Contrast this with mainland Tanzania, where no political entity above the level of village clusters and tribal segments ever emerged. The Arab sultans of the island of Zanzibar militarily dominated the mainland from the early 18th century onward. Its slave raiders operated throughout the area, but the sultanate never administered the inland population directly. By the end of the 19th century, during the period of the Third Republic in France, Tanzania had come under German rule. The colonial power controlled the territory by military force rather than by building a strong state infrastructure. Conformingly, Tanzania today remains one of the most linguistically heterogeneous countries of the world.

But didn't colonialism, such as German and later British rule in Tanzania, profoundly alter the ethnolinguistic landscape in Africa and Asia, most of which was incorporated into Western or Japanese empires by the late 19th century? Linguistic diversity rarely increased during the colonial period but was maintained or further reduced even where the colonial rulers destroyed precolonial states such as traditional kingdoms (on the Matabele in colonial Rhodesia, see Ranger 1966; on the Bakongo in Congo, see Lemarchand 1964: 193–194). More often, precolonial kingdoms were incorporated into the colonial state and they continued to assimilate smaller groups within their domains (this was the case in Botswana, as we will see). Where no such states existed previously, smaller ethnic groups often fused with larger ones in order to compete more effectively for power and status in the new political arena established by colonial governments (Peel 1989; on the Fang of Gabon and Cameroon, see Fernandez 1966). This was often enhanced by the colonial policy of bringing smaller, precolonial political communities into larger administrative entities within which assimilation processes then unfolded (see the "montagnards" in the highlands of Vietnam described by Tefft [1999]; on the Katanga, see Young 1965). Elsewhere, missionaries standardized and homogenized similar languages, thus also fostering linguistic homogenization (on the Tsonga in South Africa, see Harries 1989). Finally, migrants within colonial labor markets often learned the language of local majorities.[6]

In short, processes of homogenization during the colonial period either remained strongly influenced by precolonial states or accelerated through colonial policies, especially where imperial rule took on more direct, interventionist forms (on colonial styles, see Young 1994). The choice between indirect and direct rule, however, was again shaped by precolonial political realities. As Gerring and coauthors (2011) have shown, colonizers ruled more indirectly where they encountered centralized indigenous states. Colonial government, and thus the degree to which it fostered linguistic homogenization, was therefore profoundly influenced by precolonial political realities (but see, for Latin America, Mahoney 2010). As will be shown (see Table E.4), neither the duration nor the style of colonial rule are therefore systematically associated with how linguistically diverse countries are today.

In the Americas and the Pacific, indigenous states generally did not survive European colonization. The descendants of settlers entirely dominated the independent states founded in the late 18th and early 19th centuries. In East Asia and Europe, most states either remained independent (such as France or Japan) or had for many generations formed part of the land-based Hapsburg, Ottoman, or Romanov empires. The degree to which these independent states or the indigenous elites of imperial provinces had managed to monopolize political power and extend bureaucratic rule into the hinterland greatly influenced the process of linguistic homogenization. This can be observed in the independent states of the 19th century Americas (for Mexico, see Wimmer 1995, chapter 5) and Western Europe (as in the French case discussed above) as well as in the Hapsburg, Ottoman, and Romanov provinces before World War I. If these provinces were ruled by strongly centralized provincial governments under indigenous control, as Congress Poland before the policy of Russification set in (see Chapter 5), linguistic minorities (such as Ukrainian and Lithuanian speakers in the example at hand) gradually adopted the language of the ruling elites.

Centralizing states not only assimilated the population into a dominant language, but also left a bureaucratic and infrastructural legacy that made it easier for nation builders to provide public goods. Communist China, for example, looks back on a history of 2,000 years of bureaucratic state making, administrative centralization, and effective intervention in the daily life of ordinary subjects. This tradition greatly facilitated the task of providing public goods to the peasant masses once Mao and his followers had consolidated power. In Zaire, by contrast, the departing Belgian colonial administration, after having destroyed the small indigenous kingdoms of the interior and the coast, took everything with them—from the knowledge of how to organize a state all the way to the typewriters. There was neither the physical infrastructure nor the human capital or organizational knowledge for the independent state to provide its citizenry with even a minimal level of public services.

In many other cases in Africa and Asia, centralized precolonial states were reshaped and incorporated into the colonial administration (as we will see in the Botswana case study). As already discussed, the colonial state sometimes modified the functioning of precolonial polities in profound ways. But the state itself often adapted to and was molded by precolonial political realities and rarely completely undid what state building had been achieved before colonial conquest. While traditional states, where they survived the colonial period, sometimes competed with postcolonial governments for power and legitimacy, their deep roots in the local society made it easier for a national government to extend its authority all over the territory because the population was already accustomed to political hierarchy and bureaucratic rule and because the government could tap into a class of indigenous bureaucratic and political elites to staff the emerging administration. All of this made it easier to provide public goods in an effective and equitable way (for African evidence of such path dependency, see Gennaioli and Rainer 2007).[7] By contrast and as will be briefly discussed in Chapter 7, the duration and style of colonial rule had a more limited impact on the capacity of the postcolonial state to deliver public goods.

In China and Japan, the settler societies of the Americas and the Pacific as well as in Europe, the degree to which by the end of the 19th century political power was centralized in the hands of national or (in the case of the Hapsburg and Romanov empires) provincial elites and the degree to which they had established functioning bureaucracies influenced how far the successor governments were able to provide public goods after World War II. Compared to the former colonies of Africa and Asia, there is more continuity of state building in China and Japan, the Americas, and Western Europe from the 19th century onward. The path dependency mechanism thus operates in a more straightforward way. In short, historically achieved levels of state centralization facilitate contemporary public goods provision by leaving physical infrastructure, the know-how to run a bureaucracy, a stratum of people dedicated to serve the state, and a population used to being governed from a distant capital.

Determinants of State Centralization

According to the argument developed thus far, the historical states that had emerged by the 19th century enhanced nation building after World War II by leaving a legacy of bureaucratic capacity and control as well as a lingua franca in which political alliances could be negotiated across faraway regions. This raises the crucial question of why such states emerged in some places (China) but not others (Tanzania). To find an answer, we need to push the analysis further into the past and highlight factors that are exogenous to the history of state formation itself. In other words, we are looking for state-enabling conditions that are not in turn influenced by the process of state centralization. In the context of this broad-stroke argument, I will therefore stay away from historically more specific theories of state formation such as the one offered by Ertman (1997). If we can identify some factors that are "exogenous" to the formation of states, we can avoid the danger of infinite historical regress where the present is explained by the immediate past, which in turn is explained by the immediate past of the immediate past, et cetera ad infinitum.

Some of the most important arguments put forward in the literature come to mind, two of which highlight endogenous factors, however. First, anthropologists and historians have long argued that only economies based on agriculture or cattle herding are able to sustain a nonproductive state elite, while hunter-gatherers lack the surplus to do so (for a recent revival of this argument, see Boix 2015). As the irrigation agricultures in Mesopotamia, Egypt, and China show, there might be a "positive feedback" loop between state building and agriculture, as some states organized large hydraulic schemes that led to further intensification of agriculture. Second, Tilly (1975) famously argued that war making and state building go hand in hand, a fact well captured by his dictum that "wars made states and states made war." States extracted resources from their population to survive wars with neighboring states, while successful resource extraction and thus state building allowed them to wage more expensive wars with larger and better-equipped armies. The relationship between war and state making is therefore endogenous, assuming the form of a self-reinforcing feedback loop.

We are therefore more interested, in the context of this book, with the following three exogenous factors—though I will try, in Chapter 5, to empirically evaluate the above two arguments as well. First, Carneiros (1970) identified "environmental conscription" as a condition for the rise of the premodern agrarian state. Such "conscription" by mountain ranges (as in highland Mexico, where the Aztec state emerged) or deserts (as in Iraq, the center of ancient Babylonia) prevented the population from easily escaping the control of state builders.

Second, state formation could also be affected by climate, in line with environmentalist arguments that have recently resurged in geography and in the economic development literature (Diamond 1997; Sachs 2003). Hot temperatures and the prevalence of debilitating diseases make it more difficult to build states near the equator. Indeed, recent research has shown that such geographic conditions influence economic growth indirectly—because countries closer to the equator are governed by less well-developed states (Rodrik et al. 2004). Third, Herbst (2000) argued that low population densities, among other factors, explain why few large-scale states emerged in Africa. When people are scarce, it is obviously more difficult to extract sufficient economic surplus to nourish a standing army and a class of professional bureaucrats.

To sum up, the theory outlined above emphasizes long-term processes of political development that started well before the colonial era and the advent of nation-states. It moves from exogenous factors such as topography, climate, and population density to the slowly evolving institutions of the state, to three more temporally proximate factors: organizational density, public goods capacity, and communicative homogeneity. These then enable political alliances to spread across ethnic divides in the contemporary period of independent nation-states. In turn, such cross-ethnic alliances encourage individuals to identify more strongly with the nation.

NESTED METHODS

A Note on Temporality

Which methodological strategy is most appropriate, and what kind of empirical data do we need to substantiate this theory? The first issue to answer is whether we should indeed gather data on slow-moving historical trends rather than fast-unfolding events. As mentioned repeatedly, my theory of nation building points at the climatic forces that force the winds to blow from one direction rather than the other, and not the foaming and frothing at the edges of the breaking waves—if I may play with a metaphor introduced by Fernand Braudel (1995: 21).

Focusing on such climatic trends makes empirical sense because levels of ethnopolitical exclusion and national identification change only slowly over time, as the data show. For purposes of contrast, Figure 1.4 displays the stable configuration of Mexico, where the indigenous population has never been represented in national level government and makes up only a slowly changing share of the total population. In South Africa, by contrast, the end of apartheid dramatically changed the configuration of power, as the right-hand panel illustrates. Most countries resemble Mexico rather than South Africa, however, as the complete set of graphs for all countries demonstrates (see Figure A.1 in the online appendix at http://press.princeton.edu/titles/11197.html).

Figure 1.5 shows, for a shorter period for which data are available, how national identification changes over time—referring to the other side of the nation-building coin. The data trace average pride of citizens in their nation, as recorded in representative surveys (see Chapter 6). In most countries, responses remain fairly constant, as exemplified here by data from the United States. Cases such as Bosnia, also depicted in Figure 1.5, are rare (see the complete set of graphs in Figure A.2 of the online appendix). It therefore makes sense to focus on slow-moving processes that gradually and continuously generate differences between countries. Such slow-moving forces may also, if they reach a certain threshold, lead to an abrupt change in the power configuration (for an exploration of such threshold effects, see Pierson 2003). Not all cases à la South Africa, therefore, need to be explained through faster-moving, more eventful historical processes.

This does not mean that such faster-moving factors could not possibly play a role—they are not mere "surface disturbances," as Braudel famously declared. The actions of skilled politicians may go a long way toward creating a sense of national belonging (Miguel 2004), as I will discuss in the concluding chapter. Victory in war might have a similar effect (Sambanis et al. 2015). Governments decide to give in to pressures for minority representation or they don't, depending on the changing constellation of forces within a governing coalition (Slater 2010). Rival states might stir up discontent among ethnic

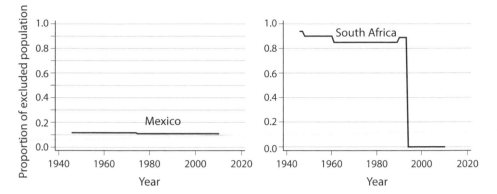

FIGURE 1.4. Size of the excluded population over time in South Africa and Mexico, 1946–2010

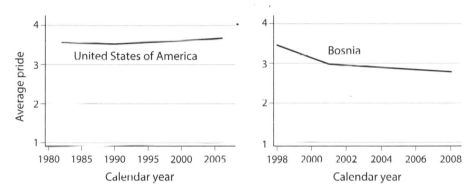

FIGURE 1.5. Average pride in country over time in Bosnia and the United States

minorities and governments might react to such outside interference by expelling ministers of minority background as "traitors" (Mylonas 2012), thus changing the configuration of ethnopolitical power. We will encounter numerous such historical events in the country case studies. However, none of them steered the course of nation building in an entirely different direction, as we will see. They seem to modify rather than reengineer the long-term historical forces on which this book focuses.

Keeping the Big Picture Alive

This emphasis on slow-moving forces that operate over the long run follows up on an older school of thinking on nation building developed by Karl Deutsch (1953), Clifford Geertz (1963), Reinhard Bendix (1964), and others. As discussed in the introduction, their work has been faulted for its methodological sloppiness, since they often cherry-picked examples to support their argument.[8] Another often-repeated criticism is that they did not give much attention to how large-scale processes such as nation building operate at the level of individuals: Why should the citizens of a newly founded state eventually embrace larger-scale identities such as the nation? The early theories of nation building, in other words, lacked a "micro-foundation."

Today the methodological and theoretical canon has decisively moved away from such evolutionary "armchair theorizing" and toward the rigorous proof of well-confined arguments derived from solid, individual-level theories. The focus is on short-term processes, operating over an election cycle, for example, rather than generation-spanning trends. Experiments on how particular institutional rules influence political behavior, manipulated in online games or in laboratories where groups of individuals distribute small dollar amounts to each other under tightly controlled conditions, have replaced historical interpretation.

Even large-N statistical analyses with countries as units of observation, which from the early 2000s onward replaced "armchair theorizing" as the macro-comparative method of choice, have fallen out of fashion. The main criticism is that these analyses can't disentangle simple correlation from actual causation. Instead, researchers now explore more disaggregated data at the subnational level, preferably where some random assignment process is at work. Ideally, a researcher manages to convince aid agencies or national governments to allocate development projects or electoral rules for parliamentary candidates by chance over some of the country's villages or electoral districts. This offers certainty about what is an independent cause (the randomly assigned "treatment") and what is an effect, thus finally exorcizing the devil of reverse causation.

There is much to be said in favor of these methodological developments. However, the price to be paid for causal rigor is steep indeed. No experiment can be run with entire countries or over periods of time that last more than a couple of years. Extrapolating from villages to countries and from one-shot experiments to generation-spanning processes remains difficult. When the kinds of questions asked become determined by the methods suitable to test causal effects, the large, macro-political developments of interest to political scientists and sociologists throughout the 19th and 20th centuries risk vanishing from sight (see the critique in Thelen and Mahoney 2015). The alternative, in my view, is to revitalize this macro-political and historical tradition by adding theoretical precision and methodological rigor to the old endeavor.

Strategic Comparisons

This book makes a modest step in that direction (for other similar projects, see Boix 2015). It combines three methods and kinds of data to substantiate the theory outlined above. I will compare the historical development of pairs of countries to illustrate how the three main mechanisms of nation building operate in the historical process. To do so most effectively, I chose "maximum variation" cases (Flyvbjerg 2006; see also Lieberman 2005: 444). The two countries differ maximally in terms of a core independent variable and, in line with the theory, in how far nation building succeeded. For example, the state of Botswana developed an exceptionally high—by African standards—capacity to provide public goods and the emerging configuration of political power was also unusually inclusive. Somalia's governments, by contrast, lacked an administration that was able to provide public services across the entire territory, and political integration across clan division largely failed.

In other words, the two cases were chosen not only because they confirm the theory (they are "on the regression line") but also because they illustrate the mechanism at work in the clearest possible way. They are, in other words, situated at *different ends* of the imagined regression line: high on the independent variable of interest and consequently high on the outcome variable; low on the same independent variable and thus consequently low on the outcome variable.

At the same time, the two countries are otherwise as similar as possible. They share a comparable historical experience, geographic location, size, and level of economic development. Holding these other factors "constant," as the social science jargon has it, it should be easier to isolate the effect of the main mechanism of interest. There is no ideal pair of countries, however, that are equal on everything else except the core variable. The case study chapters will therefore discuss other differences between the two countries and explore whether these could be responsible for the different trajectories of nation building. More often than not, however, the statistical analysis of data on all countries of the world will be more effective in ruling out such alternative explanations. Whenever appropriate, I will anticipate these statistical results in the discussion of the case studies.

There are many different typologies of how to use case studies in explanatory research. In terms of Seawright and Gerring's (2008) typology, my approach combines the "extreme case" study, where values on core independent variables are far apart from each other, with the "most similar" case study design, where countries are matched on other independent variables.[9] Mahoney and Goertz (2004) show that one needs to compare "positive" cases, where a particular event occurred or a certain institution emerged, with those where it didn't (the "negative" cases). We cannot understand nation building if we don't also study cases where it failed. One should not choose negative cases, however, that cannot possibly produce the outcome of interest. At least one facilitating condition should be present. This is true for all the negative cases discussed in this book: Somalia is linguistically largely homogeneous; thus nation building would have been theoretically possible. The Belgian and Russian states, the other two negative cases, were capable of delivering public goods (thanks to a centralized state apparatus), thus also making it feasible, in principle, to build integrated nations.[10]

The six case studies allow us to explore through which precise causal mechanisms and historical processes public goods provision, the development of organizational networks, and communicative integration brought about integrated nations. In the jargon of social science, this is called "process tracing" (Mahoney 2012). Process tracing, according to an often-cited typology (Van Evera 1997; Bennett 2010), can achieve different goals. Ideally, a case allows for what earlier methodologists (Stinchcombe 1968: 24–28) have called a "crucial experiment": the process hypothesized *must* be observed for a theory to be valid, and at the same time this historical process is compatible with *only* the proposed theory and not with any alternative argument.

My case studies unfortunately do not amount to such a "double decisive test." I indeed will demonstrate that in Switzerland early civil society development contributed to the rise of transethnic networks of political alliances, that public goods provision did the same for Botswana, and that scriptural homogeneity did likewise for China. But these historical processes could also be interpreted in the light of a different theory. Scriptural homogeneity in China could facilitate the imagining of a national community à la Benedict Anderson, which in turn helped political ties reach across ethnic boundaries. Public goods provision in Botswana could have been enhanced by its democratic tradition, which in turn encouraged parties to seek cross-ethnic constituencies, leading to an inclusive power structure. My paired case studies thus amount to a "hoop test" rather than a proof: they increase the plausibility of the theory proposed here but don't provide irrefutable evidence for it.[11]

Large *N*

I therefore use a second set of methods and analyze data on a large number of countries using statistical techniques. This will allow us to rule out some of the other possible interpretations of what happened in the six country histories. For example, we can "control for" democracy in order to disentangle its effects from the public goods mechanism proposed in my theory. In most of the statistical analysis, the sample includes all countries of the world except some microstates in the Caribbean, Europe, and the Pacific. In other parts, I will have to confine myself to about half of the world's countries, all of them situated in Africa and Asia.

Exploring these large datasets will also ensure that the hypothesized processes operate not only in the six case study countries but in the rest of the world as well. This kind of analysis will obviously be much more coarse, as many of the main mechanisms will have to be identified through less than ideal data. The statistical analysis will also be less historically informed and contextually situated than the paired case studies.

As a third methodological approach, I take advantage of dozens of multi-country surveys that have appeared over the past decades. In contrast to the previous analyses that compared the characteristics of countries with each other, the units of observations are now individuals who have filled out the survey questions. The Eurobarometer survey has now been copied in other continents as well, giving us the Afrobarometer, Asiabarometer, Middle East Barometer, and Latin America Barometer. The International Social Survey, the European Value Survey, and the World Values Survey are other important data sources. I use a combination of these datasets to explore a crucial part of the argument: that political integration across ethnic divides and national identification go hand in hand and form the two sides of the nation-building coin. As mentioned in the introduction, this analysis will cover 123 countries and 92% of the world's population.

Much has been written about the problem of interpreting statistical associations between variables in causal terms. The standard joke to show how one can mistake correlation for causation goes as follows. To prove the theory that storks bring children, all we need is data showing that there are more children born where there are many storks. This proof suffers, however, from what is called the problem of "omitted variables": the factor that causes both a high number of babies and a high number of storks nesting on rooftops is population density, which needs to be brought into the picture to truly understand where babies are born. Another common problem lies in determining the direction of causality. For example, is ethnic exclusion causing low public goods provision because rulers prefer to distribute them to their own coethnics only? Or is low public goods provision leading to ethnic exclusion, as I argue in this book?

I use some standard techniques to address these two problems. First, I sometimes add a separate independent variable for each country, for example, a 1 for Botswana and a 0 for all other countries, a 1 for Switzerland and a 0 for all others, and so on. These variables capture all kinds of country characteristics that we cannot measure and thus have to omit from the analysis, similar to the population density variable in the example of storks and babies. This is called a "country fixed effects" model. The second technique is the "instrumental variable" regression. It consists of finding a third variable that influences only public goods provision, to switch to the other example, but not ethnopolitical exclusion. We then create a new synthetic variable composed of only the part of the variation in public goods provision that is due to its association with this third variable. If this synthetic public goods variable is correlated with ethnic inclusion, we can be more certain that it is not due to reverse causation.

The combination of large-N statistical analysis and process tracing within pairs of strategically chosen countries allows me to "triangulate," as the jargon has it, between results obtained from different methodological approaches. In other words, this book is based on a "nested" research design (Lieberman 2005; see also Humphreys and Jacobs 2015) that combines comparative case studies with statistical analysis of the entire universe of cases. If we arrive at the same conclusions walking down these different avenues, this should increase the confidence in the analysis and support the causal claims made throughout the chapters.

Let me use a geological metaphor to illustrate. Imagine social reality as a large hill covered with a varied vegetation of forests and shrubs. We want to understand the geological forces that have produced the shape of the hill, its gorges, and its canyons. We dig three tunnels through the mountain, each starting from a different point situated at a different elevation and going in a different direction. If the chief engineers of the three tunnel projects can agree that the mountain has a tilted platform structure, with a layer of volcanic lava at the bottom and two layers of soft sediments on top of it, this is quite likely how the mountain is structured underneath the vegetation. Had we dug only one tunnel and started at the piedmont, we might have encountered only the lava layer and concluded that the hill must be an ancient volcano.

I conclude this chapter with a more general note on research design. As Figure 0.2 illustrates, the causal flow of the argument begins with three exogenous factors related to topography and climate. It then leads to an intermediary variable (levels of political centralization before the transition to the nation-state) that is removed from contemporary processes through a long historical time span—therefore excluding reverse causation. These contemporary processes are then traced in the case studies from 1830 to circa 1900 for Belgium, 1848 to 1900 for Switzerland, 1911 to 1950 for China, 1917 to 1989 for Russia, 1960 to 1990 for Somalia, 1966 to 2010 for Botswana, from World War II (or the date of independence) onward to 2005 in the statistical analysis at the country level, or from 1980 to 2014 for the survey data. This could be called a stacked research design: historical developments are observed at different points in time, allowing us to trace how causal processes unfold and to determine in which direction they flow. Rather than avoiding endogeneity at all costs and finding "pure" causal relationships in a laboratory cleansed from all contaminating context and history, such a research design enables us to disentangle endogenous historical processes and understand their inner logic.

We are now ready to dig the first tunnel through the mountain. It will lead us to two small Western European societies, both enjoying high standards of living and continuous democratic governance; both are divided between speakers of Germanic dialects and French, and both, of course, are famous for their chocolates. Their histories of nation building, however, diverge sharply.

2

Voluntary Organizations

SWITZERLAND VERSUS BELGIUM

Contrasting the political developments of Switzerland and Belgium will show how the early rise of voluntary organizations facilitate nation building. In the previous chapter, I argued that these organizations allow alliance networks to spread across a country's territory because they have a "built-in" tendency to link up horizontally by building bridges between coordination positions. Patronage networks, by contrast, tend to spread vertically *within* ethnic communities because they contain more open triangles and vertical brokerage positions. To show this in detail, we would need sufficiently detailed information on the structure of alliance networks for early 19th-century Switzerland and Belgium. No such information is available, however.

I therefore will focus on the historical implications of the argument: if voluntary organizations develop across the various regions of a country *before* it transitions to the nation-state, an inclusionary, multiethnic configuration of power will emerge thereafter. Why? When these organizational networks have enough time to spread across a territory, they will include members of different ethnic communities. After the transition to the nation-state, the political elite will be similarly inclusive because the new rulers of the country will rely upon these existing networks to recruit political leaders and to mobilize popular political support. An inclusive, multiethnic configuration of power then allows the population at large, including ethnic minorities, to identify as members of an overarching national community.

Switzerland

Switzerland's political history roughly conforms to this scenario. Its citizenry is composed of 71% German speakers, 23% French speakers, and 6% Italian and Romance speakers. Since the middle of the 19th century, scholars have wondered why Switzerland should have survived in the middle of a Europe increasingly dominated by linguistically uniform nation-states: German-speaking Germany, French-speaking France, Italian-speaking Italy, and so on. For those who saw a single shared language as the fundament of the modern nation-state, most prominently Ernest Gellner, Switzerland represents a major nuisance. He therefore chose to treat it as an aberration from the normal course of history (Gellner 1964: 174; Gellner 1983: 119). For those such as Max Weber (1968 [1922]: 397) who emphasized shared political history as the source of national sentiment, Switzerland was welcomed as a crown witness before the tribunal of comparative scholarship.[1]

As many other scholars have noted, Switzerland offers an interesting contrast with Belgium, Canada, Spain, and other multilingual states in the West because none of the four language groups in Switzerland has ever strived for political independence[2] or reunification with a neighboring state in which their community represents the dominant majority. This is not because the desire for being self-ruled is satisfied by giving linguistic minorities their own, autonomous province: cantonal borders in Switzerland were not drawn on linguistic grounds, and the French-German language border runs across cantons for most of its course from north to south, and such is also the case for Italian. Berne, Fribourg, the Grisons, and the Valais are multilingual cantons. Rather, it seems that ethnic difference simply is not politically relevant. There is not a single language-based political party of any significance; the attempt to found a *parti romand* that would represent French speakers was a rather spectacular failure. No major political association seeks to represent the interests of only one of the language groups. The complete lack of ethnic nationalism and separatism parallels the situation among the various language groups forming the Han majority of China, as we will see.

Switzerland is therefore best understood as a case of multiethnic nation building, where the nation is imagined as a composite of several language communities with equal claims to dignity and political power (Dardanelli and Stojanovic 2011). French and Italian speakers were, from the beginning of modern Switzerland in 1848 onward, equally or even slightly overrepresented in central government as well as the federal administration. That different language groups have lived peacefully together under one political roof became the main focus of official nationalism since its inception in the late 19th century. It is a source of considerable pride for ordinary Swiss today. Switzerland thus succeeded in both the identity and the political integration aspects of nation building.

To understand how this came about, I analyze the role of voluntary organizations during two crucial turning points that characterize the history of nation building everywhere. The first is the transition to the modern nation-state. In the case of Switzerland, it occurred after a short civil war in 1848, when a federal state replaced the loose alliance of independent mini-states that had existed for centuries. The first federal government abolished the last medieval privileges, granted the equality of all citizens in a constitution, and instituted a federal government and army. Second, I focus on periods of major political crisis when new alliance structures might emerge. This was the case in Switzerland during World War I, when for the first and only time in its history, the different language groups drifted politically apart, pulled by conflicting loyalties toward either Germany or France. World War I therefore represented a possible turning point during which history *could* have taken another path, toward the development of ethnic nationalism, a reorganization of the state into a tri-national entity, or perhaps even its breakup along linguistic boundaries—none of which occurred. The centripetal pull provided by multiethnic voluntary organizations is again crucial in understanding why.

The Early and Even Spread of Voluntary Associations

In 17th- and 18th-century Europe, an independent press and the mass production of philosophical and scientific books broke the monopoly that the Church had previously held on the print media. In Switzerland, literary societies and reading circles spread evenly all over the territory; this was not the case in Belgium, as we will see. Three historical factors contributed to this development. First, in contrast to religiously homogeneous states such as Belgium, France, or Spain, Switzerland remained divided between Catholic and Protestant cantons. This religious patchwork mirrored the political structure of the old regime: since three Alpine cantons ceased to pay tribute to Habsburg overlords in the late 13th century, Switzerland represented a loose military alliance of autonomous city-states whose shared interest was to keep the surrounding European powers at arm's length. It lacked any grand feudal or absolutist state comparable to that of neighboring France, Austria-Hungary (to which Belgium belonged before Napoleon), or Bavaria. These were able to impose a state religion on the population once the *cuius regio, eius religio* principle had become accepted in the Peace of Augsburg (1555). In Switzerland, the political competition between the cantonal governments propelled the clergy on both sides of the religious divide to invest in the reading skills of their flocks in order to immunize them against the virus of the aberrant faith. High literacy rates across the country resulted from this competition.

Second, thanks to the decentralized nature of the political system, it was more difficult for the Swiss governments to control the early bourgeois associations than it was for more autocratically ruled states such as Belgium under Habsburg, French, and later Dutch rule. The flourishing reading circles and enlightened societies included men from all estates, even peasants and artisans, provoking lively discussions whether reading novels and works of adult education represented a danger to public order and the Christian faith (de Capitani 1986: 152). But these discussions rarely motivated the authorities to suppress the associations, not the least because they often participated themselves in their activities. While urban patriciates that imitated the aristocracies of neighboring countries ruled some cantons, such as Berne, in most others long-established bourgeois elites held power—the very same elites within which these associations began to flourish. In contrast to most European societies, including Belgium, which were long dominated by a politically powerful nobility, the more bourgeois and democratic character of the ancien régime in Switzerland allowed voluntary associations to proliferate across the territory.

Third, the decentralized, rural character of industrialization also contributed to this development (Senghaas 1982). No sharp differentiations between more or less developed regions, let alone between language regions, emerged. More precisely, Switzerland's industrialization proceeded very early, again due to a lack of political obstacles as well as favorable natural conditions, including the availability of plenty of waterpower in the mountains. Industrialization embraced French-speaking regions (the watch and chocolate industries of Geneva and Neuchâtel) as well as German-speaking areas (the textile industries of Glarus and St. Gallen, the machine industries of Zürich, and later on the chemical industry of Basel). Early and even industrialization helped to spread voluntary associations across the country because it created the social classes—capitalists, overseers and administrators, traders and bankers—who were most interested in these modern forms of sociability.

Bourgeois, enlightened associations therefore flourished in almost all parts of the country. These associations were often devoted to a specific cause, to the "betterment of agriculture," to the advancement of science, to the knowledge of history, to the reform of the various cantonal armies, to the library of a literary circle. In the 18th century, there were over 100 such societies, many with a distinctively local focus—corresponding to the fragmented nature of the political system. Gradually, however, many of these societies linked up with each other to form transregional associations, in line with the theory outlined in the previous chapter. The *Dictionnaire géographique-statistique de la Suisse*, edited in 1836–1837 by Jean-Louis-Benjamin Leresche, listed 14 societies that were active throughout the entire territory of the federation (de Capitani 1986: 104–105).

The most important of these early cross-regional organizations was the Helvetic Society, founded in 1761 with the aim of uniting all progressive spirits determined to fight against the old order, reinforcing the enlightenment movement across cantonal, religious, regional, and linguistic barriers, and thus linking the different pieces of the premodern mosaic society together. Their patriotic reunions brought, at the end of the 18th century, around 200 people together (Im Hof and Bernard 1983; Im Hof and de Capitani 1983: 504–505). Another early cross-regional society was the Swiss Society for Natural Research (Schweizerische Naturforschende Gesellschaft), founded in 1797 by scientists from German-speaking Berne and French-speaking Geneva.

After the brief occupation of Switzerland by Napoleon between 1798 and 1803, new societies sprang to life that were inspired by the French Revolution. Already existing societies now started to reconstitute themselves as cross-regional organizations as well and founded German-, French-, and later Italian-speaking sections. In 1806 the Swiss Society of Artists was born, in 1807 the Helvetic Society reconstituted itself, and in 1808 the Swiss Association and in 1810 the Swiss Society for the Public Good (Schweizerische Gemeinnützige Gesellschaft) were founded. In 1811 the Swiss Society for Historical Research was formed, followed by the Swiss Society for Natural Research in 1815, the Society of Zofingen (a student association) in 1819, the Grand Loge Alpina of the Freemasons in 1822, the Swiss Society of Officers (while there was still no national army) in 1833, and the Grütli-Association in 1838 (Im Hof and Bernard 1983: 10; Andrey 1986: 576ff., 585, and passim).

While most of these associations were elite clubs, others had a much wider membership. The Federal Association of Riflemen was founded in 1824 and seven years later comprised 2,000 members (Im Hof and Bernard 1983: 20), a considerable number when compared to an overall population of less than two million (McRae 1983: 50). Roughly one in every 500 men was thus a member of a riflemen's association. Other popular associations with mass membership were the Swiss Association of Athletics (Schweizerischer Turnverein), founded in 1832 and inspired by the German gymnasts' movement, and the singers' movement that was initiated two years later under the name Le chant national. Athletes and singers praised the brotherhood of free and enlightened men and enjoyed the liberating spirit of revolutionary times. Athletic exercises were meant to overcome the restrictions of the dress codes and behavioral rules of the old regime. Singing together demonstrated every man's ability to raise his voice and to contribute to the concert of freedom and unity.

The Transethnic Nature of Associational Life

All these associations held their annual meetings in different parts of the country every year, mostly in places not known to ordinary citizens. In this way, the members of an association became familiar with other regions of what was later to become the national territory. Most associations carefully ensured that every canton was included in this system of rotating meeting places. The large majority of them—with important exceptions such as the Society for the Public Good—also rotated the presidency between cantons. Note that this system of rotating meeting places and presidencies was bounded by the borders of the confederation and did not include associations from or meetings in Germany, France, or Italy. The associational networks thus remained confined to the territory of Switzerland, even if exchanges and occasional contacts with German, French, and Italian organizations of a similar nature existed.

To what extent did these organizations succeed at integrating the different ethnic groups? The Helvetic Society can be taken as a paradigmatic case (the following draws on Im Hof and Bernard 1983: 15ff.). Before the French Revolution, there was considerable resistance to using French at the society's meetings because it symbolized the French court and therefore the absolutist order against which the Helvetic Society was determined to fight. Slowly, resistance was fading away, and after the French Revolution, French-speaking members were welcomed. In 1790, the assembly enthusiastically applauded the first speech given in French. Unfortunately, not much is known about the ethnic background of the society's members. For the Federal Association of Riflemen, however, records indicate that 1,200 (or 60%) of the 2,000 members in 1829 were Germanophones (who constituted 70% of the population). The Society for the Public Good counted 127 Francophones out of a total of 631 members (Im Hof and Bernard 1983: 20), thus again mirroring the ethnic composition of the population at large.

What vision of society and history did these movements develop? According to the ideology of "Helvetism," the ideals of the Enlightenment flourished best in the territory of Switzerland. The lack of absolutist and grand feudal states and the mini-laboratory of freedom within the limits of urban citizenry predisposed enlightened Swiss to best realize the ideals of the bourgeois revolution. The main ideas nourishing this vision of the role of Switzerland in world history came from the outside: Rousseau praised the natural democracy of Swiss herders and peasants, protected by a heroic Alpine landscape; Schiller's *Wilhelm Tell* of 1804 became a classic of patriotic playwrights.

This early patriotic movement had a distinctively republican touch. The borders of the community were never defined in ethnic or linguistic terms. Rather, all those who had fought and continued to fight against the surrounding feudal empires and the patrician elites of the Swiss city-states belonged to the community of progress that was to bring about a new social order. This typically modern notion of history as progress found expression in legends and tales that were canonized and taught by professors of Swiss history in the newly established academies. The *Histories of the Swiss* by Johannes von Müller became the standard patriotic and progressive work for about a century. Associations played a crucial role in the dissemination of this new view of history. The Society for Historical Research was founded in 1811, the General Society for Historical Research of Switzerland in 1841.

It is important to note that these patriotic associations did not develop *because* a preexisting national sentiment finally found its organizational expression, as Anthony Smith (1996) interprets the Swiss case. The idea of Switzerland as a fatherland, the place where progress and modernity would find their privileged seat, was a new concept that bore little continuity with the deep-seated cantonal identities, which had emerged from long centuries of feuding between the city-states, or with the religious frameworks within which individuals had thought and felt before the 18th century. While some early patriots were addressing humanity as a whole as the bearers of the revolution they saw coming, most originally restricted their vision of a new society to their canton (Kohn 1956: 24–25). Certainly, some other associations, especially the Helvetic Society, spread across the entire territory of the country *because* they were motivated by the goal to overcome the fragmentation of Swiss society into its cantonal compartments. Many of the Helvetic Society's members, however, were also (and perhaps primarily) members of cantonal governments, associations, and progressive clubs. Conformingly, even the Helvetic Society was proto-nationalist at best: it served the aim of uniting the forces of progress against the old, oligarchic order, and not so much of forging the various disjointed cantonal limbs into a national body. In short, these proto-nationalist organizations reached across regions and the language divide not so much because they were motivated by nationalism but because the social bases for the flourishing of civil society organizations—widespread literacy, urban bourgeoisies or educated rural elites, early industrialization—had developed throughout the territory of the old confederation.

These associations were opposed to and disconnected from the networks of conservative, anti-Enlightenment alliances centered on the Catholic Church and the Alpine heartland of the confederation. These conservative circles intended to contain and subdue the bourgeois Enlightenment movements and put faith, the observance of the traditional order, and ultramontane solidarity with other Catholic states in Europe above patriotism, rationality, and equality.

Political Integration and Nation Building after the Civil War

The short civil war of 1847 handed victory to the liberal, reformed cantons over the Catholic Special League. The reasons for this turn of events are obviously beyond the scope of the argument pursued here. Suffice to note that the victorious factions transformed the confederate state into a new national state with a central government, a constitution, a federal administration, and an army. The constitution abolished all internal customs and road taxes, established the principle of national citizenship, guaranteed the free choice of residence for all Christian citizens (and from 1866 onward also for Jews), and declared freedom of profession and trade, equality before the law, freedom of press and opinion, and universal male suffrage.

Most of the political elite of this newly founded nation-state was recruited from the liberal, bourgeois networks of associations that had emerged previously. Mirroring the ethnic composition of these associations, the new elite therefore counted members from all three major linguistic communities among its rank. Thus an inclusive, transethnic power structure developed—largely Protestant and German speaking, to be sure, but proportionally including French and Italian speakers (many of them secular Catholics) in parliament, in the central administration, and in the federal council of ministers, which represented the highest level of government. This transethnic power structure did not emerge because linguistic "minorities" successfully struggled for a balanced representation vis-à-vis a "majority." Nor did it result from an explicit power-sharing agreement between separate French-, German-, and Italian-speaking elites, as prominent theorists of consociational democracy interpret the Swiss case (see the critique of this interpretation by Rothchild and Roeder 2005).

Rather, leaders of all linguistic backgrounds formed an encompassing and enduring coalition without any political struggling by minorities and without any negotiating between representatives of the three language groups. The liberal movement that rose to power was *already* based on a transethnic network of alliances that had developed previously within the voluntary associations. The new political elites therefore took multiethnicity and the principle of equality between different language communities for granted. It is telling that the first parliament almost neglected to add a constitutional article that declared all three languages national and official. The delegate of the canton of Vaud presented a corresponding postulate, and a proposal from German-speaking Zürich was then unanimously adopted without any further debate (Weilenmann 1925: 215–224). Characteristically, there were no explicit rules with regard to the linguistic composition of the federal council, the parliament, the administration, the army, or the courts. Rather, everybody shared the implicit understanding that the different language groups should be represented within the state apparatus according to their population share. This taken-for-granted informality lasted until 1948, 100 years after the modern nation-state had been founded, when the federal council stated what had already been the case for a century: that all language groups should be equally represented in the different branches of government (McRae 1983: 136). Another 50 years passed before the constitution included a recommendation that all regions and linguistic groups should have a seat in the federal council, thus codifying a political reality that had already existed for one and a half centuries.

The result was a remarkably equitable distribution of power at different hierarchical levels of the state—the political integration aspect of nation building. According to McRae, 37% of federal councillors between 1848 and 1981 were non–German speakers while their population share amounted to only

27%.[3] French and Italian speakers occupied only slightly fewer positions in the central administration (22% since 1930) than their population share would lead us to expect, while French speakers were overrepresented in the highest-paid civil service jobs (McRae 1983: 131–135). Thus the state was never captured by a specific ethnic elite, as in Belgium, and ethnicity was never problematized or politicized.

The associational networks not only provided a transethnic elite for the new state but also allowed this elite to mobilize popular support to win national elections or a referendum. Since political parties did not form until the 1870s (Meuwly 2010), the two dominant political movements, one "radical" and one "liberal," used these associational networks to recruit followers and mobilize voters. The radicals, for example, were supported by the National Association, founded in 1835, by the Cantonal Peoples Associations, and from the 1850s onward by the veterans of a students' association (Ruffieux 1986: 682). Appealing to the shared interest of language groups was therefore never an option or a necessity when securing votes. Rather, the masses were politically mobilized through the organizational networks of either the Church or the voluntary associations. Political conflict thus pitted a premodern, hierarchical, and sacralized vision of society against the modern, secularized, and egalitarian model, Catholic against Protestant, but never French speakers against German speakers.[4]

The republican patriotism that motivated the new state elite defined the Swiss nation in distinctively nonethnic terms, as we have seen. It would never have occurred to the members of the Helvetic Society or the riflemen's association to declare German the only official language when they rose to power and national hegemony in 1848—as the French-speaking elites of Belgium had done a little bit earlier in the century. Never would these men have thought to portray the Italian-speaking part of the population as backward and to propose a politics of assimilation. Nor would French speakers exclude the German-speaking majority from the seats of power because they were less civilized, according to the Francophone point of view at the time. This is how the French-speaking elites in Belgium justified politically sidelining the Flemish majority for generations.

Correspondingly, the educational policies of the new state avoided even the slightest appearance of ethnic chauvinism or aspirations to cultural hegemony by the majority. The dominant language of the canton (and within multilingual cantons, of the municipality) became the mandatory language of instruction of the local public school system. This so-called principle of linguistic territoriality contrasts starkly with the policies adopted by many nationalizing states of the same period. Italy attempted to "make Italians," for example, by elevating Tuscanese to the national language, to be taught in all schools. The early Belgian governments tried to create a cohesive Belgian nation by teaching everybody French.

On the identity side of the nation-building coin, Swiss nationalism remained a minor part of the ideological program of the new elite after 1848.
They still saw liberalism and republicanism as the ideological fundament of
the state they had created. They were certainly patriots: Switzerland was seen
as an example to the world—the avant-garde in terms of political freedom and
equality that other states in Europe were supposed to follow, once the liberal
movements had recovered from the setbacks suffered across the Continent in
1848. They governed in the name of these universal principles rather than in
the name of the Swiss nation. Patriotism was a major motivation and cultural
force, but it remained subordinated to the liberal and republican ideals. And
while they often mentioned Switzerland's linguistic and, more importantly,
cantonal diversity and were certainly proud of it, they did not consider it a
defining feature of the state. It is therefore best to describe the early state-
building patriots as ethnically indifferent, rather than consciously and pro-
grammatically multicultural.

This changed from the 1880s onward, when an official, state-sponsored
nationalism superseded republican patriotism. This new political ideology
reacted against the French, Italian, and German nationalisms that flourished
during this period and reminded the Swiss that their nation did not really exist
from the perspective of linguistic nationalists (Siegenthaler 1993: 326; Zimmer
2003). Official nationalism was also meant to counterweigh the socialist movement that started to take root among the growing working classes, mostly
thanks to the efforts of German labor activists (Bendix 1992). Finally, Swiss
nationalism developed because the constitutional reform of 1874 introduced
direct democratic institutions and thus brought the voting (male) masses into
the political arena. The liberal Protestant elite was now forced to open their
ranks by including exponents of the Catholic party into the federal council
(from 1891 onward). They also had to renegotiate the official image of the Swiss
state by reducing the prominence of liberal and republican ideas and integrating more of the corporatist visions of society dear to the Catholic elites (Kriesi
1999: 15; Zimmer 2003, pt. 2).

The religious divide was slowly papered over, at least among the political
elite, by the new state-sponsored nationalism. At its core, it maintained that
the lack of religious, cultural, and linguistic homogeneity was not a deficit, as
pan-German and pan-Italian ideologues across the border saw it, but the very
virtue of the Swiss state. The multiethnic character of the state was no longer
taken for granted but pushed into the center of nationalist discourse. The
Swiss nation—rather than the liberal cause—became the primary source of
political legitimacy. The term "nation by will" (*Willensnation*), coined by the
liberal constitutional lawyer Hilty (1875), served as the catchword character-
izing the Swiss situation—it is still used today in almost every speech celebrat-
ing national holidays.

World War I as a Second Critical Juncture

During World War I this project of multiethnic nation-building came under increasing strain. In the preceding decades, the blossoming nationalisms of the surrounding "true" nation-states had gained some followers among Swiss intellectuals and politicians. Tensions escalated into a serious political crisis during the war. For the first and only time in Swiss history, political alliances became realigned along linguistic cleavages. The first serious crisis erupted when officer Wille, who had family connections to the German emperor and openly sympathized with Germany, was elected general of the army, a position filled only during wartime. Subsequently, several political scandals showed to the French-speaking citizens that the German-speaking elite was clearly leaning toward the Central Powers and paid mere lip service to the official principle of neutrality (Jost 1986: 746; du Bois 1983: 80ff.). Not only the elites politicized ethnicity but also the rank and file of the army, where French-speaking recruits complained about the Prussian drill on which German-speaking officers tried to insist. On the streets of bilingual cities small-scale riots broke out and speaking the "wrong" language could be dangerous in certain places at certain times (du Bois 1983: 68, 78).

Ethnic nationalism also gained ground among intellectuals. In 1916, Francophile circles founded the Ligue patriotique romande, where prominent figures such as Villiam Vogt preached hatred against the Alemannic Swiss (e.g., in his book *Les deux Suisses*). The Ligue complained not only about the Germanophile foreign policy of the national government but also about growing discrimination against French speakers in the central administration and the army (du Bois 1983: 82). German-speaking intellectuals quickly responded by founding the Association of the Swiss German Language (Deutschschweizerischer Sprachverein) and mirrored Vogt's views, for example, in the pages of the journal *Stimmen im Sturm* (Voices in the Storm) (du Bois 1983: 85).

However, such radicalism by no means dominated the debates on Switzerland's foreign policy alignments during the war; quite to the contrary. The multiethnic political elite, which had been ruling the federal state since its foundation two generations earlier, tried to cool down emotions by realigning political sentiments along the nationalist axis that they had designed in previous decades. They carefully rebalanced Switzerland's foreign policy by electing the pro-Entente, French-speaking councillor Gustav Ador after the resignation of a pro-German councillor in 1917, thus making it three French-speaking councillors out of seven. They were, all in all, quite successful with this policy of appeasement, reconciliation, and compromise. Usually, after the emotional waves of a scandal had ebbed, there were also signs of popular, transethnic nationalism: General Wille was enthusiastically welcomed in French-speaking towns and so were French-speaking army detachments parading in the German-speaking regions of the country.

Transethnic associations played a crucial role in the defense and ultimate victory of multiethnic nationalism against the challenge of ethnic competition and conflict. Especially impressive in this regard is the role of the New Helvetic Society (NHS), founded in 1914 with the explicit aim of revitalizing Swiss nationalism against the growing tide of ethnic chauvinism. During World War I, the NHS developed a consistent program of counteraction and counterpropaganda centered on the idea of Switzerland as a "nation by will."

In 1915, the NHS began to publish a patriotic Sunday newspaper to countervail the German papers that had gained some influence in the Alemannic part of the country. A bimonthly journal, the *Swiss Comrade*, addressed the young public and propagated the same patriotic spirit. A press office was opened that placed around 2,000 articles in local newspapers during the war. The society organized conferences, gatherings, and speeches across the country, including a famous speech of the poet Carl Spitteler, who admonished his fellow countrymen to remain united and to remember the spirit of brotherhood that their forefathers had breathed. A discussion between a German- and a French-speaking newspaper editor under the title "Let's Remain Swiss" was as widely received as was the intellectual Konrad Falke's essay "The Swiss Cultural Will," published by the NHS. Its president, Gonzague de Reynold, frequently attended conferences in different parts of the country (Im Hof and Bernard 1983: 17). Other associations, such as the Swiss Officers Association, the Association for Public Good, and the Association of Professors and Lecturers, played a similar role, although they did not develop a full-scale propaganda apparatus comparable to that of the NHS.

The activities of these associations effectively counterbalanced the centrifugal forces that had appeared in the political arena.[5] Equally important, they provided the micro-political glue to hold the transethnic elite together and prevent a rupture of networks of political alliances and personal friendships along the linguistic divide. The prominence of transethnic voluntary organizations in Switzerland thus explains why an inclusionary power structure developed after the crucial turning point of nation-state formation in 1848; it also helps explain why the country did not break apart along linguistic lines in the second critical juncture during World War I.

BELGIUM: FROM FRENCH ETHNOCRACY TO BINATIONAL CONSOCIATION

The history of nation building in Belgium offers an interesting contrast. In a nutshell, there were fewer civil society organizations overall and, equally important, they had not spread uniformly among French and Flemish speakers. These composed roughly 42% and 50%, respectively, of the population in 1846, while the rest spoke both French and Flemish or German (Heuschling

1851: 24). Unequal industrialization and low levels of literacy hampered the spread of civil society organizations in the Flemish parts of the country. More importantly, a large share of the industrial, commercial, and professional elites, including the high clergy, in the Flemish lands had shifted to French in the century before an independent Belgian state was founded in 1830. The social milieus within which voluntary organizations tend to flourish, in other words, were effectively French speaking even in the Flemish parts of the country.

Correspondingly, almost all voluntary associations in Belgium conducted their affairs in French, and the large majority of early publications inspired by the Enlightenment movement were printed in French. When members of these circles rose to power in 1830—governing in an uneasy alliance with conservative Catholics during the first years—they took it for granted that the official language of the independent country would be French and that the central government, the courts, the army, the universities, and the secondary schools should all be run in French. In this way, a skewed distribution of power emerged, with the minority of French speakers "capturing" the central state and its administration. Flemish intellectuals and nationalists gradually politicized the ethnic divide and grew increasingly resentful of the second-class status of their language and its speakers.

Only after World War I did this ethnocratic configuration of power change, and only well after World War II could Flemish speakers assume positions of power in the national government without having to switch to French. The power-sharing arrangement that finally emerged, after 150 years of ethnocracy, came too late to generate a strong superseding national identity à la Suisse. In the early decades of independence, too few transethnic political networks were available to build an encompassing nation, and political identities crystallized along linguistic boundaries instead. Many of the political challenges of contemporary Belgium—such as the problems that result from splitting up more and more state institutions into a Flemish and a French branch—thus stem, I will argue, from the failure of nation building in the 19th century.

Civil Society Organizations as a French Affair

The first historical turning point to focus upon is again the foundation of the modern nation-state. After a short war in 1830, Belgium split from the United Dutch Kingdom of which Belgium had become a part after the defeat of Napoleon's empire in 1815. The previous French rule over Belgium had lasted from 1794, when France's revolutionary troops swept over northern Europe. Prior to French control, the Habsburg Empire ruled Belgium for centuries, first from Spain and then from Austria. The Habsburgs managed to retain their Belgian territories after they had lost the Netherlands to independence in the 17th century.

In contrast to the stable linguistic demography of Switzerland, an increasing number of the emerging bourgeoisie in the Flemish-speaking parts of the territory shifted to French (the following draws on Murphy 1988). Language assimilation had already begun in the 13th century when the Belgian territories became part of the Duchy of Burgundy, whose administration spoke French. The process of Frenchification was reinforced after Dutch independence from Spain in the 17th century because many Flemish-speaking elites from Belgium crossed the border into the Netherlands to escape Habsburg rule. But the main driver of the process was the prestige of French and France in the 17th and 18th centuries. French became the language of cultural, political, ecclesiastical, and economic elites throughout Belgium (and Europe in general), as well as the language of instruction in the universities, with the exception of a university in Louvain that continued to teach in Latin. During long centuries, French was the language of the Hapsburg administration of Belgium, while provincial and local affairs in the Flemish-speaking parts were conducted in that language.

The Frenchification of the Flemish bourgeoisie was further accelerated during the Napoleonic period. French became the mandatory language in the courts and administrations of the entire country, and the newly founded universities and secondary schools all taught in French. The Napoleonic regime regarded French as the language of enlightenment and progress and associated Flemish with irrationality, backwardness, and conservative (Catholic) counterrevolutionary tendencies. It began an active policy of Frenchification: in 1805, Flemish was banned from academic and literary circles by decree; the publication of Flemish books and newspapers became restricted by censorship (Schryver 1981); the simultaneous publication of French translations was mandatory for all Flemish journals and other periodicals; Flemish-speaking officials in the northern provinces were gradually replaced by French speakers (Busekist 1998); and so forth.

As a result, one had to thoroughly master the master's language to make a career in Napoleon's Belgium. French spread from the high bourgeoisie and clergies downward to merchants, lower-level professionals, functionaries, and magistrates. Among the educated, only the lower clergy of the Flemish North resisted Frenchification and stuck to the language of their flock as well as the language of the guardian of the world's flocks: Latin. The seminary schools, which many of the first-generation Flemish activists attended, continued to teach in Flemish. As a side note, the assimilation of Flemish elites into French culture and language illustrates another aspect of the overall argument of the book: strongly centralized states offered incentives for linguistic assimilation. The counterfactual thus holds that if French rule had continued for another century, Flemish might well have suffered the same fate as Breton or Aquitaine in France proper and gradually disappeared.

History took another turn, however. When Napoleon's empire collapsed and Europe's borders were redrawn in Vienna in 1815, the Belgian territories were "reunified" with the northern Netherlands into a united kingdom under a Dutch king, William I. He initially tried to reverse the linguistic tide by re-Dutchifying the Flemish-speaking parts of the country, imposing Dutch as the administrative language of these provinces, shifting the language of secondary schools to Flemish, and having all French speakers learn Flemish as a secondary language. The French-speaking elites of the Flemish lands vehemently opposed this policy. In the 1820s, a petition against the Dutch-ification policy gathered 320,000 signatures, 240,000 of which came from the Flemish parts of the country, that is, from its Frenchified bourgeoisie (Polasky 1981: 41).

The Dutch king could not reverse the Frenchification of the bourgeoisie of the Flemish North. His aggressive language policy was soon abandoned by granting "linguistic liberty" to all subjects, which de facto meant that the Fran-cophone elites of the Flemish North were free to revert to French (Schryver 1981: 21). To be sure, the process of Frenchification remained confined to the elite sections of the population in the North. The vast majority continued to speak Flemish. In 1830, the year of Belgian independence, only 1.7% of the population in Anvers, 5% in Limburg, 1.6% in Oriental Flanders, and 5.3% in Occidental Flanders spoke French in their daily lives (Busekist 1998: 64).

The Frenchification of the Flemish bourgeoisie combined with two other processes to confine, as we will see in a moment, the development of civil society organizations to the French-speaking population. The first is the un-even process of industrialization. Like Switzerland, Belgium belonged to the early industrializers of Continental Europe. In the Flemish North, urban man-ufacturers built on a long tradition of textile craftsmanship. In the French-speaking South, a classic 19th-century steel industry emerged thanks to the coal reserves in the Sambre-Meuse valley. In contrast to Switzerland, however, the vast majority of the Flemish-speaking, rural hinterland was not touched by any form of industrialization and remained rooted in an agricultural, locally oriented economy and society. No parallel to the waterpower-driven, rural industrialization in central Switzerland developed in Belgium. Furthermore, for the reasons outlined above, while northern industrialization indeed cre-ated new bourgeois circles of manufacturers, merchants, and so forth, these were de facto part of the French-speaking segment of Belgian society. In other words, industrialization did not spread bourgeois social circles equally across language groups.

Second and in contrast to Switzerland's conglomerate of self-governed city-states, Belgium was ruled in a much more centralized fashion by foreign powers, the absolutist Habsburg rulers first, the strongly centralized French government under Napoleon later, and the equally centralized Dutch kingdom thereafter. This had two consequences. On the one hand, the Belgian population was almost entirely Catholic, as was the rest of the Habsburg Empire as well as France. There was no competition between churches and therefore fewer incentives for the clergy to teach the population how to read and write before the state began to educate the masses. Literacy rates in Belgium therefore tended to be considerably lower than those in Switzerland. While approximately 65% of the Swiss population could read and write as early as 1785 (calculated on the basis of Messerli 2002 and Grunder 1998), only 48% in Belgium could even sign their names in 1800 (Reis 2005).

On the other hand, the foreign rulers of Belgium had more to fear from the flourishing of new ideas, especially from any longing for national autonomy and independence. They controlled or even suppressed civil society organizations much more than was the case in Switzerland, whose cantonal governments lacked both the motivation and the capacity to do the same. In 1785, for example, the Austrian emperor Joseph II was worried about the rising influence of Freemasonry in his Belgian lands and took control of the movement, limiting the number of lodges dramatically (only three survived in Brussels, for example; Arvelle 1995: 23). While the lodges rebounded, as we will see, during the Napoleonic period, the activities of voluntary organizations remained closely monitored and restricted. The Napoleonic penal code of 1810, effective until the revolution of 1830, stated that "no association of more than 20 persons that gather every day or specific days to take care of religious, literary, political or any other matter can be formed without the consent of government and only under the conditions that the public authorities see fit" (my translation, cited in Vries and Vries 1949: 24). While the extent to which this was effectively enforced is unclear, the contrast with Switzerland, where many members of cantonal governments joined such associations, is quite instructive.

The Frenchification of the Flemish bourgeoisie, unequal industrialization across language groups, lower rates of literacy, and a more pronounced control of political life combined to limit the spread of civil society organizations in general and, more particularly, to largely confine them to the French-speaking parts of the population. To illustrate this, let us first look at the Freemasons, who played an important role in the political life of Belgium before independence (Ertman 2000).

During the Habsburg period, some Freemason lodges were made up of the nobility, some united mostly priests or mostly officers, and some had a mixed membership that included lawyers, traders, high-ranking civil servants, and businessmen. All lodges had French names and were frequented by French speakers, including the elites of the Flemish parts of the country (Arvelle 1995: 21). After the setback brought about by the policies of Joseph II, the lodges flourished again during the Napoleonic period, especially the military lodges dedicated to the cult of the emperor. Membership broadened considerably to include the bourgeoisie and comprised a total of 2,500 men, or roughly one member per 820 males. During the Dutch period, the lodges had the same social composition but broadened their aims to include education in literary and scientific matters and spreading the new spirit of enlightenment. They continued to be found across the country but comprised mostly French-speaking elites (Arvelle 1995). Conformingly, they were at the forefront in opposing the Dutchification policy of William I (Busekist 1998: 41).

The uneven distribution of early modern associations can also be seen in the press and in the book market, which fed these voluntary associations with information and ideas. Of the 17 newspapers that had existed in the pre-revolutionary period on which we focus here, only 5 published in Flemish, the mother tongue of the majority of the population. In 1841, 11 years after the revolution, the number of newspapers had increased to 80, three-quarters of which were still in French. Nine years after the revolution (data for earlier periods are not available), 197 original writings such as political pamphlets, books, and the like were published in French and only 88 in Flemish (Heusch-ling 1851: 88, 341–342). These numbers indicate that modern associational and intellectual life failed to spread across the language boundary and remained confined to French speakers of both Walloon and Flemish origins.

The Independent State: An Ethnocracy of French Speakers

The number of associations, French-speaking, increasingly politicized, Belgian nationalist, anti-monarchical, and liberal, grew over time. As in Switzerland, they played a crucial role in the foundation of the modern state. The revolution of 1830 was the combined result of the antipathy that the Dutchification policy of William I had generated among the French-speaking elites all over Belgium; the fears among the clergy that the introduction of "religious freedom" mandated by King William meant freedom for Protestant groups from the Netherlands to proselyte, under protection from the king, among the Catholic Belgians, and that his policy of establishing state schools would undermine the educational authority of the Church; the opposition among southern industrialists from the coal and steel region against the low Dutch tariffs; and inspiration by the anti-monarchical July Revolution of neighboring France (Busekist 1998; Murphy 1988; Schryver 1981).

While the support base of the Belgian revolutionaries was conformingly heterogeneous, the leadership role clearly fell to the urban groups already organized in voluntary organizations such as the Freemasons. As Witte and coauthors put it:

> There is no danger of exaggeration in the claim that the middle class was the core of revolutionary activity. It created action groups and established

opposition networks where the input of newspapers was instrumental. In every single city, it controlled resistance committees. They prepared larger protest actions, including petitions, during which they gained support of large sections of the non-intellectual part of the population. Their political know-how showed when they used the social unrest of August 10 to fan the fires of revolution. (2009: 23)

Correspondingly, after the overthrow of the Dutch monarchy, these liberal, urban, bourgeois circles rose to power and defined the contours of the new, independent state and its government. They had to share power, however, with the Catholic clergy and other conservative groups during the first 15 years. We thus arrive at the first turning point in the historical narrative: the moment when the modern nation-state is established, its constitutional principles are determined, and a new configuration of ethnopolitical power emerges.

As in Switzerland, the bourgeois associational networks and the corresponding social milieus dominated the new state, together with the conservative Catholic clergy. The crucial difference with Switzerland, however, was that these associational networks as well as the high clergy comprised almost exclusively French speakers. The new elite therefore was almost entirely French speaking as well (Murphy 1988: 50, 52), while it included, as we have seen, German, French, and Italian speakers in Switzerland. As in Switzerland, the language question was not perceived as a major political issue for another generation. The main political dividing lines separated, as in Switzerland, Catholic conservatives from liberals. As in Switzerland, the new rulers declared their own language(s) to be the official language(s) of the state. In stark contrast to the multilingual state of Switzerland, this meant that French became the sole official language of Belgium. Writes the well-known historian Henri Pirenne about the constitutional convention:

> There was less opposition between the Flemish and the Walloons (i.e. French speakers) than between the Catholics and the liberals. All belonging to the same social milieu, all speaking the same language, French, all devoted to the same cause, and for the purpose of creating a common nationality, all careful to avoid anything divisive. (1902: 440)

French became, according to Article 23 of the constitution, the language of the military, the judiciary, the central administration, and parliament. The constitution also guaranteed "free use of language," which in practice meant that the elites of the North could use French in the public administration of these regions. In contrast to Switzerland, the new state was highly centralized, modeled after neighboring France. Five years later, the new, Belgian king issued a decree mandating that all institutions of higher learning (including secondary schools) use French, while primary education continued to be provided in Flemish in the North (Murphy 1988: 63–64). The severe property restrictions on voting rights (only 2% of men could cast a ballot) effectively skewed the power configuration further in favor of French speakers, who included, as we have seen, the bourgeoisie of the northern, Flemish parts of the country.

Many leaders of the revolution hoped that these policies would transform Belgium, over the long run, into a Francophone country. One of the Jacobin leaders of the revolution, a member of the first provisional government and later prime minister, Charles Rogier, made this quite explicit in an often-cited letter:

> The first principles of a good administration are based upon the exclusive use of one language, and it is evident that the only language of the Belgians should be French. In order to achieve this result, it is necessary that all civil and military functions are entrusted to Walloons and Luxemburgers; this way, the Flemish, temporarily deprived of the advantages of these offices, will be constrained to learn French, and we will hence destroy bit by bit the Germanic element in Belgium. (cited in Hermans 1992: 72)

At that time, the erection of an ethnocratic state ruled by and for French speakers met little resistance among the Flemish majority precisely because it lacked the organizational infrastructure for mounting an opposition. The rural Flemish population remained tightly integrated into the political hierarchy established by the Catholic Church (Ertman 2000: 164). In this context, it is noticeable that as late as 1883, only 20% of children attended public schools; the rest received their primary education in Catholic schools. As Schryver (1981: 22) notes, there had therefore been "no noticeable intellectual awakening among the Flemish population." Flemish speakers had not yet, in other words, developed a politicized ethnic consciousness; their horizons of identity continued to be centered on the parish and the province, which had existed as political entities since the medieval era.

While the intellectual ancestors of the Flemish movement go back to prominent figures of the late 18th century (such as Jan Babtist Verloy), the movement started to gain momentum only after the revolution and as a reaction to the complete marginalization of the Flemish language in the new state. As often happens, folklorists and poets formed the first wave of the "national awakening." In 1836, a literary society, the Maetschappij tot Bevordering der Nederduitsche Tael- en Letterkunde (Society for the Advancement of the Study of Flemish Language and Literature), was founded. In 1841 the Taelcongres followed, and in 1842 the Nederduitsch Tael en Letterkundig Genootschap. Finally, an umbrella organization (the Taelverbond) emerged in 1844, whose first congress was attended by 500 individuals. In 1849, the Vlaemsch

Middencomiteit emerged, which raised some more explicitly political concerns (Busekist 1998; on the Flemish movement, see also Hroch 2000 [1969]: chap. 17).

This early movement generated, in 1840, a petition to parliament that was signed by 30,000 individuals (Schryver 1981: 27). It demanded that Dutch be used in official affairs in the Flemish provinces and that Ghent University be bilingual. The petition was largely ignored by the ruling Francophone elites. During the 1850s and 1860s, the movement gained momentum and became more politically courageous, demanding self-rule in the Flemish provinces and a more equal representation of Flemish speakers at the central government. The liberal political association Willemsfonds was created in 1851, and the Vlamingen Vooruit in 1858. The first liberal Flemish leagues were constituted later on, such as Vlaamse Bond in Anvers in 1866 and the Vlamsche Liberale Vereeniging in Gand in 1861, in Brussels in 1877, and in Bruges in 1878 (Busekist 1998: 83).

A first success came in 1856 with an official report that recommended elevating the status of the language: Flemish should be taught in secondary schools in Flemish provinces; Ghent University should offer courses in Flemish culture and literature; citizens should be allowed to choose the language in which they communicate with government agencies; Dutch or French should be the language in which the central government interacts with Flemish provinces; the courts should speak the language of litigants; and so forth (Murphy 1988: 66–67). In 1861, the first Flemish political party, the Meetingpartij, was founded in Antwerp. In the 1860s, finally, members of the Flemish movement won parliamentary seats in Antwerp and thus gained a minimum of representation in the political system.

The important point to underline here is that the voluntary associations and political organizations that spoke in the name of the Flemish majority all developed a full generation *after* the foundation of the modern state. In the Swiss case, by contrast, minority French speakers formed an integral part, as French speakers and speaking French, of these organizational networks well before the foundation of the modern state. The alliance networks that rose to power in the newly founded Belgian state and that set up its ethnocratic foundations were made up entirely of French speakers—including, as we have seen, a good number of individuals from the Flemish parts of the country who had assimilated into the dominant language and culture generations prior.

It is not the moment here to review in detail the political developments that eventually overcame, 100 years later, this ethnocratic power structure. In a nutshell, the Flemish movement finally gained a mass following in the 1870s. A new, Flemish-speaking bourgeoisie of professionals and white-collar workers supported the movement because they were disadvantaged by the language requirements for upward mobility in Belgian society. The movement had a series of successes, from the 1873 bill that mandated that criminal trials be conducted in Dutch in the northern provinces to the 1883 bill that allowed some preparatory courses in secondary schools to be in Flemish. The final achievement came in 1898, when Flemish was acknowledged as an official language of the country. In the 1920s and 1930s, after property restrictions on voting rights had been abolished and vast numbers of poor Flemish speakers were enfranchised, a series of reforms finally made Flemish the official language of administration, primary and secondary education, and the courts in the North and established a Flemish university in Ghent—the first serious revisions to the ethnocratic regime, giving Flemish speakers self-rule at the regional level.

The Flemish movement regained strength in the 1960s and 1970s and finally began to take aim at the national power configuration itself. After a long series of increasingly bitter battles, the Belgian state was divided into two largely autonomous, linguistically defined substates and the two language communities shared power in a much-weakened federal government. As a final step in the ethnic compartmentalization of the state, even the institutions of social security were divided up into two separate entities. The party system, which had formed during the last quarter of the 19th century, also reorganized and split along linguistic divides, giving rise to Flemish and Walloon branches of the hitherto united Christian Democrats, Socialists, and Liberals.

More than a century after the foundation of the state, then, the ethnocratic regime was finally replaced with a conflict- and crisis-prone but decisively more inclusionary power-sharing arrangement. The persistence of the ethnocratic regime over generations and the long struggle necessary to transform it explain why nation building also failed at the level of political identities. A sense of shared political destiny and loyalty to the Belgian state became ever more elusive. In the mid-1990s, only 17% and 25% of Flemish and French speakers, respectively, felt "more Belgian than Flemish/Walloon" according to survey results (Billiet et al. 2003: 246). Heated debates have emerged because the Flemish regions, whose economic development surged ahead in the deindustrialized economy of the past decades, are net contributors to the welfare state, while the French regions are net receivers (Cantillon et al. 2013). Such imbalances can also be found in Switzerland, for example in the national unemployment insurance system. But no one seems to perceive them as a matter of ethnic injustice that the government needs to address.

Conclusion

Comparing the Swiss and Belgian cases shows that nation building depends on the reach of the political alliances maintained by the elites who take control of a newly formed nation-state. Where these alliances stretched across an ethnic divide, became institutionalized, and organizationally stabilized, ethnicity was never politicized, an integrated power structure emerged, and a pan-ethnic national identity developed. Where elite networks were bounded by ethnic divisions and important segments of the population therefore remained excluded from political representation, nation building failed, political competition pitted ethnic communities against each other, and ethnic identities became more politically salient than the imagined community of the nation. The boundaries of elite political networks during the early periods of nation-state formation thus shape the prospects of nation building.

More specifically, the comparison between Belgium and Switzerland shows the important role that voluntary associations play in shaping these boundaries. Because voluntary associations facilitate horizontal linkages across a territory, the more associational networks have developed during the period leading to the creation of a nation-state, the easier it will be for the new governing elites to build alliances across ethnic divides by relying on these networks. How far and how evenly voluntary organizations spread across regions and language groups depends, as the case studies suggest, on the nature of the political system, geographic patterns of industrialization, and the rise of literacy.

But how can we be sure that there are not other differences between the two countries that explain their contrasting trajectories of nation building even better? In many respects, the two countries are very similar indeed—and these similarities obviously are not suited to explain why nation building succeeded here but not there. Both Switzerland and Belgium are divided between a prestigious "high culture" and language (French) and more peripheral cultures and languages (Alemannic and Flemish) whose speakers form, however, the demographic majority. Both countries were early industrializers, as noted above. In other respects, however, the two countries differ from each other.

Switzerland has three major language groups, while Belgium has only two of roughly equal size. Shouldn't we expect more polarized configurations to be more conflictual, as argued by Montalvo and Reynal-Querol (2005)? The answer depends on how we interpret the linguistic demography of the two countries; if we focus on a higher and politically more relevant level of linguistic differentiation, then we find that Switzerland has 63% Germanic speakers and 37% speakers of Latin languages (Italian, French, and Romance), while in Belgium the shares are 60% (59% Dutch and 1% German) versus 40%. The levels of polarization are therefore roughly comparable.

Another demographic difference is that Switzerland is also religiously heterogeneous and that the Catholic-Protestant divide crosscuts the linguistic boundary. Belgium is largely Catholic. Prominent political scientists have argued that "cross-cutting" cleavages, such as in Switzerland, balance each other out and lead to less conflict (Lipset 1960). In Chapter 5 I will evaluate this argument with systematic data from 107 countries. There is no evidence that nation building is easier when religious and linguistic boundaries crisscross each other. While Switzerland and Belgium certainly differ from each other in that regard, it is therefore unlikely that the relationship between religious and linguistic cleavages explains why nation building succeeded here and failed there.

Others may point to the different political regimes that governed the two countries during the 19th and early 20th centuries. Switzerland was a full democracy after 1848, while Belgium was governed as a semiauthoritarian kingdom after independence and only gradually, over the course of the next century, expanded democratic rights and institutions. The Polity dataset, which codes countries on a democracy scale from −10 (total autocracy) to +10 (full democracy), gives Switzerland a score of +10 from 1848 onward. Belgium starts with a −4 in 1830 and reaches +10 only in 1932, after property restrictions on voting rights were lifted. Different levels of authoritarian control certainly matter: I have argued that civil societies flourished more in Switzerland because of the decentralized and more democratic nature of the polity.

But perhaps democracy itself facilitates nation building because politicians have to seek votes in every corner of the country and cannot afford to reject supporters from a different ethnic background. Again, Chapter 5 evaluates this possibility statistically with data for 155 countries from around the world. Without going into detail here, I do find that democracy and nation building go hand in hand. But this is not, as I will show, because democracy leads to political integration across ethnic divides but because political exclusion prevents democratization. In line with this finding, the political exclusion of the Flemish majority might help explain why Belgium was so late in giving all its (male) citizens full voting rights. Conversely, early Swiss nation building made it easier to establish democratic institutions because the new rulers of the country did not have to fear empowering voters of different ethnic backgrounds.

Given these two statistical results, we can be more confident that the different trajectories of nation building in Belgium and Switzerland are indeed influenced by how the organizational infrastructure for building political alliances developed in these two countries. That the early rise of voluntary organizations fosters nation building obviously represents a tendency, not a law. Critical junctures from time to time open the space of contingency and allow imagining a different future. During World War I, Switzerland could have fallen apart along its linguistic fault lines. Belgium could have developed, in the late 19th or early 20th century, a more inclusionary power configuration giving Flemish speakers a seat at the table of central government without requiring them to assimilate into French culture and language.

But the same structural forces that shaped early nation building kept future developments on the same track: Switzerland's transethnic civil society organizations played an important role in holding the country together during

World War I, reinforcing political ties across ethnic divides and propagating a newly developed pan-ethnic nationalism. In Belgium, path dependency worked towards the opposite outcome: ambitious Flemish-speaking politicians assimilated into the ruling French-speaking elite because this was the only way to make a political career. The monolingual Flemish population was therefore continuously deprived of the leadership necessary to challenge the ethnocratic regime. To cast this idea of path dependency into metaphorical terms, there were certainly plenty of events that led the two ships to change direction, with lots of political drama on the bridge and among the rank-and-file sailors. But they did so within the range of motion that the winds allowed—no sailing ship can steer a course against the wind.

3

Public Goods

BOTSWANA VERSUS SOMALIA

This chapter focuses on the second mechanism that generates more encompassing networks of political alliances, integrating individuals from a variety of ethnic backgrounds. A well-organized, capable state that can deliver public goods—roads, schools, health services, clean water, protection from arbitrary violence, and so forth—represents an attractive partner in the ongoing exchanges between governing elites and citizens. Large segments of the population will seek to establish an alliance with the state in exchange for their political loyalty and support. In democracies, citizens are more likely to vote for such a regime. In nondemocracies, they will be less inclined to engage in everyday forms of resistance—foot-dragging, gossiping, ridiculing the rulers, or not reporting a clandestine organization opposing the regime. In democracies and nondemocracies alike, citizens will comply with bureaucratic rules and legal prescriptions and thus facilitate the implementation of public policies and the collection of taxes. They will resist the siren songs of separatists and other oppositional forces that do not accept the state in its current constitutional form.

How public goods provision generates political loyalty can be illustrated with the following anecdote from Ukraine, taken from the *New York Times* of September 14, 2014. A reporter asked a woman what she thought of the Luhansk People's Republic, which Russian separatists had just declared independent after months of fighting Ukrainian troops. "Where will they get the money?" she asked in return. "If they [the separatists] had money, they could have already started construction brigades or something. I don't care what country we live in or what it is called; I just want peace. I just want gas, water and school for the children." Over time, I argue, this woman would start to identify with a state that would provide her with what she needs for her daily survival and for her children to have a better future. She would become loyal to such a state, offering political support and thus integrating herself into the web of alliances centered on government. Eventually her children will consider themselves members of the nation in the name of which that state will govern: Luhanskian, Russian, or Ukrainian.

In this chapter, I will illustrate how public goods provision can lead to nation building by again pursuing two country histories at the macro level and over a longer period of time. As with Belgium and Switzerland, I chose two cases that conform well to the hypothesis. And as with the previous comparison, the two countries are situated at the opposite ends of the "regression line": a state that is exceptionally good at providing public goods and succeeded at nation building, and a state that provided little in terms of public services and wasn't able to politically integrate its diverse population. This time, the examples are drawn from sub-Saharan Africa, contrasting Botswana and Somalia. Both countries are characterized by extraordinarily dry weather conditions, are of similar size, had economies based almost exclusively on raising cattle or camels, were very poor at independence, and were colonized by Western powers for a roughly similar period of time.

The colonial experiences, however, also diverged from each other. Somalia was divided between a British and an Italian territory, while all of Botswana became part of the British Empire. The British ruled Botswana as well as northern Somalia without interfering much in the affairs of the local population. Italians established a more directly ruled settler colony in southern Somalia. It is perhaps useful to explore, before I begin the detailed discussion of the two cases, whether this could possibly explain the different trajectories of nation building. In the detailed analysis that follows, I will not find much evidence for such a view even though the exact nature of the colonial bureaucracy and the transition to independence mattered quite a bit, as we will see. But maybe styles of colonialism, beyond these two cases, help explain why some nations come together politically after the colonizers leave while others struggle with contentious ethnic politics or even violent secessionist conflict. In Chapter 5 I explore this possibility with a statistical analysis of a large number of countries from around the world. I find that neither former settler colonies (such as Italian Somalia) nor more indirectly ruled ex-colonies (such as Botswana) nor the former domains of particular colonial powers (British, Italian, French, Ottoman, etc.) are more or less successful at nation building. Furthermore, countries that were colonized by more than one colonial power, as was Somalia, are not less politically integrated after independence than others (in contrast to Vogt [2016]). We can therefore be more confident that the capacity to provide public goods, rather than the different colonial experience, is a crucial factor in understanding why Botswana's postcolonial fate so dramatically diverged from that of Somalia. I discuss Botswana first.

Botswana, Africa's France

Botswana is a landlocked country bordered by South Africa to the south, Namibia to the west and north, and Zimbabwe to the east. Its climate is dry, and most of the terrain is made up of the sandy Kalahari Desert, where the nomadic sections of the so-called Bushmen used to live as hunter-gatherers. The country is about as large as Ukraine, Texas, France, Spain, or Kenya but only sparsely populated by a bit more than two million individuals. They mostly live along the more fertile eastern edge of the country bordering South Africa and Zimbabwe.

Botswana is seen as one of Africa's success stories. It has sustained high levels of economic growth, mostly fueled by the discovery and exploitation of diamond fields. In contrast to other mineral-exporting countries across the continent and the world, however, Botswana's dependence on diamonds has not led to a "resource curse" with "bad governance" by rent-seeking, authoritarian elites. To the contrary, Botswana's governments are free of endemic corruption, have been democratically elected since independence in 1966, and have been able to avoid pervasive, let alone armed, conflict (Robinson and Parsons 2006; Handley 2017; du Toit 1995; Samatar 1999).

Botswana is often considered an ethnically homogeneous country, at least by African standards. Many economists believe that such homogeneity fosters economic growth and public goods provision (La Porta et al. 1999; Alesina and La Ferrara 2005; see Chapter 7). Was Botswana successful at providing public services because the vast majority of its population speaks Tswana? This interpretation overlooks the fact that the Tswana are internally differentiated into a series of smaller ethnopolitical communities (du Toit 1995: 18; Binsbergen 1991), similar to the Somali-speaking clans of Somalia.

Furthermore, Botswana was remarkably more heterogeneous in the 1930s than it is today. Strongly centralized, small indigenous states inherited from the precolonial past then leveled out this polyglot landscape through amalgamation and assimilation into the politically dominant Tswana culture and language. Linguistic and identity assimilation accelerated after independence, thanks to the legitimacy of the nation-building project pursued by successive governments. In other words, Botswana's remarkable history of state formation and nation building explains why most Batswana speak the same language today, rather than the other way around (for a more general analysis along these lines, see Chapter 7).

The nation-building project was successful, I will argue, because effective and equitable public goods provision allowed the ruling elites to extend their networks of political alliances and support across the entire territory. In a certain way, then, Botswana's story resembles that of France of the Third Republic, when various regional, peasant populations who spoke Provencal, Aquitaine, Basque, and so on were assimilated into the French nation thanks to the effective provision of public goods—schools, hospitals, roads, welfare— by the central government. *Peasants into Frenchmen* is the title of Eugen Weber's (1979) well-known book describing this process. *Tribesmen to Tswana* would perhaps be an analogous book title for Botswana.

PRECOLONIAL CENTRALIZATION IN A MOSAIC SOCIETY

Botswana was ruled for centuries by eight Tswana kingdoms.[1] They were small in terms of population size, which rarely exceeded 100,000 inhabitants. But they were hierarchically integrated and territorially concentrated, in contrast to most African kingdoms, including the militarily much more powerful Zulu and Ndebele polities to the east and south. They can best be described as centralized mini-states.[2] Most subjects of the kings were required to live in the large villages and small towns around the king's palace. The towns were composed of several villages, each village had several wards, and each ward was populated by a group of related families and governed by a headman appointed by the king (Schapera 1938; Maundeni 2002). Each ward, village, and kingdom also had an assembly of adult men (called *kgotla*) where matters of public concern were discussed. The kings and their personal advisors, the council of headmen, and the representatives of prominent and powerful families tightly controlled the proceedings of these assemblies. The kings also stood at the center of the religious system and were responsible for the spiritual welfare of their subjects. No parallel religious authority existed (Maundeni 2002). When the kings converted to Christianity in the late 19th century, abolishing polygamy, beer drinking, and rain making, their subjects adopted the same Christian denomination in a classical *cuius regio, eius religio* fashion.

Economically, the kingdoms rested on cattle breeding and agriculture. Cattle represented wealth, prestige, and power. The *mafisa* system, known from other cattle-herding groups across southern Africa, stood at the core of the political economy: apart from his personal herds, each king controlled the vast herds of his kingdom proper, which were used to provide meat for public ceremonies and to nourish the poor. More importantly, the *mafisa* system— alive and well at least until the 1970s (Murray and Parsons 1990: 160n1)—established patron-client relationships with subordinate members of the royal family and the headmen. In return for herding royal cattle, consuming the milk, and using the animals for plowing, the headmen owed loyalty and provided services to the king—a system that was sometimes described as "cattle feudalism" (see Murray and Parsons 1990: 160). A king's power also rested on his ability to ban dissenting royal family members or headmen from his realms and to confiscate their cattle, thus making them stateless, powerless, and impoverished. Strict primogeniture rules further consolidated the power hierarchy because it limited political contestation among rival princes and headmen.

Similar to other southern African kingdoms, the Tswana kings could rely on a system of age regiments to work their land or build public infrastructure. Age regiments consisted of men of a similar age, with each cohort responsible for certain duties and ceremonies. A new regiment was formed once a prince came of the appropriate age. These age groups could also be mobilized as militias in times of war. Comparatively speaking, the Tswana kingdoms were militarily rather weak, however, because they did not maintain standing armies.

The Tswana kingdoms incorporated other groups,[3] which they had either conquered or accepted as refugees from neighboring conflicts, by assigning them a new ward or village and appointing a headman. The original inhabitants of the country, many of whom had lived as hunter-gatherers, were subjugated during the 19th century and held as hereditary serfs of the royal house and the headmen. They were mostly employed as cattle herders and did not have their own wards and headmen and therefore had no political voice whatsoever. The ruling Tswana elites used the term "Sarwa" (or "Bushmen" in English) to designate these groups of Khoisan speakers (Bennett 2002; Gadibolae 1985). Other original inhabitants of the land spoke Bantu and were called "Kgalagadi." Each kingdom thus came to resemble a mosaic of groups of different ancestry and mother tongues. This was still in evidence in the 1930s and early 1940s, when the anthropologist Isaac Schapera (1952: 65) collected data for a book about the ethnic composition of the Tswana kingdoms. Before I characterize this mosaic further, a brief note on the structure of ethnic differentiations in Botswana is in order.

As elsewhere in the world (cf. Wimmer 2014: chap. 2), we find a complex system of nested categories. For example, categories A and B might belong to a superarching category α, which stands in opposition to β, which is in turn composed of categories B and D (see also Figure D.1 for an example). Not all of these levels of categorical differentiation are equally relevant at a given point in time. Furthermore, different types of categories overlap in complex ways. To simplify, we can distinguish between ethnopolitical categories—basically referring to individuals of shared ancestry who politically support each other—and ethnolinguistic categories, which refer to a group of people who speak the same language. Among the latter, various dialects of Tswana are nested into the Tswana category, which forms part of the family of Southern Bantu languages (together with Kgalagadi, Tswapong, and Birwa), which is part of the Bantu family, to which Kalanga, Herero, and others also belong, but not the various Khoisan languages spoken by the Sarwa. Generally speaking, ethnopolitical categories were more relevant well into the postindependence period. Linguistic categories, such as "Tswana," remained meaningless until the late colonial period (Wilmsen 2002: 829) and even thereafter (Selolwane 2004: 10).

The ethnopolitical categories could be used in two ways. In a narrow sense, they referred to individuals who shared common origins, had migrated together into today's Botswana, and often formed, in the past and to various degrees in the present, some kind of political unit (a ward, a kingdom, the descendants of a prince). In this narrow sense, each kingdom was dominated by what could be called its "titular" ethnic group, such as the Ngwato in the Ngwato kingdom. To compare, imagine that the German speakers of the Austro-Hungarian Empire would call themselves "Habsburgs." This is how Schapera used the term.

In a more encompassing sense, however, the subordinated groups of each kingdom might also identify with the royal house and the state. "Ngwato" might therefore refer to all subjects of the Ngwato king—independent of their origin and language. This is how colonial and postcolonial administrators and politicians often used the term "tribe" (see Bennett 2002; Selolwane 2004). Imagine that we would call all subjects of the Austrian double monarchy, including Italian, Hungarian, Rumanian, Slovakian, Croatian, and Yiddish speakers, as "Habsburgs."

Based on Schapera's (1952) list of ethnopolitical groups in the narrower, ancestry-based sense of the term, I calculated the ethnic composition of each kingdom. It turns out that the "titular," dominant ethnic groups made up between only 7% (in the largest kingdom) and 82% of the population of their kingdoms. On average, titular ethnic groups populated only 32% of the kingdoms. Even if we count all Tswana ethnopolitical groups together, they made up only 55% of the combined population of the kingdoms. In all but one homogeneous small state, the kingdoms' populations were therefore quite diverse, counting between 3 and 26 different ethnopolitical groups.

COLONIALISM LIGHT

As mentioned above, these ethnically diverse, highly centralized, and densely settled kingdoms were militarily rather weak. In the middle of the 19th century the expanding Boer settlers in search of land and water had founded their own independent, white-dominated Transvaal state and attacked one of the Tswana kingdoms. Farther west, German missionaries and traders gained influence, culminating in the establishment of the German Southwest African protectorate in 1884 (today Namibia). The Tswana kings decided that it would be safer to seek protection, especially from the expanding Afrikaners, from a European colonial power and invited the British to establish a protectorate in 1885—a rare but not unique case of invited colonialism that we will see repeated in northern Somalia.

Britain soon lost its strategic interest in the Bechuanaland Protectorate, as Botswana was called, once the Ndebele of neighboring Rhodesia (today's Zimbabwe) had been subdued by the machine guns of the British South Africa Company and its Tswana allies, the Afrikaner states had been defeated by British troops at the end of the 19th century, and Germany had lost its colonies after World War I. Bechuanaland was therefore ruled with an extraordinarily light hand. Thirty years after the proclamation of the protectorate, its administration had only 277 staff members (Lange 2009: 9), most of whom resided across the border in South Africa. Later on in the mid-1930s, only 22 colonial administrators (besides policemen) actually lived within the boundaries of the protectorate. Botswana was also spared the influx of colonial settlers—at least compared to Kenya, South Africa, the Congo, and many other African colonies. Afrikaans-speaking cattle herders did acquire some fertile lands bordering South Africa and in the Ghanzi district of the interior, but their presence and impact remained very limited indeed.

In the 1930s, the British governor passed a series of proclamations that effectively made the kings part of the colonial administration—much to the consternation of some of the most powerful kings, who had thought of the protectorate as a treaty between sovereign nations rather than a submission to a foreign power (du Toit 1995: 24–25). The backing of the British rulers, however, reinforced the power of the kings rather than weakening them. The colonial administration usually supported them in conflicts with competing politicians or unruly subjects and gave them a head start in the slowly ensuing privatization of water holes and grazing lands for cattle.[4]

The colonial government did little to nothing, until the very last years of British rule, to provide its subjects with public goods. The Tswana kingdoms, however, built a rudimentary administration and started to establish elementary schools for their subjects. They were funded first by the kings' own taxes and royal coffers, later on by the Tribal Treasuries that received a third of the colonial head tax. In 1933, there were 98 primary schools run by royal governments. After World War II, four kingdoms opened their own secondary schools—the only ones in the protectorate until the very end of colonial rule (Murray and Parsons 1990: 165–166). In total, 20–35% of Bechuanaland's population could read and write in 1950, in contrast to the estimated 1–5% of British and French Somaliland at the time (UNESCO 1957).

While thus conserving the precolonial power structure, colonial rule did change the economics of everyday life, especially with the introduction of a head tax in 1899. It was supposed to generate enough funds for the colonial administration to rule the protectorate without any net costs for London. To pay for the tax and to evade the prevalent poverty brought about by a long series of droughts, an increasing number of men began to migrate to South Africa to work in the mines (Murray and Parsons 1990: 163–164). According to du Toit (1995: 27), the number of males employed outside the protectorate rose from 2,000 in 1910 to 10,000 in 1935 and to 50,000 in 1960 (for different estimates, see Murray and Parsons 1990).

The period of indirect rule came to an end in the late 1950s, when the colonial government started to gradually invest in the education of an indigenous administrative elite in order to prepare the colony for independence. This became somewhat urgent in the early 1960s when the colonial office realized that it could not hand the protectorate over to an internationally ostracized apartheid state next door, as had long been the plan (for details, see Lange 2009). Already at the end of the 1940s, the Fitzgerald Commission recommended training Africans for the colonial administration. Progress was extremely slow, however: the first African assistant district officer was appointed in 1951, and it was not until 1959 that a second followed. By 1962, four years before independence, the colonial administration counted only four Africans out of 155 administrative and professional employees (du Toit 1995: 26–27). During the last two years of colonial rule, the British developed a focused initiative to create more staff to run the postcolonial bureaucracy (Selolwane 2004: 45ff.). The program was overseen by a small committee that allocated bursaries for students to pursue higher education abroad.[5]

At the same time, the colonial government feverishly started to build a capital city for the future independent country, raising grants and loans to the protectorate from a mere £120,000 in 1953–1954 to £1.8 million in 1964–1965 (Murray and Parsons 1990: 166). Political reforms were meant to build "modern" institutions that could govern the territory once it graduated to independence. In 1957, the Local Councils Proclamation introduced elected tribal councils to assist the kings. The Local Government Act of 1965 established nine elected district councils, which replaced the tribal councils. These councils were to form the basic units of government (du Toit 1995: 24–25, 50).

In the run-up to independence, two competing visions of the future emerged. One was put forward by the kings and their entourage. It foresaw a federalized country composed of their statelets, with the national government responsible to a legislative council appointed by the kings (Maundeni 2002: 124–125; Selolwane 2004: 12). Later, the kings advocated for a fully empowered upper house composed of their ranks (du Toit 1995: 32). The other faction was led by the former king of the powerful kingdom of Ngwato who had to resign from his throne because while studying at Oxford he married an Englishwoman. His faction included the tiny educated elite of colonial civil servants, teachers in the royal schools, and some Kalanga speakers who resented the power of the other Tswana kings (Selolwane 2004: 12). Most importantly, however, he had the backing of the colonial bureaucracy and the political elites of London who were committed to creating a modern country "fit" for independence. For reasons that are beyond the purview of this chapter (see Lange 2009), the "new men" around the former king won out and brought most of the kings to their side and into the arms of the Botswana Democratic Party (Lange 2009; Selolwane 2004: 32). In 1966, Botswana became an independent country, one of the last former colonies on the African continent outside of the Portuguese domains.

POSTINDEPENDENCE STATE BUILDING

The story that followed is remarkable. It shows that one can build an effective, modern administration almost from scratch by relying on the political infrastructure of already existing, premodern states. Two aspects of this overall process need to be distinguished and emphasized: (1) the way in which the new regime incorporated the political alliance and support networks previously centered on the kingdoms, and (2) the emergence of an efficient bureaucracy at the level of national government. I discuss each aspect subsequently.

Botswana's postcolonial state building largely relied on precolonial state institutions. To be sure, there was a sharp discontinuity in the formal political role played by the Tswana kings. As discussed above, their power was stabilized during the colonial period. But the newly independent government proceeded, in a series of political reforms during the first years of independence, to dramatically curtail their influence by introducing a highly centralized presidential system.[6] The kings lost control over the allocation of grazing land with the establishment of the Land Boards; primary education and public works were no longer the responsibility of the kingdoms but of central government; national-level policies were implemented by the District Councils and the Commissioners rather than by the rudimentary royal administrations; and most important, the kings became effectively civil servants and were—at least in theory—responsible to the Ministry of Local Government and Lands and appointed by the president (see Jones 1983; du Toit 1995: 28).

However, instead of replacing or destroying the political capacities embodied in the royal institutions, the central state incorporated them. As du Toit rightly emphasizes, the new state was built upon, not against, the Tswana kingdoms. The kings continued to represent the apex of the traditional legal system and heard all cases that touched upon customary law (du Toit 1995: 29). Furthermore, the role of the royal assemblies, chaired and controlled by the chiefs, did not diminish in the age of democratic elections. They became "important means," as Lange (2009: 14) writes, "of educating the public about political reforms and engaging them within the new institutions" and providing these new institutions with legitimacy (see also du Toit 1995: 60–62; Holm 1987: 24). Finally, the kings held ex officio positions in the District Council, Land Boards, and Village Development Committees (Maundeni 2002: 125–126) and influenced their decisions in important ways.

A case study of the Kgatleng district in the 1980s shows how much power kings still held, in effect more than the appointed "new men," independent of what laws and regulations stipulated. The king "appoints representatives and headmen, uses regimental labor, directly controls a tribal police force increased in numbers and status" (Tordoff 1988: 190–191) and so forth. His power has been "steadily increasing since independence when in theory he has been losing it" (Grant 1980: 94). Similarly, at the local level, the Village Development Committees responsible to central government worked well only if in tune with the local *kgotla* and the local headmen who were appointed by the king.

The peaceful, negotiated, and slow transition to independence is the second reason why Botswana's postcolonial government was able to build an efficient administration in such a short period of time. The Oxbridge-trained colonial officers remained as paid consultants, and the postcolonial government formed under the first president hired new expat administrators. The percentage of senior public servants who were expatriates was 89% in 1965, the last year under colonial rule, and then decreased only slightly to 80% in 1966, then to 58% in 1970, 36% in 1975, and 35% in 1986, finally reaching, in 2003, a mere 2%. Given the massive and quick expansion of the central bureaucracy, from 2,175 positions in 1964 to 6,317 a decade later and to 21,000 in 1985, this meant that the absolute number of expatriates remained largely stable (du Toit 1995: 33–34)—in remarkable contrast to the situation in Somalia, as we will see. To fill the expanding bureaucracy with local staff, the government recruited nearly all graduates of the new secondary schools and promoted them rapidly (Selolwane 2004: 47).

Most observers agree that this slowly indigenizing bureaucracy maintained high levels of professional competence, recruited and promoted on the basis of merit, and developed an ethos of dedication to the public good—coming as close to an ideal-type Weberian bureaucracy as one has seen on the African continent. The technocratic and professional mind-set of the late colonial administrators and later the expatriates laid the basis for an organizational culture that survived their gradual retreat (du Toit 1995: 58ff.; Selolwane 2004: 47–55; Handley 2017; Samatar 1999: chap. 3). In contrast to the expats funded by Western aid agencies or international organizations who pursue their own agendas and priorities, the foreign bureaucrats in Botswana remained under the political control of the government and had little influence over policy decisions, as a detailed case study of the land reform program shows (du Toit 1995: 59n39).

Reinforced by the commitment to meritocracy of the first, Oxford-educated president (Selolwane 2004: 51)—the former king of the Ngwato—this Weberian ethos manifested itself in various laws and procedures. For example, the constitution does not allow civil servants to run for public office, insulating the bureaucracy from social and political pressures and increasing its autonomous planning capacity (Holm 1987; du Toit 1995: 60–62), again in contrast to Somalia. Furthermore, the government resisted pressure for rapid promotion or salary increases and recruited and promoted strictly on the basis of merit, at least up to the 1990s when some minor problems came to the surface (du Toit 1995: 48; Selolwane 2004: 52–55, 57).

As an unintended consequence of meritocracy, Kalanga speakers ended up massively overrepresented in the higher levels of the bureaucracy. This is because they got a head start in the educational system: they were peasants, rather than cattle breeders, and sent their boys to schools once these became available, rather than to the grazing grounds to herd the cows (Binsbergen 1991: 154–155). Kalanga speakers compose roughly 11% of the population but occupied 40% of the senior public service positions in the first year of independence and remained similarly overrepresented in the subsequent decade (Selolwane 2004: 49–51). This created some complaints and rumors of ethnic favoritism. As a result, parliament launched an inquiry in 1968 and initiated an affirmative action scheme for students from remote, rural schools (Selolwane 2004: 49–51). The rumors and complaints died down, at least for two decades, and the share of Kalanga among senior bureaucrats gradually declined to 24% in 2003.

Minority overrepresentation in the administration and allegations of favoritism have politicized ethnicity in many other countries, including Somalia. In Sri Lanka, for example, Tamils were overrepresented in the colonial bureaucracy, again because of an early education in missionary schools. This led to a nationalist backlash by parties representing the Sinhala majority. When they rose to power once the country became independent, they purged Tamils from the highest ranks of the administration. A downward spiral of mobilization and countermobilization emerged that led the country into a civil war lasting decades.

Kalanga overrepresentation did not trigger a similar dynamic, I suggest, because Kalanga bureaucrats never favored Kalanga regions and populations in a systematic way, in marked contrast to the civil servants of most other countries (Franck and Rainer 2012) and in particular to Somalia's administrators, who have a reputation for channeling resources to their fellow clansmen. The meritocratic, anti-nepotist ethos and its institutional correlates prevented Botswana's bureaucrats from transforming public goods into ethnic pork. According to Holm and Molutsi (1992, cited in du Toit 1995: 59), "Staff are routinely rotated around the country without regard to ethnic identity. Promotions are not governed by concern for ethnic balance. To further combat parochialism, the Ministry of Education places better secondary students, most of whom will enter the civil service, at residential schools outside their home district."

Whether due to these measures or the professionalism and the ethos of public service inherited from the British administrators, the bureaucracy had both the capacity and the political will to distribute public goods equally across the entire territory of the country, as we will see in the next section. The skewed representation of ethnic groups in the central state was therefore largely irrelevant from the point of view of the population at large. There was no reason for common citizens to seek support from coethnics when demanding services from the state, and ethnic bonds did not acquire much political meaning.

In short, Botswana's government acquired the administrative capacity to provide public goods in a brief period of time with the help of expatriate functionaries who established an organizational culture of meritocratic professionalism that outlasted their own appointments. The bureaucracy was able to reach down to the village level because it built its institutional apparatus on the foundations laid by the precolonial, strongly centralized and legitimized states. As we will see below, the Somali governments never succeeded, largely because of their weak roots in society, to incorporate the clan system into an independent governmental architecture and remained controlled by, rather than in control of, the corresponding political forces.

PUBLIC GOODS PROVISION

This newly independent state governed one of the poorest economies in the world. It remained based on cattle breeding and agriculture before diamonds were discovered five years after independence. During the first decade, the government focused on physical infrastructure—building the new capital Gaborone first and foremost but also bituminized roads—and on internationally marketing the main export product: beef. Much has been written about the fact that the royal elite and many of the newly appointed bureaucrats and politicians were among the largest cattle owners in the country. The interests of the economic and political elites thus largely coincided and laid the groundwork for the effective management and promotion of cattle exports (Handley 2017).

However, the majority of the smaller cattle producers also profited from the way in which the state managed the economy. The Botswana Meat Commission (BMC), a para-state institution established during the last years of colonial rule, guaranteed prices against world market swings; managed foreign exchange rates without overvaluating the national currency; served the interests of cattle exporters exclusively and wasn't allowed to make a profit; and managed to gain access to European markets (as part of Britain's entry into the European Economic Community in 1973; on the BMC, see Samatar 1999). Beef exports doubled from 1971 to 1973, and as a consequence, the income of cattle owners almost tripled from 1971 to 1976 (Murray and Parsons 1990).

There is no doubt that this state-managed export regime primarily benefited the largest cattle owners and that the land reforms of the mid-1970s further advantaged the owners of large herds (Good 1992: 83).[7] But even critical observers concede that both "allowed for more effective production for the market for all cattle owners of any size, not just the biggest" (Parson 1981: 254). Robinson and Parsons arrive at a similar conclusion, stating that the export promotion scheme provided "more widespread 'trickle down' of economic benefits than any form of sectional patrimonialism in other African countries" (2006: 121; see also Handley 2017).

Indeed, a majority of households were cattle owners. In 1980, approximately 55% of all rural households owned cattle, while the rest relied on migrant labor and small-scale agriculture to feed their families (Parson 1981; Good 1992: 77). Thanks to the efficient management of the cattle industry, the majority of the rural population supported the new regime, and the ruling Botswana Democratic Party (BDP) dominated the political landscape for decades (Handley 2017). The government offered important public goods—market access, favorable terms of trade, and price stability—for large segments of the citizenry, which allowed the ruling party to build networks of alliances across the entire territory, as we will see further below.

Even more relevant for the rural segments of the population, the government massively expanded transportation infrastructure, built schools, health and sanitation facilities, and established emergency programs for periods of drought. Most of these projects were financed by a renegotiation of the Customs Union with Apartheid South Africa in 1969, which brought state revenues from customs and duties from 5.1 million pula in 1969–1970 to 12.5 million in 1972 (ca. US$17 million). In 1971 diamond production began, and four years later the government negotiated a very favorable contract with de Beers, which foresaw 50–50 profit sharing. This boosted government revenues from mining from 2.8 million pula in 1972 to 18 million in 1975 (Murray and Parsons 1990: 168). Many observers have remarked that because government institutions were set up *before* diamond money filled the coffers, Botswana established an exceptional record of good governance and was spared—like Norway—the "resource curse" haunting many other resource-rich developing nations.

Be that as it may, the resources from customs and duties as well as from diamond mining did not disappear into the private bank accounts of politicians (as government funds did in Somalia) and were not used for "white elephant" prestige projects or for building massive armies (again as in Somalia).[8] Rather, they were used to deliver public goods across the territory (du Toit 1995: 21; Taylor 2002: 4). Some standard indicators illustrate the consequences. The percentage of children enrolled in primary school went from 43% in 1970 to 84% in 2009; adult literacy rates improved from 20–35% in 1950 (UNESCO 1957) to 87% in 2013; the mortality rate of children under the age of five went from 138 per 1,000 live births in the year of independence to 53 in 2012, while infant mortality fell from 108 deaths per 1,000 live births at independence (Taylor 2002: 3) to 28 in 2012. Malnutrition among children under the age of five declined from 25% in 1978 (Taylor 2002: 3) to less than 11% in 2007. From 1973 onward, every village had a health post, and larger villages with more than 1,000 inhabitants counted on a permanently staffed clinic. The number of physicians per 100,000 individuals increased from 4 in 1965 to 34 in 2010. The percentage of households with access to drinking water went from 56% in 1981 (Murray and Parsons 1990) to 93% in 2012. The government also invested massively in physical infrastructure such as roads—an important aspect of daily life in the vast, largely rural country. Paved roads increased from 25 kilometers at independence to 8,410 kilometers in 2005, and railway traffic increased threefold. At independence, there were 2 telephone lines per 1,000 individuals and 9 in 2013 (all data from the World Bank Development Indicators except where noted).

Another example of how efficiently Botswana's government delivered public goods is the drought relief program. When in 1984–1985 the rains failed to appear, most of the US$20 million spent seemed to have reached the poor. Malnutrition increased only slightly and there was no evidence of starvation (Holm 1987: 25). The food distribution program reached 90% of all rural households and the cash-for-work project employed 60,000 individuals (du Toit 1995: 56).

As important as the average level of public goods provision is its regional distribution. As noted above, there are no indications of ethnic favoritism in how public goods were allocated, despite the massive overrepresentation of Kalanga speakers in the bureaucracy. Selolwane wrote an excellent report on ethnic politics and public administration in Botswana. She notes that the government was committed to distributing development funds "as evenly as practical across the regions where tribal and ethnic communities lived so as to mitigate against the possible politicization of ethnic inequalities" (2004: 16). Holm echoes this by observing that "almost without exception, the ruling party has distributed the results of government programs highly equitably in regional terms. One expert examining the drought relief program went so far as to conclude that the government was so obsessed with the political need not to appear to favor a particular region that it was impossible for policy makers to target the 'most vulnerable' groups" (1987: 22).

ETHNOPOLITICAL INCLUSION AND NATION BUILDING

In line with the theoretical argument introduced in Chapter 1, equitable and effective public goods provision allowed the regime to extend alliance networks across the entire country. Many different observers of Botswana's political system reach this conclusion. Murray and Parsons attribute the series of electoral victories of the BDP to "its success as the government which delivered the goods" (1990: 169) and "enriched the lives of most Batswana, particularly in the fields of education and health. The suffering they experienced during the drought of the 1960s has not been repeated during the drought of the 1980s—that is progress enough" (171). According to du Toit, the BDP "has succeeded through its technocratic priorities of growth and stability (at the expense of participation and equity), in establishing a solvent enough state which is able to deliver public goods (roads, schools, watering facilities, clinics etc.) on a non-tribal, non-regional basis. . . . Ensuring that the state is seen as neutral, not as an ethnic body . . . contributes to its legitimacy and that of the regime" (1995: 121).

It is now time to explore whether the extension of political alliance networks across ethnic divides, facilitated by equitable and efficient public goods provision, produced an inclusive configuration of power—one of the two key aspects of nation building. Botswana is a multiparty democracy with reasonably free elections and a free press. The ethnic makeup of the parliament—elected through a majoritarian, first-past the-post system—is thus a good first indicator of the power configuration and structure of alliances. In order to estimate over- or underrepresentation in the parliamentary system, we need to know more about the ethnic makeup of the population. This is no easy task since the government does not collect any systematic data on the ethnic background of individuals or the languages they speak. The census allows individuals to select only one "mother tongue," for example. The parallels to the French approach to ethnic diversity are striking.

To estimate the ethnic makeup of the population, I use two data sources. The first is the population share of the speakers of the various languages (in cluding secondary speakers). These data come from Ethnologue, a website maintained by Protestant missionaries who translate the Bible into the languages of the world to "save" its speakers. The second data refer to the population of the districts that are dominated by the various "titular" Tswana groups, which allows us to roughly estimate the population share of the ethnopolitical groups that all speak Tswana. Note, however, that many members of these "titular" groups live outside of these districts and other groups populate the Tswana-dominated districts as well, as discussed above.

Table 3.1 combines these two estimates with data on the ethnic background of members of parliament since independence (based on Selolwane 2004). Parliamentary representation largely corresponds to the population shares of different language groups—a sign of successful political integration across ethnic divides. This correspondence has increased over time because the number of seats in parliament has risen from 37 at independence to 47 in 2000 and to 57 in 2009, which gives small minorities such as Birwa, Tswapong, and Yeyi a

TABLE 3.1. Distribution of parliamentary seats by ethnic background, 1966–2000

Ethnic group	Language spoken	Estimated population share 2000	Share of district population 1991	Total population size of Tswana–dominated districts	% parliamentary seats								
					1966	1970	1975	1980	1985	1990	1995	2000	Average
Ngwato	Tswana		31.15		22	25	24	21	19	30	21	23	23.13
Kwena	Tswana		12.86		11	14	14	16	11	10	6	6	11.00
Ngwaketse	Tswana		9.73		8	8	14	13	13	10	13	11	11.25
Kgatla	Tswana		4.36		11	6	5	5	6	5	9	11	7.25
Rolong	Tswana		1.39		3	3	3	3	4	3	2	2	2.88
Tlokwa	Tswana		3.29		3	3	3	3	2	3	2	2	2.63
Tawana	Tswana		8.20		8	8	5	5	2	5	2	2	4.63
Lete	Tswana				0	0	3	3	5	3	2	2	2.25
Khurutshe	Tswana				?a	?a	?a	?a	?a	?a	?a	?a	?a
All Tswana speakers		75.71		70.96									64.88
Birwa	Birwa	1.06			0	0	0	3	2	3	4	2	1.75
Tswapong	Tswapong	0.14	2.35		0	0	3	3	2	3	2	2	1.88
Kgalagadi	Kgalagadi	2.83	2.35		3	6	5	5	6	8	6	6	5.25
Kalanga	Kalanga	10.61	3.27		11	11	11	13	15	13	17	17	12.13
Yeyi	Yeyi	1.42			0	0	3	3	2	3	2	2	1.88
Herero/Nderu	Otjiherero	2.19			?a	?a	?a	?a	?a	?a	?a	?a	
Hambukushu	Thimbukushu	1.42			0	0	0	0	2	5	4	2	1.63
Subiya/Kuhane	Subiya	0.21			?a	?a	?a	?a	?a	?a	?a	?a	
Sarwa/San	Koesan	2.78			0	0	0	0	0	0	0	0	0.00
Afrikaaner	Afrikaans	1.42	1.79		16	8	5	5	4	3	2	0	3.38
Indians	Gujarati	0.21			0	0	0	0	0	0	0	2	0.25

aMay be subsumed under "other," which are not represented in the table.

better chance to win seats in the majoritarian system of Botswana. It is especially noteworthy that Tswana speakers are slightly under- rather than over-represented: 76% of citizens speak Tswana while 65% of members of parliament are Tswana. We arrive at a similar conclusion based on an ethnopolitical definition of Tswana: the population share of the Tswana-dominated districts is 71%, still higher than Tswana representation in parliament. The second figure also indicates that many of the ethnic minorities living within Tswana-dominated districts—who often form a plurality of the population, as we have seen—vote for Tswana political leaders and thus across ethnic divides. This is confirmed by a detailed analysis of the district voting results by Selolwane (2004).

Table 3.1 does not show to which political parties members of parliament belong. The BDP has won, as mentioned earlier, every election since independence. Are the minority individuals elected to parliament mostly members of competing political parties that lose out in the electoral competition? Do the figures presented in the table therefore mask the political dominance of Tswanas? Selolwane (2004: 33–44) offers an account as detailed and convincing as possible given the limited data on the ethnic background of voters. In the early years, the opposition parties had clearly defined ethnic constituencies—one among the urban Kalinga districts of the northeast, another one among the Ngakwetse in the south, and a Yeyi and Hambukushu party (Selolwane 2004). However, as the ruling BDP lost its quasi-monopoly over time—its vote share sank from 82% in 1965 to 55% in 1999—the opposition parties won the confidence of a more diverse group of voters. Of the cumulative parliamentary seats won by opposition parties from 1966 to 2000, 69% went to politicians of the three demographically dominant ethnic groups (Ngwaketse, Kalanga, and Ngwato; Selolwane 2004: 29–30), two of which are Tswana speakers. Conversely, the BDP continued to gather support across ethnic divides. Selolwane concludes, after a detailed analysis of District Council votes, that it

> no longer holds that electoral support for political parties is influenced by ethno-tribal affiliation. Or that certain parties represent or are taken by ethno-tribal communities, to represent ethnic interests. In every electoral community now, there is much more diversity and therefore wider choice of political representation. (2004: 41)

The same is true, albeit to a lesser degree, for parliamentary elections, which show

> that Botswana elections are [not] merely a question of ethnic demographics that naturally privilege one party . . . [and that] ethnic inequalities in parliamentary representation have never been a political issue. Contrary to what Horowitz, Holm [1987] and other political analysts assert, the ruling party itself has never been a party mainly for the Tswana speaking ethnic groups. (2004: 43)

But even the authors Selolwane criticizes here agree that the BDP wins the votes of non–Tswana speakers as well, and they attribute this success to the equitable distribution of public goods across the territory. Writes Holm:

> Because of this strategy of treating all ethnic groups alike, the BDP secures a healthy following even where the opposition wins. The BDP succeeds by gaining the support of critical notables and offers them patronage to distribute to their supporters. Even in some strong opposition areas the BDP was able in the 1984 election to accrue over 40 percent of the vote. (1987: 23)

Instead of a clear ethnic voting pattern, we find a growing rural-urban divide, with a majority of the votes of urban districts and the impoverished part of the population now going to opposition parties. The BDP thus has become, increasingly, a party whose power relies on the mobilization of rural voters from a variety of ethnic backgrounds (Selolwane 2004: 37–38).

The widespread support for the governing party is also reflected at the heart of central state power, in the composition of the cabinet. The success of Botswana's nation building, defined as political integration across ethnic divides, is clearly visible in Table 3.2. The ethnic makeups of the population and of the various cabinets are almost identical. There is no overrepresentation of Tswana speakers or of any of the major Tswana-speaking ethnopolitical groups. Kalanga speakers, however, hold more cabinet seats than their population share leads us to expect—mirroring their strong position in the higher ranks of the civil service discussed above. As we will see in a moment, this encouraged politicians to raise the issue of Kalanga overrepresentation in recent decades; comparatively speaking, however, ethnicity did not become the main bone of contention in Botswana's political arena. Also evident from Table 3.2 is the dramatic overrepresentation of Afrikaans-speaking, white segments of the population—a legacy of the colonial regime. Over time, however, their share of cabinet posts declined very steeply indeed.

No discussion of Botswana's nation building is complete without at least mentioning that the Khoisan-speaking groups, many of whom previously lived as hunter-gatherers, remain completely excluded from the political system. The Bantu majority widely despises them as "less civilized," "remnants of the stone age," as people of a different, supposedly inferior racial stock. They are stigmatized by their past as serfs of the royal houses, dispossessed from much of their ancestral lands, which have been converted into private grazing fields, and scattered over much of the country. The only political capital they can muster is their status as "indigenous populations" and one of the few surviving communities with memories of a hunter-gatherer past. Both ensure them the attention and support of international NGOs and advocacy groups such as Survival International. This has not yet translated into political representation

TABLE 3.2. Distribution of cabinet posts by ethnic background, 1966–2005

Ethnic group	Language spoken	Estimated population share 2000	Share of district population 1991	Total population size of Tswana-dominated districts	% cabinet posts									
					1965	1970	1975	1980	1985	1990	1995	2000	2005[a]	Average
Ngwato	Tswana		31.15		25	22	36	27	19	29	25	35	27	27.22
Kwena	Tswana		12.86		0	11	14	20	19	18	13	12	5	12.44
Ngwaketse	Tswana		9.73		13	11	14	13	19	18	13	6	9	12.89
Kgatla	Tswana		4.36		0	11	0	0	6	6	0	6	0	3.22
Rolong	Tswana		1.39		13	0	0	0	0	6	6	0	5	3.33
Tlokwa	Tswana		3.29		0	11	7	7	0	0	0	0	0	2.78
Tawana	Tswana		8.20		13	0	0	0	0	0	6	0	0	2.11
Lete	Tswana				0	0	0	0	6	6	0	0	0	1.33
Khurutshe	Tswana				0	0	0	0	0	0	?[b]	0	?[b]	0.00
All Tswana speakers		75.71		70.96										73.67
Birwa	Birwa	1.06			0	0	0	0	0	0	?[b]	0	?[b]	0.00
Tswapong	Tswapong	0.14	2.35		0	11	7	7	6	6	0	6	0	5.38
Kgalagadi	Kgalagadi	2.83	2.35		0	0	7	7	6	0	13	12	9	6.75
Kalanga	Kalanga	10.61	3.27		13	11	7	13	13	12	13	18	27	14.25
Yeyi	Yeyi	1.42			0	0	0	0	0	0	0	6	5	1.38
Herero/Nderu	Otjiherero	2.19			0	0	0	0	0	0	?[b]	0	?[b]	0.00
Hambukushu	Thimbukushu	1.42			0	0	0	0	0	0	?[b]	0	?[b]	0.00
Subiya/Kuhane	Subiya	0.21			0	0	0	0	0	0	0	0	0	0.00
Sarwa/San	Koesan	2.78			0	0	0	0	0	0	0	0	0	0.00
Afrikaaner	Afrikaans	1.42	1.79		25	11	7	7	6	0	6	0	0	4.63
Indians	Gujarati	0.21			0	0	0	0	0	0	?[b]	0	?[b]	0.00

[a]Data from Makgala 2009.

[b]May be subsumed under "other," which are not represented in the table.

in the Botswana state, however, as Tables 3.1 and 3.2 demonstrate. Quite often, they attempt to shed the stigma of their origins by "passing" into the Tswana majority. This brings us to the second aspect of nation building to be discussed here: the shifts in the ethnocultural landscape that political integration brings about.

ASSIMILATION AND POLITICIZATION: A CHANGING ETHNIC LANDSCAPE

Equal political representation of all major ethnic groups means that overall, with the exception of recent developments to be discussed in a moment, ethnicity is much less politicized in Botswana than in many other African states— or in Belgium, for that matter. Correspondingly, ethnic boundaries remain fluid and ambiguous. Individuals often hold multiple identities and move back and forth between different modes of identification: a person might identify as Tswana speaker in one context but as Ngwato in another (emphasizing ethnopolitical identities in the larger sense) and as Kuhurutshe in yet another (emphasizing ethnopolitical identities in the narrower sense). There is plenty of intermarriage between individuals of different backgrounds, and individuals often claim a different mother tongue than do their parents (Selolwane 2004: 5–6). As was the case in the last quarter of the 19th century in France, the effective and equal distribution of public goods and the political integration that it enabled made it attractive for minorities to shift identities—and to be accepted by majority members as such.

Especially among the younger generation, fewer and fewer speak minority languages and many have started to identify either with the Tswana "titular" ethnic group or with the Kalanga if these form a local majority (Selolwane 2004: 6; Binsbergen 1991: 160). In the 2001 census, 90% of citizens selected "Tswana" when asked what their mother tongue was (only one choice was allowed, explaining the divergence with the Ethnologue estimates). Kalanga parents, as Werbner (2002: 739) notes, often give their children Tswana names to help them pass into the majority. He also discusses language assimilation among Kgalagadi, Yeyi, and Kalanga in Ngamiland as well as Khoisan speakers all over the country (Werbner 2002: 734). Nyati-Ramahobo (2002: 21) mentions several cases in which minorities adopted the language and cultural patterns (such as patrilineal descent or the marriage customs) of the dominant Tswana groups.

Cultural assimilation and identity shift explain why the ethno-demographic patterns of the late colonial period differ so considerably from those of today. Data limitations make it impossible to be more certain about this, but Table 3.3 at least allows some plausible speculations. It lists four kinds of ethnic diversity data at different points in time. The first data point is from the census of 1946 and tabulates responses to the question: What is your tribe? This means that individuals were allowed to choose what they saw as their eth-nopolitical affiliation (for possible problems with these data, see Nyati-Ramahobo 2006). The second set of data comes from Schapera, who in the 1930s and 1940s meticulously collected information on all the ward heads and sub-ward heads of the eight Tswana kingdoms. As noted above, he focused on ethnopolitical identities in the narrower sense as defined by ancestry from a common stock. He also noted migration histories going back to the 18th century, which often explained why a particular group of families arrived in which particular kingdom. These first two data can be broken down by the seven Tswana kingdoms and are shown in the first seven columns. The last two columns refer to the contemporary period and are for the country as a whole. The first is the population share of the speakers of specific languages around 2000, based on Ethnologue's estimates. These include those who speak the idiom as their second language. The last column shows estimations, from the 2001 census, of the share of the population that mentioned a specific language as their first.

Without taxing the reader's patience with too much detail, Table 3.3 suggests that minorities gradually assimilated into and identified with the Tswana majority, a process that started in the precolonial and colonial period and accelerated in the course of postcolonial nation building. The first seven columns show that many more individuals self-identified with the titular ethnicity in 1946 than their ethnopolitical origins in the 18th and 19th centuries would suggest, with the exception of the Tawana kingdom. This must be the result of an identity shift during the precolonial and colonial periods, when other Tswana groups adopted the identity of the dominant, "titular" Tswana ethnicity. This is also true for Kgalagadi (again with the exception of those living in the Tawana kingdom), who were the original inhabitants of the country subsequently conquered and subjugated by the Tswanas. They seem to have gradually adopted Tswana language and identity.[9]

The last three columns demonstrate that the share of minorities was vastly higher in the 1930s and 1940s—whether measured by self-identification or by ethnopolitical origin—than in the 2000s, based on either estimates of language speakers by Ethnologue, which includes secondary speakers, or the 2001 census return where respondents could list only one language spoken at home. Over the course of only two generations, the share of Tswana jumped from 55% in 1946 to over 75% in 2000. While we cannot be sure that all individuals who listed Tswana as their mother tongue in 2000 also identified with the Tswana category, the figures certainly illustrate the degree of linguistic assimilation that occurred since the colonial period. The only exception to that pattern is that of the largest minority of Kalanga speakers.

Table 3.3. Ethnic self-identification in 1946, ethnic origins, and contemporary linguistic affiliation (in percent of population)

Ethnic group	Language spoken	Ngwato 1946 Census	Ngwato Schapera	Kwena 1946 Census	Kwena Schapera	Tawana 1946 Census	Tawana Schapera	Ngwaketse 1946 Census	Ngwaketse Schapera
Ngwato	Tswana	18	7	0	0.5	0	8.5	0	3
Kwena	Tswana	1	5	66	48	0	9	0	5
Ngwaketse	Tswana	0		0				80	45
Kgatla	Tswana	0	1.5	15	12			15	20
Rolong	Tswana	0	0.5	0		0		0	0.5
Tlokwa	Tswana	0		0	0.8			0	1
Tawana	Tswana	0		0		19	43	0	0.5
Lete	Tswana	0	2	9	8	0	18		
Khurutshe	Tswana	5	7	5	6			0	7
Other Tswana	Tswana	3	3	0	6.5				
Total Tswana		27	26	95	81.8	19	78.5	95	82
Birwa	Birwa	10	7			0	3		
Tswapong	Tswapong	11	[a]	0		0		0	
Kgalagadi	Kgalagadi	4	8	4	11	5	3	4	15
Kalanga	Kalanga	22	26[b]			2			
Yeyi[c]	Yeyi	0.7	0	0		32	0[d]	0	
Herero/Nderu	Otjiherero	1	2			14	11		
Hambukushu	Thimbukushu					13	0[d]		
Subiya/Kuhane	Subiya		3			1			
Sarwa/San	Koesan	9	1[d]			9	0[d]		
Total population		100,987		39,826		38,724		38,557	

[a]Schapera doesn't consider Tswapong an ethnic group since it is a regional term turned ethnonym.
[b]Schapera points to the varied origin of Kalanga groups; here, I included Pedi–Kalaka, Seleka Kalaka, Tebele–Kalaka, Nyai.
[c]Koba were classified as Yeyi.

This brings us to the history of Kalanga political activism. Before entering this discussion, however, it should be reiterated how little ethnicity was politicized in postindependence Botswana overall, in stark contrast to many other African countries. The reason, I have argued, is that the newly established, professional bureaucracy provided public goods effectively and equitably across the territory. This helped build far-reaching networks of alliances and support such that all major ethnic groups ended up with adequate representation in the center of power. This in turn depoliticized ethnicity, as it had in a similar way in Switzerland.

How political integration depoliticizes ethnicity is illustrated by the first episodes of Kalanga activism. These events might well have represented a cru-

| Kingdom/District | | | | | | Population share in all 7 kingdoms, 1946 census | Estimated population share, 2000 Ethnologue | Population share with mother tongue, 2001 census |
| Kgatla | | Lete | | Tlokwa | | | | |
1946 Census	Schapera	1946 Census	Schapera	1946 Census	Schapera			
1	0			0	3			
0.6	5	0	2	0	7			
82	55	0		0	11			
0		0		0				
3	5	0	10	100	49			
0		0		0				
		100	82	0	5			
				0	7			
5	16							
91.6	81	100	94	100	82	55.72	75.71	78.2
						4.04	1.06	0.7
0		0		0		4.44	0.14	0.3
2	7					3.81	2.83	3.5
0.3	1			0	3	9.22	10.61	7.9
0		0		0		5.24	1.42	0.3
						2.57	2.19	0.6
						2.01	1.42	1.7
						0.15	0.21	0.4
1	0					5.11	2.78	1.8
20,111		9,469		2,318		249,992		

[d]Schapera (1952: 99) explains Yeyi, Sarwa, and Hambukushu were subjugated to the ruling Tswana elites and thus had no ward head of their own, which explains why they don't appear on his list.

cial turning point during which alliance networks could have realigned along ethnic divides—similar to what could have happened in Switzerland during World War I. Here are the details: The Bakalanga Students Association was founded in 1945 as a reaction to the imprisonment of a prominent Kalanga notable who had struggled against Ngwato overrule and was punished by the colonial government. The association wanted to promote the writing of the Kalanga language and the education of Kalanga children. In the postcolonial period, however, the founders of the movement became spokesmen for the Botswana Civil Service Association because they had entered the postcolonial government, and later the Confederation of Commerce, Industry, and Manpower, an entrepreneurial group (Werbner 2002: 740). They were, in other words, co-opted into the expanding power structure of the independent state, became part of its inner core, and shifted from ethnic advocacy to quiet assimilation: Binsbergen (1991: 157) notes that Kalanga members of the ruling party often played down their Kalanga background and no longer advocated their language or its recognition by the state.

The second episode concerned Kalanga overrepresentation in the bureaucracy. As noted above, this led to complaints and a parliamentary inquiry in the early days of independence, after which the issue died down. In the mid-1980s, two separate strands of activism and public debate reemerged. Rumors spread that a group of civil servants and businessmen founded a company that explicitly excluded Kalanga such that they could not profit from the land privatization scheme implemented at this time (Werbner 2002: 747). On the other hand, Kalanga students founded the Society for the Propagation of the Ikalanga Language. The society did not gain many followers, however, and limited itself to cultural activism such as the organization of festivals (Werbner 2004: 54). This is, I argue, because the masses of Kalanga speakers remained tied into the networks of alliances centered on the state, thanks to the effective and equitable distribution of public goods by subsequent postcolonial governments. Still, the society's activities were public enough to encourage the foundation of a Tswana cultural organization, Pitso ya Batswana, which opposed such minority activism and promoted the active citizenship of every Batswana, independent of ethnic background (Werbner 2004; Taylor 2002: 23).

Ethnicity was more seriously politicized during a fourth episode. In 1995 Kalanga members of parliament started to demand an amendment to the constitution that would recognize the non-Tswana tribes. Currently, only the eight Tswana kings have permanent seats in the House of Chiefs, while four additional seats rotate between representatives of the other ethnic groups (Bennett 2002: 14n42; Selolwane 2004: 14). Tswanas thus enjoy a different constitutional position than ethnic minorities, a fact against which minority elites started to mobilize, under Kalanga leadership. They also started to question why Tswana was the only official African language in the country (Taylor 2002: 23) and to pressure members of the political elite with a Kalanga background to "come out" and support their demands.

In 2000, Kalanga activists held what would become an annual cultural festival at the stone ruins of an ancient Kalanga city built around 1400 and thus before Tswana immigration—indicating that "we were here before you" (Werbner 2002: 735). They were, in turn, accused by counteractivists such as Pitso ya Batswana of planning to establish minority rule over the country—a fear that was nourished by the fact that the judiciary was already dominated by Kalanga (Selolwane 2004: 53–54). The Tswana chiefs joined the choir of critics of the proposed amendment and argued that permanent representation in the House of Chiefs by groups that lack established kingdoms would undermine the institution of kingship itself and therefore the very foundation of Botswana (Makgala 2009).

This was the first time in the history of the country that public debates were framed in ethnic terms. To date, Kalanga activists have not achieved any constitutional changes, nor have other languages been recognized as national languages, let alone are they taught in schools. Remarkably, however, these public debates remain confined to issues of representational politics and have not led to a shift in political alliance networks and their reorganization along ethnic divides. This was shown quite clearly in the above analysis of the support base of political parties and the ethnic composition of the cabinet.

To conclude, nation building à la Botswana (or *à la française*, for that matter) comes with a price: minorities are pressured to assimilate into the dominant Tswana language and culture—the absolute *horribilum* for a multiculturalist vision of a just society dear to politicians and political philosophers in the developed West. In contrast, however, to other assimilationist nationalisms, the Botswana version not only promises political participation and equal access to public goods but actually realizes them. It is therefore not surprising that very large portions of the minority population have embraced Botswana nationalism and its association with Tswana language and culture. This includes, it is worth noting, the small group of Afrikaans-speaking whites. During the early years of independence, according to one ethnographer, they "appl[ied] for citizenship, register[ed] as voters, and pin[ned] posters of Seretse Khama [the first president of independent Botswana] on their walls" (cited in du Toit 1995: 53).

Somalia: A History of Nation Destroying

Somalia stretches like a tilted L, roughly 350 kilometers in width, around the Horn of Africa. It is situated across the Gulf of Aden from Yemen, east of the Ethiopian highlands and northeast of Kenya. It is only slightly larger than Botswana. Its climate is equally dry and arable land very scarce as well (1.5% of the surface in Somalia and 0.5% in Botswana). Like Botswana's, Somalia's society and economy long revolved around cattle, mostly camels, but also sheep and goats. However, Somalia's population was five times larger and counts 11 million today. And unlike Botswana, a majority of that population—as much as three-quarters in the mid-20th century (Lewis 1988: 174n16; Laitin and Samatar 1987: 22)—lived a nomadic life.

Camels served as a medium of exchange, including for dowry payments and as compensation for homicide, an important conflict resolution mechanism in a society that lacked a centralized state. Somalia's modern economy continues to depend on livestock, quite similar to Botswana. In 1980, for

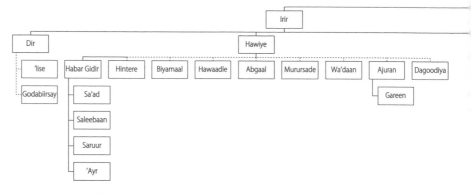

FIGURE 3.1. A simplified genealogical map of Somali clans (without southern agricultural clans)
Source: Adapted from Laitin and Samatar 1987: Figure 2.1.
Note: Broken lines indicate that intervening ancestors are not shown.

example, three-quarters of export earnings came from selling camels, sheep, and goats, mostly to Saudi Arabia (Laitin and Samatar 1987: 101). Unlike Botswana, however, Somalia is not blessed with any significant mineral wealth and remains a poor agricultural society.

Most Somali adhere to the Muslim faith and speak the same language—which should facilitate establishing ties across regions and thus nation building, according to the theory outlined previously. Somali society is characterized by other kinds of divisions, however: those of clan and lineage. Lineages and clans are groups of families that descend from the same male ancestor. The further removed in the genealogical tree a common ancestor, the larger the group of related families. Lineages and clans ally with and oppose each other according to a segmentary logic (Lewis 1994): all families united in a lineage should oppose members of another lineage when a murder, theft of livestock, or competition over grazing grounds involves any member of these two groups. If these same issues pit more distantly related individuals against each other, however, larger units—groups of lineages patrilineally related to each other—come into play, thus the term "segmentary" lineage system.

This principle also translates into politics. In the postcolonial period, clans and families of clans that are, again, related through patrilineal ties competed with each other for political power and patronage. Lineages (or *mag* in Somali) comprise anything from 200 to 2,000 families, while clans count at least a couple thousand families. Clan families are correspondingly even larger. The Darood, for example, have as many as one million individual members. Beyond the segmentary principle of alliance formation, ties to the patrilineage of a man's mother—reinforced by a tradition of solidarity between mothers and their sons—also play an important political role (Laitin and Samatar 1987: 30), as we will see. Figure 3.1 gives an overview over the main clans and clan

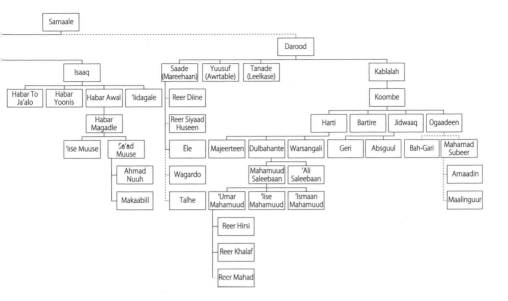

families of Somali society. Not all intervening generations are shown here, and the figure does not include the southern agricultural clans.

In the South, the fertile valleys of the Jubba and Shebeelle rivers allow for the production of sorghum, corn, and (in the 20th century) bananas. Bantu- and Oromo-speaking peasants settled on these lands before they were conquered or displaced by nomadic Somali groups. The colonization of the southern territories continued for centuries. As a result of these developments, the genealogical principle has been supplanted by a different form of social and political organization: local, landowning lineages form the hierarchical center around which dependent, client lineages of a variety of northern origins are grouped together with conquered Bantu peasants or hunter-gatherer groups (such as the WaBoni) who became dependent serfs—quite similar to the fate of the Sarwa in Botswana. And similar to what happened in Botswana, these client and serf clans often assimilated into the culture of the dominant lineage or were even absorbed completely by rewriting genealogies or through a formal adoption procedure (Lewis 1994: chap. 6). As we will see, however, assimilation has not proceeded and accelerated to the same degree as in Botswana. In southern Somalia in the 1950s, adopted client lineages still remembered and insisted on their "true" northern origins (Lewis 1994: chap. 6, 144).

PRECOLONIAL SOCIETY WITHOUT STATE

The reason is that no centralized states had emerged in either the nomadic North or the sedentary South of Somalia that could have provided strong enough incentives for more complete ethnic assimilation. To be sure, in the

Middle Ages up to the 1700s, the highly centralized, irrigation-based sultanate of Ajuran in the southern interior had dominated and incorporated the surrounding tribes as well as the coastal cities populated by Indian and Arab traders. It soon disappeared, however, and a sort of political devolution followed. In the nomadic North, the segmentary lineage system prevailed well into the colonial period and beyond.

The core political institution of the nomadic groups was the ad hoc councils that gathered to resolve a specific conflict. While all members of the assembly had the right to speak, powerful or prestigious men de facto dominated the proceedings, as was the case in the assemblies of the Botswana kingdoms. Unlike in Botswana, however, there were no kings or other institutionalized centers of political authority. Disputes were resolved through informal contracts, called *heers*, rather than by royal decree. The councils elected "sultans" and were given advice by religious notables, but neither of these held any power (Lewis 1994) and cannot be considered formal political offices comparable to the headman, councillors, and kings of the Tswana chiefdoms. Religious figures, such as the spiritual leaders of Sufi orders, lived in small compounds where they cared for the sick or those displaced by clan conflicts. They were generally respected by the nomadic clans but had no political authority over them (Lewis 1994: 56). The most famous of these leaders, Sayyid Muhammad (the "mad mullah" of British colonial historiography), founded a local branch of the new Saalihiya mystic order in the late 19th century. He soon rallied a series of clans against the invading Ethiopian troops and later on against the British colonial government. His support was based on a shifting alliance of clans held together by his charisma rather than by any institutionalized government (Lewis 1988; Laitin and Samatar 1987: 57–58).

This was also true for another group of power brokers, the famed Somali poets. They composed long recitals shaming, ridiculing, or praising political and religious leaders and were often patronized by them. Their poems traveled quickly around the entire Somali territory, facilitated by memorizers who went from oasis to oasis and from village to village or by cassette recorders and radios later on. They too wielded moral but no institutionalized political power (Laitin and Samatar 1987: 34–41).

In the agricultural South, some of the landowning clans held more real authority over their communities. But even the most powerful sultan of Somalia, the head of the Geledi clan in the South, had no private body of followers, owned no land personally, and had to rule via consensus (Laitin and Samatar 1987: 42–43). Large swaths of Somali territory thus were effectively stateless. This was not true, however, of the coast, the only place where "any degree of centralized government was established and maintained, however irregularly, over long periods of time" (Lewis 1988: 33).

But the authority of these states was confined to trading cities, similar to the Swahili towns such as Lemu and Zanzibar farther down the coast. Situated at the end of the caravan routes coming from the interior, they exchanged camel skins and meat, slaves, ivory, ghee, Ostrich feathers, and rare gums for textiles and porcelain with traders from Arabia, India, and beyond. The cities usually counted only a couple thousand inhabitants. Some of these city-states on the Gulf of Aden such as Berbera and Zeila became nominally dependent on the Ottoman Empire during the 18th and early 19th centuries, similar to the mini-states in the Persian Gulf such as Abu Dhabi and Doha. Those in the South, especially Mogadishu, had to acknowledge the sovereignty of the Oman Sultanate across the Gulf, and after the split of that sultanate, of its southern offshoot centered in Zanzibar in what is today northern Tanzania (Lewis 1988: 39). The administrative footprint, however, of both the Ottoman Empire and the Zanzibari Sultanate was extremely light and consisted of a handful of representatives and tax collectors per town only. The city-states never managed to subdue the nomads of the hinterland. These could mobilize tens of thousands of warriors against which the feebly fortified coastal cities stood little chance (Lewis 1988: 34–35). Only the Majeerteen Sultanate (a clan of the Darood family) situated at the Horn managed to gain effective control over the interior and represented a territorial state comparable to some of the more powerful and populous Tswana kingdoms. It remained independent from both the Ottoman Empire and the Oman Sultanate by signing a treaty with Britain in 1839. In the 1920s, Italy ended its long-lasting sovereignty through military conquest.

In short, history did not produce centralized polities comparable to the Tswana kingdoms, except for the Majeerteen Sultanate. The overwhelming majority of the population lived as nomads and governed themselves by the system of segmentary lineages, under the guidance of elders, clan leaders, and Sufi sheikhs who wielded a great deal of moral authority but little effective political power. As we will see, this past carried into the colonial period by making a system of indirect rule—akin to Bechuanaland—rather difficult to establish, as there were no indigenous authorities on which indirect rule could rely. The absence of state institutions was thus cemented during the colonial period, in a development that ran parallel—but in opposite directions—to the strengthening of the Tswana kingdoms under British rule.

THE COLONIAL PERIOD: ABSENTEE AND SETTLER IMPERIALISM

The colonization of Somalia is too complex a history to be recounted here. Suffice it to say that Ethiopia, France, Britain, and Italy all vied with each other, and in varying alliances, for control over Somalia. Colonial projects also differed markedly. France and Britain were mostly interested in controlling the supply and transfer routes around the Horn of Africa to the Far East and later in securing passage through the Suez Canal. Ethiopia sought to conquer further territory in the plains southeast to its highland core. Italy wanted to establish a settler colony similar to British Kenya or Rhodesia and thus show its European peers that it too belonged to the civilizing, conquering nations of superior power and prestige (Hess 1967).

Somalia was subsequently divided between a British territory in the North, stretching parallel to the coast of the Gulf of Aden, and an Italian territory covering the rest of the country, gained first via protectorates and lease agreements and later through military conquest. Ethiopia managed to conquer and retain the Ogaden, a vast stretch of arid land in the interior, while France incorporated what is today Djibouti in her colonial domains. After Italy lost her colonies in World War II, the South came under British military administration until 1949, when the UN decided to give the South as a trusteeship back to Italy to prepare it for independence in 1960. The North remained a British protectorate. In 1960, finally, the British and Italian territories unified to form the independent state of Somalia. The following narrative will thus have to bifurcate and treat the British and Italian colonial experiences separately.

In the North, Somali clans worried about the growing influence of Abyssinia and thus "readily consented to British protection" (Lewis 1988: 46) by signing a series of treaties in the 1880s. British colonial rule was extremely light. No attempt was made to control the interior, and only three consuls were positioned in the port cities, funded by port revenues. The interior was basically left to itself, as there was "no pervasive system of ingenious chiefs and consequently no basis for a true system of indirect rule." Titular "clan leaders and elders of lineages were in many cases officially recognized and granted a small stipend" (Lewis 1988: 105). These clan and lineage elders thus provided the link between the British district commissioners and the population at large and were sometimes given judicial power since the administration lacked the capacity to process cases.

The school system remained thoroughly underdeveloped. Sayyid Muhammad rose up against British rule because he had heard that missionary schools converted Muslim Somali children to Christianity. British administration then outlawed missionary schools to calm the situation. Three government-run schools were established in 1905 but closed shortly thereafter. Later plans were given up because the interior clans resisted paying for schools where their children would be turned into infidels.[10] The situation changed only slowly after the World War II. In 1952, a vocational school, a girls' school, and a secondary school were opened.

Given the lack of educated locals, the rudimentary colonial administration was run with the help of Indian and Arab clerks (Lewis 1988: 115; according to Laitin and Samatar [1987: 106], they were Kenyans). In 1956, when Her

Majesty's government decided to grant northern Somalia independence in 1960, hasty preparations were made: Somali officials were promoted to senior positions in the administration and the police. A legislative council with appointed clan representatives was established, enlarged by a dozen elected members later on (Laitin and Samatar 1987). Some 65 Somalis were sent to study abroad, mostly in the United Kingdom (Lewis 1999 [1961]: 282).

In 1958, a mere 30 of the 200 bureaucrats in the colonial administration of the British North were Somali. But by early 1960, all six district commissioners of the police force were Somali and a Somali assistant commissioner of police was nominated.[11] Interestingly enough, the result of this Somalianization policy was starkly different from that in Botswana. Government departments were seen as "belonging to" and favoring members of specific clans and lineages. The agricultural department in the last years of colonial rule, for example, was perceived as a Dulbahante institution since Dulbahante clan members (of the Darood clan family) were the first ones appointed to its administrative positions (Lewis 1999 [1961]).

To sum up, the British colonial administration had very little impact on the nature and structure of political alliances, which remained organized, in the stateless society of northern Somalia, along the principles of lineage and clan solidarity. Little colonial state capacity was built, and there was virtually no administrative infrastructure on which the postcolonial government could rely to provide public goods to the northern population.

In the Italian South, the situation was quite different as the Italian government aimed to create an agricultural colony for Italian settlers. Correspondingly, the colonial state built administrative capacity to provide public goods to the Italian settlers rather than the southern Somali population as a whole. A more centralized and direct form of rule than in the North emerged. The governor in Mogadishu appointed Italian residents as heads of districts and provinces, who were advised by government-funded Somali chiefs and elders (in Italian *capos*, a term that has survived to the present day). These *capos* were in charge of a rural police force numbering around 500 in 1930. The governor also appointed *kadis* (a traditional Ottoman term), who administered cases of customary and Islamic law concerning the Somali population. The regular police force counted 1,475 Somalis and 85 Italian officers. The colonial bureaucracy remained rather light: around 1927, the civil service employed 350 Italians and 1,700 Somalis and Arabs.

By the end of World War II, roughly 9,000 Italian settlers lived in the colony, most of them on the banana plantations that had been established in the fertile riverine regions. These plantations formed the core of the colonial enterprise. The problem for the colonial settlers was how to get locals to work for them, and various forms of monetary incentives and forced labor were tried, mostly targeting the long-sedentary Bantu groups. The colonial government invested heavily in making these export enclaves viable, all the while neglecting the rest of the colony and its indigenous population.[12]

Education was mostly left to the Catholic missionary schools. In 1928, there were eight such schools, where until 1928 Italian and Somali children were taught together. The impact was modest as there were only about 1,800 Somali and Arab pupils in these schools in 1939 (Lewis 1988: chap. 5). The situation changed quite markedly when the UN entrusted Italy to lead the territory to independence. In 1952, a UNESCO-supported five-year program for schooling the population was initiated. By 1957, 31,000 children and adults were enrolled in primary schools, 246 in junior secondary schools, 3,316 in technical institutes, and around 200 in higher education (Lewis 1988: 149). In 1950, the School of Politics and Administration opened in Mogadishu to train Somali officials and politicians. In 1954, the Higher Institute of Law and Economics was founded (which would later become Somalia University College). Generous bursaries were given to the most promising students for studies abroad, mostly in Egypt and Italy. By 1956, all districts and provinces were directed by Somali administrative officials. All these various initiatives to school the Somali population and train civil servants bypassed the nomadic majority of Somalis in the South, however.

The main focus of the Italian administration remained the production and commercialization of bananas, as they had been during the colonial period. They served a peculiar, mercantilist aim: buying bananas cheaply and selling them at a high price in Italy to finance the grants needed for the Somalian dependency. But the colonial enterprise was never profitable. In the mid-1950s, after the return of Italians as UN trustee administrators, the local revenue from imports and exports was £2 million, but the administration of the territory cost £5 million (Lewis 1988).

In contrast to the late colonial bureaucracy of Botswana, then, the Italian Somali administration, including its senior-level Somali civil servants, did not help the nomadic, cattle-breeding majority of Somalis gain access to world markets or make them more competitive. The state monopoly on bananas continued to profit Italian plantation owners, commercial interests, and the Italian state itself rather than the population at large (Laitin and Samatar 1987: 105).[13] Correspondingly, little progress was made during the colonial period in building the necessary administrative capacity to govern the interior territories in a more direct way and to provide their populations with public goods, a capacity on which the postcolonial government could have built. Italian colonial rule in the South certainly had a much greater impact than British rule did in the North, giving rise to a broader urban stratum of Western-educated colonial bureaucrats and a comprador bourgeoisie. But it remained focused on the Italian-dominated export industry and did little to establish state institutions outside of these enclaves.

NETWORKS OF POLITICAL ALLIANCE BEFORE INDEPENDENCE

Absentee colonialism in the North and settler-enclave colonialism in the South therefore did not change the principles according to which the majority of the population built political alliances. The logic of clan solidarity can be easily discerned in the politics of anticolonial nationalism that emerged both in the North and in the South. To be sure, compared to precolonial politics, higher levels of segmentation in the genealogically framed system of loyalties became important because the political arena now expanded to include the entire colonial domain (a process noted around the world; see Wimmer 2014: chap. 3). Political alliances now comprised entire clans and clan families, while lower-level, lineage solidarity lost political appeal and import (Lewis 1999 [1961]: 284–285). In both colonial territories, early nationalist movements emerged among the urban, educated sections of the population, and especially among the slowly emerging class of bureaucrats, police officers, and other employees of the colonial administrations. These organizations all pursued the goal of unifying the Somali-speaking territories, now scattered over British, French, and Italian Somalia as well as Ethiopia and northern Kenya. And they all aimed at overcoming clan division and fostering a unified national community. This proved to be a rather elusive goal, however, as can be seen in the political development of both the South and the North.

The Somali Youth Club, founded in 1943 in Mogadishu, counted some 25,000 affiliates a couple of years later. Soon, a group of Majeerteen subclans splintered away, and the renamed Somali Youth League (SYL) became more heavily Darood. The southern, agricultural clans of Rahanweyn and Digil founded their own party, the Patriotic Benefit Union, later renamed HDMS (Lewis 1988: 122–124). In the municipal elections of 1954 in the South, 22 parties competed for seats, all of which could be clearly identified with a particular clan, with the exception of the SYL, which continued to have a broader support base. Correspondingly, the SYL won the first general elections in 1956, and the SYL formed the first Somali government, still under Italian trusteeship.

The SYL government tried to balance clan interests by assembling a government in which all the major groups were represented. The prime minister and two other ministers were Hawiye, two ministers Darood, and one Dir. This caused resentment among the Darood, however, who formed roughly half of the membership of the SYL (while only 30% were Hawiye) (Lewis 1988: 122–124). Tellingly, the northern clans within the Italian territory that were somewhat underrepresented in the government soon founded their own party (the Greater Somali League) (Laitin and Samatar 1987: 65–66). The southern, agricultural clans, whose party, HDMS, had lost the elections, complained that its members were discriminated against by the new government when it came to filling positions in the civil service, now rapidly Somalianizing.

After partial elections in 1959, a new government again under the victorious SYL was formed, and some HDMS ministers were added to the extended clan coalition (Laitin and Samatar 1987: 160). The SYL-led government attempted, through various means such as individualizing punishment for homicide or reducing the statutory authority of clan leaders, to undermine the role of clan solidarity in everyday life and build an integrated Somali nation. Parties were forbidden to take on clan names, and the client status of landless clans was eliminated (Laitin and Samatar 1987: 147ff.). These policies did not undermine the logic of clan politics, however, as the postcolonial history of alliance building will show.

In the British North, the National Unity Front (NUF) emerged as one of the most important nationalist organizations. In 1959, one year before independence, the British enlarged the Advisory Council, meant to guide Britain in the decolonization process, by adding elected members and allowing, for the first time, the formation of political parties. Half of the seats went to the NUF, mostly supported by a group of Isaaq clans. Other Isaaq clans, however, sided with the Somalia National League. Darood and Dir clans tended toward the SYL (which had boycotted the elections), as did their clan brethren in the South.

To summarize, colonialism didn't transform the precolonial political structures, marked by the absence of centralized states, in a profound enough way to put the country on a different path of political development once it shook off the colonial yoke. In the North, the colonial state left only a feeble imprint and in the South, the Italian administration remained focused on the export-oriented settler enclaves without profoundly altering the web of political alliances and loyalties among the Somali majority. Correspondingly, politics in the emerging colonial and postcolonial arenas were shaped by the continuing appeal of clan and, increasingly, clan family loyalties. Political movements, as soon as they broke out from their urban, educated milieus into the nomadic hinterland, were either directly dependent on a single clan or clan family or represented unstable alliances of such clans and clan families—the shared rhetoric of Somali nationalism notwithstanding.[14] Weakly developed state institutions, inherited from the precolonial past and largely preserved during colonial rule, also made it difficult for postcolonial governments to provide public goods in an efficient and equitable way across the territory. This, in turn, discouraged establishing durable cross-clan alliances, as is shown in the following section.

THE FIRST DECADE OF INDEPENDENCE: CLAN CLIENTELISM AND COMPETITION

After a series of tumultuous events, the British protectorate and the Italian trustee territory finally became an integrated, independent country in 1960. In Botswana, the British continued to pay higher-level, expatriate civil servants for a decade, as we have seen. The British administrative tradition thus shaped a whole generation of civil servants after independence. In northern Somalia, Britain paid the salaries of its administrators for only six months after independence (Lewis 1988: 165, 172). Italy also financed, in part, the stipends of a team of Italian experts serving the newly independent Somalian government. But they soon left the country and were not permanently employed by the Somali government. In both the North and the South, therefore, the influence of expat administrators on the emergent administrative culture was short-lived.

The capacity to provide public goods was further hampered because two colonial administrations had to be fused into a single bureaucracy. It took three years to integrate the two very different administrative and legal systems, including different salary scales, promotion procedures, trades and tariffs, legal provisions, and so forth. The lack of basic infrastructure made things even more difficult: there was no telephone line between North and South and no regular flights except for police aircraft (Lewis 1988: 171). Perhaps more important, no common administrative language existed since the various elite factions had not been able to agree on which Somali script to use (Laitin 1977)—a notable contrast to China, as we will see in the next chapter. English emerged as the de facto administrative language, which produced a certain dominance of northerners in the rapidly growing national bureaucracy.[15] Somali law followed in other aspects the Italian rather than the British model in allowing civil servants to run for office (Lewis 1988: 73, 204). A professional class of administrators disinterested in gaining political power therefore could not emerge, again in contrast to Botswana.

This fragmented, embryonic, politicized administration had virtually no tax base beyond the tariffs it collected from imports and exports—a legacy of the resistance that the interior clans had mounted against any form of taxation, in turn the consequence of long centuries of living without a state. Somalia therefore became one of the most aid-dependent countries in Africa: it received approximately US$90 per capita through the 1960s, twice the average of other newly independent African states. Foreign aid was mostly used to enlarge the bureaucracy and the military instead of providing public goods to the population at large. By 1976, 15 years after independence, the administration had ballooned to 72,000 employees, roughly half of the Somali workforce that received a regular salary (Laitin and Samatar 1987: 107–108). The Soviet Union, with which the Somali government soon forged an alliance, provided US$11 million in military aid in 1963 (Lewis 1988: 200–201) and annual loans of US$50 million in subsequent years (Laitin and Samatar 1987: 78), which were used to build up an army of 14,000 soldiers in a handful of years.

However, this newly enlarged bureaucratic and military apparatus was not able to expand its authority into the rural, nomadic areas and put an end to endemic clan conflict (Laitin and Samatar 1987: 85). In Botswana, by contrast, the first moves of the independent government were to transform the kings into civil servants and to integrate their authority into a newly centralized political system, thus building on the political infrastructure of the kingdoms.

For these various reasons, the independent Somali state was not able to provide public goods in an effective and nondiscriminatory way across the territory: there were no precolonial states to incorporate into the postcolonial political edifice, no colonial tradition of investing in public goods was there to be inherited, the postcolonial state was fragmented due to the dual imperial legacy, and no meritocratic tradition of bureaucratic rule emerged. The newly appointed officials behaved in similar ways as they had during the colonial administration: they indulged in the "widespread and time-honored Somali practice . . . of distributing national resources through clans, rather than through an impartial system of selection and distribution" (Laitin and Samatar 1987: 30). Referring to the first years of independence, Laitin and Samatar illustrate how pervasive corruption was by pointing at "government cars [that] were used as private taxis; government medicine [that] was on sale in local pharmacies." "The big men," they continue, "provide jobs, lucrative construction permits, outright cash payments, and other forms of patronage to certain influential clan members and their families in return for the latter's ability to deliver the clan's support" (46).

This distribution of favors to fellow clan members further politicized clan divides. Under these circumstances, it was difficult to establish alliances between the national government and citizens independent of clan connections. For the masses of Somalis, there was no direct public assistance or any form of support for the poor (Laitin and Samatar 1987: 47), nor were there substantial programs that would have benefited agricultural workers or livestock herders (Laitin and Samatar 1987: 85), as was the case in Botswana. Given the lack of public goods provision, the average citizen saw no reason to identify with or provide political support to the government directly. Its limited resources could be accessed only by activating one's ties to clan chiefs with connections to the government (Lewis 1988: 166), who in turn delivered their clan's votes to politicians (Lewis 1994: 170). This gave clan identities and loyalties a new meaning.

Clan politics, within and between political parties, therefore dominated the political history of the first decade of independence. The details of the fast-changing coalitions between parties and clans are too complicated to be of interest here. A short summary must suffice. At the beginning, it seems that the inherited North-South divide was the most heavily politicized cleavage. This became clear in the 1961 constitutional referendum, which was opposed by almost all northern parties and clans as it shifted the power center to the South, locating parliament and the capital in Mogadishu. Disaffected northern junior officers unsuccessfully staged a coup in that same year.

Over time, however, new alliances across the former colonial border emerged, many of them influenced by the logic of clan solidarity. The Darood clans who supported the United Somali Party (USP) in the North joined the Darood-dominated, southern Somali Youth League, while the Dir wing of the USP could now support the Hawiye clans of the South. The expanded political arena also offered incentives to found new parties with both northern and southern clan elements, as the short-lived Somali Democratic Union and the more stable Somali National Congress show (Lewis 1988: 176). The latter included northern Dir and Isaaq clans but also important Hawiye elements from the former Italian parts of the country—all united in the attempt to counter the dominance of Darood, particularly Majeerteen politicians during the first decade of independence. Indeed, it seems that the politically dominant clans during that first decade were the Hawiye from central Somalia, the Isaaq from the North, and especially the Majeerteen from the former eponymous sultanate on the Horn (Laitin and Samatar 1987: 92), who supplied one out of two presidents and two prime ministers out of three.

But these larger clan blocs gradually dissolved and alliances again formed along narrower clan and lineage identities—the opposite, in other words, of nation building. To briefly summarize, after the 1964 national elections, two Darood candidates from the SYL engaged in a bitter rivalry for the position of prime minister. And after the presidential elections of 1967, with an Isaaq president and prime minister and the Darood still divided from the 1964 feud, the fragile anti-Darood coalition by Dir, Isaaq, and Hawiye clan families (all patrilineal descendants of Irir) lost its raison d'être and the appeal of the Somali National Congress as an anti-Darood party diminished. Further fragmentation followed. In the 1969 elections, 62 parties, most of which represented narrower clan interests, competed with each other. The more broadly based SYL won again. Indicating the opportunistic nature of politics in independent Somalia, all but one member of the opposition parties defected after the election to join the government party SYL, hoping to get a piece of the pie and distribute it to their clan supporters.

Interestingly, processes of assimilation, well under way in the southern agricultural regions, came to a halt when clan and lineage ties were politicized in this way and the political arena fragmented. In Botswana, more and more of the former client groups adopted the dominant Tswana identity over time, as we have seen. In postcolonial Somalia, however, the southern client clans rediscovered their northern origins and allied with the corresponding parties and party factions (Lewis 1994: 144).

SIAD BARRE'S REGIME: CLANISM AS BOOMERANG

The chaos of the 1969 elections provoked a bloodless military coup under the leadership of the charismatic major general Siad Barre, much to the satisfaction of large segments of the public. The coup offered a second critical juncture during which major alliances were reshuffled and history could have taken another turn. Similar to the critical juncture of World War I in Switzerland or of episodes of Kalinga activism in Botswana, however, the existing alliance networks were established enough to resist fundamental restructuring and Somalia traveled further down the path of political fragmentation. I will show that this was in no small part because the state continued to lack the capacity to provide public goods to the population in a sustained and equitable way. Despite serious efforts especially at the beginning of its reign, Siad Barre's regime therefore wasn't able to build lasting alliances with the citizenry outside of the grid of clan alliances. He had to increasingly rely on the support of the handful of clans related to his family, thus narrowing the ruling coalition and excluding important segments of the population from any meaningful representation in national government.

The beginnings were promising, whether or not one harbors any sympathies for the political ideology of the new regime. The military junta distanced itself from party politics and jailed corrupt and divisive politicians. It propagated a new ideology that combined "scientific socialism" with Islam. Talking in clan terms or mentioning clan names was forbidden; the regime decreed that strangers in everyday encounters should address each other as "comrade" rather than the traditional clan term "cousin." It portrayed multipartyism and clanism, synonymous with nepotism and corruption, as anachronistic barriers to a brighter socialist future. It set up a new state structure, with an all-military Supreme Revolutionary Council at the top, aided by a civilian Council of Secretaries. A powerful National Security Service (NSS) was formed, and National Security Courts held unchecked judicial powers. Military officers replaced civilian district and regional governors in the first years of junta rule. Clan leaders were rechristened as "peace seekers" and integrated into the bureaucratic apparatus. In theory, they could be posted in any part of the country.

The new regime sought to build institutions within which alliances with citizens could be formed, independent of clan ties. Unemployed urban men were recruited into a people's militia, called Victory Pioneers, to lead local development projects and organize civics classes for the population at large. New provincial boundaries were drawn, cutting across clan territories, and subdivided into 64 new districts. A revolutionary council was set up in each province, presided over by a military governor and supervised by a regional NSS chief as well as a representative of the president's Political Office. An "orientation center" was built in each province, meant to replace the lineage associations (which were banned). These centers provided space for educational and recreational activities, including a library with Marxist literature, and organized weekly "orientation" meetings during which the local population received ideological training. All secondary school students were required to attend a military camp where they were ideologically "trained" as well.

The population was encouraged to hold their weddings at the orientation centers, hoping that a revolutionary, modern form of wedding ceremony would replace the traditional exchange of bride wealth at clan weddings. The regime also provided (in theory) for burial expenses to further weaken clan solidarities, banned blood-compensation payments that lay at the heart of the clan system, and imposed the death penalty for murder, hoping to further undermine the logic of clan conflict and solidarity (Lewis 1983: 154–157).

How did this newly erected bureaucratic apparatus fare in terms of public goods provision? Some serious efforts were made that should be noted. Barre decreed an official Somali script in 1970, and airplanes dropped grammar texts in Somali on the one-year anniversary of the revolution. A literacy campaign closed all secondary schools for an entire year so that teachers and students could teach nomads how to read and write—a campaign similar to that in other communist countries in the developing world. According to government figures, the literacy rate jumped from 6% in 1970 to 55% in 1975. As Laitin and Samatar (1987: 83) note, however, these figures are likely exaggerated.

In 1974, the government introduced a cooperative scheme for nomads so that they would share desert resources more peacefully and more efficiently. Fourteen cooperatives were created, with each family receiving 500 to 700 acres of exclusive grazing land as well as access, in times of drought, to common land. With the help of international agencies and Kuwaiti funding, the government also created more ambitious range cooperatives, but "these associations have achieved little," as Laitin and Samatar (1987: 112) note. Beyond these rather scattered efforts, little was done to help cattle breeders market their product.[16] Unlike in Botswana, no systematic attempt was made to enhance productivity, marketing, or access to global markets.

Lacking the capacity for routine operations, the government could provide public goods only through short-term, all-out operations similar to the military-style campaign launched to teach the nomads how to read and write.[17] In 1974, a terrible drought endangered the livestock and life of northern nomads. The emergency relief, organized with logistical and material support from the Soviet Union, Sweden, and other countries, was remarkably efficient and saved the lives of tens of thousands of individuals—in contrast to the disasters brought about by previous famines in neighboring Ethiopia. Again with financial and logistical support from the Soviet Union, 90,000 nomads were subsequently resettled in the South and on the East Coast in a Stalin-style operation that sought to turn the camel herders into farmers and fishermen, despite the traditional distaste for fish among nomads. Agricultural cooperatives were founded in the South and irrigated newly cleared land, with substantial support from the World Bank and again Kuwait. These state-owned cooperatives employed the ex-nomads as salaried farmers and sold their maize, beans, groundnuts, and rice to the government. By the end of the 1970s, however, "with rain again bringing rich grass to the grazing fields, many men returned to their homes in the hope of restoring their flocks" (Laitin and Samatar 1987: 113). The fishing cooperatives were also not self-sustaining and produced less and less: from thousands of tons to less than 500 tons after the Soviet advisors had left.

Public goods provision was hampered not only by the lack of institutional capacity but also by the resurgence of corruption. As noted earlier, the junta initially denounced corruption and clan nepotism and punished some of the civil servants who had exhibited the most egregious behavior (Laitin and Samatar 1987: 79). But soon enough, these efforts evaporated and corruption became endemic again. Among other factors, this was because Barre shifted to Somali as the official language of the country, once a script to write Somali was adopted, replacing English as the de facto language of the bureaucracy. Those who held advanced degrees from abroad, as many of the most senior officials did, lost their privileged position and were now meant to "obey the commands of those who were their inferiors in terms of education and intelligence . . . because they were members of the colonizing regimes in our country," as Barre himself put it (quoted in Laitin and Samatar 1987: 84). Corruption and bribery spread again and "made the citizenry ever more cynical toward its government," as Laitin and Samatar (1987: 95) remarked. "It is well known," they continue, "that government ministers and middlemen skim up to 40 percent of each contract as a private payoff. . . . Only on-the-job corruption makes it possible for these [government] workers to provide their families with a decent urban existence. Corruption, like tribalism, has reached epidemic proportions" (96; cf. also 119).[18]

Overall, then, the government was not able to provide public goods on a large enough scale and in an equitable, sustained enough manner to encourage political alliances to shift away from clans and lineages toward the institutions of the state and its agents. Because the state lacked basic infrastructural capacity, public goods had to be provided through military-style campaigns that lasted a couple of years only, as with the literacy campaign and the drought relief program, rather than through more permanent institutional channels. Cross-clan alliances between the center of government power and the population could not be sustained and clan clientelism slowly resurged and strengthened the corresponding loyalties, discouraging the population from identifying with the national project.

The power base of the regime, while more broadly based and inclusionary during the first months of its rule, gradually narrowed down to certain clans and clan families. Nation building thus remained beyond the reach of the revolutionary leaders who so desperately sought it. Initially, the junta appointed ministers in line with meritocratic principles (Laitin and Samatar 1987: 90).[19] However, this soon changed and networks of political alliances quickly re-

TABLE 3.4. Distribution of cabinet seats (1960–1969) and Supreme Revolutionary Council seats (1975) over clan families

	1960	1966	1967	1969	1975
Darood					
% seats	42	37	33	33	50
Population share	20	20	20	20	20
Hawiye					
% seats	28	19	22	28	20
Population share	25	25	25	25	25
Digil and Rahanwiin					
% seats	14	18	17	11	0
Population share	20	20	20	20	20
Dir					
% seats	0	6	6	0	10
Population share	7	7	7	7	7
Isaaq					
% seats	14	19	22	28	20
Population share	22	22	22	22	22
Total seats	14	16	18	18	20

Source: Lewis 1983: 166. Population shares are from the CIA World Factbook and need to be considered rough approximations.

aligned along clan divisions. In 1971, a coup by disaffected army officers failed, and Barre called out the leaders of the Majeerteen clans as those who had orchestrated it. As discussed above, members of these clans had held the keys to political power throughout the preceding decade and felt left out in Barre's regime (Laitin and Samatar 1987: 91). Barre subsequently abandoned merito-cratic recruitment and began to favor members of his own clan, Mareehaan, the clan of his mother, Ogadeen, also of the Darood clan family, and the clan of his son-in-law, Dulbahante, again of the Darood family (Laitin and Samatar 1987: 92; Lewis 1983: 165–166). Including the Dulbahante was strategically important because their lineages lived in the North while the Mareehaan and Ogadeen were mostly populating the South. This so-called MOD coalition (for Mareehaan, Ogadeen, and Dulbahante), as it was known secretly in Somalia at the time, also included some of the politically weaker clans of Hawiye, Isaaq, and even Majeerteen. They were represented in the army and government, in an attempt to form a broader ruling coalition. This is shown in Table 3.4.

Darood overrepresentation increased dramatically during Barre's regime, jumping from 33% to 50% of seats with a population share of only around 20%. But the actual power configuration of Barre's military dictatorship is not ad-equately reflected by such data. The command structure was steep indeed and centered on the president, his top generals, the National Security Service chief, and the chief of the president's Political Office (cf. Lewis 1983: 166; see also Laitin and Samatar 1987: 97). Members of other clans were appointed to positions in the Supreme Revolutionary Council, for example, an Isaaq vice president and foreign minister, but they did not wield much independent power. Barre appointed them only because they adhered to the personality cult that he had crafted around himself and were thus his willing lackeys (Lewis 1983: 178). It is therefore only a slight exaggeration to speak of Barre's regime as a Darood ethnocracy—similar to Assad's Alawi regime in Syria and the dominance of Sunni Arabs in Iraq under Saddam Hussein, both of whom hid their narrow power bases, as did Siad Barre, with appeals to pan-Arab solidarity.

How much did the lack of capacity to provide public goods impede the formation of alliances across clan divides and force the regime to gradually narrow the ruling coalition, until it ended up with the MOD alliance? Given the limited documentary evidence (and I should add my even more limited expertise in Somalian matters), this is rather hard to determine. The extent to which weak public goods provision affected alliance formation becomes more evident, however, in the final years of Barre's rule. From the mid-1970s onward, the regime no longer attempted to politically integrate the hinterland by providing public goods through punctual campaigns. Instead, the populist-nationalist goal of national unification became paramount (Laitin and Samatar 1987: 88). In 1977, Barre launched a war to wrestle the Ogaden, inhabited by Somali nomads, out of Ethiopian hands. After a Soviet-supported military buildup, the war initially proceeded well and produced a wave of nationalist enthusiasm. The Somali army was defeated by Ethiopian and Cuban troops, however, as soon as the Soviet Union decided to switch to the Ethiopian side in the middle of the conflict. Hundreds of thousands of refugees, the large majority of them from the clan of Barre's mother, the Ogadeen, fled from Ethiopian reprisals across the border.

The government initially housed these refugees in camps of up to 60,000 people, where they were entirely dependent on the UN High Commissioner for Refugees. The Ogadeen refugees were then resettled among the northern Isaaq clans by military force. In the Isaaqi's eyes, the regime channeled public goods in the form of international assistance exclusively to the clans closely allied with the regime. "Clan discrimination" against Isaaq further increased when Barre started to recruit Ogadeenis from the refugee camps as well as members of the Ogadeeni-dominated, anti-Ethiopian Western Somali Liberation Front (WSLF) into militias that were supposed to maintain order in the restless North but soon started to harass the Isaaqi population. In light of the skewed distribution of public goods, such as international aid and protection from arbitrary violence, Isaaqi elites started to break away from the regime, further narrowing its power base. Isaaqi officers deserted from the army and in 1980 established a militia to counter WSLF dominance and protect the Isaaqi population from its abuses. The government quickly counteracted by depriving these army units of weapons or transferring them to other parts of the country. The Ogadeen "colonization" of the North also included "seizure of property and economic favoritism at Isaaq expense," as Lewis notes (1983: 180). Armed militias among non-Isaaq clans (mostly Darood but also some Dir) were encouraged to attack Isaaq nomads. No serious development activity was undertaken by the national government in the North, which further alienated Isaaqi politicians and their followers.

The skewed distribution of public goods in favor of the ruler's mother's clan finally led to open political and later military opposition. Isaaqi politicians founded, in Saudi and British exile, an exclusively Isaaqi political party, the Somali National Movement (SNM). It demanded the ouster of Barre, the federalization of the country, and a new social order based on traditional *heer* contracts. Soon after the foundation of the party in 1981, a local branch appeared in the northern city of Hargeisa, whose members deplored the lack of any government-run social services in their area and sought to improve the situation through self-help organizations. The regime arrested the group's leaders and set up a surveillance system in which every 20 families were supposed to be supervised by an official of the government party. In 1982, a group of prominent Isaaq elders denounced the "economic discrimination against Isaaq merchants and traders in favor of Darood officials and refugees." In return, the regime accused two senior Isaaq members of government of stirring up unrest and threw them in jail, further alienating Isaaqi constituencies and galvanizing support for the SNM.

Soon armed confrontations broke out between followers of the SNM (reinforced by deserting army officers with Isaaq roots) and the government. This was the second violent domestic conflict that the regime had to face. The first had erupted shortly after the Ogadeen war was lost and Majeerteen officers, who resented the fall from power their clansmen had held during the 10 preceding years of civilian rule, staged an unsuccessful coup. Its survivors then founded a guerrilla movement, the Somali Salvation Democratic Front, with headquarters in the archenemy's territory, Ethiopia.

A spiral of repression, political mobilization, and increasing guerrilla activity unfolded. It finally led, in the late 1980s, to a multifront civil war during which the army bombarded, in 1988, the cities of Hargeisa and Burao targeting Isaaq civilians. The most conservative estimates set the number of civilian casualties of this genocidal campaign at 50,000. A third major guerrilla force, largely based on a Hamiya clan alliance, finally overthrew Siad Barre in 1991. His regime was the last to have held control over the entire territory of Somalia. Since he was forced into exile, a series of complexly interwoven civil wars, foreign interventions (by the United States under UN mandate and repeatedly by Ethiopia), and secessions (of the former British territory in the North and the former sultanate of Majeerteen at the Horn) have shattered what state infrastructure he was able to build. Somalia stands today as a prime example of what has come to be known as a "failed state."

The detailed history of how Somalia fell apart is not the main focus of this chapter. Rather, the point to emphasize here is that the Barre regime was not able to establish a durable bureaucratic infrastructure to provide public goods, on a routine basis, to the population at large. This would have enabled him to extend networks of alliance and support across the territory and to circumvent clan leaders by gaining the loyalty of individual citizens independent of their clan background, as was the case in Botswana. The military government was quite effective at campaign-style operations: increasing literacy by sending teachers and students to the nomadic hinterland, providing for starving nomads during the drought crisis, and resettling some of them in the South and on the coasts. But it lacked the infrastructural capacity to create a sustainable and effective administration. Without such routine bureaucratic capacity, it is difficult to provide security, administer justice, develop infrastructure, and enhance the economic welfare of the citizenry at large. Without effective and equitable public goods provision, the regime wasn't able to extend its bases of support beyond its own narrow clan circles.

Three main reasons for the weakness of the Somali state have been identified: it lacked a legacy of state centralization from the precolonial and colonial past; a notoriously non-meritocratic, nepotistic culture had emerged in the hastened transition from colonial rule; and bureaucratic elites linked with citizens through the ties of clan clientelism, further undermining the state's capacity to provide public goods equitably and impartially. Despite favorable conditions such as linguistic homogeneity, nation building failed because the postcolonial state was not able to provide an attractive enough exchange partner to trade the provision of public services for the political loyalty and support of its citizens.

Communicative Integration

CHINA VERSUS RUSSIA

This chapter focuses on the third mechanism that facilitates the spread of alliance networks across a territory and thus nation building: communicative integration. In China, political elites from all regions of the country could easily converse with each other in the common writing system. In the Russian Empire, by contrast, communication across ethnic divides was more difficult because the population spoke many tongues written in different scripts. China transitioned to the postimperial period without any serious challenges to its territorial integrity, leaving the Tibetan and Muslim Uighur situations to the side for the purposes of this chapter. Postimperial nation building succeeded in terms of both political integration and identification: all governments that ruled after the abdication of the emperor in 1912 recruited their members from across the major regions of the vast country; a Han-Chinese national identity became firmly rooted in the minds of elites and ordinary citizens alike.

In Russia, ethnic nationalisms flourished after the revolutions of 1905 and 1917, which led to the overthrow of the Romanov dynasty. In 1917 Finland, Poland, the Baltic states, Ukraine, and the Transcaucasian states declared independence—most of which the red armies subsequently reconquered either during the Russian Civil War or during World War II. The Soviet Empire fell apart a second time along its ethnic fault lines when Communist rule came to an end in the mid-1980s. This chapter shows that an important part of these diverging stories of nation building is that a shared medium of communication held China's population together, fostering political ties between people who spoke different languages, while Russians remained fragmented into dozens of languages written in different scripts, thus impeding the formation of alliance networks across the territory.

China's Silent Dogs

Using China to illustrate how communicative integration eases nation building seems, at first sight, to be rather counterintuitive. Despite the official image as a largely homogeneous country populated by the Han majority, which represents over 90% of the population, this majority is de facto extraordinarily diverse and speaks in many, mutually unintelligible tongues. They include not only the well-known Mandarin and Cantonese languages but also a range of other idioms, many of which also cannot be understood mutually, that are spoken in the southern parts of the country.

A uniform Chinese script, not intimately tied to or derived from any of these languages, overlays the polyglot landscape, however. Polyglossia, in other words, combines with scriptural homogeneity, which facilitated building and maintaining political ties across a vast population speaking different tongues. China's Babylon, to use a biblical metaphor, was held together by the shared writing system. In theoretical terms, therefore, monoglossia and monographia have similar consequences for nation building.

Monographia enabled effortless communication between faraway individuals, facilitated the exchange of political ideas, and made it easy to form a polyglot political faction. In the imperial period, such factions proposed different interpretations of the classical canon of Confucianism and tried to oust each other from the inner circles of power. While initially often formed around provincial nuclei, these political alliance networks never remained confined to a particular language group and always ended up with a multilinguistic constituency. Consequently, when the last emperor abdicated in 1912 and the country became a modern nation-state, no movement advocating the autonomy or even independence of the Cantonese-, Xiang-, or Ming-speaking areas of the empire arose, as was the case among linguistic minorities in Russia during these years. Kuomintang and Communist cliques remained as cross-regional and polyglot as had been the factions of the imperial period. The dogs of linguistic nationalism therefore never barked. Nation building—both on the level of political integration and in terms of popular identification—superseded linguistic divides within the Han majority. The next sections describe how this story unfolded.

POLYGLOSSIA AND MONOGRAPHIA

Figure 4.1 gives a broad overview of the linguistic heterogeneity of contemporary China. It shows the areas where different Chinese languages are spoken as well as those of non-Chinese-speaking minorities, most importantly Tibetan-, Mongolian-, Korean-, and the various Thai- and Turkic-speaking communities at the outer fringes of the country.

This chapter focuses on linguistic diversity within the Han majority. I am not concerned, therefore, with the Tibetan situation or the fate of the Muslim, Turkic-speaking population in the northwestern province of Xinjiang, or the "tribal" minorities in Yunnan or Ghuizou, or the Miao of the Southwest. The Chinese empire from the 17th century onward had conquered these areas, and they were governed—and some would say continue to be governed—as internal colonies.

Linguistic diversity among the Han population is in fact considerable. Precisely because this diversity was never politicized, the Sinitic languages spoken by Han Chinese in different regions are commonly referred to as "dialects." But from a linguistic point of view, based on the criterion of mutual intelligibility, they clearly represent separate languages. "A language is a dialect with an army," the linguist Max Weinreich is supposed to have once said, and the various Sinitic languages never had one of their own.

Figure 4.2 details the phylogenetic relationship between the Sinitic languages and dialects. Recent experimental research (Chaoju and van Heuven 2009) shows that this tree more or less accurately describes how far individuals can understand each other: the further removed two languages are in the tree, the less their speakers understand each other. While individuals who speak different Mandarin languages might be able to grasp the meaning of each other's utterances, this is definitively not the case between speakers of Mandarin and the southern languages or between those who speak different southern languages.

This linguistic heterogeneity is combined, however, with scriptural homogeneity. All Chinese dynasties managed their administrative affairs largely in this script, and philosophers, poets, and essayists used it as well. Contrary to popular belief in contemporary China, the centralized empire did not emerge *because* of the uniform classical script. When the Qin reunited the empire late in the third century BC and gave it the shape that would last for millennia, a great variety of scripts were still in use. Scriptural homogeneity was not achieved until the early Tang dynasty (in the 7th century), a full millennium after the empire had emerged in its classic form (Xigui 2000: 147ff.). Scriptural uniformity was the consequence of political centralization, rather than the other way around.

Over time, two different versions of the script emerged that were adapted to different contexts: a classical version used by government officials and in "high" cultural genres such as poetry, and a less formalistic, "vulgar" variant (called *baihua*) in which popular novels were written and into which the statements of illiterate defendants in courts were transcribed (Wei 2015: 285). It is

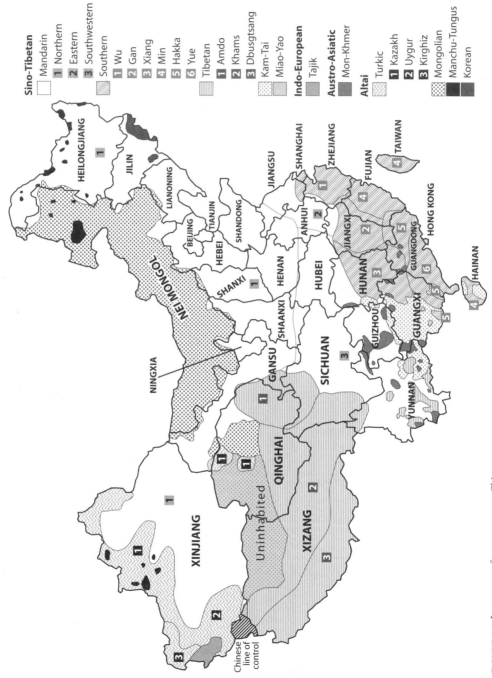

Sino-Tibetan

Mandarin
1 Northern
2 Eastern
3 Southwestern

Southern
1 Wu
2 Gan
3 Xiang
4 Min
5 Hakka
6 Yue

Tibetan
1 Amdo
2 Khams
3 Dbusgtsang

Kam-Tai

Miao-Yao

Indo-European

Tajik

Austro-Asiatic

Mon-Khmer

Altai

Turkic
1 Kazakh
2 Uygur
3 Kirghiz

Mongolian

Manchu-Tungus

Korean

HEILONGJIANG **1**
JILIN
LIANONING
BEIJING
TIANJIN
HEBEI
SHANDONG
SHANXI **1**
SHAANXI
HENAN
JIANGSU
SHANGHAI
ANHUI **2**
HUBEI
ZHEJIANG **1**
FUJIAN **4**
TAIWAN **4**
HUNAN **3**
JIANGXI **2**
GUANGDONG **6**
HONG KONG
GUIZHOU **5**
GUANGXI **5**
HAINAN **4**
YUNNAN **5**
SICHUAN **3**
GANSU **1**
NEI MONGOL
NINGXIA
QINGHAI **1**
1
XIZANG **2**
3
XINJIANG **1**
1
2
3
Uninhabited
Chinese line of control

FIGURE 4.1. Languages of contemporary China

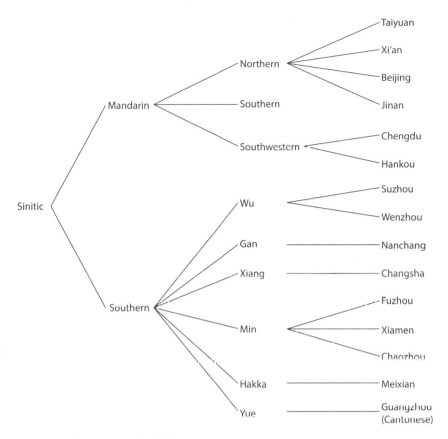

FIGURE 4.2. Language tree for Sinitic
Source: Adapted from Chaoju and van Heuven 2009: 712.

important to note that both versions of the script are logogrammatic. Each sign represents a particular word, not a sound as in phonogrammatic scripts, such as the Latin alphabet. To understand a sophisticated text, thousands of signs therefore need to be memorized. In an agricultural society, which China was well into the 20th century, only a tiny segment of the overall population would be able to write and read a text in a logogrammatic script.

What do the signs actually represent? A small proportion is pictographic, that is, the signs directly outline the object signified. The strokes for the tree sign, for example, resemble a tree. Another group of signs are ideographic and represent more abstract concepts but also in direct ways. The sign for the number 1, for example, consists of a single horizontal stroke. Over 90% of the signs, however, are what linguists call phonosemantic compounds: they are based on the pictogram of a similarly sounding word, but additional elements of the sign clarify that a different word is meant.

This raises an important question: Which of the variety of languages spoken throughout the empire does this script refer to? The short answer is none—at least if we follow Wei's (2015) excellent analysis of the question. The connection between sound and meaning, while at the basis of the phonosemantic compounds, became increasingly lost as the languages evolved over thousands of years. In contrast to European languages, therefore, the Chinese writing system disconnects sign from sound. Classical Chinese was pronounced differently depending on the actual language spoken by a person. As Wei puts it,

> The pronunciation of a given character or morpheme is not in any way dictated by the written script. Instead, it is subject to different executions depending on the readers' regional tongues and the tradition of *wendu*, a vocalizing practice that accommodates some Mandarin influences but retains distinctive local pronunciations and, in many cases, presents compromises between the Mandarin and regional phonologies. (2015: 289)

Conversely, none of the actually spoken languages developed their own writing system that would have been closer to their phonological reality. It is important to note that the plain, "vulgar" *baihua* version of the script also did not conform to any of the languages spoken in the empire but remained as distant from these vernaculars as the classical, more formal version—attempts by late 19th-century reformers to identify *baihua* as the equivalent to European vernaculars notwithstanding.

The Chinese script thus allowed speakers of different languages to communicate with each other—using brush and paper—even though they would not have understood each other when reading the text aloud. In this way, the communicative disadvantage of polyglossia was overcome by monographia. As the administration of the empire rested on written communication, monographia represented a decisive advantage. The memorial system exemplifies this. It was codified during the Ming dynasty and allowed an uncensored, secret communication between the emperor and the governors of the provinces (Guy 2010). The governors wrote memoranda on political, military, and fiscal affairs to the emperor, who then annotated and returned the memo. These exchanges could be rather lengthy: in the early 18th century the Southwestern governor Ortai sent memorials that ranged between 3,000 and 9,000 signs. The emperor's responses were comparatively terse, numbering between 240 and 670 signs. The distance was such that it took three and a half months until the governor had a response from the imperial palace.

Beyond the imperial administration, the uniform script allowed literate men from all corners of the empire to communicate with each other even if they spoke very different languages. As Elman (2013: 49) notes, "A literatus from Shanxi in the North-west could bridge the vernacular gap with his south-eastern Cantonese colleague, even if communication only occurred in written form using a brush." As we will see, the sinographic script thus enabled politically ambitious men to form alliances with each other that stretched across the entire, polyglot territory of the empire. This was true for the late imperial period as well as the 20th century.

Monographia was all the more important because unlike in other empires (such as the Ottoman realms), elites and nonelites alike spoke the local languages (Wei 2015: 258), such that the elite was fragmented by linguistic diversity as well. This brings us to the question of what role Mandarin played during the imperial period. While some scholars think that most literati throughout the empire mastered spoken Mandarin from the early 15th century onward (Elman 2013: 48–49), others are more skeptical. According to Wei (2015: 270ff.), Mandarin indeed served as a sort of lingua franca for officials, traveling monks, and merchants across different regions. However, attempts to ensure that all state officials would be able to converse fluently in Mandarin failed. Emperor Yongzheng (1723–1736) tried to force literate men from the southern provinces to go through eight years of Mandarin training before considering employing them as administrators. When his son succeeded to the throne, he admitted that the policy had failed, and he no longer required Mandarin training for southern officials. By the middle of the 19th century, the Mandarin curriculum in southern provinces had been largely forgotten.

Thus, even the educated elite often spoke Mandarin poorly, if at all (Wei 2015: 287). Furthermore, Mandarin itself was fragmented into a series of distinct languages and dialects such that native speakers of Mandarin often had difficulty understanding each other. "Even in the early decades of the twentieth century," writes Wei (2015: 266), "people from the same Mandarin-speaking region sometimes found it hard to communicate among themselves using what they assumed to be Mandarin, let alone communicate with those from other regions." Quite tellingly, the president of a newly founded university in Peking complained in the 1920s that if professors wanted to ensure that their students had understood the lectures (held in Mandarin), they would have to hand out their lecture notes written in the classical script (Wei 2015: 266n9).

POLITICAL CENTRALIZATION, MONOGRAPHIA, AND ELITE RECRUITMENT

It is now time to discuss the political development of China and how monographia shaped political alliance networks throughout the centuries. In terms of periodization, I distinguish between the Ming dynasty (1368–1644), the

Qing dynasty (1644–1911), and the republican period that followed, punctuated by the Japanese invasion and the Chinese civil war, which ended in the victory of the Communists and the proclamation of the People's Republic of China in 1949. For the purpose of this analysis, the most important turning point is the transition from empire to nation-state when the last emperor abdicated in 1912. I will thus take a close look at the nature of political alliances during the late Qing empire and then briefly trace their evolution through the republican and Communist periods.

The Ming and Qing periods are, for the purpose of this general discussion, similar enough that they do not need to be treated separately. The one significant difference, however, concerns the composition of the imperial household and entourage. The Qing had conquered the empire from the north and were of Manchu ethnic origin, speaking Manchu among themselves and using a distinct written script for palace communication and diplomatic notes until the end of their reign. From 1800 onward, however, the Manchu elite no longer spoke Manchu but the northern Mandarin dialect of their capital, Peking. The conquering Manchus and their Mongolian and Han allies of the early days remained organized according to the military principles that had given them the upper hand in armed confrontations with the Ming forces: they were divided into groups of bannermen with different prestige and privilege, a military ruling caste of sorts. The rank-and-file bannermen were supposed to retain their military prowess and resist assimilation into the court culture of Han China. Overall, however, the bureaucratic, fiscal, and military administration of the empire relied on the same organizational principles, modes of elite recruitment, and cultural bases as those of the preceding Ming dynasty, even if important posts (such as provincial governors) were preferentially given to individuals of Manchu origin.

The political system resembled a steep pyramid of authority. The emperor obviously stood at the top, surrounded by eunuchs whose lack of descendants freed them from clan and family loyalties, making them more dependent on and therefore more loyal to the emperor. The central administration in Peking, divided into ministries, oversaw provincial administrations, which in turn oversaw prefectural, district, and county officials. The army, also directly responsible to the emperor, was similarly organized along a straightforward pyramidal scheme. It offered a less prestigious career track compared to the bureaucracy. The censorship office, a separate, independent branch of the administration, oversaw and spied upon the rest of the government apparatus to discover irregularities in administration and tax collection (Kiser and Tong 1992). Such irregularities were a constant problem for the Ming and Qing dynasties, which had lost control, compared to previous emperors, over local affairs and thus had to cede much power, at the local level, to the landed gentry (Wei 2015: 283–284).

The Chinese empire developed a unique way to recruit bureaucrats into the various branches and levels of this administrative machinery. Unlike other large-scale premodern polities, the Chinese empire never relied on a hereditary nobility because it tried to prevent an autonomous social stratum from emerging and competing with the emperor for political power. Instead, the empire recruited its administrators and generals—leaving the Manchu privileges aside for a moment—through a system of examinations (the following relies on Elman 2013).

To be a candidate for these exams required literacy in the classical Chinese script, usually acquired in childhood through clan schools or private teachers. The system comprised three government-administered, academic examinations leading to three hierarchically ordered titles—from the licentiate to the "doctorate." The more demanding examinations were held in the provincial capitals and the "doctorate" exam in the metropolis. Those who passed the first level were exempt from taxes and given a small annual stipend of rice to allow them to become independent of agricultural pursuits and live the life of a scholar/politician. The three degrees also led, though not in uniform ways throughout the centuries, to different tiers of administrative appointments by the emperor. The highest officeholders such as governors or overseers of the salt monopoly came from the ranks of those who had passed the "doctorate" exam. Men reached this level usually at an advanced age after a life spent studying for the exams.

In theory, anybody could become a candidate for the exams. In practice, sons of graduates were much more likely to apply for and much more likely to pass the exams. Still, social mobility in China was far more common than in any other premodern state (Ho 1962). Since passing these exams became increasingly difficult (only 1% passed the exams in the late 18th century according to Elman 2013: 125), especially as population growth in the 18th and 19th centuries far outpaced the growth of the administration, the system produced a constant surplus of literate, classically trained men who either failed the exam or could not acquire an appropriate government position after passing. In the early 19th century, there were about 1.1 million licentiate degree holders out of a population of 350 million. Only 2.2% of these were able to pass the provincial and palace degrees and thus were eligible for positions in the imperial administration. An additional 2 million were candidates for local examinations but had not been able to pass them yet, raising the total to about 3 million classically trained individuals, a figure that increased to 4 to 5 million after 1850 (Elman 2013: 245). This literate stratum of society represented the political elites, and the following analysis will concentrate on the alliance structures that emerged within this stratum.

The exam subjects remained largely constant throughout the Ming and Qing dynasties. They were based on a particular interpretation of the Chinese classics and of Confucianism—often branded "neo-Confucianism" in the 20th century by Western scholars. The exams tested fluency in the Chinese script, knowledge of the five classics in literature (such as the Four Books) and of imperial genealogies, poetic skills, and the mastery of an argumentative essay, which had to take a prescribed, syllogistic form. All in all, it required, in the late Ming, memorizing about 520,000 signs (Elman 2013: 155). It should be mentioned that from 1815 onward, the empire was less inclined to penalize the outright sale of licentiate titles, an illegal practice that had existed for centuries. Between 1837 and 1848, the emperor even legalized title sales in order to raise money for a treasury depleted by war expenditures—a practice greatly resented by those who had earned their degrees through years of hard study.

To bring the story back to the argument outlined in the theory chapter: an extraordinarily high level of political centralization generated, over long periods of time, a homogeneous communicative landscape—albeit in the case of China in the form of monographia rather than monoglossia. The examination system encouraged ambitious men from around the empire, whatever their mother tongue, to acquire the scriptural skills necessary to succeed. This in turn allowed the empire to recruit from all corners of its realms, giving rise to a polyglot bureaucratic elite, as we will see. Thus, monographia allowed integrating a variety of ethno-linguistic communities into the imperial polity—and it continued to have this effect during the republican and Communist periods.

Imagine if the examinations had been held in one of the Mandarin idioms, let's say the northern Mandarin variant that the Communists later declared the "national" language. Speakers of southern Chinese languages would have been severely disadvantaged in the competition for political power. The bureaucracy would have become dominated by northern Mandarin speakers—not unlike how Turks surged to prominence in the Ottoman Empire once Ottoman was replaced with Turkish or how German speakers gained control of the Habsburg Empire once German replaced Latin as the language of administration. In terms of the well-known paraphrasing of the Habsburg situation by Ernest Gellner, "Ruritanians" who spoke the language of the peripheries would then have been ruled by "Megalomanians" who spoke the language of the imperial center, once it declared its own tongue the official language of administration.

Monographia was not the only enabling condition, to be sure for a multilingual elite to emerge. Perhaps equally important was the conscious design, by the Ming and Qing courts, to recruit from across the regions of the vast empire. This was achieved through the quota system, which fixed—though with variations over time—how many licentiates and provincial degrees could be acquired in each county and province. The quotas could be abolished, reinstated, enlarged, or reduced to reward or punish particularly loyal or unruly areas of the empire. The important point here is that without monographia, such a policy would have been virtually impossible. The academic quality of the degree holders would have varied dramatically were the avenues of upward mobility restricted to those who were fluent in a particular Chinese language. Imagine the contemporary European Union—comparable in population size to the Qing empire—with Flemish as the only official language whose mastery would determine the career prospects of bureaucrats in Brussels.

It is now time to examine to what extent this system indeed produced a balanced power configuration that included individuals from all major language communities. Table 4.1 combines two data sources. The first is Chang (1967 [1955]), who compiled figures of licentiate degree holders from the various provinces. These figures are based on unrepresentative samples and include those who had bought their titles in the 19th century. If I included only the regular titleholders, the provincial shares in the total number of degree holders would remain largely the same. The figures include both civilian and military licentiates—there were two separate examination systems with varying degrees of permeability between them.

The data in the second part of the table provide details about those who had passed the "doctorate" exams, almost all of whom subsequently served high offices in the empire. They thus formed the highest echelon of the Qing state. These figures are derived from the complete lists of degree holders that Ho (1962) assembled. Since these lists also contain information on the degrees held by the ancestors of a successful candidate, Ho was able to calculate rates of social mobility. Here, I show the percentage of doctors whose 14 male ancestors over the previous three generations held either no title whatsoever or only one licentiate degree. From this, we can calculate differences between the average rates of upward mobility across provinces.

No clear pattern of advantage or disadvantage emerges from Table 4.1. For ease of inspection, negative differences from the average are highlighted in italics. Some Mandarin-speaking provinces, such as Honan, Anhwei, Hupei, and Szechwan, were disadvantaged in terms of their shares of licentiate as well as palace degree holders. But other Mandarin-speaking areas, such as Hopei, Kiangsu, and Shansi, were advantaged in both. Among the provinces where southern language predominated, the Hakka- and Yue-speaking province of Kwangtung ("Canton") as well as Xiang-speaking Hunan were disadvantaged on both levels. Wu-speaking Chekiang as well as Kam-Tai- and Hakka-speaking Kwangsi were advantaged on both, however. The same holds true if we look at patterns of intergenerational mobility.

TABLE 4.1. Licentiate and palace degree holders per province, Qing dynasty

| Province | Dominant language | Licentiates (regular and irregular, civilian and military | | Highest graduates | | Upwardly mobile highest graduates |
		In % of population	% difference from national average	In absolute numbers per 1 million inhabitants	% difference from national average	% difference from national average
Hopei (or Pei–Chihli, Chili)	Mandarin, northern	4.1	64.8	117	31.1	*–5.7*
Honan	Mandarin, northern	2	*–19.6*	81	*–4.9*	5.5
Shantung	Mandarin, northern	1	*–59.8*	100	14.1	*–3.2*
Shansi	Mandarin, northern	2.7	8.5	108	22.1	3.6
Shensi	Mandarin, northern	5	101.0	59	*–26.9*	15.1
Kansu	Mandarin, northern	Included in Shaanxi		Included in Shaanxi		
Liaotung, Fengtien	Mandarin, northern			91	5.1	20.3
Kiangsu	Mandarin, southern	2.5	0.5	93	7.1	*–8.5*
Anhwei	Mandarin, southern	1.7	*–31.7*	41	*–44.9*	0.9
Hupei	Mandarin, southern	1.1	*–55.8*	64	*–21.9*	10
Szechwan	Mandarin, southwestern	0.6	*–75.9*	38	*–47.9*	16.7
Kweichow	Mandarin, southwestern/ Miao–Yao	1.8	*–27.7*	116	30.1	6.9
Yunnan	Mandarin, southwestern/ various Tibetan /Miao–Yao	2	*–19.6*	94	8.1	4.7
Kiangsi	Gan	2.4	*–3.5*	99	13.1	*–4.4*
Kwangtung	Hakka/Yue	1.8	*–27.7*	63	*–22.9*	0.9
Kwangsi	Kam–Tai/ Hakka	4.7	88.9	90	4.1	*–2.3*
Fukien	Min	1.7	*–31.7*	117	31.1	*–2.7*
Chekiang	Wu	5	101.0	130	44.1	3.6
Hunan	Xiang	2.2	*–11.6*	45	*–40.9*	16.7

Source: Chang (1967) and Ho (1962).

Note: Negative differences from the average are highlighted in italics.

POLITICAL ALLIANCES IN IMPERIAL CHINA

We've now laid the foundations to examine how political alliances formed in imperial China and during the transition to the nation-state—with important consequences for nation building in the post-imperial period. Until the Taiping Rebellion in the mid-19th century, the peasant masses were not actively participating in the power struggles of the empire. They remained under the control of the local landowning gentry who also provided the vast majority of candidates—successful or not—for the various examinations and thus formed the local bureaucratic elite. The literati struggled against each other to gain the favor of and influence those at the top of the political pyramid. Since access to the highest echelons depended on examination success—and subsequently on the appointment decisions by the emperor and his advisors—control over the examination system itself became one of the main political prizes to win.

To gain or maintain influence and to foster each other's bureaucratic careers, ambitious titleholders formed patron-client relationships with each other. Clients supported their patron politically and in return were granted protection and career promotion. Following Hucker (1966), we can distinguish between different types of such patron-client ties. First, "officials who had passed the same doctoral examination [together] ('the class of 1526') considered themselves lifelong comrades who owed political loyalty to one another, and for their whole careers they were like politically subservient disciples of the senior officials who had been their examiners." Similar bonds were forged among those who had passed lower-level exams together. Qing attempts to undermine such loyalty, for example by banning rites of gratitude to the teachers of examination compounds, were largely unsuccessful (Elman 2013: 223; further references documenting examiner-candidate patronage can be found in Kiser and Tong 1992: 313–314).

Second, similar patronage ties developed between superiors and inferiors in government agencies and the military. They tended to last for their entire careers, even if the officials were subsequently posted to different agencies or regions. Thus, writes Hucker, "the adherents of one powerful minister intrigued against those of another, or officials from one region intrigued against those of another region, or officials of one agency against those of others" (Hucker 1966: 46).

Third and most important for empire-wide politics, influential scholars/bureaucrats developed various interpretations of the "Way Learning," the neo-Confucian orthodoxy, which implied different ideals of the gentleman-scholar-administrator and different notions of legitimate power. More often than not, however, the differences remained confined to more subtle matters of textual interpretation, poetic style, and so on. But they mattered greatly because depending on which interpretative school was favored by the examiners, candidates fared more or less well in the examinations.

At various times, especially during the Ming dynasty, such schools of interpretation organized around privately owned study academies that trained potential candidates. The famous Donglin Academy in the late Ming period proposed a purified, puritanical ideal of the righteous scholar/bureaucrat who was supposed to stand up for moral values independent of expediency and thus of the opinions of his superiors. After initially gaining much ground in the examination system and thus in the inner circles of power, Donglin adherents were brutally purged from the administration (Dardess 2002). Subsequently, the Restoration Society adopted some of Donglin's principles and was able to gain considerable influence by placing several general secretaries (the highest post in the administration), members of the Hanlin Academy (which oversaw Confucian orthodoxy and the intellectual part of the examination system), provincial governors, and so on. According to Elman, it formed "the largest political interest group ever organized within a dynasty, and examination success was its time-honored route to power" (Elman 2013: 89–90).

After the overthrow of the Ming, the Qing rulers tried to prevent the resurgence of such large-scale factions by prohibiting literati from gathering to discuss philosophical and political issues or forming local academies (Wakeman 1972: 55; Levine 2011: 876). Despite close control and supervision, however, various intellectual reform movements resurged during the 19th century. The Xuannan Poetry Club and the Spring Purification Group, for example, "followed a similar organizational trajectory as the Donglin Academy had, scaling up literary associations into oppositional pressure groups within the central government bureaucracy. In the 1830s, the Spring Purification association united literati around a morally activist political platform, seeking to rescue the Qing court from domestic and foreign crises" (Levine 2011: 876).

Polachek (1991) analyzed the Spring Purification movement in some detail. His study allows us to observe how a large-scale political alliance network developed from a literary organization to a political faction of networked officials/poets. The literary circle formed in Peking to read and discuss poetry during springtime. It drew together a cluster of individuals who had either failed in the "doctoral" examination or had succeeded (two were Hanlin Academy members) but were in danger of losing their patron or had advocated a literary style that was currently out of favor. One core member was an ambitious bureaucrat who had served in different parts of the country in important posts and had accumulated a varied set of clients whom he protected. In other words, all early members of the Spring Purification movement were relatively peripheral in the power structure of the capital at the time. Unlike most factional groups in imperial China, then, this group was not formed around an examiner and those who successfully passed the exams he administered, but represented a composite of various disaffected individuals.

Later on, this group of intellectuals/poets/politicians allied itself with one of the contenders for the position of the grand secretary. He was a prominent examiner and controlled appointments, intermittently, to lower-level examination posts. The Spring Purification poetry readings were held, as Polachek shows, when this person was in charge of examinations and during the period of the imperial exams. In this way, promising club members were brought to the attention of the examiners in the hope that this would help them pass the exam. Such manipulation of or even control over the examination system and thus over the appointment process was typical for imperial factional politics, as noted above.

More to the point, the Spring Purification group was also typical in that it united individuals of various regional and thus linguistic backgrounds from around the country, as the biographical sketches provided by Polachek illustrate. They were united—apart from their desire to gain power—by a shared interpretation of the scriptural canon and by their love for a certain style of poetry. In other words, monographia allowed men from different linguistic backgrounds to form a shared outlook on the political world, build alliances with each other, and thus produce and institutionalize a transregional, transethnic network.

To make the counterfactual explicit, imagine if each of the various language groups in imperial China had developed its own phonogrammatic writing system, perhaps even using different scripts (say, Latin for the Mandarin languages and Arabic for the southern, as was the case in Russia). The formation of political ties across these language divides would have undoubtedly been more difficult, and we would observe fewer cross-regional, multilinguistic alliance networks such as gathered under the umbrella of the Spring Purification group. Rather, factions would have formed among men who could understand each other effortlessly because they spoke and wrote the same language.[1]

Writing in the shared script itself played an important role in the formation of alliances across linguistic divides. While the Spring Purification Society remained largely confined to the capital, other and more successful such movements used letters and pamphlets as the main means of recruiting new members from across the country into the alliance network. The way in which the early Donglin Academy mobilized followers is a good example. "The primary extension of the Donglin group into politics," writes Wakeman (1972: 51), "was the work of [the academy's founder] himself, via both a stream of letters sent to friends throughout the empire, and a series of widely disseminated pamphlets. In fact, his interference—for he was still a commoner and had no bureaucratic rights as such—in two major appointment cases in 1607 and 1620 created a countrywide sensation," which was brought to the attention of the literati class by copying and distributing these pamphlets.

Monographia continued to play an important role in the formation of alliances later on in the Qing dynasty and closer to the transition to the nation-state in 1911. Despite the imperial ban on forming associations, many sprang into existence after a series of humiliating defeats of the imperial armies, first against Western powers in the Boxer wars, as a consequence of which China lost control over coastal trading towns such as Hong Kong and Shanghai, and, more importantly, after the war with Japan in 1895 ended in the loss of Taiwan as well as control over the Korean client state.

New scholarly associations emerged among literati (the following draws on Wakeman 1972). They shared the reformist goals of earlier associations but added some moderately modernist points to their programs. They sought to blend the Confucian heritage with elements of Christian charity and concern for the masses, Japanese war-proneness, as exemplified by the *samurai* warrior ethos, and Western constitutionalism. Sometimes these associations even advocated for a parliamentary assembly that would perfect the union between the emperor and the people, a proposal that was adopted by the emperor during the last years of his reign.

The first of these associations was the Study Society for Self-Strengthening—the equivalent of the Helvetic Society founded in Switzerland a century earlier. Later on, such associations proliferated throughout the empire, increasingly with a less Peking-focused outlook. Many associations confined membership to a province or even a district, mirroring the idea of popular sovereignty. The literati men who founded these associations communicated with each other mostly in writing, using the shared sinographic script. They often copied each other's ideas found in tractates, learned expositions, and pamphlets distributed throughout the empire. Notably, none of these associations raised language issues or questioned the unity of the empire—quite the opposite: the shared goal was to reform the empire in its existing political outlook and territorial extension to better resist the encroachments by Japan and the barbarian West.

A second group of politically active networks was composed of a distinct, if overlapping, group of individuals who hailed from the same social background as the reform-minded literati. They had acquired a modern education at missionary schools in China (which flourished after the anti-Western Boxer Rebellion was brutally subdued by an alliance of mostly Western powers), at British schools established in Hong Kong, and at universities in Japan, where the court sent promising students after it abolished, in a dramatic decision in 1905, the examination system on which the empire had rested for thousands of years. Japan represented the model nation for modernist elites in China since the successful Meiji Restoration. In the early 1900s, the community of students in Japan numbered in the thousands. Most of them came from elite backgrounds and many of them had previously passed the licentiate exam in China (cf. Harrison 2001: 101–102). Not surprisingly, then, their regional composition was about as balanced as was the licentiate population in China overall. More precisely, they came mostly from central China (Hunan and Hupei), the Guangdong region, Shanghai and the lower Yangtze area, as well as Szechwan (Fairbank 1987: 152–153).

From their Japanese teachers as well as from Chinese intellectuals who had been exiled to Japan, they learned the language of liberal constitutionalism and modern nationalism—as refracted through Japanese translations. They became convinced that in order to withstand the pressures of Western and Japanese imperialism, the Manchu dynasty had to be overthrown and replaced by a republican government ruling in the name of the Chinese (Han) majority (more on early republican nationalism below). Their ideas started to be widely disseminated and understood—thanks to the shared sinographic script—among the literati of China proper. Many of the reform associations that had sprung up in late imperial China became aligned with one or the other of these early republican, nationalist associations.

In the context of this chapter, we are particularly interested in how these associations gradually fused with each other, giving rise to a remarkably polyglot alliance structure. The Guangdong-based Furen Literary Society (composed mostly of Cantonese speakers), for example, later merged into the Revive China Society founded by Sun Yat-sen (a Cantonese speaker as well), who later emerged as the preeminent nationalist, anti-Manchu leader. The Revive China Society in turn merged with the Chekiang-based Restoration Society and other provincial revolutionary organizations from other linguistic regions of the country into the Chinese United League (or Tongmenghui). The Chinese United League was founded in 1905 under Japanese tutelage and comprised a variety of cross-regional alliances. Writes Fairbank: "The Alliance of 1905 was a Japanese-arranged marriage of provincial groups in which Central China supplied the most members and leaders. . . . The Cantonese contingent was second" (1987: 154). Only a few years after its foundation, however, the Chinese United League had branches in Guangdong, Szechwan, Wuhan, Shanghai, Hangzhou, Suzhou, Anqing, Fuzhou, and Tianjin and counted half a million members. The first political party in Chinese history, the Kuomintang, emerged out of the Chinese United League to contest the first elections after the overthrow of the Qing dynasty in 1912—which it won with overwhelming popular support.

The printing industry, which started to flourish after the turn of the century (cf. Fairbank 1987: 141ff.), greatly helped coordinate ideas and strategies between like-minded local groups throughout the country as well as the exile community in Japan and thus helped bring them under a shared organizational roof. Technological innovations made the rapid printing of texts with Chinese characters possible and enabled the production of daily newspapers that were read across the country. They were often printed in the coastal concession cities such as Shanghai, beyond the reach of the imperial censors (Harrison 2001: 111ff.). Printed materials were also the main tools for mobilizing support beyond the immediate circle of activists. These included the popular comics (*manhuas*) with minimal texts, many criticizing the Qing government and traditional, "feudal" society in general. Needless to say, monographia greatly facilitated the production and dissemination of these texts and thus made it easier to mobilize broader political support among the polyglot population.

AFTER THE QING: THE STRUGGLE BETWEEN TWO TRANSREGIONAL ALLIANCE NETWORKS

The revolution of 1911 brought an end to thousands of years of dynastic rule. The particulars of historical events are not of interest here, nor can I explore in any detail postrevolutionary political developments. Suffice it to say that a period of instability followed when the military and political authority structure of the empire collapsed. Factional fighting among various regional generals (or warlords) ensued until the Kuomintang was able to establish a one-party authoritarian regime in 1928. Japanese intervention and occupation followed in 1931; a prolonged civil war between the Kuomintang under its generalissimo Chiang Kai-shek and the Communist Party of China ensued, which ended in the latter's victory in 1949.

The end of the empire certainly offered a critical juncture during which linguistic nationalisms could have developed, similar to what occurred when Russia's Romanov dynasty collapsed. The Chinese state could then have fallen apart into a series of linguistically more homogeneous states. This, however, did not happen, nor did anyone ever attempt to move history in that direction. To see why, I suggest looking at the ethnoregional composition of the alliance networks that dominated postimperial China, leaving the complexities of the warlord period aside.[2] We have already seen how the alliance network of the Kuomintang developed from the early nationalist associations through a series of mergers, which brought literati from around the country under a shared organizational umbrella. It is now time to briefly tell the story of the Chinese Communist Party (CCP)—the main contender for power during the postimperial period.

The party was founded in the early 1920s by a group of intellectuals under Soviet tutelage. Until 1928, both the Kuomintang and the CCP were organized as Leninist parties and overseen by Soviet political agents. The leadership of the CCP was mostly trained in the Soviet Union, while many Kuomintang cadres went through a Japanese education, as discussed above. Moscow was hoping that the "bourgeois" Kuomintang would reestablish a unified country that could then be taken over by the revolutionary CCP. During this period of alliance, most CCP members were also members of the Kuomintang, and the social origins and regional composition of both groups greatly overlapped.[3] The CCP remained militarily weak and counted only few members. It finally acquired a mass membership after the May 30 incident of 1925, during which British policemen killed protesters in Shanghai, sparking nationwide anti-imperialist protests and riots. Tens of thousands of students and members of the urban middle class who had participated in these demonstrations now joined the CCP.

The Kuomintang became aware of Moscow's strategy later on and in 1927 violently purged CCP members from its ranks, with the help of underworld gangs from Shanghai. The CCP subsequently tried to establish its own territorial base from where to fight the Kuomintang (and the Japanese) during the long march across China under the leadership of Mao. The two parties fought each other more or less continuously from 1927 onward except during a Moscow-sponsored alliance meant to help the struggle against Japan, which lasted from 1937 to the Japanese defeat in 1945.

We are now ready to consider the linguistic composition of the political alliance networks formed within the Kuomintang and the CCP. Table 4.2 was calculated on the basis of data provided by North (1952). I again take the birth province of individuals as an indication of their linguistic background. The table shows that neither the Kuomintang nor the CCP was strictly representative if we analyze the data by provincial origin. Some smaller and less developed provinces in the North were underrepresented in both alliance networks. The Kuomintang alliance contained more members of the economically dynamic, coastal regions of the South where non–Mandarin speakers were dominant. This is because the commercial, capitalist bourgeoisies allied with the Kuomintang, especially after its drift to the right once the Communists had been purged from its ranks. For similar political reasons, the CCP included more representatives of the populous peasant provinces of the interior—including a very significant overrepresentation of individuals born in Mao's home province Hunan.

If we aggregate the data by language group, however, no clear pattern emerges. In both the Kuomintang Central Executive Committee and the CCP Central Committee, northern Mandarin speakers were generally underrepresented (with the exception of Shansi province). Some southern or southwest-

TABLE 4.2. Regional origins of Kuomintang and CCP Central Committee members

Province	Dominant language(s)	Kuomintang Central Executive Committee members, 1924–1945			CCP Central Committee members, 1945			CCP Politburo members, 1921–1951
		In % of total	Difference between population in 1926 and representation, %	% over- or under-representation	In % of total	Difference between population in 1950 and representation, %	% over- or under-representation	In absolute numbers
Hopei (or Pei–Chihli, Chili)	Mandarin, northern	4.5	−3.9	−49.3	0	−6.8	−100.0	
Honan	Mandarin, northern	0.4	−7.3	−100.1	0	−7.8	−100.0	
Shantung	Mandarin, northern	2.4	−5.1	−71.8	2.3	−6.4	−73.4	1
Shansi	Mandarin, northern	3.1	0.5	18.4	6.8	4.3	168.7	1
Shensi	Mandarin, northern	2.8	−1.0	−27.8	2.3	−2.8	−54.9	1
Kansu	Mandarin, northern	1.4	−0.2	−12.3	0		−100.0	
Liaotung, Fengtien	Mandarin, northern							
Kiangsu	Mandarin, southern	8.4	0.9	12.7	11.4	3.0	35.6	5
Anhwei	Mandarin, southern	3.5	−0.9	−22.3	2.3	−3.1	−57.1	4
Hupei	Mandarin, southern	4.2	−2.0	−34.4	11.4	6.5	131.7	5
Szechwan	Mandarin, southwestern	5.9	−5.4	−50.5	13.6	2.6	23.3	1
Kweichow	Mandarin, southwestern/Miao–Yao	3.5	1.1	46.6	2.3	−0.4	−13.4	
Yunnan	Mandarin, southwestern/various Tibetan/Miao–Yao	1.7	−0.7	−31.7	0	−3.1	−100.0	
Kiangsi	Gan	8.4	2.4	41.8	11.4	3.0	35.6	1
Kwangtung	Hakka/Yue	15	7.0	91.8	2.3	−3.9	−62.7	2
Kwangsi	Kam–Tai/Hakka	3.1	0.5	18.4	2.3	−1.2	−33.7	
Fukien	Min	2.8	−0.4	−12.3	6.8	4.5	193.3	
Chekiang	Wu	12.9	7.6	152.4	0	−4.1	−100.0	1
Hunan	Xiang	8.7	−0.2	−2.0	27.3	21.4	364.6	8

Source: North (1983).

ern Mandarin-speaking provinces were underrepresented in the Kuomintang, others in the CCP, and the same goes for the non-Mandarin-speaking provinces. Both alliances comprised a good number of individuals from all over the country and the same could be said of the small politburo of the Communist Party—even if Hunan overrepresentation in that body is somewhat more striking. The data thus show that during the postimperial period, alliances continued to form independent of language affinity, as they had during the late Qing.

A more detailed study of the Kuomintang confirms this analysis. Table 4.3 lists the major political factions within the Kuomintang (based on North 1952). As the names of the cliques already suggest, only one of them, the Northeast Army Clique, was based on the shared regional origin of its members (who were mostly born in Liaotung and had formed a clique of allied warlords before joining the Kuomintang). All the others were held together by other kinds of commonalities. For example, the Sun Fo Clique comprised the followers of Sun Yat-sen's son, Sun Fo. The Political Science Clique was centered on General Chang Chun, Sun Fo, and T. V. Song. They represented businessmen, professionals, and officeholders, quite a few of whom were fluent in English and educated in Japan or the United States. The Central Committee Clique, headed by Chen Li-fu and his brother, was notable for its fervent anticommunism and represented the interests of big landowners. The Whampoa Regeneration Clique was made up of the graduates of the Whampoa military academy where Chiang Kai-shek had taught. A prominent member was Ho Ying-chin, who had studied with Chiang Kai-shek at the military academy in Tokyo (the above is based on Bagby 1992: 45–46). It seems that alliances formed on the basis of similar principles as under the Qing: political strongmen developed clientelist ties with those who graduated from the same schools in the same year, who served under them in bureaucratic or military institutions, or who shared their political convictions.

Among the Communists, factions also developed independent of linguistic commonality. This is evident from the early analysis of Chao (1955), who discusses all kinds of possible splits within the newly established Communist regime but never mentions language or region. The only possible schism detected in the otherwise monolithic power structure was a possible conflict between

> a newly-developed bureaucratic-technician class and the older type of Party bosses. . . . Already a number of persons have risen to national prominence on the strength of their professional or technical abilities. When this group becomes sufficiently numerous and strong, it may challenge decisions of the Party hierarchy on economic or technical grounds. Some older Communists who lack technical education may also feel resentful toward

TABLE 4.3. Political factions in the Kuomintang Central Executive Committee

Political orientation	Name of faction	No. of members
Left	Kuomintang left	7
	Sun Fo Clique	8
	Reorganization Clique	11
	The Middle Group	16
	Communist Party Rebels	4
	European–American Clique	28
	Local cliques	106
Pro–Chiang Kai-shek	Party veterans	12
	Whampoa Regeneration Clique	22
	Direct affiliates	32
	Quasi–direct affiliates	9
	Officials (military)	16
	Naval Clique	2
	Political Science Clique	14
	Northeast (Manchurian) Army Clique	10
	Overseas	10
	Officials	9
Right	Central Committee Clique	117
	Chu Chia-hua Clique	10

Source: North 1952.

these new men because of their privileges and quick promotions. (Chao 1955: 153)

If we jump forward in time to China under the recent presidency of Hu Jintao (2003–2013), a similar picture emerges. According to Li,

One coalition might be called the "elitist coalition," led by former Party chief Jiang Zemin, and now largely led by Vice President of the PRC Zeng Qinghong. The core faction of this elitist coalition is the so-called Shanghai Gang, including prominent leaders such as Huang Ju, Wu Bangguo, Chen Liangyu, Zeng Peiyan, and Chen Zhili. Like their patrons, Jiang Zemin and Zeng Qinghong, many rising stars in the elitist coalition are princelings (those who rose to leadership via family connections). . . . Some are returnees from study abroad (so-called haiguipai). An overwhelming majority of returnees come from, and work, in the coastal regions. These leaders often represent the interests of entrepreneurs, the emerging middle class, and the economically advanced coastal provinces (China's "blue states"). . . . The other coalition can be identified as the "populist coalition" led by President Hu Jintao and Premier Wen Jiabao. The core faction of the populist coalition is the Chinese Communist Youth League (CCYL), the so-called tuanpai who worked in the national or provincial leadership in the League in the early 1980s when Hu Jintao was in charge of that organization. Most of the populist coalition's members have advanced their political careers through local and provincial administration, many have leadership experience in rural areas, and many have worked in the fields of Party organization, propaganda, and legal affairs. Like Hu Jintao and Wen Jiabao, leaders of the populist coalition often come from less-developed inland provinces (China's "red states" or more commonly known in China as "yellow states"); they usually have humble family backgrounds. Leaders of the populist coalition are more effective in addressing the concerns and needs of the population at the grassroots, especially the so-called "vulnerable social groups" such as farmers, migrant laborers and the urban unemployed. (2005: 3)

The formation of these two transregional alliances—connecting hundreds of thousands of bureaucrats, party members, business elites, and everyday citizens into hierarchical patronage relationships—continues to be facilitated by monographia, which allows like-minded speakers of different tongues to communicate with each other in writing and form alliances. Both coalitions therefore comprise leaders of different regional and linguistic origins, as was the case for other Chinese factions since at least the Ming.[4]

THE INVENTION OF THE HAN NATION

It is now time to analyze the nationalist ideology that developed after the overthrow of the imperial order. More specifically, why did none of the non-Mandarin language groups of the South claim the mantle of national autonomy for itself? In the late Qing and early republican period, a rich intellectual debate ensued on how to translate the Western concepts of race, ethnic group, nation, people, and nation-state into the Chinese context and how exactly to define the boundaries of the imagined community in whose name the post-dynastic state was to rule.

Some argued for the existence of a "Chinese race" comprising several other sub-races, such as the Mongolians, Tibetans, Koreans, Japanese, and Siamese. Others maintained that these formed separate races altogether and that the Han Chinese represented a distinct racial stock, as did (a point of agreement among most) the Manchu. When the Japanese empire later created a puppet state named Manchuria, most intellectuals abandoned the idea of a separate Manchu race and subsumed the Manchu under the Chinese race, thus trying to undermine the legitimacy of the Japanese imperial project. Another point of discussion was whether these different non-Han races (or sub-races of the Chinese) should remain separate from the Han majority or whether they should eventually be absorbed by and melded into, as Sun Yat-sen hoped, the Han race and its state.

Others focused on the concept of nation, which was translated into the term *minzu*, previously reserved for foreign tribes (Harrison 2001: 104). They suggested that the Chinese nation comprised a series of different nationalities, including the Han, Tibetans, Mongols, Manchus, and Muslims. Another hotly debated question concerned the historical origin of the Chinese/Han nation or race: Was it descended from a single ancestor (such as the Peking man whose skeletal remains were discovered in the early 1920s)? Or were there originally several different racial stocks or national groups that subsequently fused, over time, into a single race or nation? Was this Han/Chinese race/nation of Western, Mesopotamian origin or born on indigenous soil? Was the mythical Yellow Emperor who ruled during the third millennium BC the ancestor of the Han only or of all the five nationalities/races of contemporary China?

The details of these debates, summarized by Leibold (2012), are not of interest here. It suffices to note that the five nations theory became official doctrine under the republican and nationalist governments from 1912 to 1949 (Harrison 2001: chap. 5), which also embraced the idea that the Yellow Emperor was the founding ancestor of all five national groups. On the political level, republican governments granted some symbolic representation and a minimal degree of self-rule to the four minority nations—as had been the case under the Qing.

It is striking that in all these debates the internal homogeneity and political unity of the category "Han" remained uncontested—while there was much debate as to whether it represented a race, a nation, or a people and what its relations to other races or nations should be. The ethnonym "Han" had already emerged in its contemporary meaning during the early modern Ming dynasty (Elliott 2012). In the context of the revolutionary, anti-Qing propaganda of the 19th and early 20th centuries, it acquired a new political meaning. Members of the "Han" majority were defined, in the imperial tradition, as descendants of the subjects of the Han dynasty (roughly second century BC to second century AC)—but now reinterpreted in nationalist and republican terms as representing "a people" of equal citizens. All inhabitants of "inner China"—over which subsequent dynasties had ruled for many centuries—who lived sedentary lives were included in the category and distinguished from the formerly nomadic, "barbarian" Manchus that the nationalists portrayed as usurpers of political power. Whether or not they conceived "the Han" as a race or a nation or a people, all participants in these debates agreed on which segments of the population were Han, that they formed an overwhelming majority of

China's population, that they were unified by a shared political history and common culture, and that they needed to be somehow distinguished from Manchus, Koreans, Tibetans, Mongols, and the minorities of the southwestern periphery.

It is fascinating from a comparative point of view that the concepts of "race," "nation," and "ethnicity" were never applied to any of the language groups that together composed the Han majority. In other words, Chinese intellectuals and politicians could not conceive of speakers of Mandarin, Wu, Min, Guo, and so forth as peoples of different historical ancestry, cultural origins, and future political destiny. As far as I can see through my nonexpert eyes, the scholarly literature (Elliott 2012; Harrison 2001; Dikötter 1991) has failed to wonder about this fact—with the exception of a short article by Wang (2001). Most analyses imply that the Han majority represented a natural, self-evident category waiting to be called a race or nation and do not problematize the linguistic heterogeneity within the Han category. While contemporary scholars debated whether modern Chinese nationalism broke with traditional Confucian universalism or whether this universalism was de facto always restricted to the Han (Duara 1993), no one wondered why language groups never developed nationalist aspirations. Rather, Chinese intellectuals and politicians applied the category of "nation" or "race" to a linguistically highly heterogeneous population—similarly to late 19th-century Switzerland and in dramatic contrast to Romanov Russia, as we will see. Imagine, to give a contrafactual example of similar scale, that 19th century Western Europeans would have applied the newly popular concept of the nation to all subjects of Charlemagne's medieval empire, united by Christendom and Western civilization.

To be sure, the intellectual material to imagine language groups as nations, particularly the language nationalism developed by German philosophers and scholars during the 19th century, was available to Chinese intellectuals, as it was to nationalists in Eastern Europe, Romanov Russia, the Balkans, and the Arabic-speaking parts of the Ottoman Empire who eagerly relied upon it. Liang Qichao, perhaps the most influential theorist of nation and race of the period, extensively quoted the German philologist Max Müller, according to whom "blood is thicker than water, but language thicker than blood." Liang Qichao embraced this idea but considered it relevant only for the very remote past of Chinese history: linguistic differences were slowly eroded, over thousands of years, through the mixing of different language groups (nations) into the dominant, expanding Huazu lineage of the Yellow Emperor (Duara 1993: 26).

Similarly, the Stalinist concept of the nation—famously defined as groups with a shared language, a territory, minimal economic self-sufficiency, and a specific culture—was applied only to the non-Han minorities during the

Communist era. Mirroring Stalinist nationality policies, the Communist regime identified over 50 minority "nationalities" and granted them some sort of symbolic self-rule under the guidance of the party. But no one during the 20th century ever imagined the Cantonese or the Wu speakers around Shanghai, for example, as a "nationality," although they could tick off all the items on Stalin's list: a common language, specific territory, economic cohesion, and distinct cultural features.

Thus, what Wei noted so perceptively regarding an earlier period continued to hold true for the 20th century: "There was a sense of local affiliation, belonging, and pride that could be expressed through the use of common spoken languages and dialects, but nowhere . . . could be found exact analogies to the essentialist assumptions of early modern and modern European vernacularization: the linkages between tongue and blood and among language, religion, and ethnicity" (2015: 281).

This is true even for the Cantonese, whose cultural prestige (after all, the classic poetry rhymed in Cantonese), economic dynamism, and geographic separation from the North would predestine them to embrace an ethnonationalist project (Wang 2001). To be sure, as Carrico (2012) discusses, one can find today some radical regionalist websites run out of Guangdong. But the authors of these websites argue their case by complaining that the centrality of Guangdong in the history of China has not been acknowledged enough by northerners—rather than assuming a separate historical origin and destiny for the Cantonese people, as a standard nationalist rhetoric would have it. Perhaps more popular than this peculiar form of centripetal minority nationalism, however, is a recent reappropriation of the Han mythology in the youth culture of Guangdong. In line with a long tradition of imagining one's own province/language as forming the core of the common Chinese civilization (cf. also Siu 1993), a particular fashion emerged among young Cantonese that consists of wearing costumes imagined to be typical of the Han dynasty. The idea seems to be that the Han majority, with which these adolescents obviously identify, should fashion folkloristic costumes similar to those of the officially recognized minorities.

The dogs of linguistic nationalism remained silent, I argue, because the alliance networks inherited from the late Qing period and reknit along similar structural patterns under republican, nationalist, and communist governments stretched across regions and linguistic frontiers. This became evident when we analyzed the composition of Qing, Kuomintang, and Communist political elites. While in Switzerland polyglot networks emerged due to the early development of civil society networks that stretched deep into the general population, it was China's monographia that played a similar role in facilitating the horizontal spread of network ties across linguistic divides. Scriptural homogeneity reduced the transaction cost of political communication and thus allowed the propagation of ideas and the knitting together of associational and patronage networks across the vast territory and polyglot population of the empire. Just as monographia provided the communicative cement to politically integrate the imperial state over thousands of years, it fostered nation building in the modern period of mass politics.

The contours of the nation—imagined as a Han race or nation—followed those of these polyglot alliance networks. The counterfactual, again, would be a situation where the Kuomintang had emerged from southern, non-Mandarin-speaking networks of political alliances communicating in Cantonese (akin to the networks of Flemish speakers in Belgium), while the Communists would have recruited leaders and followers exclusively from the Mandarin inlands and the North (similar to the French speakers of Belgium). A drifting apart of the country along the ethnolinguistic divide, for example during the warlord period following the collapse of imperial authority in 1911, would have been much more likely.

Speculating beyond the Han Chinese case of polyglot monographia, we might ask whether monoglot heterography has the opposite effects, as the theory would predict. In order not to stray too far from the case at hand, we can look to the northern border of China and wonder why a pan-Mongolian nationalism never gained traction. Mongolian speakers are divided between the independent state of Mongolia that emerged from the former Chinese province of Outer Mongolia and the current Chinese province of Inner Mongolia. Calls for reunification have lost their appeal over the past 50 years and today represent a marginal voice on either side of the border (Bulag 1998). After the overturn of the Communist regime in Mongolia, political elites developed an official nationalism that emphasized the superior nature of the Kalkha Mongols, the majority of Mongolia's citizenry, because they directly descended from the subjects of Genghis Khan. They portrayed Inner Mongolians across the border as degenerate cousins who had lost their cultural virtues through centuries of admixture with Han Chinese. Inner Mongolian intellectuals, in turn, also hesitate to embrace a pan-Mongolian nationalism, not the least for fearing to break the unity of China with which they identify. In other words, another dog of nationalism that never barked loudly enough to be heard. Inner Mongolians write their language in the ancient Mongolian script while Mongolians from Mongolia have used, since the 1946 alignment with the Soviet Union, the Cyrillic script. Perhaps this impeded written communication between political elites, the spread of propaganda and ideas across the border, and thus the emergence of a more encompassing imagined community?

Coming back to China proper, her history of nation building conforms quite well to the theoretical story outlined in the first chapter, as we have seen. Extraordinarily high levels of premodern state centralization produced a homogeneous communicative space—through monographia, rather than monoglossia—which in turn made it easier to build alliances across regions, which in turn resulted in an ethnically balanced power configuration at the center—from the Qing dynasty all the way to present-day Communist China. Political integration across linguistic divides then fostered political identification with the Han Chinese nation. The various linguistic minorities of the South never imagined themselves as candidates for a project of national autonomy let alone separate statehood.

The Russian *Völkergefängnis*

Of all the late 19th-century states in the world, the Russian Empire perhaps resembles Qing China the most—except with regard to the diversity of written languages. Both empires ruled over enormous populations—400 million around 1900 in China and 180 million in Romanov Russia, two and a half times the population of the United States at the time. Both China and Russia had roughly the same amount of arable land. More importantly, both remained independent polities throughout the 18th and 19th centuries—even if China's sovereignty was compromised from the failed Boxer uprising onward. Both formed important centers of civilizational gravity with elaborated high cultures, and both elites saw themselves standing at the very center of human history. There were no restraints on the absolute power of the two emperors up to the very last decade of their rule. Furthermore, China's and Russia's historical developments run on parallel tracks: the imperial order broke down in China in 1912 and in Russia five years later, and both countries became ruled by Communists thereafter.

One important difference, however, is that the Russian Empire is of much more recent origin. While China's emperors controlled their core territories for 2,000 years, the Russian tsars conquered theirs only from the 16th century until the late 19th century—not enough time, one could argue, to assimilate the peripheral populations into the culture of the center. Does this explain China's success at nation building and why the Russian Empire fell apart? I will come back to this alternative explanation in the concluding paragraphs of this chapter and show that there is not much evidence supporting it.

THE ROMANOVS CONQUER BABYLON

Romanov Russia conquered its domains in three waves (the following is based on Kappeler 2001). The first lasted from the 16th century to the 18th and rolled over the areas that had previously been ruled by the Golden Horde, a Turco-Mongolian dynasty that had splintered off from the unified Mongolian khanate sometime in the 14th century. Russia first conquered the khanate of Kazan in the middle Volga area east of Moscow. The Astrakhan khanate further south at the mouth of the Volga along the shores of the Caspian Sea soon saw the same fate. The peoples of the great Eurasian Steppe stretching from the Carpathian Mountains all the way to the Korean border were gradually subdued as well. During this first wave of expansion, Romanov Russia also absorbed the Cossack state in what is today southern Ukraine, the Crimean and Nogai Tatar khanates (the latter on the steppes north of the Caucasian mountain range), the Mongolian Kalmyk state known as the Dzungarian khanate (situated east of the Caspian Sea), and the Bashkirs in the Ural Mountains.

The second wave rolled westward in the 17th and 18th centuries. The long-existing Polish-Lithuanian state was swallowed without encountering much resistance. Estonia, Latvia, and later Finland were taken away from the Swedish Empire after victory in war. Bessarabia, a Romanian-speaking province, was snatched away from the Ottomans. The third wave rolled south- and eastward during the 19th century and was mainly triggered by geopolitical competition with the British Empire. Romanov troops and governors now encountered much more sustained military resistance from the tribally organized nomads of the Kazakh Steppe as well as the mountain peoples of Caucasia, who were subdued in decade-long, brutal campaigns. In the case of the Circassians, it ended with the forced expulsion of the entire population. The Romanovs also incorporated, on the other side of the Caucasian mountain range, the small khanates inhabited by Christian Armenians, the Georgian kingdoms, and the Shiite Turkic populations (later called Azerbaijanis) that had for centuries been vassals of the Persian Empire. The eastward movement further extended the empire's control over the Eurasian Steppe, where it conquered—in ruthless military campaigns that resembled those of the Western colonial powers in Africa—the nomads of Turkmen or Kazakh origin as well as the old Silk Road khanates of Bukhara (in today's Uzbekistan) and beyond, all of which adhered to the Muslim faith. A final push further eastward deep into the Siberian tundra brought Russian control to the Bering Strait and temporarily even beyond to Alaska.

As a result of this history of expansion and conquest, the empire was remarkably multilingual, with Russian speakers making up not even half of the population around 1900. As Table 4.4 shows, based on the first census in Russian history, the empire represented a true eldorado for linguists, with most of the language families of Eurasia represented among the polyglot subjects of the emperor.[5] Korean as well as Finnish, Turkish, Yiddish, Russian, and Iranian languages could be heard on the streets of imperial Russia.

Moreover, polyglossia combined with heterography well into the Communist period. Most Muslim populations wrote in the Arabic script. This was true, for example, for Kazakh, Azerbaijani, Tatar, and Crimean Tatar. Finnish, Polish, German, and the Baltic languages were written in modified Latin

TABLE 4.4. Language groups and their main characteristics, 1897

Language family	Language group	Language subgroup	Main area of settlement	% population	Majority religion	% can read among those 10 and older	% personal nobility
Indo–European	Slavic	Eastern Slavic					
		Russian	West	44.31	Russian Orthodox	29.3	0.84
		Ukrainian	West	17.81	Russian Orthodox	18.9	0.16
		Belorussian	West	4.68	Russian Orthodox	20.3	0.16
		Western Slavic					
		Polish	West	6.31	Catholic	41.8	0.78
		Southern Slavic					
		Bulgarian	West	0.14	Russian Orthodox	29.8	NA
	Baltic	Lithuanian	West	1.32	Catholic	48.4	0.08
		Latvian	West	1.14	Lutheran	85	0.08
	Iranian	Tadjik	Middle Asia	0.28	Sunni	3.4	0.01
		Ossetian	Caucasus	0.14	Russian Orthodox	7.1	0.2
		Kurdish	Transcaucasia	0.08	Sunni	NA	NA
		Roma (Gypsies)	Diaspora	0.04	Russian Orthodox	NA	0
	Armenian	Armenian	Transcaucasia	0.93	Armenian Gregorian	18.3	0.55
	Romance	Romanian (spoken by Moldavians)	West	0.89	Russian Orthodox	8.8	0.17
	Germanic	German	West/Diaspora	1.43	Lutheran	78.5	0.96
		Yiddish (spoken by Jews)	West	4.03	Jewish	50.1	0.07
		Swedish	West	0.01	Lutheran	98	NA
	Hellenic	Greek	Diaspora	0.15	Greek Orthodox	36.7	0.3
	Finnish	Finnish	West	0.11	Lutheran	98	NA
		Estonian	West	0.8	Lutheran	94.1	0.05
Uralic	Finnish	Mordvinian	Volga/Urals	0.81	Russian Orthodox	9.8	0
		Votiak (Udmurts)	Volga/Urals	0.33	Russian Orthodox	9.8	0

Family	Subgroup	People	Region		Religion		
		Cheremis (Mari)	Volga/Urals	0.3	Russian Orthodox	9.8	0
		Zyrian (Komi and Komi–Permiaks)	North	0.2	Russian Orthodox	NA	NA
		Karelian	North	0.17	Russian Orthodox	NA	NA
		Izhora (Ingrians)	North	0.01	Russian Orthodox	NA	NA
		Vep	North	0.02	Russian Orthodox	NA	NA
		Lappish	North	0	Russian Orthodox	NA	NA
	Ugric	Ostiak (Khanty)	Siberia	0.02	Russian Orthodox	5	0.01
		Vogul (Mansi)	Siberia	0.01	Russian Orthodox	5	0.01
	Samoed	Samoyed (Nentsy, etc.)	North	0.01	Shamanist/animist	NA	NA
Altaic	Turkic–Tatar	Chuvash	Volga/Urals	0.67	Russian Orthodox	9.8	0
		Azerbaidjani	Transcaucasia	1.15	Shiite	16.5	0.09
		Turkmeni	Middle Asia	0.22	Sunni	3.4	0.01
		Turkish (Crimean Tatars)	Steppe	0.18	Sunni	16.5	0.09
		Gagauz	West	0	Russian Orthodox	NA	NA
		Kazakh	Middle Asia	3.09	Sunni	3.4	0.01
		Karakalpak	Middle Asia	0.08	Sunni	3.4	0.01
		Tatars (of Siberia and along the Volga)	Volga/Ural/Siberia	1.5	Sunni	16.5	0.09
		Bashkir (including Teptiar)	Volga/Urals	1.14	Sunni	26.2	0.03
		Nogai	Steppe	0.05	Sunni	NA	NA
		Kumyk	Caucasus	0.07	Sunni	7.1	0.2
		Balkar	Caucasus	0.02	Sunni	7.1	0.2
		Karachaian	Caucasus	0.02	Sunni	7.1	0.2
		Uzbek (Sarts)	Middle Asia	1.43	Sunni	3.4	0.01
		Kirgiz	Middle Asia	0.51	Sunni	3.4	0.01
		Uigur	Middle Asia	0.08	Sunni	3.4	0.01
		Khakassian	Siberia	0.03	Russian Orthodox	5	0.01
		Shor	Siberia	0.01	Russian Orthodox	5	0.01
		Iakuts	Siberia	0.18	Russian Orthodox	5	0.01
		Altaian	Siberia	0.03	Russian Orthodox	5	0.01

TABLE 4.4. (*continued*)

Language family	Language group	Language subgroup	Main area of settlement	% population	Majority religion	% can read among those 10 and older	% personal nobility
Altaic (*cont.*)	Mongol	Burian	Siberia	0.23	Sunni	5	0.01
		Kalmyk	Steppe	0.15	Sunni	4.1	0.02
	Marchurian–Tungus	Tungus (Evenks), etc.	Siberia	0.05	Shamanist/animist	5	0.01
Koreanic	Korean		Diaspora	0.02	Russian Orthodox	NA	NA
Caucasian	Southern	Georgian	Transcaucasia	1.08	Russian Orthodox	19.5	1.04
		Mingrelian	Transcaucasia	Incl. in Georgian	Russian Orthodox	NA	NA
		Svan	Transcaucasia	Incl. in Georgian	Russian Orthodox	NA	NA
		Adzhar	Transcaucasia	Incl. in Georgian	Russian Orthodox	NA	NA
	Northwestern	Kabardinian	Caucasus	0.08	Sunni	7.1	0.2
		Circassian (with Adygei)	Caucasus	0.04	Sunni	7.1	0.2
		Abkhaz	Transcaucasia	0.06	Sunni	NA	NA
	Northeastern	Chechen	Caucasus	0.18	Sunni	7.1	0.2
		Ingushetian	Caucasus	0.04	Sunni	7.1	0.2
	Dagestan	Avar	Caucasus	0.17	Sunni	7.1	0.2
		Lezgian	Caucasus	0.13	Sunni	7.1	0.2
		Darginian	Caucasus	0.1	Sunni	7.1	0.2
		Lak	Caucasus	0.07	Sunni	7.1	0.2
Paleo–Siberian		Chukchi	Siberia	0.01	Russian Orthodox	5	0.01
		Koriak	Siberia		Shamanist/animist	5	0.01
		Iukagir	Siberia		Shamanist/animist	5	0.01

Source: This table is based on Kappeler 2001: 395–99, 402–3, 407.

Note: Some linguists claim that Georgian forms its own separate language family.

alphabets, while Armenians and Georgians had been writing their idioms in their own, unique scripts for more than 1,000 years. Russian was obviously written in Cyrillic. The Mongolian script was used for Kalmyk. A speaker of the Ugric language Finnish used to the Latin alphabet could not read and understand a letter or a political pamphlet written in the northern Caucasian language of Georgian in Georgian script. The average literate person speaking the Slavic language Russian and used to reading and writing in Cyrillic could not decipher a tractate written in the Turkic language Tatar and in Arabic calligraphy. The contrast to China's monographic situation is rather obvious.

This linguistic and scriptural heterogeneity was not laid out on a level political playing field. In the non-Russian areas especially of the west, the noble elites and the bonded peasant population that toiled on their estates were often of different ethnic origins. A Polish-speaking nobility ruled over Ukrainian-, Belorussian-, and Lithuanian-speaking peasants. The descendants of the German crusader orders that had conquered the Baltic lands in the Middle Ages continued to rule over Estonian- and Latvian-speaking peoples. The Swedish nobility was of preeminence in the Finnish lands. In Central Asia, the nomadic, Turkic-speaking populations and the indigenous populations of eastern Siberia were governed by Russian administrators and generals.

These various ethnic hierarchies combined with the fragmented linguistic and scriptural landscape, I argue, to impede political alliance networks to stretch across ethnic divides. This in turn politicized ethnic differences and finally led to the dissolution of the empire along ethnonational divides, first in the revolution of 1917 and a second time, after the Soviets had reconquered the Romanov empire with military force, when Communist rule ended in 1989.

POLITICAL POWER STRUCTURES, ALLIANCES, AND MOBILIZATION

It is not easy to prove this argument in a "smoking gun" test based on detailed historical evidence. Such evidence is available only for one (even if important) case: for the mobilization of the Jewish population by the socialist Bund. For the rest of the analysis, evidence will be more circumstantial. I will show that networks were indeed confined, throughout the 19th century and especially during the early 20th, by linguistic boundaries without showing in fine-grained detail that this was so *because* it was difficult to communicate across linguistic divides.

To be sure, some transethnic political networks emerged during the century before 1917, especially during the late 19th century when radical, revolutionary parties began to flourish underground. With very few exceptions, however, these transethnic movements represented ethnic conglomerates, that is, they were composed of often fragile alliances between linguistically defined political factions. These conglomerates quickly fragmented along their ethnolinguistic fault lines in the course of the revolutionary events of 1917.

The Political Order of the Ancien Régime

Before I discuss in detail how political alliance networks clustered along linguistic divisions, I should briefly outline the main characteristic of the political order of the Romanov empire. It differed sharply from how the Chinese emperors ruled over their domains. There was no empire-wide recruitment into the higher echelons of the bureaucracy through examinations. Rather, the political hierarchy rested on the estate order that Peter the Great had codified, along northern European models, in the late 17th and early 18th centuries. The estates were defined by the state and it policed who had the right to claim which title and thus to claim membership in which estate. At the top of the system we find the caste of hereditary nobles, many of whom were also large landowners. For exceptional service to the state, a person could be elevated to a nonhereditary status of nobility. From these ranks of nobles, the state recruited its highest functionaries and most of the officers of the army. For example, roughly 70% of the employees of the Ministry of Justice at the end of the 19th century and 85% of those working for the Ministry of the Interior at the eve of World War I were of noble origin. Of those appointed to the State Council, which advised the tsar on matters of fiscal and legal policy, 90% were nobles (Lieven 1981: 382–383, 402).

Various intermediary estates followed further down the ladder: the clergy, honorary citizens, merchants, urban commoners, gilded craftspeople, and the frontiersmen turned into an estate of armed peasants (the famed Cossacks). At the bottom of the pyramid we find the serfs of the noblemen, who had sharply reduced personal rights (e.g., to freely choose one's spouse) and could not leave the land but were sold together with the soil until the tsar freed the serfs in 1861. A special category in the estate system was the *inorodtsy*, or "allochthon peoples." They consisted of Jews, on the one hand, and the mountain tribes of the Caucasus, the hunter-gatherers of Siberia, and nomadic herders of the steppe, on the other hand. These groups were all considered culturally too alien or backward to merit full citizenship but were given the right to administer their own affairs until they were assimilated or civilized enough to become Russian subjects.

The estate system provided the organizational grid to incorporate new territories into the empire. In general, the hereditary nobility of conquered peoples continued to rule over their domains. The tsar recognized their authority over the dependent peasant population and translated their status into the Russian estate system by officially granting them a certain title and associated privileges. This is how Poland-Lithuania, Transcaucasia, the Baltics, and Finland were incorporated into the empire. In Muslim areas, however, the landowning elites were ennobled but their dependent peasants remained free. In areas without hereditary, landowning nobilities, the *inorodtsy* status applied. In the conquest of Central Asia during the late 19th century, however, even some sedentary agricultural groups such as the Uzbeks were classified as *inorodtsy*.

In administrative terms, the newly conquered areas were governed through the same system as the rest of the empire, even if some adjustments were made locally (see Pipes 1997: 4ff.). They were divided into provinces (governorates), which in turn comprised several districts. Deviating from this standard scheme, in the minority areas newly conquered in the 19th century several governorates were responsible to a governor-general, usually a high-ranking general of the army who acted as a viceroy and held absolute powers unchecked by the courts or any other organ of the state. At the local level, tribal or other "traditional" authorities were granted political authority over their subjects as well as some judiciary powers that had no parallel in other parts of the empire.

We are now ready to discuss the nature of political alliances. At the court, factions of nobles allied with one or the other prince vying for influence over the emperor's decision; powerful clergy and their mostly noble allies did the same. In the army, cliques of officers competed for promotion, and so on. Outside these centers of power, how did political alliances form and how far did they stretch across the various linguistic divides? Rather than offering the full panorama of empirical configurations, which would take me far beyond my scholarly competence, I will focus on a series of important cases that shaped the course of political developments in the early 20th century. These will concern the Polish-, Finno-Baltic-, Ukrainian-, Tatar-, Georgian-, and Yiddish-speaking lands of the empire. In each of these cases, alliance networks coalesced along linguistic divides because reaching the masses, an increasingly important goal of the anti-tsarist political movements of the 19th century, was much easier in a script and a language that the general population understood. Only in the Jewish case will I be able to offer some direct evidence for this conjecture. In the other cases, the evidence is more circumstantial and some other, historically specific mechanisms need to be considered as well.

Poland

In the Polish case, three such additional factors played an important role in confining alliance networks to Polish speakers. The Polish nobility, who had dominated a Polish-Lithuanian state from the Middle Ages until the late 1700s, was incorporated *tel quel* as the ruling elite of a semi-independent entity called

Congress Poland. Already established alliances among the Polish noblemen, often determined by familial relationships and histories of previous competition and alliances, therefore remained politically salient and meaningful. Most of these preexisting alliances, obviously, were confined to fellow Polish speakers. Expanding the Romanov empire by incorporating existing nobilities, in other words, conserved monolinguistic alliance networks.

Second, Congress Poland had its own all-Polish school and university system, its own separate army units, and a military academy that taught exclusively in Polish, further confining elite friendships and alliances to the Polish community. Imagine if in Qing China Guangdong would have had its own army unit and military academy where officers would have been trained in Cantonese written in a different alphabet than the classical Chinese script.

Third, the memories of independent statehood provided politically ambitious Polish noblemen with a model for the future. They thus confined their networks of alliances to other Polish nobles (who made up as much as 20% of the population) in order to one day achieve the dream of renewed independent statehood, a dream first couched in terms of rights to dynastic succession rather than in a modern nationalist discourse. The peasant population, whether speaking Polish, Belorussian, Lithuanian, or Ukrainian, as well as the Jewish town dwellers, remained largely excluded from these networks of agitation and mobilization and thus also indifferent to the proto-nationalist cause of the Polish nobility.

Later on, these networks of alliances were reconfigured within all-Polish associations, the most important of which was the Freemasons. They brought the Polish noblemen into enlightened milieus similar to those that we encountered in Switzerland and among French speakers in Belgium at the time. Within these monolinguistic networks a genuine Polish nationalism emerged, greatly influenced by the German linguistic nationalism that started to spread in the early 19th century among intellectuals across Eastern Europe (but not, as we have seen, in China).

Polish nationalism soon had its first cataclysmic encounter with the Romanov state. After the tsar's regent had disregarded for decades many of the constitutional freedoms granted to Congress Poland, forbade the Freemasons and suppressed other patriotic associations, censored the Polish press, manipulated Polish political life through his secret agents, and planned to send Polish troops to help roll back the Belgian nationalist revolution of 1831, members of the Polish military academy rose in arms. The uprising was violently subdued by the imperial armies. More than 10,000 Poles who had instigated or supported the rebellion went into exile, where the movement split into an aristocratic and a more recently developed democratic wing led by intellectuals. This exiled political elite was more disconnected from their Russian-speaking peers than ever before.

A second full-scale uprising, still largely supported and carried out by the noble stratum alone, occurred in 1863, sparked by resistance against the draft into the Russian army. The military defeat at the hands of the tsarist forces was again crushing; hundreds were executed and thousands (some historians claim tens of thousands) deported. As before, the peasants (with the exception of some Catholic Lithuanians) failed to support the rebellion and sometimes even sided with the imperial forces.

This seems to have changed after the tsar adopted a policy of Russification to prevent future Polish rebellions. The tsar thus gave in to the rising Russian nationalist forces that wanted to break the power of the disloyal Polish nobility and who were carried away, more generally, by the tide of nationalist, increasingly racialized ideologies that swept over the globe. The main elements of the Russification policy pursued after 1863 (see Kappeler 2001: 252–261) were that Russian replaced Polish as the language of administration, justice, and education (down to the village level) in Congress Poland; that the rights of the Catholic Church were curtailed; and that Russians ousted Poles in the administration of the Polish lands.

Outside of Congress Poland, the Ukrainian, Belorussian, and Lithuanian languages were banned, in a move to break Polish influence over the peasants of the former Polish-Lithuanian state and to turn them into loyal subjects of the tsar. In the Baltic provinces, Russian was introduced as the official language of state institutions down to the municipal level, including of the courts, and as the language of instruction in schools (from 1881 to 1895); in addition, the German university in Tartu was Russified. Romanian was no longer a school subject in Bessarabia and subsequently outlawed as a language for church services. The German schools of the Volga settler communities had to shift to Russian in the 1890s. Georgian was no longer a language of instruction in Georgia in the 1870s, and a similar fate befell Armenian church schools in the 1880s. In 1903, the possessions of the Armenian church were confiscated. The Azerbaijani language and Muslim educational institutions, however, were spared because the Russification policy targeted Western, Christian populations only (on the variegated policies of Russification, see also Miller 2008).

Most of these measures were undermined by a network of underground schools (such as those maintained by Lithuanians) or were simply not pursued long and consistently enough to make Russian the spoken language of the Christian minorities.[6] Russification policies were softened in 1895 and completely abandoned after the revolution of 1905. Writes Kappeler: "In the medium term the coexistence of Russian, German, Polish, Hebrew-Yiddish, Armenian, Georgian, Tatar and Arabic high languages and high cultures was not replaced by the Russian language and Russian culture. Rather, it expanded to encompass an even greater variety of literary languages and high cultures" (2001: 318).

Contrary to China, then, political centralization in the Russian Empire did not have a long enough history to erode cultural differences through slow-moving, voluntary processes of assimilation. The Russification policy lasted only one generation and was imposed from the center without any support from below. More importantly, learning and speaking Russian clearly wasn't attractive enough for minority elites given that they remained excluded from the highest echelons of power, as we will see. In China, equal access to the highest levels of imperial power encouraged non-Mandarin-speaking elites to adopt the Confucian cultural canons propagated by the center, including the uniform script.

Perhaps equally important was timing: Russia's attempt to culturally homogenize its Christian populations came at a point when many Western minorities already had developed nationalist aspirations. This all but guaranteed that Russification would be perceived as "language loss" and a betrayal of the traditions of one's national ancestors. Rather than undermining the appeal of nationalist movements, the policy strengthened these by driving rank-and-file members of ethnic minorities into the arms of their respective nationalists. Exceptions are Bessarabia, parts of Ukraine, and Belorussia where nationalism was slow to develop and where considerable parts of the population adopted Russian as their language and identity during the second half of the 19th century.

To come back to Poland, the tsar had hoped that by freeing the serfs and granting them even more generous access to land in the Polish provinces than in the rest of the empire, he would win their loyalty and prevent the emergence of mass support for Polish nationalism. But the persecution of the Catholic Church after 1863, the suppression of Polish elementary schools and their replacement by schools that taught in Russian, the restrictions on the Polish press, and the closing of Polish-speaking universities all produced the opposite effect and brought the masses of the Polish-speaking population on the side of Polish nationalists. The nobles now extended alliances to the freshly minted citizens (the former serfs) to form a linguistically defined political bloc: the first parties with a mass following that emerged toward the end of the 19th century were all almost exclusively focused on the fate of the Polish-speaking population of the empire. The Polish Socialist Party appealed to the rising Polish working class, while the National Democrats catered to the middle classes with a more chauvinist and anti-Semitic discourse.

As we will see, these parties gained an almost complete monopoly on the votes of the Polish masses once the tsar agreed to hold elections after 1905. To understand why, we should keep in mind that only about 40% of the Polish-speaking population could read (see Table 4.4) at the end of the century, and only half of those with reading skills could also read in Russian (Kappeler

2001: 313)—the policy of Russification notwithstanding. Thus the pool of the population that could understand a pamphlet written in Russian or follow Russian newspapers was limited to about one-fifth of the Polish population. Political mobilization in the age of mass politics therefore proceeded within linguistically homogeneous compartments.

While the *tel quel* incorporation of the Polish nobility, the memory of previous statehood, the romantic nationalism that it helped nourish, and the anti-Catholic repression that formed part of the Russification policy certainly also played a role, we should not underestimate how language difference shaped the formation of political alliances as soon as politics was no longer the exclusive affair of educated elites. This becomes even clearer in the case of Finland and the Baltics.

Finns, Estonians, and Latvians

In these northwestern corners of the empire, none of the other three factors was at play, but political networks also fragmented along linguistic lines and ethnic differences became as thoroughly politicized as in the case of Poland (the following relies on Kappeler 2001: 221ff.). Estonians, Latvians, and Finns lacked a high culture and tradition of statehood comparable to that of Poland, Georgia, Armenia, Ukraine, or the Crimean Tatars. They had never been ruled by their own nobilities that could subsequently have been incorporated into the Russian state. We can therefore exclude previous statehood, written high culture, and indigenous nobility as necessary factors for the development of ethnonationalism in the Russian Empire. Instead, we can focus more directly on how linguistic differences shaped the structure of alliance networks.

In the Baltic northwest, the population learned how to read and write much earlier than elsewhere, as Table 4.1 shows. Among Finns, Estonians, and Latvians, 98%, 95%, and 85%, respectively, of the population over the age of 10 years old was able to read in 1897—massively more than the 30% of Russian speakers who were literate at that time. The Lutheran church, to which almost all Finns, Estonians, and Latvians belonged, was responsible for the early spread of literacy, an advantage that these regions maintained even after the Russian state began to standardize the educational system across its domains. According to Lutheran creed, a direct, unmediated understanding of God's word is crucial. The church thus taught the peasants and townspeople to read and write in the vernacular languages rather than in German or Swedish, the language of their noble overlords. The early freeing of the serfs in Estonia and Latvia in 1816 and the fact the Finns had never known personal serfdom also contributed to the spread of literacy and the eventual rise of a stratum of independent, politically conscious farmers. Note also that despite the Russification campaign mentioned above, only half of literate Latvians, fewer than a third of Estonians, and even fewer Finns were able to read Cyrillic Russian by the end of the 19th century (Kappeler 2001: 313). This linguistic and scriptural divide shaped how networks of political alliances formed subsequently, as we will see.

The first signs of interest in the Finnish, Estonian, and Latvian languages came from Swedish and German intellectuals who from the 1820s onward formed folkloristic societies—similar to the Flemish study groups founded at the same time in Belgium. Subsequently, Finns, Estonians, and Latvians joined choral clubs and attended singing festivals, in the three respective languages. These and other enlightened associations blossomed throughout the lands, as they had in Switzerland around the same time. Finns, Estonians, and Latvians did not, however, sing together with their Russian peers (as French- and German-speaking Swiss had done) because enlightened organizations had barely spread to the masses of illiterate Russian serfs. Among educated segments of the population, Russians spoke an Indo-European language written in Cyrillic, while Finns and Estonians spoke a Uralic language written in the Latin alphabet. Ties of alliance and support between organizations were correspondingly more difficult to establish and a common outlook on the political world never developed.

From 1860 onward, partly as a reaction to the Russification policies pursued by Moscow after the second Polish uprising, the patriotic movements split into a moderate, status quo-oriented wing and a more radical wing that sought to overthrow alien rule by German Baltic nobles or their Swedish equivalents on the other side of the Gulf of Finland. Until the late 19th century, most demands remained confined to language issues, however: primary schools should teach exclusively in the local vernacular; court proceedings should be held in the local languages; and so forth. In short, Finnish and Baltic patriots pleaded to end the language discrimination that their coethnics had been subject to for centuries—quite similar to the demands of the early Flemish nationalist movement, as we have seen. Nothing comparable ever emerged in China because the common script did not require a uniform spoken language, and the educational system was therefore equally accessible from all corners of the land.

Making Ukrainians

Mass political mobilization in the Ukrainian-speaking parts of the empire developed much more slowly than in the northwest. Not only did Ukrainians lack an indigenous nobility, as did the Baltics and the Finns, but literacy levels were much lower as well: not even 20% of Ukrainians could read around 1900. Not until the last quarter of the 19th century did some student groups emerge to advocate the reading and dissemination of Ukrainian literature and poetry in order to beat back the assimilatory pressure coming from Moscow and the Russian speakers of Ukraine. A series of provincial organizations emerged that were dedicated to the study of Ukrainian folk life. They were inspired by the ideals and goals of the *narodniks*. A brief side note on this specifically Russian political movement is perhaps in order.

The *narodniks* (best translated as "populists") were spearheaded by descendants of the Russian nobility in the 1860s and 1870s. They developed an anarcho-agrarian vision of a just society, foreseeing a return to the "original communism" of the peasant villages whose members traditionally shared ownership of land. One of the core ideas of the *narodniks* was that intellectuals and avant-garde political leaders should learn the cultural ways of the peasant masses—which inevitably meant, as it turned out, to speak its many different tongues and appreciate its manifold ethnic traditions.

In Ukraine, so-called *hromady* organizations (derived from the word for peasant communities) were initially largely apolitical and mainly attracted Ukrainian high school and university students. About 20 of these *hromady* were united, together with other more explicitly nationalist student groups, in 1897 into a clandestine General Ukrainian Organization with 450 members committed to spreading the literary use of Ukrainian (Subtelny 2009: 280–284).

This cultural nationalism was quickly radicalized when these various alliance networks coalesced into a new, *narodniks*-inspired political party, the Revolutionary Ukrainian Party (RUP). The RUP used the existing *hromady* networks to spread its influence into the provincial towns and peasant villages. Originally radically nationalist, the party soon became more concerned with social issues—not the least in order to become more attractive to the peasants who still had not adopted a nationalist outlook on the world but largely identified as members of a particular village community. The RUP soon splintered into a socialist group that became the Ukrainian wing of the Social Democratic Labor Party and a separatist National Ukrainian Party. The remainder of the RUP rechristened itself the Ukrainian Social Democratic Labor Party. In 1905, the liberal wings of the Ukrainian movement formed a separate Ukrainian Democratic Radical Party (Pipes 1997: 10–11). This liberal party and the renamed RUP subsequently dominated the political arena in the Ukrainian-speaking lands.

These parties launched propaganda campaigns, in Ukrainian, among the Ukrainian-speaking peasantry to convince them that they formed part of a separate, Ukrainian nation dominated by Polish nobles, exploited by Jewish merchants, and suppressed by the Russian tsar. At the same time, Ukrainian as a written language was increasingly adopted by the small segments of the population that had previously been taught to read and write in Russian, further helping to spread nationalist ideas written in the vernacular language. Language-based nationalism was so successful that all Ukrainian parties combined received roughly 70% of the vote in the 1917 elections.

Tatars

The role of language and scriptural diversity in shaping networks of alliances becomes again more evident in the case of the Tatar and, more generally, the Turkic-speaking populations of the empire. They were all of Muslim faith, with the exception of some tiny Siberian groups as well as the Gagauz in Bessarabia. The educated elites of the Crimean and Volga Tatars played the leading role in raising the political consciousness of Turkic-speaking Muslims. Their activities illustrate well how written languages can confine networks of alliances. As the population was scattered over a noncontiguous terrain stretching from the mountains of the Hindu Kush all the way to what is today Ukraine, the printing press and the distribution of newspapers played an important role in the mobilization of political support. To be accessible to the literate public, the overwhelming majority of these publications were written in the Arabic script, with which most were familiar thanks to the Koran schools, and in the Volga Tatar language, which represented a kind of lingua franca among Turkish-speaking groups. The rest of the empire's population obviously could never read a Turkish text written in Arabic and were therefore excluded from the emerging communicative space. By 1913, there were 16 periodicals and 5 daily newspapers; 430 nonreligious books were printed in a total of 1.5 million copies (Pipes 1997: 13–15; but see Geraci 2001: 26 for the suppression of Tatar publications in Kazan).

Perhaps equally important, Kazan Tatar intellectuals crafted a modernizing version of Islam. It was disseminated not only through the flourishing printing press but also through a system of private primary and secondary schools, which were largely financed by wealthy merchants from Kazan and Baku. A generation of students was taught modern subjects and reformed Islam in their own native tongues—largely tolerated by Moscow, whose Russification policy was exclusively aimed at the Christian groups of the West. The worldview of Turkic speaking youth was cast in a separate and distinctive shape, molded by modernist Islamism. Their networks of adolescent friends and acquaintances remained confined to coethnics, making it more difficult to build alliances across linguistic divides later on in life.

But even before this new school system emerged, as Geraci's (2001) historical study of the city of Kazan shows, Tatar and Russian speakers had almost no social contact with each other, whether among the peasantry or the bourgeoisie. This is all the more remarkable because Russians had conquered the city in the 16th century, and Tatars and Russians had therefore lived side by side for 400 years. There is almost no evidence, Geraci writes, that Russians and Tatars knew each other's languages (Geraci 2001: 37, 41, 45; with the exception of Orthodox missionaries). The fact that written publications were either in Arabic or in Cyrillic and that children were taught different languages in separate schools certainly did not facilitate the social integration of the different quarters of the town.

The new Tatar Muslim schools produced a generation of leaders who were personally familiar with each other and who lived in the same linguistic, political, and cultural universe established by the print media. They soon formed political associations and parties—confined to other readers of Arabic, speakers of Turkic languages, and adherents of Allah. Among these was the liberal Union of the Muslims (Ittifak) established at congresses of Muslim political leaders and intellectuals in 1905 and 1906, where it was also decided that Muslim representatives in the newly elected duma would form a separate caucus. At the same time, more narrowly defined parties emerged that catered to specific linguistic communities rather than the Muslim population as a whole. These were often more radically nationalist and socialist. Some Volga Tatar intellectuals founded a local counterpart of the Russian Socialist Revolutionary Party, while in Azerbaijan, the Moslem Democratic Party Mussavat was formed. Mussavat originally had a pan-Islamist orientation but turned Azerbaijani nationalist in the course of the 1917 revolution.

Georgians

The situation in the Caucasus was rather more complicated and diverged considerably between the Georgian, Armenian, and Azerbaijani regions (the following draws on Kappeler 2001: 220–234). Here, I will focus exclusively on Georgia, which followed Polish developments up to a certain point but then took an interestingly different path. The Georgian nobles, who composed 5% of the population, were large estate holders and became incorporated into the Russian nobility in a similar way as their Polish peers, albeit only after decades of struggles to have their status recognized by the imperial state.

After the forced unification of the formerly independent Georgian church with the Russian Orthodox Patriarchate, a mild cultural nationalism centered on Georgian history and language emerged among the nobility. Compared to the Polish networks of nationalist associations that mushroomed during the same period, however, it remained rather marginal. For Georgian nobles, nationalism was less attractive than were anti-bourgeois, revolutionary ideologies because their economic status had declined often precipitously—despite the favorable terms on which their serfs were freed—and because an Armenian commercial middle class had risen throughout the Georgian territories. Many Georgian nobles had studied at Russian universities in the last decades of the 19th century—under the policy of forced Russification—and had linked up with the radical political movements of the time, mostly of socialist and communist inclinations. The nationalist components of their ideological visions remained initially marginal.

This did not mean, however, that they founded or joined organizations with a multilingual composition, comparable to the anti-imperial groups formed in the Japanese exile and on the Chinese mainland during these years. A case in point is the Georgian Social Democratic Party, which became the most important political force of the region, enjoying the support not only of the small local proletariat but also of the educated classes and parts of the peasantry (Jones 2005).

In 1903, the national-level Social Democratic movement split into a Bolshevik faction in favor of a direct takeover of the revolutionary movement by a tightly knit avant-garde party of professional revolutionaries. The Menshevik, on the other hand, favored an alliance with liberal political forces to first complete the bourgeois revolution. The Georgian Social Democrats joined the Menshevik faction and actually dominated, together with Jewish intellectuals and politicians, that party, putting Russians into a minority position. Because the alliance networks assembled under the Menshevik label resembled a conglomerate made up of different linguistic pieces, the Menshevik were more receptive to nationalist demands than were their Bolshevik counterparts. Not surprisingly, the Georgian Social Democrats adopted, around 1910, the principle of nonterritorial autonomy for the Georgian nation and the Menshevik faction followed suit some years later.[7]

Perhaps I should briefly explain where the idea of nonterritorial autonomy came from. After the Second International, Austrian Marxists suggested that the socialist movement needed to pay more serious attention to the nationality problem because they expected national sentiment to increase rather than decrease in the course of economic development, contrary to what Marx, Engels, and Rosa Luxemburg had assumed. The solution advocated by Bauer and Renner was to grant cultural and linguistic autonomy to individuals of the same national background, independent of where they lived. Many Russian minority nationalists adopted this doctrine in the first decade of the 20th century (Pipes 1997: chap. 1), and so did the Georgian Social Democrats and Menshevik.

That Georgians dominated the Menshevik became clear in the first fully democratic elections in Russia, held for a constituent assembly after the February Revolution of 1917 (i.e., before the Bolshevik putsch in October of that year). The Mensheviks received only 3.2% of the overall vote and the Bolsheviks 25%. In Georgia, however, a full 75% voted for Mensheviks—the fruits of the political alliances that the Georgian Social Democrats had built over the previous decades with peasants and workers who spoke their tongue. It is noteworthy that among the 20% of the Georgian-speaking population that was able to read at the end of the century, only a third (or 7% of the Georgian population overall) was also able to read Cyrillic Russian. Thus, Georgian networks were institutionally integrated within empire-wide parties while Polish networks were channeled into separate, Polish parties. But in both cases, I suggest, the communicative ease provided by a shared language made these networks crystallize along linguistic divides as soon as larger segments of the population entered the political arena as voters.

Jews

I could not muster any direct evidence for the role of linguistic commonality in the formation of monoethnic political alliances among Poles, Finns, Baltics, Tartars, and Georgians. Such evidence is available for the Jewish case. Jewish intellectuals and politicians played an important role in the development of the various revolutionary organizations—quite simply because Jews remained, together with the *inorodtsy* nomads of the Central Asian steppes and the Caucasian mountain tribes, excluded from full citizenship rights throughout the 19th century, were the victims of anti-Semitic agitation and propaganda increasingly endorsed by the tsarist regime, and suffered from a series of pogroms (especially after the assassination of Tsar Alexander II in 1881) that were at least tolerated, if not actively instigated, by Russian authorities. Jews had, in other words, very good reasons to oppose the autocratic regime and to actively seek its overthrow. In any case, this is not the place to recount the details of the political mobilization of the Jewish intelligentsia—one branch into Zionism, the other into various revolutionary organizations.

I will instead focus on the most important of these organizations, the Bund, which played a crucial role in the development of the Social Democratic Labor Party within which it operated until 1903. Notably, among all the branches of that party, the Bund was the most successful in mobilizing mass support. It had 23,000 members in the early 20th century, while the Russian branch counted only 8,400 (Schapiro 1961: 160). The Bund was able to gather the support of the Jewish population by propagating its program in the vernacular language spoken by the majority of the Jewish small-town dwellers in the west. Writes Schapiro:

> The decision of the Bund to use Yiddish as the language of propaganda was also due to quite empirical reasons—it was the only language in which a mass Jewish audience could be reached. (It is interesting to recall in this connection that when, in the 1870s, one of the pioneers of the Jewish revolutionary movement in Vilna, Lieberman, insisted on Hebrew as the language of propaganda, it was also for a practical and not nationalistic reason: Hebrew, he thought, was the best literary vehicle for training revolutionar-

ies among Talmudic students. . . . Expediency, then, was at any rate the origin of the "nationalism" of the Bund, as it would later be described by its opponents [i.e., the Bolsheviks during the 1903 Congress of the party), and probably the main motive underlying the doctrine of national cultural autonomy for the Jews which the Bundt ultimately evolved. (1961: 156–157)

This analysis can be substantiated by a direct quote from L. Martov (born Tsederbaum), the future leader of the Mensheviks and thus Lenin's main opponent in the factional struggles of the first quarter of the 20th century. Earlier on, he had helped organize the Jewish workers of Vilnius. Referring to these early days of political mobilization, he describes the shift in the Bund's tactics from a nonethnic, class-based strategy to the nationalist strategy that later came to define the Bund:

> In the first years of our movement [i.e., the Bund], we expected everything from the Russian working class and looked upon ourselves as a mere addition to the general Russian labor movement. By putting the Jewish working-class movement in the background, we neglected its actual condition, as evidenced by the fact that our work was conducted in the Russian language. Desiring to preserve our connection with the Russian movement . . . we forgot to maintain contact with the Jewish masses who did not know Russian. . . . Obviously, it would be absurd to further restrict our activity to those groups of the Jewish population already affected by Russian culture. . . . Having placed the mass movement in the center of our program, we had to adjust our propaganda and agitation of the masses, that is, we had to make it more Jewish [by shifting to Yiddish]. (quoted in Pipes 1997: 27)

While initially of a purely pragmatic nature, mobilizing the Jewish masses in Yiddish (or Hebrew) had its own side effects: it created a communicative space within which it became easy to imagine Jews as a modern nation with a shared political destiny (quite à la Anderson). It took only a little bit more than a decade until the Bund (in 1901) adopted a genuinely nationalist political program—defining Jews as a nation and advocating nonterritorial autonomy in line with Austro-Marxist principles, which obviously suited the Jewish diaspora especially well. At the same time, the Bund abandoned the straightforward "class-struggle first" position that dominated the thinking of the Russian leaders of the Social Democratic Labor Party (on the evolution of the nationality policies of major revolutionary parties, see Pipes 1997: 21–49).

The case of Jewish mobilization also helps clarify how exactly the linguistic diversity mechanism operates. As is well known, Jewish political elites were also fluent in Russian. The reason the Bund resorted to Hebrew or Yiddish in its publications and speeches is not that its leaders could not understand what their Christian Russian peers were saying or writing. Rather, they mobilized rank-and-file followers in Yiddish or Hebrew because fluency in Russian among the less well-educated segments of the Jewish population was much more limited—even if among the most developed of all minorities (see below). The networks of followers that they built, relying on the strategic advantage of communication in the vernacular, were thus confined to speakers of that language. What matters for the mechanism that this chapter explores, in other words, is the linguistic diversity of the literate population at large rather than that of the political elites.

Ethnic Voting Patterns

The Jewish case suggests that the masses in Romanov Russia were mobilized along separate ethnic tracks because of the advantages of addressing them in their vernacular languages, rather than because the political activists were nationalists. Over time, however, as these alliance networks developed within separate linguistic compartments, nationalism became an increasingly plausible way of defining political communities. How national communities were imagined was already preconfigured, conversely, by who met with whom, whom one could trust in the fast-changing political environment of the early 20th century, and with whom one shared the goal of gaining political power. Even the non-nationalist political parties with a mass following, most importantly the Social Democratic Labor Party, therefore ended up as patchworks of national alliance networks—Georgian, Jewish, Polish, Lithuanian, Ukrainian, Russian, and so on—rather than genuinely transethnic political organizations comparable to the Kuomintang or the Chinese Communist Party (or any of the Swiss political parties, for that matter).

It should also be noted that among most language groups, literacy in Russian was much lower than it was among the Jews. As was the case with other diaspora groups such as Armenians and Germans, Jews who could also read in Russian outnumbered those who could read only in Yiddish or Hebrew. Only half of Poles who could read could also read Russian around 1900; in the case of Lithuanians, Estonians, and Georgians, fewer than a third; and in the case of Latvians, fewer than half (Kappeler 2001: 313). If the practical advantages of political mobilization in the vernacular language explain why Jewish activists sought to build monoethnic networks, it must have played an even larger role for the leaders of these other groups.

In China, by contrast, anti-imperial agitators during the end of the 19th century could use the common Chinese script to build transregional, multilinguistic alliance networks. Thus the nation was imagined within the boundaries of this scripturally homogeneous space. In late Romanov Russia, multiple national aspirations emerged and the landscape of identities was as fragmented as were the networks of political alliances that shaped it: parallel nationalisms of Russians, Ukrainians, Georgians, Armenians, Estonians, and so on flourished and competed with each other.

To be sure, not all the major parties in Romanov Russia had an ethnolinguistic connotation similar to that of the Mensheviks. The Socialist Revolutionary Party, which inherited the populist, peasant-focused tradition of Russian radicalism and gained a majority of the votes in the 1917 elections, had a rather more balanced linguistic composition (Perrie 1972; Jews were massively overrepresented as well, however). But in general, voting and political mobilization largely proceeded within linguistically defined population blocs, as became apparent in the 1917 elections. As mentioned above, Ukrainian national parties received 70% of the votes in the corresponding regions, where the cities were largely inhabited by non-Ukrainians (Poles and Jews in the main; the following draws on Kappeler 2001: 362–363). Yiddish, Polish, and German speakers, in turn, voted almost en bloc for the respective national parties, the Zionist parties now winning out over the Bund in the case of the Jewish vote. In Transcaucasia, Georgians voted for "their" party, the Mensheviks, as discussed earlier, while Armenians voted largely for the federalist-nationalist, "bourgeois" Dashnak Party, and Azerbaijanis for the Muslim Democratic Musavat Party. Only 5% voted for Bolsheviks or the Socialist Revolutionaries in Transcaucasia. In the Middle Volga and Ural area, Tatars and Bashkirs voted in the majority (around 55%) for separate, ethnically defined lists. Similarly in Central Asia, Kazakh parties won three-quarters of the votes in the province of Uralsk. The only exception to this pattern of ethnic voting is the northwest, where the Bolsheviks were able to gather the votes of non-Russian minorities as well—almost entirely through local, ethnically defined branch parties, however. In all, 40% of Estonians voted for the Bolsheviks (the rest of the votes going to Estonian national parties), as did 72% of Livonians and 51–63% of the inhabitants in the provinces with a Belorussian majority, where national parties obtained only about 1% of the vote.

WHO RULED?

Our understanding of ethnic politics in Romanov Russia would be incomplete without a brief discussion of the ethnic composition of the tsarist regime against which these various political movements struggled. Given the lack of political ties across ethnic divides, we would expect that most minorities would not be represented in the inner circles of power, unlike the situation in Qing China. At the very top of the political pyramid, however, the Romanov state was more representative of the ethnic makeup of the population than was Qing China, which was ruled by a tiny Manchurian elite. The tsar and his family as well as the high nobility were of Russian-speaking and Russian Orthodox background. Apart from the imperial household and its entourage, the power center of the empire consisted of the top echelons of the administration and the army. Here, the comparison with Qing China leads to opposite conclusions.

Table 4.5 gives an overview of the religious background of the political-military elite. Unfortunately, there are only limited data on the mother tongues spoken by members of this elite. Since there is a great deal of overlap between religion and language, however, we can draw some conclusions about the linguistic representativity of the regime as well. The more limited information on the linguistic background of elite members will be discussed further below. Leaving details aside, Table 4.5 shows two outstanding characteristics of the configuration of ethnopolitical power. First, Russian Orthodox individuals were clearly overrepresented at the top of the civilian administration. While making up 70% of the population, almost 90% of the 215 State Council members (which advised the tsar on budgetary and legal matters) were Orthodox under Nicholas II, and the same is true of those who held one of the top 568 administrative positions. The army was comparatively more multiethnic: 77% of the officers in 1867 and 85% in 1903 were Russian Orthodox.

Second, in both the administration and the army, Lutherans, almost all of whom were of German background, were dramatically overrepresented. While not even counting 3% of the population, 12% of the State Council members, 7% of the top-ranking administrators, and a full 27% of the generals in 1867 were of Lutheran faith. In the army, the share of Lutheran generals declined to 10% in 1903, a consequence of the Russification policy, but it remained at 14% among the top generals. Clearly, the German minority formed part of the ruling coalition of the Romanovs.

Identifying Germans by religion vastly underestimates their role in the imperial state because only the Baltic German nobles retained their Lutheran religion, while many others had over time converted to Russian Orthodoxy. Lieven (1981) gives a detailed breakdown of the membership in the State Council and notes that of the 61 non-Russian members, 48 were of German origin, and only 16 of these (the Baltic nobles) were Protestant—and thus show up in Table 4.5. Given the dynastic logic of imperial politics, the role of Germans in the Romanov empire perhaps does not come as a surprise: the Romanovs were linked, from the late 18th century onward, to previous Russian emperors through the maternal line only and in the male line descended from northern German nobles.

Because political alliances in the Russian Empire rarely crossed ethnolinguistic divides, as we have seen above, it is not surprising that all other groups—Poles, Jews, Tatars, and so forth—were massively underrepresented

TABLE 4.5. Representation of ethnoreligious groups in the administration and army of the Russian Empire

Religion	% of pop.	Main language groups	% of pop.	Administration	
				% members of the State Council (1894–1914)	% top 568 positions (1894–1914)
Russian Ortho-dox	69.3	.		87.9	89.9
		Russian	44.31		
		Ukrainian	17.81		
		Belorussian	4.68		
		Georgians	1.08		
Lutheran	2.8			12.1	6.9
		Germans	1.43		
		Finns	0.11		
		Estonians	0.8		
Catholic	9.1			0	3.2
		Poles	6.31		
		Lithuanians	1.32		
Armenian Or-thodox	0.9	Armenian	0.93	0	0
Muslim	11.1			0	0
		Azerbaidjani	1.15		
		Kazakh	3.09		
		Tatar	1.5		
		Bashkir	1.14		
		Uzbek (Sarts)	1.43		
Jews	4.5			0	0
		Yiddish	4.03		

Source: Based on Kappeler 2001: 300–301.
Note: Values in parentheses are included in the main figures based on religious affiliation.

in the inner circles of power (with the partial exception of Polish army generals in 1867). The Jewish and Muslim communities, which together represented roughly 14% of the empire's population, were almost completely excluded from any representation in the centers of power. The Russian-German ruling house and their noble allies held a firm grip on the state, and even reinforced it after the second Polish uprising when Russian chauvinism spread among the political elites.

		Army			
% officers in 1867–1868	% generals in 1867–1868	% captains in 1903	% colonels in 1903	% generals in 1903	% top generals in 1903
77		80.9		84.9	81.7
		(1.5)		(0.3)	
7	27	4.2	7.3	10.3	14.7
		(1)			
14		12.9	5.9	3.8	3.6
			·		
1		1.1		0.4	0
1		0.9		0.6	0
0	0	0	0	0	0

We arrive at a similar conclusion by looking at Table 4.4 again, which lists language groups and, in the last column, the share of the population that was elevated to personal (nonhereditary) nobility as a result of outstanding service to the state. These figures allow us to estimate rates of upward political mobility, given that noble status was a key to a career in the imperial government or army. The category of personal nobility included, during the 19th century, those who had achieved a high rank in the military or the administration or who were members of one of the imperial orders, such as the Order of Saint Stanislaus created to reward loyal Polish servants of the dynasty.

Table 4.4 adds more nuance to the findings based on the religious background of elite members. Importantly, we can now differentiate between different Russian Orthodox ethnicities. The share of the ennobled among Ukrainians and Belorussians, who adhered to Russian Orthodoxy but did not speak Russian, amounted to only a fifth of the share among Russians proper. We also discover that there were even more ennobled among Georgians than among Russians. This is well reflected in the prominent role that Georgians played in the politics of the late empire, on the sides of both the tsar and his revolutionary enemies, as we have seen. We can thus conclude that most of the Russian Orthodox in the highest ranks of the administration and the army, as revealed by Table 4.5, are most likely to have been Russian speakers, with a small contingent of Georgians on the side. Table 4.4 also confirms the extraordinary position of Germans in the imperial power structure: their share of personal nobility was noticeably greater than that of Russian speakers. With the exception of Armenians and Poles, all other groups had an almost negligible chance of making a career in the administration and army—quite a contrast to the situation in the Qing empire, where rates of upward mobility were similar across regions and language groups.

TWO BREAKUPS OF THE RUSSIAN EMPIRE

Given this unequal configuration of ethnopolitical power, its increasing tilt—as a consequence of the Russification policies—toward Russian speakers, and the confinement of political alliance networks within linguistic boundaries, it is not surprising that opponents of the regime with a minority background increasingly leaned toward radical nationalist ideologies. Eventually, they advocated secession from the empire and founded a series of separate nation-states, leading to the breakup of the empire. To be sure, the revolutionary movements popular among the Russian majority proved to be decisive in the events of 1905 and 1917. To recall, the 1905 revolution forced the tsar to make some democratic concessions, on which he backtracked soon thereafter. The February Revolution of 1917 overthrew the dynasty, and in the October Revolution of that year the Bolsheviks putsched themselves to power. A civil war followed, which the Bolsheviks won decisively in 1922.

In none of these events did minority nationalists play a crucial role. But the weakening of the imperial center prepared the ground on which minority nationalism mushroomed, radicalized, and rapidly gained political power, eventually leading to the disintegration of the empire in 1918. For the purposes of this chapter, it suffices to briefly follow the developments after the October Revolution (the following draws on Pipes 1997; for a summary of the complex developments, see Smith 2013: chap. 2). Initially, most of the nationalist parties and the minority segments within umbrella parties waited to see whether the Bolsheviks, once they had seized power in Petrograd, would keep their promise to grant the right of self-determination to all of the empire's peoples. This promise had been reiterated in a Bolshevik declaration of November 2, 1917. After Lenin dissolved the Constituent Assembly in January 1918, however, it became clear that his party would try to rule the country through a tightly controlled, centralized apparatus and that it was privileging class struggle over the principle of national self-determination.

A month later, the nationalist parties on the empire's periphery declared their provinces sovereign nation-states: Finland, Estonia, Lithuania, Ukraine, the Moldovan Republic (the former Russian province of Bessarabia), Belorussia, and the Transcaucasian Federation, which in the summer of 1918 fell apart into Georgia, Armenia, and Azerbaijan. In Turkestan, a provisional Muslim government attempted to take power, supported by a Turkmen National Army. In Kazakhstan, the Alash Party declared an independent Kazakhstan— after a bloody war pitching Kazakh nomads against the Russian settlers who had invaded their lands since the 19th century. In the southern Ural, a central *shura* (council) of Bashkirians declared itself autonomous, and in the northern Caucasus a coalition of mountain tribes and Cossacks created an independent Mountain Republic of the Northern Caucasus.[8]

In many regions, the nationalists competed with White Russians, Bolsheviks, and a range of other groups for military and political power. World War I greatly complicated the situation and brought occupation by the Central Powers from Saint Petersburg all the way to Rostov on the north shores of the Black Sea. British troops intervened in Central Asia, Ottoman forces in the Caucasus, and so on. In the end, the Bolsheviks accepted Finnish sovereignty and had to give in to Baltic and Polish independence as well. By 1921, however, the Red Army had reconquered the rest of the imperial domains from Ukraine and Belorussia to Central Asia and from Transcaucasia to Siberia. In 1924 the Uzbek khanates of Bukhara and Kiva were subdued by military force as well. The Baltic states, western Belorussia, and Moldavia were able to maintain independence for a generation only. They were reconquered by Soviet troops during World War II, such that the postwar Soviet Union ended up with the same territory as the Romanov empire, with the exception that Finland and Poland were permanently lost to the nationalist cause.

It is beyond the scope of this chapter to fully discuss the politics of ethnicity in the reconquered Soviet empire. I limit myself to a broad outline aimed to show that little transethnic nation building occurred during the seventy years of Soviet rule, despite a serious effort by the communist regime from the 1950s onward. The victorious Bolsheviks initially even deepened the fragmentation of the political landscape along linguistic divides. They alphabetized and educated minorities in their own languages, a policy pursued more or less consistently until the late 1950s. They granted "titular nations" privileged access to the bureaucracies of newly formed republics, whose boundaries were drawn on the basis of linguistic geography (Martin 2001). Each major language group would find its home in a Soviet Socialist Republic (SSR), such as the Ukrainian SSR. Autonomous republics within these SSRs were the domains of smaller ethnolinguistic communities, such as the Moldavian Autonomous SSR. Autonomous oblasts were created for even smaller groups, such as the Jewish oblast somewhere far east at the Chinese border, and autonomous districts for tiny minorities. Ethnographers helped identify the various ethnolinguistic groups (now termed "nationalities" following Stalin's definitions) and delimit their territories (Hirsch 2005); linguists standardized the languages and created Latin and later Cyrillic alphabets to write them; artists composed operas and wrote novels or revolutionary plays in the local vernaculars.

Lenin, Stalin, and their successors hoped to tame the spirit of linguistic nationalism by containing it in these institutional vessels. Indeed, during the next seven decades, the nationalist movements demobilized entirely. It is somewhat unclear if this was because minority elites found plenty of opportunities to advance their political careers within the SSRs—even if national autonomy often resembled a paper construction rather than a lived political reality, given the unchecked power of the Communist Party apparatus controlled by Moscow. Or perhaps secessionist aspirations simply died down under the weight of repression. During the Stalin era and beyond, the Soviet state deported millions of minorities perceived as disloyal to Siberia (Martin 2001: chap. 8), executed hundreds of thousands of counterrevolutionary individuals or sent them to labor camps, including many "bourgeois nationalists" who did not praise the Soviet nationalities model loud enough, and did not shy away from using hunger as a weapon to subdue unruly minority populations (as in Ukraine during the famine of the early 1930s; Martin 2001: chap. 7).

Be that as it may, linguistic divisions continued to confine the networks of political alliance and patronage that emerged within the one-party regime, as they had done under the tsar. The system of titular nations at the level of republics, autonomous republics, oblasts, and districts encouraged forming political machines within these monolinguistic spaces. The existence of such ethnic clientele networks is well documented. Willerton (1992), for example, shows in detailed case studies of Azerbaijan and Lithuania how such mono-ethnic patronage networks operated and how they insulated themselves with more or less success from any attempts by Moscow to break their grip on provincial politics (see also Hale 2013 for the continued relevance of these networks in post-Soviet elections in Russia).

Given the scarcity of transethnic political alliances, it is not surprising that Russians dominated the highest echelon of power as much as they had done under the Romanovs. In the politburo and the central committee of the party, in the council of ministers, among the chairmen of the state committees, and among the generals of the army, Russians usually occupied about 85% of the positions, while they made up only slightly more than half of the population (Hajda and Beissinger 1990; Encausse 1980: 126; the data refer to the 1970s and 1980s). Minority representation at the center of power only increased when there was a powerful patron. Under the Georgian Stalin, Georgian membership in the politburo reached its peak; under Khrushchev, Ukrainians were overrepresented; and so on (Rigby 1972). The contrast with Communist China is instructive and shows that nation building—in its political integration aspect—largely failed in the Soviet Union.

The same was true on the identity side of the nation-building coin. A new Russification policy attempted to foster a unified national community—to little avail. From the Khrushchev years onward, the regime introduced compulsory Russian classes in schools throughout the country (Grenoble 2003). Many of the primary schools of smaller linguistic minorities had to shift entirely to Russian. The communist regime saw the Soviet Union no longer as a multinational model state that had solved the "problem" of bourgeois nationalism by allowing it to flourish culturally while containing its political ambitions. Rather, the party now portrayed the country as the homeland of a "Soviet people" whose members communicated with each other in Russian. The regime embarked on a path of forced assimilation, envisioning the eventual "convergence and fusion of peoples" into a single Soviet, Russophone melting pot (with regard to the Brezhnev period, see Grenoble 2003: 58).

The policy did not erode the linguistic diversity of the Soviet Union, however. There were few incentives to embrace Russian and the new national identity of the "Soviet people," given that the political center continued to be dominated by Russians and that the political careers of minorities were mostly confined to their republics where speaking the local vernacular represented an advantage. Table 4.6 lists the percentage of individuals of each of the major groups who ceased to speak their own language and adopted Russian as their native tongue. The data refer to the time span after the onset of the Russification policy under Khrushchev in 1953 and before the end of empire in 1989. As the table shows, the larger groups and those who were titular nations of an SSR (the Transcaucasian, Baltic, and Central Asian republics) or an autonomous republic within these SSRs were slow to adopt Russian. Census data also allow us to calculate the percentage of individuals who shifted their identity from one ethnic group to another. Between 1959 and 1970, only 1% of the population did so, and almost all of these individuals were of "mixed" descent and started to identify as Russian as soon as they were old enough to fill out a

TABLE 4.6. Russification by language group and type of autonomy, 1959–1989

Language	Russification in %	Language	Russification in %	Type of autonomy	Russification in %
Koriak	37.5	Rumanian	3.2	Soviet Socialist Republic	1.9
Korean	29.6	Balkar	3.2		
German	26.6	Ossetian	2.1	Autonomous Soviet Socialist Republic	6.4
Karelian	23.3	Adygei	1.9		
Chukchi	22.6	Abkhaz	1.8	Autonomous oblast	3.3
Mansi	21.6	Lezgin	1.8	Autonomous district	18.7
Evenk	19.8	Kurd	1.6	Other	8.7
Udmurt	19.3	Uyghur	1.6		
Komi	19.0	Hungarian	1.5		
Finnish	18.9	Karachai	1.2		
Komi–Permiak	17.6	Avar	1.1		
Khanty	16.5	Kazakh	1		
Chuvash	14.3	Dargin	1		
Mari	14.2	Ingush	0.9		
Polish	13.9	Kabardin	0.7		
Belorussian	13.2	Kumyk	0.7		
Gypsy	12.7	Chechen	0.7		
Nenets	12.6	Karakalpak	0.7		
Mordvin	10.9	Lithuanian	0.6		
Bulgarian	10.6	Tuvin	0.6		
Khakass	9.7	Azeri	0.5		
Tatar	8.6	Latvian	0.4		
Bashkir	8.6	Georgian	0.4		
Buriat	8.5	Turkmen	0.4		
Yiddish	7.2	Tajik	0.3		
Ukrainian	6.6	Kirgiz	0.3		
Gagauz	6.6	Uzbek	0.2		
Dolgan	6.0	Kalmyk	0.1		
Greek	5.3	Estonian	−0.3		
Altai	4.3	Cherkess	−0.4		
Moldovan	3.8	Armenian	−0.7		
Sakha	3.7				

Source: Based on Kaiser 1994; reproduced in Gorenburg 2006: Table 1.

census form of their own (Gorenburg 2006). The contrast with the assimilation processes documented for Botswana is quite obvious.

During the thaw of Gorbachev's glasnost, nationalist aspirations were rekindled, especially in the Baltic, in Transcaucasia, as well as in Ukraine and Belorussia. This does not come as a surprise, given how linguistically defined networks had been reinforced through the titular nationality principle and

that most linguistic minorities lacked representation in the center of government power. When authoritarian rule softened under Gorbachev, another
critical juncture emerged during which history could have taken another turn.
The Soviet Union could have democratized within its existing borders. Had
nation building succeeded during the communist era, the Soviet Union could
have joined India and China as a third country of gigantic proportions hosting
a heterogeneous population held together by dense ties of political alliances
and a shared national identity.

For the reasons outlined above, however, history again didn't take this turn.
The Soviet empire fell apart after the Baltic provinces declared independence
and headed a new parade of sovereignties that marched west to east across the
imperial domains. When Yeltsin successfully resisted a putsch by Soviet generals who aimed to save the empire, it was clear that the Soviet Union would not,
as it did in the early 20th century, try to reconquer the renegade provinces.
The role of language difference and how it structures political alliance networks became clear during the process: minority republics declared independence from the Soviet Union sooner if their populations had maintained their
own languages and resisted shifting to Russian, as Hale (2000) has shown.
Presumably, the less assimilated populations had also developed fewer ties of
political alliance and support with the Russian majority.

I conclude by briefly addressing a concern raised at the beginning of this
chapter: Could it be that the Russian and Chinese trajectories of nation
building diverge because China looks back on a much longer history of statehood? After 2,000 years under a common political roof, who would imagine
struggling for a separate state despite the civilizational identity shared with
fellow Chinese? Note that this would be a separate mechanism from the
process of linguistic assimilation into the language of the state, which indeed
takes time to unfold. The question therefore is whether a long history of
statehood encourages nation building apart from its indirect effect via linguistic homogenization.

There are reasons to doubt whether that is indeed the case. Comparing
groups within Russia, we have already seen that the Tatars of Kazan, who lived
under Russian governments for four centuries, developed only few political
ties with Russians and no shared identity emerged. Conversely, such ties were
more frequent among Georgians, for example within the Menshevik faction,
although Romanov Russia had conquered their lands centuries later. We arrive
at a similar conclusion by comparing across countries with the help of the
datasets to be explored in more detail in the next chapter. I find that a very
long history of statehood *à la Chine* does not enhance political integration
across ethnic divides. What matters for the prospects of nation building in
the 20th century is whether a centralized state had emerged by the late 19th

century—even if its history doesn't reach back thousands of years but is of more recent historical origin, as in the case of Russia.[9] Russia and China therefore don't diverge from each other in that regard. This should make the argument pursued in this chapter more plausible: that the scriptural uniformity of China helped establish political ties across linguistic divides and forge a common identity, while the linguistic and scriptural heterogeneity of Russia represented a handicap its nation builders could not overcome.

5

Political Integration

EVIDENCE FROM COUNTRIES AROUND THE WORLD

We have now come to the end of the *tour du monde* that led us from Europe across Africa to East Asia. Comparing across, rather than within, the three pairs of case studies, the reader may wonder whether the argument really holds. For example, why didn't Somalia's linguistic and scriptural homogeneity help in building alliances across clan divides if such homogeneity played an important role in China? And why did Switzerland not fall apart along its linguistic divides, as did Romanov Russia and the Soviet Union? One might also ask how other countries fit into the picture. Wouldn't India's polyglot population predispose the country to a fate similar to that of Russia? And yet none of the major non-Hindi regions developed separatist ambitions. What about the early development of civil society in the United States that Tocqueville described in such detail in the early 19th century: Why did it not help building networks of durable alliances across the racial divide after the US Civil War?

We also need to ask if factors emphasized by other researchers, for example democratic institutions or colonial legacies, impede or enhance nation building as well; perhaps they do so in more important ways than public goods provision, civil society development, and linguistic diversity. While I have discussed many such factors in the six case studies—by showing, for example, that colonialism didn't profoundly alter the trajectories of political development in Somalia and Botswana—they are not part of my theoretical framework. The historical narratives therefore treated them as contingent and specific to the cases at hand. But do they shape nation building in other countries in more systematic ways?

The only way to address these concerns is to explore a very large number of cases from around the globe. This is what this chapter accomplishes, using datasets that cover the entire world over long stretches of time. We thus transition from a narrative mode of analysis, through which I showed that the three proposed causal mechanisms indeed shaped the six country histories, to a statistical mode of inquiry: the three causal processes will now be identified in the form of average statistical effects over thousands of observations. At the same time, we can also explore whether alternative accounts of nation building are supported by the empirical evidence.

The analysis proceeds in three steps that closely follow the theoretical argument outlined in Chapter 1. In the first step, I show that high capacity to provide public goods, well-developed voluntary organizations, and linguistic homogeneity are statistically associated with more inclusive configurations of power in which both ethnic minorities and majorities are represented in central government. The dependent variable will be the share of the population that remains excluded from such representation. This first step will therefore tread on the same ground as the three preceding, qualitative chapters—but we will fly over much more terrain and at a much higher altitude from where not many historical details will be visible, only the mere contours of the political topography.

The second step will take us further back into history, exploring how the conditions that favor nation building after World War II have previously emerged. As argued throughout the preceding chapters, I will show that governments are better able to provide public goods and the population speaks fewer languages if the territory was already governed by a centralized state in the 19th century. The dependent variables will be linguistic homogeneity and public goods provision, measured in a variety of ways.

In a third step, I push the inquiry further down the historical road by asking why centralized states have emerged in some places but not others—thus going beyond the discussions of the previous three chapters. Levels of state centralization in the late 19th century will serve as a dependent variable to explore some of the classical arguments already summarized in Chapter 1: that states developed where there were enough people to economically support an unproductive political elite; that they emerged only in temperate climates free of debilitating diseases; that they resulted from a self-reinforcing process of war making and state building; and so on.

The First Step: Explaining Ethnopolitical Integration

Do voluntary organizations, public goods provision, and linguistic homogeneity foster nation building beyond the six cases discussed in the previous chapters? To measure these three factors across countries and decades, I will have to use rough proxy variables. The statistical analysis will therefore not pay much attention to historical sequences, chains of events, differences between regions of a country, and the like. This allows me, on the bright side, to identify general patterns of nation building that hold across most countries of the world, thus complementing the more fine-grained analysis of the preceding chapters.

MEASURES FOR THE POLITICAL DEVELOPMENT ARGUMENT

To measure how far voluntary organizations have developed in a society, I rely on a dataset that Schofer and Longhofer (2011) have assembled. It counts the number of nongovernmental organizations per capita, based on an encyclopedia of such groups. It covers many countries and all years from 1970 to 2005 (for descriptive statistics, see Appendix Table C.1). Unfortunately, these data do not include government-controlled voluntary organizations, prominent in many communist countries and beyond, but only NGOs. Theoretically, a communist women's organization, to give an example, is as useful in establishing political alliances across ethnic divides as is an association of carpenters, as long as membership in these organizations is not mandatory. It is quite likely, then, that this measurement underestimates the development of voluntary organizations in the communist world—and there is not much I can do about this. On a more positive note, additional analysis shows that the higher the number of voluntary associations per capita the more ruling elites rely on patronage to gain followers.[1] This supports my claim that patronage and alliances between the state and voluntary associations represent two alternative ways in which ruling elites gain the support of the population at large.

There is also no ideal way to measure state capacity (see discussion in Hendrix 2010), let alone how capable it is of providing public goods. The unresolved problem in this field is that we can measure capacity only by looking at the outputs produced by the state, such as the number of government-run schools or health clinics. However, outputs depend not only on capacity but on policy choices as well: some governments want to improve the health of their population, others want to build up an army. Until better solutions are at hand, I follow the standard approach and focus on measuring outputs. First, I will use the proportion of adults who can read and write (in line with La Porta et al. 1999; Gennaioli and Rainer 2007), which is strongly influenced by public school systems as well as state-led alphabetization campaigns, such as those discussed in the case of Somalia.[2] The data were assembled from various sources (see Wimmer and Feinstein 2010) and cover most countries of the world since the early 19th century.

The second, less often used measurement is the length of railroad tracks per square kilometer. Data are again available from the early 19th century onward (Wimmer and Feinstein 2010). Such long data series will allow me to evaluate whether a statistical association between public goods provision and nation building is indeed brought about by a long-term process, as the theory maintains: if literacy and railroads in 1900 predict nation building in 2005, then we are indeed dealing with slow-moving, quasi-glacial processes here.

Railroads, provided and maintained by the state, often represent a public good in themselves—though some railroads also serve military purposes or transport natural resources, rather than people, or run (at least initially) without any state subsidies. Still, railway length comes closer to a measurement of public goods provision than the government share of GDP. This and other commonly used indicators of state capacity don't distinguish between different types of government expenditures, most importantly, between military and other outlays.[3] Since I will use literacy rates and railway track length as two alternative measurements of public goods provision, they will be integrated into two separate statistical models.

To measure linguistic diversity, I use the earliest available data, which were assembled by Soviet ethnographers in the 1950s and 1960s. Fearon and Laitin (2003) used these data to calculate the probability that two randomly chosen individuals speak the same language. Linguistic data are ideal for the specific purpose at hand since we need an "objective" description of the communicative landscape that disregards the political relevance of linguistic divides. To be sure, this measurement does not take into account that some societies are linguistically diverse but scripturally homogeneous, as in the case of China. However, China is unique in that regard. There are only two other countries that use a logogrammatic script, Japan and Korea, and both are linguistically largely homogeneous. A linguistic fractionalization measure is therefore good enough to capture the communicative barriers that might impede the formation of political alliances across a society.

COMPETING ARGUMENTS: POLITICAL INSTITUTIONS, HISTORICAL LEGACIES, GLOBAL PRESSURES, ETHNO-DEMOGRAPHIC CONFIGURATIONS

The political development argument outlined in the previous chapters contrasts with a series of other approaches in comparative politics and political sociology, briefly mentioned before. It is time to bring these alternative views back into the picture. I discuss the most prominent arguments as well as the data available to evaluate them empirically.

Political Institutions: Democracy, Proportionalism, and Parliamentarianism

Many comparative political scientists and political theorists believe that democracy represents, at least in the long term (Huntington 1996; Diamond

1995), the most effective institution to promote ethnic inclusion and nation building—so much so that some authors and policymakers use the terms "nation building" and "democratization" synonymously (Dobbins 2003–2004). After all, democracy encourages political leaders to reach beyond the narrow circle of coethnics and seek votes across ethnic divides, one could argue. The political leaders of ethnic minorities, on the other hand, can organize freely in democracies (Diamond 1994), pressure for participation, and offer themselves as partners to form winning coalitions. Competitive elections, finally, can bring about a shift in government and thus minimize the risk that ethnic minorities remain permanently excluded from representation in the executive. Democracies should therefore be less exclusionary than nondemocratic regimes.

To test this hypothesis, I use the well-known Polity IV dataset and a scale that measures how democratic or autocratic a country's system of government is. As mentioned before, this scale ranges from –10 to +10, and I use the standard cutoff point of +6 to identify democracies. "Anocracies" are defined as regimes that display both autocratic and democratic features (ranging from –6 to +6 on the combined scale). Autocracies contain no democratic elements (–6 to –10 on the combined scale).

Political scientists have also debated whether some democratic institutions foster nation building more than others. Are parliamentarian systems such as Great Britain's (Linz 1990; Lijphart 1977) or presidential systems à la the United States (Saideman et al. 2002; Roeder 2005; Horowitz 2002; Reilly 2006) more conducive to political inclusion? Another, closely related debate concerns the rules according to which voters elect members of parliament. Some scholars maintain that proportional systems, as opposed to majoritarian rules such as in the United States, encourage multiple parties to share power with each other and thus allow minority parties to gain a seat at the table of government (Lijphart 1994, 1999).[4] These various debates have crystallized around two positions: Centripetalists advocate a US-style combination of majoritarianism and presidentialism, which is supposed to encourage politicians to reach across ethnic and racial divides and build broader coalitions. Consociationalists, on the other hand, argue that proportional systems of representation are more likely to give minority parties and candidates a chance, and parliamentary systems then allow such parties to gain influence in coalition governments, leading to more inclusive regimes overall.

To evaluate these competing hypotheses, I rely on three datasets: Gerring and Thacker (2008) have coded whether a political system is presidential, mixed, or parliamentarian, as well as proportional, mixed, or majoritarian. These data are available from 1946 onward and for democracies and anocracies only. I also use a more fine-grained coding of political institutions provided by a team of researchers from the World Bank (WB) (Beck et al. 2001), which includes autocratic regimes as well but only years after 1975. Finally, the equally granular dataset from the Institutions and Elections Project (IAEP) (Regan and Clark 2011) covers all countries from 1972 onward. The results for the WB and IAEP data, which are substantially identical to those based on Gerring and Thacker's data, are shown in Appendix C.

Historical Legacies: War, Empire, or Slavery

A second group of approaches highlights the historical legacies of war or imperialism, thus linking the prospects of nation building to Europe's conquest and century-long domination of the world. According to the colonial legacy approach, imperial governments often recruited members of ethnic minorities into the administration (such as Tamils in British Sri Lanka) or into the colonial army (such as Berbers in French Morocco). These groups were seen as more loyal to the foreign rulers because as minorities they depended on their promotion and protection. Once the colonizers left and the country became independent, such historically privileged minority groups dominated the postcolonial state as well (Horowitz 1985: chaps. 11–13).

There are two versions of the colonial legacy argument, a weaker and a stronger one. According to the weak version (Chandra and Wilkinson 2008), independence rarely changed the power configuration inherited from the imperial past. For example, the dominance of the Tswana kings during the colonial period allowed politicians from the Tswana majority to occupy most positions of power in the governments of newly independent Botswana. Where minorities ruled during the colonial period, however, they would continue to do so after independence. The weak version thus folds into a general path-dependency argument: power configurations tend to change slowly except when turned upside down by revolution or war. I cannot test this argument in a systematic way because data on colonial configurations of power are available for a few countries only (ibid.).

The stronger version argues that countries with a colonial past should be less successful at nation building than countries without such a past since it is *only* in colonial polities that minorities were systematically promoted. Russia, Switzerland, and China should therefore be more politically integrated and inclusive than Somalia, Botswana, and Belgium. To test this stronger version of the argument, I count the percentage of years since 1816 that a territory was controlled by an imperial or colonial power (most data are from Wimmer and Min 2006).

Other authors believe that *how* colonial governments ruled mattered and that not all styles of colonial rule had the same consequences for postcolonial nation building. Mahoney (2010; see also Olsson 2007) argues that mercantilist forms of colonial domination, based on natural resource extraction, controlled trade, and a sharply drawn boundary between conquerors and conquered, leave behind a legacy of internal colonialism that hampers nation building. By contrast, "liberal" forms of colonial domination, which combine free trade with a more lax political control of the native population, allowed postcolonial governments to integrate majorities and minorities into an encompassing coalition. Since most Spanish colonies were conquered during the mercantilist period, former Spanish domains should be less inclusive especially compared to former British territories that were ruled by "liberal" colonial regimes most of the time.

Others have argued that the French ruled their colonies more directly than other colonial powers, through a colonial bureaucracy staffed with assimilated locals from various ethnic and regional backgrounds. This diverse group of assimilated bureaucrats then often dominated the postcolonial government. Former French colonies should therefore exhibit lower levels of ethnopolitical inequality than the former domains of other colonial powers (Blanton et al. 2001; Ali et al. 2015). All data on former colonial and imperial masters were adopted from the work of Wimmer and Feinstein (2010). They coded the maximum percentage of a country's territory that was ever controlled by a specific empire.

This is certainly not an ideal way of evaluating whether styles of colonial rule matter. As is well documented in the historical literature, the same imperial power might have ruled different colonies in different ways. The small states on the southern shore of the Persian Gulf, for example, were only nominally part of the Ottoman Empire, while Greece and Bosnia were ruled through military governors appointed by the sultan. Styles of rule also changed over time within the same colony. A more fine-grained analysis is therefore in order. Several measures of the actual style of colonial rule are available, all for a dramatically reduced number of countries.

Acemoglu and coauthors (2001) calculated the mortality rate of European settlers and soldiers in different colonies around the world. This serves as a proxy variable to estimate whether European legal and bureaucratic institutions were transferred to overseas territories: they did so where European settlers could survive. These data are available for 70 countries only (for a criticism of the quality of these data, see Albouy 2012). In the context of this chapter, this variable is a good measure of how suitable a colony was for European settlers. It thus should capture the different colonial experiences of Botswana and Somalia, for example.

Another aspect of colonial rule is the extent to which it replaced indigenous political institutions or, on the contrary, relied on them. Lange (2005) counted how many court cases in the various British colonies were decided by "traditional" courts presided over by indigenous, local judges and how many were decided by colonial courts. These data are available for 35 former British colonies and measure "directness" of colonial rule.[5] Alternatively, we can rely on economic data: the per capita expenditure of the colonial or imperial government of a territory shortly before independence. Higher expenditures indicate that the colony was ruled more directly because maintaining a modern bureaucracy is more expensive than providing a traditional king with a stipend. All expenditure data have been converted to constant US dollars and weighted by the GDP of the colonial territory (data from Wimmer and Feinstein 2010). The sample comprises 83 countries for this measure.

A second legacy argument is that societies with a history of slavery face serious obstacles to building integrated nations after emancipation, similar to the United States before the civil rights movement (Winant 2001). Racially identified populations of dark complexion, they argue, bear the stigma of a slave past, and lighter-skinned groups and individuals will continue to prevent their ascent to positions of political power. This argument is difficult to test without global data on the historical prevalence of slavery (currently available only for Africa). But we can at least see whether countries whose populations are marked by racial difference are also those with starker ethnopolitical hierarchies. The Ethnic Power Relations dataset has recently been amended with a coding of how ethnic categories are differentiated from each other: by language, by religion, by profession (such as in India's caste system), by cultural traditions, or by race (Wimmer 2015). A high share of racially marked groups should lead to a higher share of the population excluded from representation in national government.

A final legacy argument concerns the role of war and conflict. The history of war in the modern world, as I have argued elsewhere (Wimmer 2013), is to a large extent driven by the formation of new nation-states, the settling of borders between them, and ethnopolitical struggles over who controls their governments. The ideal of an ethnically homogeneous nation-state has sometimes been realized through the assimilation of minorities, but sometimes through wars that redrew national borders along ethnic territories and expelled minority populations through violence. Nation building could be easier in such more homogeneous states with a history of ethnonationalist war. Another possible mechanism could be that total war between states mobilized ethnic majorities and minorities alike. War mobilization reinforced national identities and reduced the salience of domestic ethnic divides in view of the grand antagonism toward the enemy nation across the border. Popular nationalism might then lead to political integration of minorities and majorities into an encompassing coalition—the opposite of what I have argued so far. Minorities could also "prove," through volunteering for the army, resisting defection, or in the course of actual fighting, their loyalty to the state and were perhaps rewarded, at the end of the war, with political representation in national government.

To test these bellicist theories of nation building, I rely on two variables, both from the Wimmer and Min (2009) war dataset. The first counts the number of ethnonationalist wars, including ethnic civil wars and anticolonial wars of independence, that have occurred from 1816 until the first year of data on ethnopolitical exclusion (1946 or the year of independence for newer countries). The second variable counts the total number of wars of any type within the same time span. It includes wars between states that sometimes led to border adjustments and thus more homogeneous societies and/or strengthened ties of national solidarity and thus facilitated the political integration of minorities.

World Polity: The Global Diffusion of Multiculturalism

The democracy and historical legacies arguments refer to domestic political factors. Other authors point at global, transcontinental forces that shape ethnopolitical configurations around the world. According to John Meyer and collaborators, a rational world culture based on the normative principles of the Enlightenment has emerged over the past 200 years and eventually come to dominate societies around the world (Meyer et al. 1997). Since the American civil rights movement, this canon includes the idea that minorities need to be politically empowered and their representation in the political system guaranteed. Corresponding policies—such as reserved parliamentary seats, electoral district engineering, quotas at the cabinet level, and so forth—diffused widely around the world (Kymlicka 2007).

World culture theory seeks to explain differences between countries as well as differences over time. I test both aspects separately. The more linkages a country maintains to the centers of global culture and power, the more elites and nonelites are exposed to world cultural models and the more the ranks of government should open to hitherto excluded groups. To evaluate this hypothesis, I use two measurements, one referring to a top-down and the other to a bottom-up mechanism of how world culture diffuses. In the top-down mechanism, government elites are exposed to world culture by participating in global institutions, such as the various organizations of the UN. I will use data on how many international governmental organizations a country has joined (Pevehouse et al. 2004).[6]

The bottom-up-mechanism operates through international nongovernmental organizations such as the Ford Foundation, Amnesty International, and Human Rights Watch. They transplant global ideas of multicultural justice and minority representation into civil societies around the world. Sometimes (as is the case with the Ford Foundation) they even directly encourage excluded minorities to politically mobilize. Eventually, civil society actors will have gained enough momentum to force the government to open its ranks to hitherto excluded minorities. The number of international nongovernmental organizations per capita (based on Smith and West 2012) will be used to test this argument.

With regard to changes over time, world polity theory hypothesizes that the average country should become more and more inclusive as world cultural models gain ground around the world. This trend should accelerate from the 1970s onward, as by this time the global hegemon, the United States, had finally overcome racial restrictions on voting rights and minority empowerment entered the canon of global norms. This argument can be tested statistically with "natural cubic splines coded on calendar time." This cryptic term refers to a simple device that enables tracing nonlinear trends in how the passing of time is associated with levels of ethnopolitical inclusion in the world. It could discover, for example, a gradual increase in inequality until 1957, then a decrease for a decade, followed by a sharp increase thereafter; or it could describe a continuous decline from the 1970s onward—in line with expectations of world polity theory. These trends will be graphed to ease interpretation.

Cross-cuttingness: Ethno-demographic Cleavage Structures

A final argument pertains to the structure of ethnic cleavages, briefly referenced in the chapter on Switzerland and Belgium. Shouldn't nation building be more difficult in a society where religious and language boundaries reinforce each other, as in Romanov Russia, compared to Switzerland, where French and German speakers are also divided into Catholic and Protestant segments? This argument was prominent in the 1960s and 1970s, when political scientists such as Lipset (1960) and others (e.g., Rae and Taylor [1970]) analyzed how the "cleavage structure" of a society influences political conflict and cooperation. In sociology and anthropology, a long line of scholars stretching from Simmel to Evans-Pritchard and Blau have made similar arguments (for an overview, see Selway 2010: 118–120).

Selway (2010) has recently studied ethnic conflicts from this perspective, arguing that countries are less conflict-prone when linguistic divides cut across religious boundaries. He calculated, on the basis of survey data from around the world, a measurement of the degree to which religious and linguistic boundaries overlap (1 if there is perfect overlap, 0 for complete cross-cuttingness). These data are available for 107 countries. I will use them to assess to what extent the ethno-demographic cleavage structure of a society enhances or inhibits nation building.

DEPENDENT VARIABLE AND MODELING APPROACH

Levels of ethnopolitical inclusion (the political integration aspect of nation building) will be measured with data from the Ethnic Power Relations (EPR) dataset (Wimmer et al. 2009). EPR includes 156 countries and 733 politically relevant ethnic categories. A category is politically relevant if at least one actor (a political movement, or a party, or an individual) with some minimal resonance in the national political arena claims to speak for this category or if outsiders consider the category to be relevant by discriminating against group members. EPR does not code individuals, parties, or movements as "representing" an ethnic group if these actors cannot acknowledge their ethnic background in public or publicly pursue group interests. In line with constructivist notions of ethnicity, the list of relevant categories can change over time, and categories can fission or fuse. EPR is based on an encompassing definition of ethnicity (see, e.g., Wimmer 2008) that includes groups with a distinctive religion, language, race, culture, or profession (as in caste systems).

EPR lists the political status of each ethnic category for each year by evaluating whether group members can be found at the highest levels of executive government, such as the cabinet in parliamentary democracies, the ruling circle of generals in military dictatorships, the politburo in communist countries, and so on. The measurement is thus independent from whether a country is ruled as a democracy or not. Levels of representation are measured through an ordinal scale. It ranges from monopoly power (total control of executive government by representatives of a particular group) to dominance (some members of other groups hold government positions), senior partner in a power-sharing arrangement, junior partner, representation at the regional level (e.g., in a provincial government), powerless, and discriminated against (i.e., targeted exclusion from any level of representation). For the purposes of this chapter, I calculate the share of the population that is either discriminated against, powerless, or represented in regional governments only; these populations are all excluded from representation in national government. The dependent variable therefore will be the population share of these excluded groups.

A few points about the statistical modeling approach are in order. First, most variables change over time, with the exception of the linguistic fractionalization index for which there are unfortunately no historical data. We can therefore pool all observations for all years and all countries together into a single dataset that uses country-years as units of observation.[7] Thus the dataset contains Somalia in 1960 (the first year of independence), Somalia in 1961, all the way to Somalia in 2005, as well as Botswana in 1966, Botswana in 1967, and so on. Included are all years between 1946 or the year of independence and 2005 for the 156 countries of the world that have an area of more than 50,000 square kilometers and a population of at least 1 million individuals.

All statistical models will have to take the ethno-demographic composition of the population into account (or "control" for it, as social scientists would say). Imagine a country with only two ethnic groups, each 50% of the population.

The size of the excluded population is either 0% or 50%. In a country with 10 groups with a 10% share of the population each, the size of the excluded population can be 0%, 10%, 20%, and so on up to 90%. All models will thus include controls for the number of groups as well as for the population share of the largest group.[8]

MAIN FINDINGS

I proceed in a stepwise fashion, separately evaluating each group of theories discussed above.[9] Table 5.1 tests the various historical legacies arguments. Models 1 and 2 in Table 5.1 show that contrary to a bellicist theory of nation building, we don't find more inclusive governing coalitions in countries that experienced many ethnonationalist conflicts in the past (Model 1) or many wars of all types (Model 2). It is therefore unlikely that nation building is easier when ethnic cleansings and border adjustments through war produced more homogeneous populations or when wars with neighboring states kindled the fires of nationalist enthusiasm and reduced the political salience of domestic ethnic difference. We will see (Models 4 and 8 in Table 5.4) that countries that fought many ethnonationalist wars in the past are also not linguistically more homogeneous today—raising further doubts about the bellicist theory of nation building.

According to Model 3, countries that spent many years under imperial rule since 1816 are not more exclusionary than those less affected by imperialism. This runs against the strong variant of the colonial legacy argument. Regarding styles of colonial rule, it turns out that former French dependencies are more exclusionary compared to countries never under foreign rule, contrary to expectations; but so are former British dependencies, thus raising doubts about whether the difference between direct and indirect colonial rule matters for postcolonial nation building. We will see that the statistical effects of having been a British or French colony disappear once I add measurements for public goods provision, linguistic homogeneity, and the number of voluntary organizations into the equation (see Table 5.3). Model 3 in Table 5.1 also indicates that former Spanish colonies do not exclude larger shares of their populations, as would be the case if mercantilism left a legacy of internal colonialism difficult to overcome through postcolonial nation building after World War II. Models 4–6 evaluate with continuous variables whether different styles of colonial rule affect nation building. Model 4 uses a measurement of settler mortality, Model 5 measures indirect rule with the proportion of cases handled by customary courts, and Model 6 uses another indicator of direct rule: the per capita expenditures by imperial governments prior to independence. None of these three variables is significantly associated with ethnopolitical exclusion. We are forced to conclude that none of the different colonial legacy arguments is supported by evidence.

Model 7 in Table 5.1 explores whether societies with a legacy of slavery continue to exclude dark-skinned populations from government representation. The independent variable here is the share of the population identified on the basis of its racial distinctiveness. There is no significant association with the share of the excluded population, however. We arrive at a somewhat more nuanced but similar conclusion if we shift to an analysis with groups, rather than countries, as units of observations (the results are not shown here). Racial groups are more likely to be politically discriminated against than ethnic groups marked by a distinct language or religion. But culturally defined categories (such as the indigenous populations of Latin America) or the caste groups of South Asia are even more likely to be politically oppressed than racial groups (for details, see Wimmer 2015). In short, there is no consistent evidence that racial difference prevents nation building more than other kinds of ethnic divisions.

In Table 5.2, I evaluate whether ethno-demographic cleavage structures, global influences, or democratic institutions affect the prospects of nation building. Model 1 in Table 5.2 shows that countries in which religious and linguistic cleavages cross-cut each other, such that few members of a particular religious group also speak the same language, are not more politically inclusive than countries where linguistic and religious boundaries overlap—in contrast to what the cross-cutting cleavage argument would expect.

According to Model 2, the more international organizations a government joined, the smaller the share of the population it excludes from power. It seems that nation building is more likely in countries whose governments are well integrated into the world polity and thus exposed to hegemonic notions of minority rights and multicultural justice. This statistical association, however, will again disappear as soon as we introduce public goods provision, linguistic diversity, and the number of voluntary organizations in the models of Table 5.3. The second measurement for the world polity argument refers to the "bottom-up" mechanism of how world cultural models diffuse around the world. The number of international nongovernmental organizations per capita, however, is not significantly associated with the share of the excluded population in Model 3 of Table 5.2. It does not seem that organizations such as Human Rights Watch and Amnesty International transmit global ideas about minority empowerment very effectively into local political arenas around the world.

How about the changes over time that world polity theory predicts? Model 2 in Table 5.2 shows that one of the measurements for the time trend is statistically significant. We can understand what this means by letting the model

TABLE 5.1. Historical legacies (generalized linear models of the proportion of population excluded from representation in government)

	Past ethno-nationalist wars	Past wars	Duration and domains of imperial rule	Settler mortality	Indirect rule	Direct rule	Legacy of slavery
	1	2	3	4	5	6	7
No. of ethnonationalist wars fought between 1816 and first year of data, Wimmer and Min 2006	0.0272 (0.117)						
No. of wars fought between 1816 and first year of data, Wimmer and Min 2006		-0.0112 (0.037)					
Duration of imperial past (proportion years under colonial or imperial rule since 1816), Wimmer and Feinstein 2010			-0.6932 (0.509)				
Maximum % of territory ever governed by Spain, Wimmer and Feinstein 2010			0.1883 (0.472)				
Maximum % of territory ever governed by Habsburgs, Wimmer and Feinstein 2010			-0.3401 (0.417)				
Maximum % of territory ever governed by Ottomans, Wimmer and Feinstein 2010			0.5877 (0.371)				
Maximum % of territory ever governed by Russian empire, Wimmer and Feinstein 2010			0.4225 (0.5)				
Maximum % of territory ever governed by French empire, Wimmer and Feinstein 2010			0.6555* (0.345)				

	(1)	(2)	(3)	(4)	(5)	(6)	(7)
Maximum % of territory ever governed by British empire, Wimmer and Feinstein 2010			0.6039* (0.349)				
Maximum % of territory ever governed by Portugal, Wimmer and Feinstein 2010			0.7969 (0.606)				
Maximum % of territory ever governed by Ge, Be, Eg, It, Neth, US, China, J, Thai, Swe			0.3862 (0.379)				
Mortality rate of European settlers during colonization (logged), Acemoglu et al. 2001				0.0666 (0.121)			
Indirect rule (% cases decided by customary courts), Lange 2005					0.0121 (0.011)		
Gov. expenditures per capita before independence (standardized), Wimmer and Feinstein 2010						−0.0514 (0.210)	
Population share of ethnoracial groups, Wimmer 2015							0.4306 (0.4218)
Natural cubic splines on calendar year	Yes	Yes	Yes	Yes	Yes	Yes	Yes
Ethno–demographic controls	Yes	Yes	Yes	Yes	Yes	Yes	Yes
Observations	7,138	7,138	7,134	3,604	1,122	3,604	6,782[a]

Note: Robust standard errors in parentheses. Constant not shown.

[a] The sample is restricted to countries in which ethnicity is politically relevant.

*$p < .1$

TABLE 5.2. Cleavage structure, world polity, and political institutions

		Dependent variable: Proportion of excluded population			DV: Change in the proportion of excluded population next 5 years	DV: Transition to democracy in the next 10 years
	1	2	3	4	5	6	7

	1	2	3	4	5	6	7
CLEAVAGE AND WORLD POLITY VARIABLES							
Degree of overlap between linguistic and religious categories, Selway 2010	−0.2145 (0.802)						
Number of membership in IGOs, Correlates of War Project		−0.0159*** (0.005)					
Number of international NGOs per capita, logged, Union of International Organizations			−0.1168 (0.075)				
POLITICAL INSTITUTIONS VARIABLES							
Democracy, lagged, Polity IV (reference: autocracy or anocracy)				−0.9460*** (0.219)	−1.1050*** (0.305)		

Fully proportional systems, Gerring and Thacker 2008 (reference: other systems)					0.4463 (0.278)		
Fully parliamentary systems, Gerring and Thacker 2008 (reference: other systems)					-0.0550 (0.346)		
Democratic transition during past 5 years (reference: no transition)						-0.02455 (0.0164)	
Proportion of excluded population, EPR							-0.915* (0.4667)
CONTROL VARIABLES							
Natural cubic spline on calendar year 1	Yes	0.0178** (0.008)	Yes	Yes	Yes	Yes	Yes
Natural cubic spline on calendar year 2	Yes	-0.0065 (0.008)	Yes	Yes	Yes	Yes	Yes
Ethno–demographic controls	Yes	Yes	Yes	Yes	Yes	Yes	Yes
Number of observations	5,195	6,542[a]	5,826	6969[b]	3,387[c]	6,176	4,439[d]

Note: Robust standard errors in parentheses. Constant not shown. Models 1–5 are generalized linear models; model 6 is a linear regression; model 7 is a logistic regression.

[a]The sample is restricted to years before 2001.

[b]The sample excludes years of war or anarchy.

[c]The sample is restricted to democracies and anocracies because of missing values on the proportional/parliamentary systems variables for autocracies; it also doesn't include years of war or anarchy.

[d]The sample is restricted to nondemocratic regimes.

*p < .1
**p < .05
***p < .01

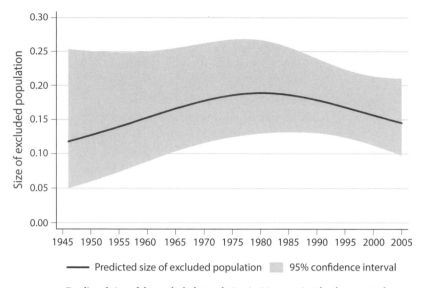

FIGURE 5.1. Predicted size of the excluded population in 98 countries that became independent after 1945

predict the average level of inclusion in each calendar year and then assembling these predictions into a graph. We don't see the expected downward trend in Figure 5.1 but an inverted U shape. To produce this figure, I included only countries that became independent after 1945. If older countries were included in the calculations, we wouldn't be sure whether the trend is due to changes *within* countries over time or because we added new countries to the pool of observations as time passes. A graph with all countries included would be even less encouraging for advocates of world polity theory.

Model 4 in Table 5.2 evaluates whether certain kinds of political institutions offer incentives to build integrated nations. Indeed, democracies are on average more inclusionary than autocracies or anocracies, a result that I will further interpret below.[10] Are particular types of democratic institutions more effective at fostering nation building than others? Model 5 shows that neither proportional representation nor parliamentarism is associated with more inclusion—a finding that runs against important strands of the literature that emphasized the inclusionary power of consociationalism. These results are based on Gerring and Thacker's (2008) data (which exclude autocracies) but also hold if we use the World Bank dataset on political institutions to code parliamentarism and proportionalism (see Appendix Table C.4), or when we rely on the IAEP data (see Appendix Table C.5), or when observations are restricted to democracies only (see Appendix Table C.6)—one could argue that proportionalism and parliamentarism can be effective only in democratic polities.

We are thus left with the finding that democracy and nation building go together. As Model 7 demonstrates, however, the causal arrow points in the other direction than expected by those who believe in the inclusionary nature of democracy: minority regimes (such as Iraq under Saddam Hussein or Syria under Assad) are much more reluctant to democratize during the ensuing five years than governments that rest on a broader ethnic coalition (see Horowitz 1993: 21–22; Tilly 2000: 10; the same holds true when using a 10-year time window).[11] This suggests that democratic regimes are more inclusionary because exclusionary regimes will remain autocratic rather than because democratization breeds inclusion and tolerance. Indeed, Model 6 shows that in recently democratized countries, the proportion of the excluded population does not change over the next five years (the same holds for the next 10 years). In any case, the association between nation building and democracy will no longer be statistically significant once we introduce the political development variables, to which I now turn.[12]

The first panel of Table 5.3 (5.3A, Models 1–9) shows the results with literacy rates as the measure for public goods delivery by the state. The second panel (Models 10–18 of 5.3B) uses the length of railroad tracks per square kilometer for the same purpose. I discuss the results of both panels conjointly. The first model in each panel (Models 1 and 10) shows full support for my argument. The more literate a population or the more railway tracks on a territory, the more voluntary associations per capita, and the more linguistically homogeneous the citizenry, the smaller the share of the population not represented in central government. As discussed in the introduction (see Figure 0.2), these associations are not only statistically significant but also substantially important: increasing the percentage of literate adults by one standard deviation or 28%, adding one more voluntary association per five individuals (also a standard deviation), and raising the likelihood that two randomly chosen individuals speak the same language by 28% (again a standard deviation) all reduce the percentage of the excluded population by over 30%. Railroads have an even bigger effect: one standard deviation denser tracks (or 30 kilometers more per 1,000 km²) reduces the excluded population by over 65%.

One could argue, however, that the statistical association between the two public goods variables and nation building is generated by other mechanisms that don't have anything to do with how attractive it is for citizens to form a political alliance with government elites, as maintained by my theory. For example, literacy in a shared language could strengthen overarching, national identities, as foreseen by Anderson (1991). This in turn could increase tolerance toward minorities and thus help overcome resistance to their full political integration. This is not the case, however, as Appendix Table C.9 shows.[13] An alternative mechanism for railroads could be that they were built to wage war and to expel unruly ethnic minorities, which in turn would decrease the

TABLE 5.3A. Testing the political development argument I (generalized linear models of proportion of population excluded from executive government, Models 1–9)

Models with % adult literates as public goods variable	1	2	3	Country fixed effects 4	Cross-section with IVs set at 1900 or 1960 and DV in 2005 5	Heterogeneous countries only 6	Heterogeneous countries only 7	Homogeneous countries only 8	Homogeneous countries only 9
POLITICAL DEVELOPMENT VARIABLES									
% literates among the adult population	-0.0112** (0.006)	-0.0104* (0.006)	-0.0113* (0.006)	-0.0016*** (0.000)		-0.0078* (0.004)		-0.0327*** (0.009)	
% literates among the adult population in 1900					-0.0157** (0.006)				
Total no. of associations per capita, 1970–2005, Schofer and Longhofer 2011	-21.7368** (9.105)	-17.5692* (9.878)	-15.4155* (9.193)	-0.0102*** (0.003)			-26.4312** (11.997)		-40.7667* (22.831)
Linguistic fractionalization, Soviet Atlas, Fearon and Laitin 2003	1.3399** (0.552)	1.2087** (0.604)	1.3023** (0.552)		1.0793* (0.594)	0.6390 (0.633)	0.4025 (0.670)	2.3644*** (0.915)	1.1672 (1.289)
ADDITIONAL CONTROLS									
GDP per capita, Penn World Table (inter- and extrapolated)		-0.0154 (0.027)							

Population size, averaged between Fearon and Laitin 2010, WDI, Penn World Table		−0.0030 (0.000)							
Maximum % of territory ever governed by French empire, Wimmer and Feinstein 2010			−0.1901 (0.442)						
Maximum % of territory ever governed by British empire, Wimmer and Feinstein 2010			0.0018 (0.351)						
Number of membership in IGOs, extended to 2005, Correlates of War Project			−0.0033 (0.006)						
Democracy, lagged, Polity IV (reference: autocracy or anocracy)			−0.3577 (0.262)						
Natural cubic splines on calendar year and ethno-demographic controls	Yes	Yes	Yes	Yes	Yes	Yes	Yes	Yes	Yes
Observations	4,611[a]	4,601[a]	4,584[a]	4,611[a]	144	3,858	2,539[a]	3,280	2,072[a]
Number of countries	147	147	147	147	144	87	82	68	65

Note: Robust standard errors in parentheses. Constant not shown.

[a]Missing values on the number of associations per capita variable before 1970 and for 8 countries.

*p < .1
**p < .05
****p < .01

TABLE 5.3B. (continued, showing Models 10–18)

Models with railroad density as public goods variable	10	11	12	Fixed effects 13	Cross-section with IVs set at 1900 or 1960 and DV in 2005 14	Heterogeneous countries only 15	Heterogeneous countries only 16	Homogeneous countries only 17	Homogeneous countries only 18
POLITICAL DEVELOPMENT VARIABLES									
Length of railway tracks (km) per 1,000 km^2	-0.0215*** (0.006)	-0.0198*** (0.006)	-0.0201*** (0.006)	0.0001 (0.001)		-0.0191*** (0.005)		-0.0174** (0.009)	
Length of railway tracks (km) per 1,000 km^2 in 1900					-0.0196*** (0.007)				
Total no. of associations per capita, 1970–2005, Schofer and Longhofer 2011	-21.1631** (9.495)	-17.6888* (10.047)	-16.0260* (9.452)	-0.0062** (0.003)			-26.4312** (11.997)		-40.7667* (22.831)
Linguistic fractionalization in 1960, Soviet Atlas, Fearon and Laitin 2003	1.4111*** (0.530)	1.3033** (0.589)	1.3819** (0.549)		1.1499** (0.519)	0.8122 (0.653)	0.4025 (0.670)	1.0476 (1.247)	1.1672 (1.289)

ADDITIONAL CONTROL VARIABLES

	(1)	(2)	(3)	(4)	(5)	(6)	(7)	(8)	(9)
GDP per capita, Penn World Table (inter– and extrapolated)		-0.0132 (0.026)							
Population size, averaged between Fearon and Laitin 2003, WDI, Penn World Tables		-0.0000 (0.000)							
Maximum % of territory ever governed by French empire, Wimmer and Feinstein 2010			-0.0681 (0.388)						
Maximum % of territory ever governed by British empire, Wimmer and Feinstein 2010			-0.0102 (0.353)						
Number of membership in IGOs, extended to 2005, Correlates of War Project			-0.0011 (0.006)						
Democracy, lagged, Polity IV (reference: autocracy or anocracy)			-0.3306 (0.244)						
Natural cubic splines on calendar year and ethno–demographic controls	Yes	Yes	Yes	Yes	Yes	Yes	Yes	Yes	Yes
Observations	4,611ᵃ	4,601ᵃ	4,584ᵃ	4,611ᵃ	149	3,858	2,539ᵃ	3,280	2,072ᵃ
Number of countries	147	147	147	147	149	87	82	68	65

Note: Robust standard errors in parentheses. Constant not shown.

ᵃMissing values on the number of associations per capita variable before 1970 and for 8 countries.

*p < .1

**p < .05

***p < .01

proportion of the excluded population. At first glance, there is some support for the first part of this argument since ethnonational wars have sometimes led to better-developed rail systems (see Model 6 in Table 5.4), and they also increased literacy rates (Models 3 and 7 in Table 5.4). However, we already saw in Table 5.1 (Models 1 and 2) that countries that fought many wars are neither more nor less successful at nation building. It is therefore unlikely that wars enhance nation building indirectly by increasing a state's capacity to provide public goods.[14]

Models 2 and 11 in Table 5.3 add two variables that influence a very wide range of phenomena and that we therefore need to consider here as well: economic development and population size. Are rich countries such as Switzerland better at nation building because there are more resources to share? Is political integration across ethnic divides easier in small countries like Botswana simply because the absolute numbers of individuals with a minority background are lower and the chances that they form part of a powerful network therefore higher? This doesn't seem to be the case. In both models with railways and those with literacy rates, GDP per capita and population size are not significantly associated with ethnopolitical exclusion.

Models 3 and 12 add all variables that were statistically significant in previous models from Tables 5.1 and 5.2, including the democracy variable for which I have identified a reverse causation problem. Adding these variables doesn't change how literacy rates, railroad density, voluntary organizations, and linguistic heterogeneity influence nation building. However, all the other variables are not statistically significant anymore: democracies are not more successful at politically integrating minorities, nor are countries that are members of many international organizations; it is also no longer a disadvantage to have been colonized by the British or French empire. This lends additional support to my argument that we need to focus on slow-moving, domestic processes of political development to understand nation building rather than on colonial legacies, world polity pressure, or political institutions.

SENSITIVITY, CAUSAL HETEROGENEITY, AND REVERSE CAUSATION

The remaining models in Table 5.3 as well as parts of Appendix C address concerns that the previous results might not mirror real-world causal processes but represent statistical artifacts. First, one could argue that some governments are more inclusionary than others for reasons that are not captured by any available data and therefore not evaluated in the previous statistical models. For example, the small-town character of Swedish society combined with the Lutheran religious tradition could have created a benevolent mentality of tolerance that subsequently enhanced nation building. There are no data on such mentalities. But perhaps they are more important to understand nation building than the three mechanisms that my theory highlights. Perhaps, statistically speaking, the variables associated with my theory would no longer be significantly associated with ethnopolitical inclusion had we integrated data on these cultural mentalities into the models. This is the "omitted variable problem" I mentioned in the introduction.

To evaluate this possibility, we can use country fixed effects models. To return to the example, such a model tests whether an increase in the number of Swedish voluntary organizations leads to a decrease in the share of the excluded population in Sweden—net of the fact that this share is already low for the cultural reasons mentioned above. In other words, fixed effects models don't compare across countries but only over time within them. This is done by adding a separate variable for each country of the world, thus a variable that assumes the value of 1 for Sweden and 0 for all other countries. We therefore take all stable characteristics of each country into account: the mentality of its population, the geography, its historical past, and so on.

Models 4 and 13 report the results of two country fixed effects models.[15] They do not include linguistic fractionalization since there are no time-varying data available and we therefore cannot assess if changes within countries over time affect ethnopolitical inclusion. The literacy and number of organizations variables are significantly associated with ethnopolitical exclusion, as in the previous models. In other words, even if we take a range of country specificities into account—mentalities, geographies, and histories—we still find that nation building is enhanced by public goods provision and well-developed civil societies.[16] Unfortunately, however, the railways variable is no longer significantly associated with ethnopolitical exclusion in Model 13. This may be because some countries increased their capacity to provide public goods from the 1960s onward but built freeways instead of railways. In other words, the railways variable is perhaps not ideally suited to trace how public goods provision changes over time within countries, but better at capturing differences between countries.

Models 5 and 14 in Table 5.3 address a second concern. Are we really dealing with long-term developments that evolve slowly over time, as my theory foresees? So far, we can't tell because in the previous models, I tested statistical associations across all country-years (remember that the data are composed of observations on Botswana in 1966, Switzerland in 1946, China in 2005, etc.). The results could therefore be driven by short-term fluctuations rather than long-term trends. A government could provide many public goods in a particularly good year and also include all minorities in its ruling coalition in that same year. When the economy turns sour in the following year, that same government might provide fewer public goods and also expel minority representatives from the cabinet.

To explore this, we can shift to a different research design and measure ethnopolitical exclusion with one observation at the end of the data series in 2005. If we are dealing with long-term trends, then countries that had provided few public goods a long time ago should still be more exclusionary in 2005. We have assembled data that measure literacy rates and railway density in 1900 (Wimmer and Feinstein 2010). The linguistic fractionalization data collected by Soviet linguists refer mostly to the early 1960s, almost half a century before 2005. Unfortunately, the count of voluntary organization starts only in 1970, 'and for many countries considerably later. According to Models 5 and 14, countries that provided lots of public goods more than a century ago and had linguistically homogeneous populations half a century ago turn out to be more inclusionary in 2005, thus supporting the idea that long-term trends are at work here, rather than short-term fluctuations.

Models 6–9 and 15–18 in Table 5.3 explore a third concern: whether we need to distinguish between different causal pathways leading to nation building. In the more homogeneous countries of Europe and East Asia, wars, ethnic cleansings, and secessions have done much to reduce the obstacles for successful nation building. Many countries of the Global South have inherited more diverse societies from the colonial era. Perhaps nation building in the more homogeneous countries has nothing to do with public goods provision or the rise of voluntary organizations. To evaluate this possibility, I explore subsamples of more or less heterogeneous countries.

Models 6 and 7 as well as 15 and 16 refer to heterogeneous countries with a religious-linguistic fractionalization index above the average.[17] Models 8 and 9 as well as 17 and 18 do the same for more homogeneous countries. To avoid collinearity problems when using a reduced number of observations, the public goods provision and voluntary organizations variables are run in separate models, hence there are three models for each subset of countries. The results suggest that public goods provision and voluntary associations influence nation building in both diverse and homogeneous countries. Not surprisingly, there is generally no association between linguistic diversity and ethnopolitical inclusion because countries ended up in either of the two subsamples precisely based on their levels of diversity.

Fourth and most importantly, we need to evaluate whether the previous results are due to reverse causation: perhaps inclusionary regimes provide more public goods to the population because they don't restrict access to coethnics, as do ethnocracies. They may also provide a more fertile ground for the flourishing of voluntary organizations, which ethnocratic regimes might very well suppress. Inclusionary governments also offer more incentives to learn the dominant language since minority individuals can hope to make a political or administrative career. Linguistic heterogeneity might thus decrease over time, as the Botswana case suggested. In other words, nation building could result in better public goods provision, denser networks of voluntary organizations, and more homogeneous populations, rather than the other way around.

To evaluate these reverse causation issues, I use a statistical technique called "instrumental variable" regression. The basic idea is to find a third variable (the "instrument") that is causally related to the independent variables of interest (public goods provision, linguistic heterogeneity, or voluntary associations) but not the dependent variable (the population share of excluded groups). We can then create a synthetic, new independent variable composed only of that part of the variation in the original independent variables that can be explained by the instrument. This new, synthetic variable is thus purged, as it were, of the effects that the dependent variable might have on the original independent variable (the reverse causation). The synthetic variable can now be used as an appropriate new independent variable. For this to work, however, the instrumental variable should influence the dependent variable exclusively through the original independent variable. We thus have to be careful to ensure no alternative causal pathways exist leading from the instrumental variable to the dependent variable.

It is not easy to find good instruments for the four main independent variables in Models 1 and 10 in Table 5.3. The analysis, which can be found in Appendix C, is therefore rather preliminary. I use the average suitability for agriculture as an instrument for railway density (railways don't usually lead into a desert); the number of foreign Catholic priests and Protestant missionaries in 1923 for literacy rates after World War II (as priests and missionaries tried to teach colonial subjects to read and write); the number of past ethnonationalist wars fought before World War II for the density of voluntary organizations (since armed conflict destroys associational life); and the heterogeneity of agricultural suitability across the regions of a country for linguistic diversity (because regions with different economic bases in the preindustrial age tend to be separated by ethnic boundaries today, following Michalopoulos 2012).

To ensure that these instrumental variables don't influence ethnopolitical inequality through other causal pathways, I ran a series of "placebo" regressions with subsamples of countries with very high or very low values on the original independent variable (see Appendix Table C.10). To illustrate, if the effect of agricultural suitability on ethnopolitical exclusion is mediated exclusively through railways, suitability for agriculture should *not* affect levels of exclusion in countries without any railroads. All four instrumental variables pass this simple test.

The results of the instrumental variable regressions, reported in Appendix Table C.11, support the main argument in quite unequivocal ways. All the instrumented variables are highly significant in the expected direction. This means that we can be more certain that a dense web of voluntary organizations, language homogeneity, and a state that is capable to provide public goods are causes of nation building, rather than the other way around.

The Second Step: State Building and Political Development

It is now time to ask where these three ingredients of successful nation building come from. In Chapter 1 and in some of the country case studies I argued that much depends on a previous history of state formation. More precisely, strongly centralized states—such as the Tswana kingdoms and imperial China—leave a legacy of linguistic homogeneity and of the infrastructural capacity to provide public goods effectively and equitably. Voluntary associations, by contrast, develop independently of state building: centralized states can either suppress their flourishing (as in Belgium) or encourage it by providing them a shared political enemy (as in Romanov Russia).

It is now time to see whether this argument holds for a larger universe of cases, again using statistical analysis. How can we measure historically achieved levels of state centralization? I use two indicators. The first is meaningful for African and Asian countries, most of which came under Western or Japanese colonial rule during the last decades of the 19th century. Here, path dependency refers to whether indigenous states had existed before colonization. The data are based on the Human Relations Area Files (HRAF) assembled by anthropologists on the basis of thousands of ethnographies each describing the economic, social, political, and cultural features of a particular precolonial society. The data contain information on whether these societies were governed by states, defined as an institution with at least three hierarchical levels of authority. Müller aggregated these data to the country level (1999; for other recent use of these data for Africa, see Gennaioli and Rainer 2007). He estimated the contemporary population share of each of the ethnic groups represented in the HRAF. This allows us to calculate the proportion of today's population that was governed by states before the Western colonial powers arrived.

The HRAF data are not meaningful for the settler societies of the Americas and the Pacific, which largely destroyed existing precolonial polities. They are also not available for Europe because Western countries rarely became ruled by foreign powers and in the East, in the Hapsburg, Ottoman, or Romanov domains, imperial rule had already lasted for sometimes hundreds of years. We can use another data source to measure 19th century levels of state centralization that is meaningful for the Americas and Europe as well. Economists turned to the *Encyclopædia Britannica* as a source to assemble what they call the "state antiquity index" (Bockstette et al. 2002). They coded for each 50-year period over the past 2,000 years (1) whether a government above the tribal level ruled over the territory of today's countries, (2) whether that government was controlled by local elites (rather than foreign imperial powers), and (3) how much of today's territory was ruled by that government. The resulting index runs from 0 to 50. To make this measurement as compatible with the HRAF data as possible, I use the version of the index that refers to the period between 1850 and 1900—in other words, the immediate precolonial period that corresponds to the HRAF data. In most countries in the Americas and in Europe, nation building became part of the political agenda of state elites once the masses of (male) citizens had been enfranchised, in the last decades of the century, and thus had entered the political arena. In most cases, the post-1850 period is therefore the appropriate reference point for the path dependency argument. The state antiquity data are missing for only eight countries represented in the EPR dataset.

We can now evaluate whether the history of state formation until the late 19th century indeed influences whether states have the capacity to provide public goods and how many languages their populations speak after World War II. Table 5.4 reports the results. The first four models use the precolonial state centralization measure. It is highly significant and with large coefficients. The countries of Africa and Asia that were governed by a centralized state before colonization have longer railroad tracks today (Model 2), more of its citizens are literate (Model 3), and its population speaks fewer tongues (Model 4, which has fewer observations because the dependent variable does not vary over time). In line with theoretical expectations, precolonial centralization is not associated with how many voluntary organizations we count per capita (Model 1). We arrive at similar results with the state antiquity measurement, which is meaningful for the Americas and Europe as well: the more developed indigenous states were in the late 19th century, the longer are railway tracks (Model 6) and the more literate (Model 7) and the less linguistically diverse is the population (Model 8) from the end of World War II onward. This second set of models has many more observations and covers almost the entire world.

The models of Table 5.4 include a series of other, theoretically meaningful independent variables, many of which have been the focus of previous research. I will discuss them only briefly here. Rich countries (measured through a GDP per capita variable) can build more railways, alphabetize their populations easier, provide a fertile ground for voluntary associations, and host a less diverse population. Democratic governments, again measured with a continuous scale reaching from total autocracies to full democracies, are known to provide more public goods and to encourage the formation of voluntary associations. Topography, measured as the difference between the highest and lowest elevation in a country, could influence railway construction as well as how many languages are spoken in a country. As discussed earlier, previous ethnonationalist wars could increase linguistic homogeneity through ethnic cleansings or state partitions along ethnic divides; they would also increase the length of railway tracks if these were mainly built for military purposes; and, as mentioned earlier, such wars destroy networks of voluntary associations. Finally, I replicate Schofer and Longhofer's (2011) model to explain how many voluntary organizations we count per capita: I add regime change as well as the number of international nongovernmental organizations (which

TABLE 5.4. Explaining public goods provision, associational density, and linguistic heterogeneity

	DV: Number of associations pc	DV: Railway density	DV: Proportion literate adults	DV: Linguistic fraction-alization	DV: Number of associations pc	DV: Railway density	DV: Proportion literate adults	DV: Linguistic fraction-alization
	1	2	3	4	5	6	7	8
Proportion of population ruled by states before colonization, HRAF, Müller 1999	-0.0000 (0.001)	9.2753*** (2.962)	0.7622*** (0.228)	-1.6707*** (0.315)				
Index of degree of state centralization between 1850 and 1900, Putterman 2006					-0.0001 (0.000)	0.2751** (0.137)	0.0133* (0.007)	-0.0230*** (0.007)
GDP per capita, Penn World Table (inter– and extrapolated)	0.0001*** (0.000)	0.1512 (0.234)	0.0535** (0.026)	-0.0609*** (0.015)	0.0015*** (0.000)	1.6985*** (0.390)	0.2207*** (0.056)	-0.0399*** (0.013)
Combined autocracy and democracy score, –10 to 10, Polity IV	0.0000 (0.000)	0.287** (0.124)	0.0170* (0.009)	0.0050 (0.007)	0.0001** (0.000)	0.3673*** (0.139)	0.0263* (0.013)	-0.0034 (0.006)
No. of ethnonational wars fought between 1816 and first year in data, Wimmer and Min 2006	0.0002 (0.000)	0.9964 (1.543)	0.2125* (0.124)	0.0326 (0.171)	-0.0023*** (0.001)	4.8374* (2.574)	0.2517** (0.103)	-0.0899 (0.101)
Difference between highest and lowest elevation (in m), Fearon and Laitin 2003	-0.0003** (0.000)	-0.3339 (0.446)	-0.0537 (0.051)	0.1703*** (0.063)	-0.0008 (0.001)	-2.8230*** (1.010)	-0.0234 (0.044)	0.1003** (0.042)
Regime change during past 3 years, Polity IV (reference: no regime change)	-0.0003 (0.000)				-0.0014** (0.001)			
Number of international NGOs on territory, Smith and West 2012	0.0000 (0.000)				0.0000 (0.000)			
Observations	2,513	3,776	3,776	76	4,361	6,665	6,665	141

Note: Robust standard errors in parentheses. Constant not shown. Models 1–4 without Europe and the Americas. Models 1 and 5 without values on dependent variable before 1970. Models 4 and 8 are cross-sectional. No time trend is included in these models to avoid collinearity. Models 1, 2, 5, and 6 are linear regressions. Models 3, 4, 7, and 8 are generalized linear models.

*p < .1
**p < .05
***p < .01

measure World Polity influences) to the list of independent variables in Models 1 and 5. As the table shows, many of these expectations are confirmed in the statistical models, especially in Models 5–7 where the number of observations is much higher.

How much does 19th-century state centralization affect postwar public goods provision and linguistic heterogeneity—beyond the fact that the associations are all statistically significant? To compare the sizes of effects, we can again express independent and dependent variables in standard deviations. A standard deviation, to recall, measures how much two-thirds of the observations differ from the mean value. This enables us to compare effects across variables that are measured in different units (kilometers or percentages) and that show different ranges of variation: the data points of some variables cluster tightly around the average, while other data might be more widely dispersed.

Especially in the models with the precolonial centralization variable, the effects are sizable: increasing the percentage of the population that lived under states in the precolonial era by 40% (a standard deviation) increases railway density by a third of a standard deviation, or roughly 10 kilometers per square kilometer. GDP, the master variable of the social sciences that is important for all kinds of other outcomes, offers a good comparison. It is not significant in Model 2 and its effect size is very small compared to the precolonial centralization variable. Increasing the share of the population that lived in precolonial states by 40% increases postwar literacy rates by almost a third of a standard deviation as well, or roughly by 9%—a slightly more powerful effect than that of GDP. The association with linguistic heterogeneity is even stronger, amounting to more than half a standard deviation: 40% more population under precolonial states increases the chances that two randomly chosen individuals in the early 1960s speak the same language by 17%. This effect is more than three times that of GDP.

The effects of the state antiquity index are comparatively more modest but still substantial. If we increase the index by a standard deviation of 12 points (out of a maximum of 50), then we can expect to see 4 kilometers more railway per square kilometer, 4% more adults who can read and write, and a 10% higher chance that two citizens speak the same language. GDP is three to four times more effective than state antiquity in these models when we seek to explain public goods provision, but only two-thirds as influential in the models with linguistic heterogeneity as the dependent variable.

The Third Step: Determinants of Inherited Statehood

In the previous section we saw that states built by the late 19th century facilitated public goods provision after World War II and assimilated the population into the dominant language, leaving behind a more homogeneous linguistic landscape.[18] These findings raise the crucial question of why such centralized states developed in some places, such as China, but not others, such as Somalia. We can evaluate some of the most important arguments put forward in the literature with existing data, albeit in a somewhat tentative way.

I shift dependent variables again, now trying to explain the shares of the population governed by states before colonization or, in a second set of models, the state antiquity index. I use another version of the state antiquity index that adds points if an indigenous state has persisted throughout centuries. In the previous analysis, I used a snapshot describing the extent to which indigenous states had developed by the second half of the 19th century. This was appropriate for evaluating how late 19th-century statehood influenced postwar public goods provision and linguistic heterogeneity. Here, we assume a longer perspective that disregards more short-term fluctuations in indigenous statehood such as brought about by 19th-century colonialism.

A number of hypotheses about how to explain the rise of the territorial, hierarchically integrated state will be discussed. I begin with Tilly's (1975) seminal study of the mutually reinforcing relationship between war making and state building. We can test whether precolonial states developed in territories where many wars between states were fought from 1400 to 1900. The data come from a list of wars assembled by historian Peter Brecke (2012). We coded whether these were civil or interstate wars, on which territories of today's states they were fought, and which states participated. Since Tilly assumed wars to have a slow, cumulative effect on state building over generations, using this very long, five-century time span seems appropriate. The causal relationship goes in both directions (or is "endogenous," in social science jargon), a fact well captured by Tilly's already quoted dictum that "wars made states and states made war." We should also note an obvious bias in the data: centralized states usually maintain a literate elite that can narrate the heroic battles fought by their princes and dukes, while societies without states might fight equally heroic and costly wars whose tales are forgotten over generations. If we do find an association between war frequency and statehood, we therefore have to interpret it cautiously.

Second, we can test a classical evolutionary argument that has been made repeatedly since the publication of Lewis Morgan's *Ancient Society*. The invention of agriculture gave rise to the state, so the argument goes (see Harris 1969), because it generated the necessary economic surplus to support a nonproductive political elite. Another, more complex and more interesting explanation was recently put forward by Boix (2015). The agricultural products of sedentary peasants can be appropriated through war, he argues. Peasants started to protect themselves from marauding bands of warriors by either submitting to a monarchical state or organizing defense on their own in a republic.

How can we test these two arguments empirically? According to classical evolutionary thinking, state building is a cumulative process, with higher levels of centralization building upon lower ones. Thus the greater the amount of time that has elapsed since agriculture was introduced on a territory, the more likely a centralized state should have emerged. I adopt data on the years since the agricultural transition from Putterman (2006).

Third, I hypothesize that states emerged in rugged topographies with low valleys and high mountain peaks (data on elevation differences are from Fearon and Laitin 2003). This is in line with anthropologist Carneiros's (1970) theory of "environmental conscription" as a condition for the rise of the premodern state. Peasants cannot run away from state builders who attempt to extract resources from them if they are surrounded by high mountains (as in highland Mexico and Oaxaca, where the Aztec and Mitla states emerged) or inhospitable deserts (as in Iraq, the center of ancient Babylonia). The elevation difference variable thus captures only one mode of confinement and disregards the fact that flat, hot deserts can have the same effects as rugged, cold mountains.

Fourth, geography and climate may also constrain or enable state formation, in line with environmentalist arguments prominent in the economic development literature (Sachs 2003). Hot temperatures and the prevalence of debilitating diseases near the equator should make state building more difficult to initiate and sustain. Indeed, research has shown that geography influences economic growth because countries closer to the equator are governed by less well-developed states (Rodrik et al. 2004). To evaluate this argument, I use absolute latitude as a variable, in line with the literature on economic growth.[19]

Fifth, I explore Herbst's (2000) theory according to which low population densities and difficult transport conditions explain why comparatively few indigenous states developed in Africa. Without enough people to sustain it, a state cannot be built. When trade is hampered by rough terrain, the economy cannot produce the necessary surplus to maintain a state elite. Data on population density in 1500—long before levels of statehood are measured, to avoid reverse causation problems[20]—are from Putterman and Weil 2010. Transport conditions can be approximated with elevation differences. This time, however, we would expect a negative association with levels of state centralization: more rugged terrain, less state formation.

Finally, we need to discuss whether preexisting ethnic heterogeneity influences state building later on. A diverse population, speaking in different tongues or adhering to different religions, might make it more difficult to erect a common political roof. This would be the opposite of the argument that I have made so far: that centralized states, where they have emerged by the late 19th century, subsequently *generated* lower levels of diversity because they assimilated their subjects into the dominant language and culture. Both processes would result in the same statistical association between high levels of state centralization and low linguistic diversity. How can we know in which direction the causal arrow points?

I again pursue an instrumental variable approach here. Linguistic diversity is instrumented with two variables. As in previous models (see Appendix Table C.11), I use the degree to which the various regions of a country are suitable for agriculture (differences in the survival strategies of regional populations gave rise to ethnic boundaries between them). How can we be sure that ecologically more heterogeneous territories don't also facilitate state formation—which would make the measure unsuitable as an instrument? Some authors have argued that countries situated between ecologically diverse regions developed centralized states because traders, who buy products in one region and sell them in another where they don't grow locally, demanded protection from strong rulers (Fenske 2014). But no one has made the argument, to my knowledge, that the same applies for ecological diversity *within* countries.

I also use a second variable: the heterogeneity of elevation differences within regions (from Michalopoulos 2012).[21] A country with a flat plain on half of its surface and a mountain range on the other half (think of Iraq) would score a high value on this variable. As with the first instrumental variable, we again assume that such a country would provide a fertile ground for ethnic difference to emerge (between Kurds in the mountains and Arabs in the plains, to remain in the example) as a result of adaptations to different local habitats. There is no historical or theoretical argument linking diversity in elevations across regions to processes of state formation.

Now that I have discussed six major theories of state formation and the measurements used to test them, we are ready to discuss the results displayed in Table 5.5. Precolonial state centralization is the dependent variable in Model 1, and state antiquity in Models 2–4.[22] Many results differ considerably across these two sets of models. I rely only on those that are consistent and on those where the divergences can be plausibly explained. Territories with many wars fought since 1400 are more likely to have developed indigenous states around the world (Model 2) but don't show higher levels of precolonial state centralization in Africa and Asia (Model 1). Perhaps this divergent result is due to different geographic coverage of the two dependent variables. Perhaps Tilly's argument holds only for Europe and the Americas (cf. the discussion in Rasler and Thompson ND).[23] Indeed, a history of warfare enhances the formation of indigenous states in Europe and North America (Model 3) but not outside of the West (Model 4).[24] This interpretation is in line with other research showing that precolonial societies in Africa and Asia that were frequently attacked from the outside did not develop more centralized political

TABLE 5.5. Explaining levels of statehood in the past (two-stage least squares instrumental variable models on inherited levels of statehood, first stage not shown)

	Dependent variable: Precolonial centralization	Dependent variable: State antiquity		
	Asian and African countries only	All countries	Western countries only	Non–Western countries only
	1	2	3	4
Linguistic fractionalization, instrumented	−1.0927** (0.504)	0.2780 (0.244)	0.9105 (0.787)	0.0282 (0.164)
Number of interstate wars fought between 1400 and 1900, Brecke 2012	0.0007 (0.002)	0.0008** (0.000)	0.0011* (0.001)	0.0013 (0.001)
Difference between highest and lowest elevation (in m), Fearon and Laitin 2003	0.0798*** (0.029)	0.0148* (0.009)	−0.0059 (0.029)	0.0184** (0.009)
Absolute latitude, Michalopoulos 2012	0.0043 (0.008)	0.0033* (0.002)	−0.0003 (0.006)	0.0059* (0.003)
Population density in 1500 (logged), Putterman and Weil 2010	0.0539 (0.041)	0.0636*** (0.015)	0.1189*** (0.042)	0.0531*** (0.018)
Thousands of years since transition to agriculture (standardized), Putterman 2006	−0.0859 (0.074)	0.0711*** (0.022)	0.0023 (0.066)	0.0670** (0.028)
Observations	74	134	48	86
R–squared	0.371	0.374	−0.241	0.483

Note: Robust standard errors in parentheses. Constant not shown.

*p < .1

**p < .05

***p < .01

systems (based on the HRAF data: Osafo-Kwaako and Robinson 2013: 17).[25] I leave it to others to explain why wars might have played a different role in the histories of Western and non-Western societies.

We find the opposite with regard to elevation difference, which is supposed to test the environmental conscription argument as well as the idea that difficult conditions for transporting trade goods impeded state formation. A rugged terrain enhanced state building everywhere, in line with the theory of environmental conscription, except in Western countries (Model 3). Seen together with the previous results, it seems that wars in the early modern period might indeed have propelled the formation of states in the West, while mountain ranges confining the peasant population had similar consequences outside of the West.

Geographic distance from the equator is not consistently associated with state formation: the variable is insignificant for the African and Asian countries in the model with precolonial centralization (Model 1) but significant for non-Western countries when the state history index serves as the dependent variable (Model 4). There is also no consistent support for the argument that an early transition to agriculture enhanced state building. But indigenous states seem to have flourished where population density was high in 1500 (Models 2–4), in line with Herbst's reasoning, while there is no association with the other measurement of state formation, precolonial state centralization (Model 1). I hasten to note here, however, that Model 1 would produce a statistically significant association between population density and precolonial state centralization if we did not instrument linguistic fractionalization. I conclude that early modern population density could well be an important factor possibly around the world for explaining where states formed in subsequent centuries.

Next, I explore whether states homogenized the languages spoken by their subjects or, conversely, whether states could not emerge where the population spoke many different tongues. Model 1 shows a negative association between the instrumented linguistic fractionalization variable and precolonial statehood. We would be tempted to think that diversity impedes state formation. The models with state antiquity as a dependent variable, however, lead to a different conclusion, since the instrumented fractionalization variable is consistently insignificant. We thus don't arrive at a solid result that would hold for both measurements of state formation (see also Ahlerup 2009). But we do know for certain, thanks to a temporal lag of roughly 60 years between the two measurements, that the centralized indigenous states of the late 19th century subsequently homogenized the linguistic landscape à la Botswana (Table 5.4, Models 4 and 8). Whether an already low level of diversity facilitated building such states cannot be answered in more conclusive terms without data on the linguistic makeup of the world in the early 19th century. Only a massive effort at collecting such data would allow us to disentangle more precisely how state formation interacts with diversity.

Conclusion

This chapter explored the long-term dynamics of nation building with data from countries around the world, thus complementing the case studies offered in the previous three chapters. The theoretical framework remained the same: assuming an exchange theoretic perspective, I distinguished between a resource, an organizational, and a communicative aspect of political alliances. These alliances will stretch across ethnic divides and throughout a territory if state elites have the infrastructural capacity to provide public goods and thus become more attractive exchange partners for citizens; if associational networks have developed that will make building transethnic coalitions easier;

and if few linguistic barriers hamper the exchange of information and thus the establishment of wide-reaching relationships of alliance and support. Where centralized indigenous states had emerged by the late 19th century, postwar governments inherited their infrastructural capacity to deliver public goods and a more homogeneous population, both of which facilitated nation building. Such centralized states were not spread evenly around the world of the 19th century: they were more likely to have emerged where there were enough people to sustain a nonproductive state elite; in a topography that made it difficult for peasants to escape state builders (outside of the West); and where intense warfare had forced ruling elites to build stronger states (in the West).

This chapter also evaluated alternative accounts of nation building: that it is fostered by democracy or consociational institutions; that it was more successful under global pressures to offer minorities avenues of political representation; that it was more difficult after a divisive colonial experience, a history of slavery, or where religious and linguistic boundaries reinforced each other. While I did not find any support for these arguments, this does not mean that they are entirely irrelevant. After all, the statistical approach pursued in this chapter captures only average effects across many countries and years. Many cases are not situated "on the regression line" and therefore not well explained by such models. If one were more ambitious and searched for a complete explanation of all cases, for example using Qualitative Comparative Analysis as a technique (Ragin 1989), one might find that democratization or specific colonial experiences are important factors in understanding a particular subset of countries or a specific historical period.

This chapter was also not able to explore some other factors and mechanisms that could affect levels of ethnopolitical inclusion. For example, it disregarded the policies of neighboring states or regional hegemons that might affect the decision of whether or not to grant political participation to minorities (see Mylonas 2012). It also paid little attention to the elite bargains that shape the power configuration over the short run (see Acemoglu and Robinson 2006; for Africa, see Roessler 2011).

Obvious data limitations should be noted as well. As I've frequently noted, we currently don't have data on linguistic diversity or voluntary organizations before the 1960s. More important for the present argument, there are no data on the structure of political alliance networks for more than a handful of countries. I therefore could not show empirically that the reach of these alliance networks determines the power configuration in national government—a crucial element in the relational theory of nation building proposed here. However, the three-country comparison offered rich detail about how these networks developed over time, how they were related, in the historical process, with public goods provision, language heterogeneity, and voluntary organizations, and how they in turn shaped the ruling coalition after the transition to the nation-state. I hope, therefore, that the four chapters combined will convince the reader that it is worthwhile to pursue the relational perspective advocated by this book: to see nation building as a matter of political alliances between rulers and ruled and to identify the historical forces that encourage these alliances to reach across ethnic divides.

6

Identifying with the Nation

EVIDENCE FROM A GLOBAL SURVEY

It is now time to look at the other side of the nation-building coin: the emergence of national identities. The case studies have already suggested that individuals of diverse ethnic backgrounds embrace a national identity if they see themselves represented in national-level government. Conversely, they will find their ethnic identities more meaningful than the idea of a national community of solidarity and shared political destiny if their alliances are confined to coethnics and if no coethnic can be found among the governing elite. Swiss identify more strongly and more positively with the nation than do Belgians, who see themselves primarily as either Flemish or Walloon. National identities are also more strongly rooted in Botswana than in Somalia (important currents of Somali nationalism notwithstanding) and definitely more among the polyglot Han majority of China than they were among the average citizens of the Romanov empire or the Soviet Union. In short, the straightforward argument that I pursue here is that identification with the nation follows from political representation.

This chapter explores this hypothesis with data from around the world. I found a multitude of representative surveys that ask the same simple question: "How proud are you to be a citizen of your country?" It was asked in 123 countries, and we have the answers of 770,000 individuals. These 123 countries represent about 92% of the world's population. Many of these surveys also gathered information on the ethnic background of respondents. This allowed me, with a team of research assistants, to link the surveys with the Ethnic Power Relations dataset to determine to what extent these ethnic groups were represented at national-level government and how this affects the national identity of its members. This was possible for a subsample of 165,000 individuals from 224 ethnic groups living in 64 countries.

Previous research used similar data sources, usually with smaller samples of around 30 countries. Many scholars have suggested that demographic minorities will identify less positively with the national community than majorities and have offered a series of different explanations why this might be so. Building on the theoretical foundation outlined in Chapter 1, I will argue that it is not so much demographic size but political power and representation that explain which individuals are more proud of their nation. Members of minorities that are politically dominant (such as Alevi in contemporary Syria) should identify as positively with their nation as do politically dominant majorities (such as Koreans in South Korea) that see themselves more unproblematically as legitimate owners of the state.

A Power Configurational Theory of National Pride

I should first clarify what exactly "national identity" means. It is a contested concept, perhaps because of the morally ambiguous role that nationalism has played over the past two centuries of world history. Many researchers have therefore sought to distinguish more benevolent forms of national identification from others, differentiating "patriotism" from "chauvinism" (cf. Coenders et al. 2004), or a supposedly less bellicose "Western" nationalism from a war-prone "Eastern" version (Kohn 1944), or a citizenship- and state-centered "civic" from a more intolerant, ancestry-based "ethnic" variant (see discussion in Brubaker 1999). A second axis of discussion revolves around whether a strong identification with the nation can develop only when ethnic identities have weakened or whether, on the contrary, ethnic and national identities can reinforce each other, as maintained by multiculturalists.

This chapter is not concerned with these two discussions. Rather, it seeks to understand which citizens see their nation in a more positive light than others—independent of the strength of such identification vis-à-vis ethnic identities and independent of whether these identities assume a civic or ethnic, patriotic or chauvinistic form. Such positive identification has important and largely positive consequences, as it goes hand in hand with more effective government (Ahlerup and Hansson 2011), support for the welfare state (Qari et al. 2012; but see Shayo 2009), and less resistance to paying taxes (Konrad and Qari 2012).[1] It is also important to note here that national pride is conceptually and empirically distinct from how individuals evaluate their current government. Some citizens, that is, may continue to be proud of their nation, even though a particular government may betray what they perceive as core principles and values of the nation.

How does such positive identification with a nation emerge? A more detailed discussion of the exchange theoretic model of political identities is now in order. It assumes that nation-states have played a crucial role in the dissemination of national identities, even if these might have originally been crafted by intellectuals or anticolonial movements.[2] The basic proposition is that individuals who regularly exchange resources—including "soft" resources such as recognition or prestige—with each other will eventually identify with a shared social category, a notion of "us" that includes all stable exchange partners and excludes others.[3] Who exchanges resources with whom is also influenced by social categories that are already considered relevant and legitimate because these might come with the normative expectation that members establish relationships with each other. New social categories either are introduced from the outside or develop endogenously when exchange relationships within a society change (for details, see Wimmer 2008).

Following this logic, I do not expect citizens to embrace a national identity—perhaps despite intense nationalist propaganda by governments and state intelligentsias—if they have not already established durable exchange relationships with the central government. They will identify primarily with other, subnational or transnational social categories, depending on the contours of the exchange networks they have spun. If individuals of the same migrant origin support each other wherever they live around the world, they will develop a diasporic identity and be proud of their community's heritage. If villages or neighborhoods are key to the provision of public goods and remain detached from national-level alliance networks, a strong local patriotism will emerge (see the "neighborhood nationalism" in Back 1996). If politicians mobilize ethnic ties to provide public goods independent of the central government or to gain power outside of national alliance networks, their followers will be proud of their ethnic background, rather than of the nation (cf. Congleton 1995).

To understand who identifies more positively with the nation, we therefore need to analyze the power configurations at the center of the state: which ethnic communities are represented in national government and are thus more closely tied into the exchange relationships between citizens and the state. These exchange relationships often come with tangible benefits: a long line of research has shown that citizens receive more public goods from coethnic political leaders (for a sample of 139 countries, see de Luca et al. 2015),[4] expect such rewards in return for voting for a politician (for urban Ghana, see Nathan 2016) and evaluate coethnic incumbents accordingly (for Uganda, see Carlson 2015), and perceive pervasive discrimination by bureaucrats of a different ethnic background (for three postcommunist countries, see Grodeland et al. 2000). Conversely, leaders are more attentive to the demands and preferences of their coethnic citizens (for South Africa, see McClendon 2016; for the

United States, see Broockman 2013). Chapter 8 will offer some direct evidence, based on the analysis of survey data from Afghanistan, that public goods provision, in turn, leads citizens to identify more closely with the national community. Beyond these tangible advantages, political representation by coethnics also comes with a sense of empowerment and symbolic ownership of the state. I have to leave it open how important these symbolic gains are compared to the political and material benefits that alliances with governing elites often bring.

To describe different configurations of ethnopolitical power, I introduce a slightly more complex version of Tilly's polity model (1975) than the one outlined in Chapter 1. Tilly distinguished between members of the polity—the political actors and their constituencies who are represented at the highest level of government—and those who remain without connections to governing elites. In the analysis of Chapter 5, I used this basic distinction to determine how far nation building had succeeded. The lower the population share of excluded groups, the greater the degree of political integration across ethnic divides.

For the purposes of this chapter, further distinctions should be made, depending on whether the polity is composed of more than one actor group (the left panel in Figure 6.1) or whether it has a more monopolistic structure (the right panel in Figure 6.1). In coalition regimes, senior partners can be distinguished from junior partners according to their relative power. Outside of the polity, some groups might hold regional power, for example in a provincial government, all the while remaining excluded from representation in central government. Further down the political pyramid, other groups might not be represented in either national or provincial government. And finally, discriminated-against groups are actively prevented by more powerful actors from rising to political prominence.

We can now introduce a series of empirical hypotheses, based on the exchange theoretic principles outlined above, about which ethnic group's members and which country's citizens we expect to be more proud. First, members of the polity should develop a more positive attitude toward the nation than excluded groups. Second, discriminated-against groups should identify the least positively with the nation, given that they do not maintain any beneficial exchange relationships with members of the polity. Third, at the country level, we expect citizens of countries with a large share of the population without representation in national-level government to be less proud of the nation.

Fourth, we need to add a more dynamic perspective because the boundaries of the polity may expand or contract; groups move up or down in the political hierarchy depicted in Figure 6.1: elections, ethnic civil wars, popular revolts, or outside intervention may empower some ethnic elites and their constituencies while pushing others from the seats of government. Following the theoretical premises outlined above, we expect groups whose political sta-

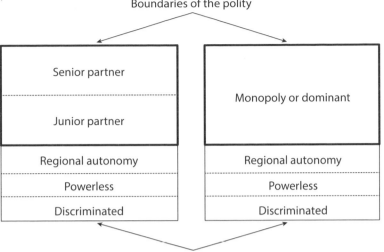

FIGURE 6.1. Configurations of ethnopolitical power

tus declined in the past to see the nation in less positive terms than those whose status remained stable. For example, whites in the United States should be less proud after the election of President Obama. Such status loss is conflict-prone, as we know from both large-N research (Cederman et al. 2010) and qualitative case studies (Petersen 2002). More important in the present context, it reduces national pride because if a citizen's political status declined, her exchange relationship with the political center will be less favorable than before.

We need to add another consideration to the simple exchange theoretic arguments made so far. Identification with the nation depends not only on one's power status but also on how far one can trust that this status will be maintained in the future. Thus, the prospect of stability enhances a positive view of the national community whereas uncertainty reduces pride. Two additional hypotheses can be formulated. Citizens of countries with a fragmented polity (the left panel in Figure 6.1) should be less proud of their nation than those living under a more monopolistic power configuration (the right panel). Because sanctioning noncooperative behavior across ethnic divides is more difficult (Habyarimana et al. 2007), power-sharing regimes are generally more unstable. This raises the prospect that the coalition could break apart, reducing trust in the future political status of polity members.[5] This, in turn, should make them less proud of their country.

Finally, struggles over the boundaries of the polity have led to armed violence in many countries around the world. Such violence tends to "unmix" ethnic groups (Kaufmann 1996) and destroy alliances that cross ethnic divides. Political elites distrust each other's intentions and find it difficult to establish cooperative alliances in the aftermath of war. We thus expect less national pride among members of groups that experienced many ethnic civil wars in the past. The same should be true for the country level: citizens of countries with a history of repeated ethnic conflicts should be less proud of their nation than citizens of peaceful countries.[6]

Other Perspectives

THE DEMOGRAPHIC MINORITY HYPOTHESIS

To date researchers have focused on other ways in which the ethnic background of individuals may affect their national pride. A distinguished group of scholars believes that individuals who are members of demographic minorities identify less positively with the nation. Reformulated into the language of continuous variables, national pride should increase with the size of a group. Three explanations have been put forward, two of which rely on sociopsychological arguments.

The first is the in-group projection model, as elaborated by Mummendey and Wenzel (2007; Wenzel et al. 2007). It assumes a situation of nested categories of identity, as when several ethnic groups are "nested into" a nation. Members of a lower-level category (an ethnic group) tend to think that their own characteristics (such as the language they speak) are prototypical for the higher-level category (the nation) as well. This allows them to perceive their own group as representative of the higher-order category and identify with that category. This perception is empirically more plausible if their group constitutes the demographic majority.

Staerklé et al. (2010) introduced a second sociopsychological argument to explain why larger ethnic groups should be more proud of the nation. Following Sidanius's social dominance theory, they expect an "ethnic asymmetry" in how strongly members of different subgroups identify with a superordinate category and with its legitimizing myths such as nationalism (Pratto et al. 2006: 281). Dominant groups see themselves as embodying and representing the superordinate category while subordinate groups maintain a more ambivalent attitude toward the encompassing category. In principle, the theory allows for the possibility that demographic minorities are socially dominant and thus more identified with the overarching category. In Staerklé et al.'s (2010) study of national identification and nationalism, however, dominance is exclusively identified through group size. Majorities should be more proud of the nation than minorities, they argue, because they perceive themselves as the legitimate "owners" of and representatives of the country.

Political scientists have introduced a third argument about why group size matters for national pride (Robinson 2014). However, they assume that larger groups should identify *more* with their ethnic community and see the nation in less positive terms. While an earlier generation of scholars expected that ethnic affinities would wither away during the course of national political integration, more recent scholarship suggests that ethnic identities become more salient because competition for political power and patronage increases in postcolonial societies. Robinson suggests that members of large ethnic groups are better able to compete in the national political arena and thus come to identify more with their ethnic category. By implication, therefore, they see the national community in less positive terms.

All three arguments take for granted that demographic majorities are always politically dominant. However, we need to distinguish demographic and political aspects from each other, rather than assuming that all countries resemble a prototypical Western nation, where a single demographic majority has historically dominated the state, such as whites in the United States, Germans in Germany, and so on. Around the world, configurations of ethnopolitical power are more complex.

In many countries—almost all African countries south of the Sahara, Belgium, Switzerland, Canada, Macedonia, Malaysia, and India, to name just a few states are ruled by a coalition of ethnic elites rather than by a single majority and its representatives. This is the case for roughly a third of all country-years in the EPR dataset. Furthermore, in 23 countries of the postwar world—Bolivia, Liberia, Angola, South Africa, Iraq, Jordan, Rwanda, Syria, Nepal, Taiwan, and so on—demographic minorities dominated the state and excluded all others from meaningful political participation. Should we not expect, for example, that Sunni in Iraq under Saddam Hussein identified more with the Iraqi nation and were more proud of its achievements—despite being a demographic minority—than the demographically dominant, but politically marginalized Shia? We therefore need a theory and data that can capture these more complex configurations as well.

Furthermore, all three demographic minority arguments assume that dominant groups remain dominant over time and subordinate groups remain subordinate. After all, demographic balances between minorities and majorities tend to change very slowly. In many countries of the world, however, configurations of power change faster than demographic trends. In Mali, for example, the carousel of coups and civil wars from which the country has suffered since the early 1990s has shifted groups within and outside of the polity at least four times. Overall, only 42 countries in the world have not experienced a change in the ethnopolitical configuration of power since World War II.[7] As argued above, groups that lose political status should identify less with the nation and, conversely, recently empowered groups should develop a new sense of national pride.

Finally, social dominance theory is not quite specific enough as to what dominance actually means, perhaps because as a general theory it seeks to explain many different phenomena. To do so it makes the simplifying assumption that each society is dominated by a group that monopolizes economic resources, social status and prestige, health, housing, political power, and so on (Pratto et al. 2006). However, symbolic, social, economic, and political dominance do not need to coincide. Economically and socially dominant groups such as whites in post-apartheid South Africa or Chinese in Malaysia, for example, might not dominate national government. To explain national identification and pride, we therefore need a more specific theory that relates to political power and representation, rather than to a more general "social dominance."

The numerous empirical tests of the demographic minority hypothesis have reached rather conflicting conclusions, due perhaps to these various theoretical ambiguities or because each study is based on a different set of countries. Using individual-level data, Smith and Kim (2006) report that in only 13 out of 33 International Social Survey (ISS) countries are individuals with a minority background less proud of the nation. By contrast, Staerklé et al. (2010) show that members of ethnic, linguistic, and religious minorities evaluate their country in less positive terms in these same 33 ISS countries. And then Masella (2013) finds that minority individuals don't identify less with the nation in 21 countries that completed the World Values Survey (WVS).

Using group-level data, some authors have investigated whether larger groups identify more positively with the nation than do smaller ones. The findings are again conflicting: Masella (2013) analyzes majorities and minorities separately and finds that larger groups are generally less identified with the nation in the 21 countries of the WVS. In Robinson's (2014) sample of 246 groups in the 16 African countries that took an Afrobarometer survey, however, larger groups identify *more* with the nation than with their ethnic groups. Elkins and Sides (2007), finally, find that the size of minorities is not associated with national pride in 51 countries that completed the WVS.

At the country level, we would expect more heterogeneous populations—made up of a large number of small groups—to identify less positively with the nation overall. However, according to Masella (2013) this is not the case, and Robinson (2014) arrives at the same conclusion using Afrobarometer data for 16 countries. According to Staerklé et al. (2010), by contrast, minorities in heterogeneous countries see their nation less positively than minorities in homogeneous countries (while there is no association for majorities). This finding is based on 33 ISS countries.

THE INSTITUTIONALIST ARGUMENT

The neo-institutionalist tradition in political science also offers an argument about how national pride relates to ethnicity. According to this school of thinking, which social category an individual identifies with depends on the incentives provided by the institutional framework. Elkins and Sides (2007) have applied this approach to the problem of national pride and evaluated the consociational theory discussed in the previous chapter. Minorities in countries that elect members of parliament through proportional systems should identify more positively with the country and nation because they are more likely to be represented in parliament and executive government. Federalism should have the same consequences or it could—as argued by "centripetalist" authors (Roeder 2005)—increase minority identification with the autonomous province and decrease attachment to the nation as a whole. Identifying 90 ethnic minorities on the basis of the Minorities at Risk dataset and using various waves of WVS for 51 countries, the authors show that both majorities and minorities are less proud in countries with proportional representation. Minorities express more national pride in federal countries, but the same does not hold for majorities. They conclude that consociational institutions have "at best mixed effects" on national pride.

This important research suffers from some of the limitations of the data it uses: the Minorities at Risk dataset mostly includes disadvantaged groups, and there is no information on actual representation in regional or national government. It is therefore difficult to answer the research question asked by institutionalists. One would first have to evaluate whether proportional representation and federalism indeed increase minority representation at the national or regional level, respectively (proportionalism doesn't increase national-level representation, however, as shown in the previous chapter). In a second step, one would then see whether representation goes along with national pride. This second question is what this chapter aims at, using a theoretical model and empirical data that will allow us to address it in more precise terms.

Data and Measurements

DEPENDENT VARIABLE

Most researchers have worked with a relatively small sample of countries, using either the ISS module on national identities or the WVS. However, a large number of surveys—organized by the various continental barometer organizations—have asked at least one comparable question: "How proud are you of your XY nationality [in some surveys: to be a citizen of XY]?" Most of the surveys allow respondents to choose from four responses ranging from "very much" to "not at all." The question asks specifically about pride to be "Swiss," for example, rather than pride in "your country." Immigrants or ethnic minorities are therefore unlikely to understand this question as referring to their country of origin or to a neighboring country where coethnics represent the dominant majority (such as Croatia from the point of view of Bosnian Croats). Equally important, the question is clearly about pride in the national community of citizens (proud to be Belgian) and not about pride in one of its component groups, such as the nationalities of multinational states (Flemish and Walloon).

Drawing on Latinobarometer, AsiaBarometer, Afrobarometer, the WVS, the European Value Survey, and the ISS, we were able to assemble a dataset that covers 123 countries from South Africa in the south to Russia in the north, from Japan in the east to the United States in the west, from very small countries such as the Maldives and Luxembourg to very large ones such as China and India. As mentioned previously, the dataset contains representative samples for roughly 92% of the world's population. Appendix Table D.1 lists the countries, surveys, and survey waves covered by the data.

While representative at the country level, these surveys obviously did not draw representative samples of all ethnic groups with the same political status—for example, all discriminated-against individuals in Bolivia or all members of the polity in Russia. In one of the analyses below, however, I will compare national pride between different status groups within each country. There is no way to assess whether this problem affects the results in systematic ways. But it is reassuring that the results remain largely unchanged when I exclude status groups with fewer than 100 individual responses (ca. one-fifth of all groups).

To further explore this issue, I took advantage of the fact that 43 of these status groups were sampled in different surveys, for example, a first time by the ISS in 2004 and then by the WVS in 2009. I calculated how similar the responses of group members were in these two surveys. As Appendix Figure D.2 shows, there is no systematic relationship between the size of the samples and the degree to which responses resemble each other across surveys. If small sample sizes were a systematic problem, then the responses to the two surveys should diverge more the smaller the sizes of the samples.

But what does the "how proud are you of your nationality" question actually measure? Two related issues need to be discussed. The first refers to the underlying sentiment captured by the question. I follow Bollen and Medrano (1998) in distinguishing attachment from moral identification. Attachment refers to how strongly individuals believe that they form part of one community rather than another. Moral identification implies a positive evaluation of one's community's standing in the larger world, independent of how important membership in that community is for one's overall identity. For example, Germans might feel very identified with the German nation but not evaluate Germany's historical role in positive terms (see Giesen and Schneider 2004). Indeed, I find a very weak correlation[8] between answers to the question about national pride and whether respondents identify primarily with the nation or with their ethnic group (the latter question is asked in only some of the surveys). Clearly, the pride question refers to the moral, evaluative component of national identification rather than the strength of the attachment. I also note here that responses to the pride question are only weakly correlated (at .16) with how survey respondents evaluate the current government of their country. Empirically, therefore, pride in one's nation is distinct from approval of its government.

Second, we also need to discuss the extent to which individuals around the world understood the pride question in similar ways (metric invariance in technical jargon) and whether ticking the same box actually means the same thing across countries (scalar invariance).[9] To statistically test for either metric or scalar invariance, one needs more than one question relating to the same underlying concept. Since I am working with only one question, I cannot offer a technical test of metric and scalar invariance here. But Davidov (2009) showed on the basis of multiple questions asked in the ISS survey that respondents did understand a series of similar pride questions in the same way across countries. He also demonstrated, however, that similarly proud individuals did not necessarily tick the same answer box in different countries.

As previous research seems to be inconclusive due to different country samples and limited sample sizes, among other possible reasons, I think that the advantage of being able to use data from a very large number of countries outweighs the possible problems with scalar invariance (in line with the reasoning and research strategy of Elkins and Sides [2007]). Furthermore, this issue will affect only the country-level analysis. In the group-level model presented below, country fixed effects ensure that we compare groups within rather than across countries. Scalar invariance problems therefore could possibly affect only half of the results presented below.

With this caveat about comparisons across countries in mind, I now briefly describe how the 770,000 individuals from around the world answered the pride question. As Appendix Table D.2 with descriptive statistics shows, the world's populations are on average surprisingly proud of their countries: the global average is 3.4, thus in between "somewhat proud" and "very proud." The standard deviation is also small: two-thirds of all individuals around the world are between 2.7 (a bit less than "somewhat proud") and "very proud" of their nationality. Most of the European populations are far less proud of their respective nations than are those of the rest of the world. The same is true for some Central and East Asian countries. The least prideful are Germans, and among the most proud are Laotians, Ghanaians, and the population of Trinidad and Tobago.

The average pride of ethnic groups varies quite a bit more. In line with the expectations of my theory, Muslims in Serbia, Russians in Latvia, and Albanians in Macedonia—all with a history of sustained discrimination—are among the least proud (close to "not very proud" on average), while among the proudest we find Uzbeks in Uzbekistan and Creoles in Trinidad and Tobago.

ETHNICITY-RELATED VARIABLES

In order to test the power configurational argument of national identification, I again rely on the EPR dataset (see Wimmer et al. 2009) but now use the more fine-grained scheme of coding the political status of ethnic groups. In line with the more detailed version of the polity model outlined earlier, EPR describes the political status of ethnic groups with a seven-tiered scale. It ranges from monopoly power, a position of dominance (with only token representation of other ethnic communities), senior and junior partners in power-sharing governments, regional autonomy, no representation at either the national or regional level (or "powerless" for short), all the way down to discriminated against (see Figure 6.1; for more information on EPR coding rules, see again the online appendix to Wimmer et al. 2009).

With a team of research assistants, we connected the ethnic background information that individuals gave in the survey to the ethnic categories listed in the EPR dataset. An individual who ticked the "Serbian" box in the World Values Survey for Yugoslavia, for example, was identified with the EPR group "Serbians" and given the corresponding political status (member of a "dominant" group). This was possible for 64 countries and 224 groups, representing roughly a third of all ethnic categories and almost half of the countries covered by EPR. Of all the ethnic categories listed in any of the surveys, we found a match in the EPR dataset for about half of them. We took advantage of the fact that many systems of ethnic categorization are segmentally nested, which allowed using many-to-one and one-to-many matching procedures (for details see Appendix D).

In addition to the political status categories, EPR contains information about the total number of ethnic conflicts fought since 1945, defined as armed confrontations between rebel groups and government troops that cost more than 25 individual lives. To test whether a decline in political status decreases pride in the nation, I created a variable that indicates whether a group had recently moved down in the seven-tiered hierarchy. For example, the political status of non-indigenous Bolivians declined from "dominant" to "junior partner" after the election of the indigenous Evo Morales to the presidency.[10]

The EPR dataset also offers a series of indicators describing the power configuration at the national level. This will allow us to use the full, 123-country dataset, including countries for which there was no information on the ethnic background of individuals in the surveys. Three variables are of interest here. First, the size of the excluded population measures the proportion of regionally represented, powerless, and discriminated-against groups—in other words, the share of the population that remains outside of the polity. This measurement served as the core dependent variable in the previous chapter. Now, the population share of excluded groups will be used as an independent variable to show that political integration leads to national identification. This analysis therefore complements the more fine-grained investigation of how the political status of an ethnic group affects the national pride of its members. Second, the "power-sharing" variable indicates whether the polity is made up of one (as in the right panel of Figure 6.1) or more (as in the left panel of Figure 6.1) ethnopolitical elites. As discussed, power sharing should reduce confidence in the future political status of polity members and thus national pride. Third, I count the number of ethnic armed conflicts in a country's history since 1945—the same variable that I will also use for the analysis at the group level.

OTHER COUNTRY-LEVEL VARIABLES

Obviously, other aspects of a country's history and current condition will influence national pride. I tested every country-level variable that has ever been used in quantitative research as well as a number of additional, theoretically meaningful variables. Table 6.1 lists these 26 variables as well as the data sources. In addition to standard variables such as GDP per capita, linguistic and religious diversity, and population size, it includes an index of globalization, various variables to test historical legacy arguments, some variables to explore the consociational theory evaluated by Elkins and Sides (2007), a series of variables related to the history of war and the contemporary military power of a country, some economic variables emphasized by previous research, and adult literacy rates that refer to Anderson's (1991) theory of nationalism as propelled by the rise of reading publics. To use all 26 variables in a single statistical model would overburden it. I therefore proceed in a step-by-step fashion, testing each variable individually and then retaining those that were significantly associated with national pride for future analysis.[11]

INDIVIDUAL-LEVEL VARIABLES

To explain national pride, we also have to take into account differences between individuals. All surveys contain similar questions about the basic characteristics of individuals (for details, see Appendix D). This allows us to take into account that men are usually more proud of their country than are women, married individuals more than unmarried ones, older individuals more than younger, and less educated more than better educated. Pride could also be influenced by an individual's political outlook because nationalism usually goes hand in hand with a right-wing orientation. Although we could not find corresponding questions in all of the surveys, we can at least measure whether or not "politics is important" to the survey respondents around the world. I also included the question of whether "religion is important" since

---

TABLE 6.1. List of country–level control variables and data sources

GLOBALIZATION

Index of global integration, extended 2012–, Konjunkturforschungsstelle of the ETH Zürich

POPULATION CHARACTERISTICS

Population size, interpolated, logged, World Bank World Development Indicators

Adult literacy 15+ (in %), interpolated and extended, UNESCO/Wimmer and Feinstein 2010

Percentage Muslim population in 2010, Pew global surveys

Religious fractionalization, Alesina et al. 2003

Linguistic fractionalization, Alesina et al. 2003

WAR AND MILITARY

No. of wars fought since 1816, Wimmer and Min 2006

No. of wars lost since 1816, Correlates of War Project

Share of global material capabilities, in %, logged, Correlates of War Project

Military expenditures in 1000s of current USD, extended 2007–, logged, Correlates of War Project

War of independence, Wimmer and Min 2006 plus Correlates of War Project for some countries

ECONOMICS

GDP per capita in constant USD, inter– and extrapolated, logged, World Bank World Development Indicators

Human Development Index, interpolated, United Nations Development Programme

Gini index of inequality, interpolated, United Nations University Wider, World Bank Development Indicators for some countries

Landlocked country, Wikipedia

HISTORICAL LEGACIES

Former British dependency, Wimmer and Min 2006

Axis power during World War II

Ever a communist country

Former German dependency, Wimmer and Min 2006

Number of years since 1816 with constant borders (incl. provincial), Wimmer and Min 2006

Years since foundation of first national organization (means centered), Wimmer and Feinstein 2010

Years since independence, Correlates of War Project

POLITICAL INSTITUTIONS

Combined autocracy (–10) to democracy (+10) score (interpolated), Polity II, Polity IV Project

Average Polity II score between 1816 and 1990, Polity IV Project

Federation or federal system, extended from 2005–, Institutions and Elections Dataset

Proportional or mixed electoral system, extended from 2005–, Institutions and Elections Dataset

---

religious individuals might identify more positively with the nation if membership in the nation is defined on the basis of religion (as in Poland, for example). I also add some basic information on the social class background of individuals.[12] Since we are not interested in how individual difference affects national pride, the table with results doesn't show these variables, though they are included in the statistical models.

Results

A brief note on the statistical modeling approach is in order before I can move on to the results. In line with most previous research using similar data sources, I use a multilevel approach to take into account that individual responses to the pride question are influenced simultaneously by their individual characteristics, by the characteristics of the ethnic groups they are a member of, and by the specificities of the countries in which they live. We will therefore consider individual-level variables, ethnic group variables, and country variables to explain why some individuals have greater pride in their nation than others.[13]

The appropriate specification is an ordered logit model because the outcome is a rank order, ranging from "not proud at all" to "very proud."[14] Because the data are composed of a very large number of different surveys, I checked whether the results change when we take into account the specific survey to which an individual responded. This would be the case if a survey was conducted at a moment of heightened nationalist anxiety, for example, or if the survey asked the pride question after some other questions that had already prepared individuals to focus on their national identity. The main results with "survey fixed effects" remain unchanged.

Let me first discuss which of the 26 country characteristics are *not* associated with national pride. The details of this analysis can be found in Appendix D.[15] Most important, the citizens of more diverse countries are not less proud of their nation, as soon as I take some other country characteristics into account (Model 1 in Appendix Table D.4).[16] Contrary to the demographic minority argument, it doesn't seem to matter much if the citizens of a country speak many or few different languages or believe in the same or many different gods. Some other interesting non-results should be mentioned. Countries that fought many wars with other states since 1816 are neither more nor less proud than more peaceful countries (Model 3 in Appendix Table D.3), nor are countries that lost those wars less proud (Model 13). Isolated countries don't differ from those that are integrated into the global economy (Model 1), democracies don't differ from autocracies (Model 24), and rich countries are no different from poor countries (Model 5).

We are now ready to evaluate the power configurational hypotheses with Table 6.2. In a first step, I investigate whether the political status of ethnic groups influences how proud their members are. To begin with: Are members of ethnic groups that are not represented in national government less proud of the nation than members of the polity? Model 1 has two levels (individuals and ethnic groups) and uses country fixed effects, a technique introduced in the previous chapter. It takes into account all stable characteristics of each of the 64 countries—its unique climate, its geography, its specific historical past, and so on. This also means that groups are compared within countries, rather than across them. We thus avoid the problem of scalar invariance discussed earlier. This model includes the 224 ethnic groups for which we could match the ethnic categories of the surveys with those of EPR.[17]

In line with the theory elaborated above, Model 1 of Table 6.2 shows that all status groups without representation in national-level government are less proud than members of the polity. And in keeping with the second hypothesis, the effect is particularly pronounced for discriminated-against groups, whose members are, on average, two standard deviations less proud than included groups. Groups that enjoy some political representation in provincial governments are also less proud than included groups. This is compatible with the theory, since members of such groups are expected to develop alliances with regional, rather than national, government. Correspondingly, they should be proud of that region or province, rather than the nation.

Model 1 also shows that members of larger ethnic groups are neither more nor less proud of their nation than are members of smaller groups—again in contrast to the demographic size argument. But maybe these results are distorted because most excluded groups are considerably smaller than included groups, such that we already capture the consequence of size with the political status variables? If I restrict the sample to demographic minorities only, I again do not find that smaller groups are less proud than more populous ones (results not shown). Even among minorities, in other words, larger size does not increase national pride.[18]

Also according to Model 1, members of groups that lost political status in the recent past are less proud of their nation than those that maintained their political status or even improved it. The effect is rather small, however. Again in line with expectations, members of groups that have engaged in many armed conflicts are less proud of their nation than those with a peaceful past. The size of the effect is considerable here, as one additional armed conflict in the past would imply a bit more than half of a standard deviation decrease in national pride.

Model 2 evaluates the same arguments at the country level. Since there are no group-level variables in this model, we can take advantage of the entire set of 123 countries. The theoretical expectations are again fully met: the larger the share of excluded groups, the less proud a country's population is overall. If political integration fails, in other words, the imagined community of the nation means much less to its members. The more ethnic armed conflicts were fought since 1945, the less proud citizens are—thus replicating the previous finding at the group level. Finally, when power is shared between two or more ethnic elites (thus corresponding to the left panel of Figure 6.1), individuals are less proud on average. According to the theory, such countries are more conflict-prone than are more monopolistic regimes, which makes individuals fear that their current political status will not be maintained in the future. A lack of confidence in one's future political status in turn reduces national pride.

TABLE 6.2. Multilevel ordered logit regressions on pride in one's nation

	1	2
INDIVIDUAL–LEVEL VARIABLES		
Gender, age, education, social class, marriage status, importance of politics, and religiosity	Yes	Yes
ETHNIC–GROUP–LEVEL VARIABLES		
Group size, EPR	0.127	
	(0.134)	
Regional autonomy (reference: included groups), EPR	−0.329**	
	(0.104)	
Powerless (reference: included groups), EPR	−0.130*	
	(0.054)	
Discriminated against (reference: included groups), EPR	−1.519***	
	(0.124)	
Lost power in recent past (reference: no power loss), EPR	−0.358***	
	(0.036)	
Number of ethnic conflicts in group history since 1946, EPR	−0.426***	
	(0.075)	
COUNTRY–LEVEL VARIABLES		
Country fixed effects	Yes	No
Size of the excluded population, EPR		−0.103**
		(0.038)
Powersharing (reference: no power sharing), EPR		−0.207***
		(0.018)
Number of ethnic conflicts in country history since 1946, EPR		−0.083***
		(0.014)
Number of years since 1816 with constant borders (incl. provincial), Wimmer and Min 2006		0.005***
		(0.000)
Former British dependency (reference: never a British dependency), Wimmer and Feinstein 2010		0.939***
		(0.199)
Axis power during World War II (reference: all other countries)		−0.723*
		(0.342)
Federalist country (reference: non–federalist), IAEP		−0.215***
		(0.018)
Number of individuals	170,257	768,244
Number of ethnic groups	224	0
Number of countries	64	123

Note: Standard errors in parentheses. Constant not shown.
*$p < .1$
**$p < .05$
***$p < .01$

It is now time to briefly discuss other country characteristics that are considered in Model 2 and that are significantly associated with national pride. These variables were retained from the previous model-building steps documented in Appendix D.[19] If a country has existed for a long time within its current borders, its citizens will be more proud, perhaps because meaningful exchange relationships between government and citizens need time to develop and institutionalize. Federalist countries have less proud populations. Again, this makes sense from an exchange theoretic point of view: in such countries, many citizens will have developed meaningful alliances with their provincial governments, rather than with the elites of the capital.[20] Former British dependencies are more proud overall—perhaps due to the prestige and power of the globally dominant Anglophone culture. The citizens of countries that fought on the side of the Axis during World War II are less proud, most likely due to the humiliation of defeat and the shame associated with the atrocities committed by Axis powers in Europe and East Asia.[21]

Before concluding, I would like to briefly discuss whether the main findings could be the result of reverse causation. Perhaps dominant groups punish ethnic communities with a critical stance toward official nationalism by preventing any of their members from rising to power in national government. In this way a lack of pride among excluded groups would be the cause and not the effect of their political disadvantage. Similarly, one could argue that ethnopolitical conflict results from a lack of national pride (see Sambanis and Shayo 2013), rather than the other way around.

Unfortunately, none of the standard ways to evaluate this possibility is feasible, given the nature of the data. It is difficult to imagine an instrumental variable that affects group status but not pride. Manipulating pride in one's country in an online or laboratory setting is unrealistic because subjects would likely not find it credible if a certain political status was randomly assigned to their ethnic group. Alternatively, we can remain within the data universe explored so far and follow the responses of group members across surveys and then see whether a change in power status leads, in the next survey, to a change in pride, as the theory predicts.

There are only eight groups whose political status changed between two surveys that are reasonably close in time to each other. Of these eight groups, three (whites in the United States, Taiwanese in Taiwan, and Slovaks in Slovakia) were less proud of their nation after their power status declined. Two (Asians and Zulus in South Africa) became more proud after their representation in central-level government improved. One additional group (the Sunni of Iraq) experienced a severe civil war during the same year in which their power status improved. The net effect of these two conflicting trends was a decrease in pride. Two other groups (both from Bolivia), however, did not conform to expectations. While far from conclusive, this analysis supports the idea that access to power induces pride, rather than the other way around.

A similar analysis is not possible for the conflict mechanism because there is only one group in the dataset that was sampled twice before a conflict broke out, such that we could assess whether there was a decrease in pride preceding the onset of violence. This is what we would expect if a lack of pride produced conflict, rather than the other way around. But I can compare average levels of pride of the groups that were surveyed before a first conflict broke out (it is 3.53 on the 4-point scale) with those that have never experienced any conflict since 1945 (which is lower at 3.45) and with those that were surveyed for the first time after a conflict had already occurred (which is yet lower still at 3.43; the difference with the 3.45 of groups without conflict is almost significant at conventional levels with a t-value of 1.6). Sample sizes for the groups surveyed before war are very small, however, and we should not rely on these results too much.[22] But they clearly suggest that conflict reduces national pride, while a lack of pride does not seem to be one of the drivers of conflict.

Conclusions

All the previous chapters explored the political integration aspect of nation building, asking under which conditions an inclusive regime emerged in which ethnic minorities and majorities alike were represented in national-level government. The preceding pages focused on the identity part of the nation-building equation: Which individuals, ethnic groups, and citizenries identify more positively with the nation? In line with the power configurational theory of identity formation, I showed that national pride follows from political inclusion. If individuals maintain meaningful exchange relationships with the state, they will embrace the nationalist narrative crafted and disseminated by political elites and their intellectual allies. Conversely, individuals will be less inclined to see the nation in a positive light if their ethnic community is not represented in national-level government or even discriminated against by those in power, if it was involved in armed conflict in the past, or if it recently lost representation in central-level government.

By contrast, ethnic demography seems to matter little: the citizens of religiously or linguistically diverse countries, such as Tanzania and Switzerland, are not less proud of their nation than are the citizens of largely homogeneous countries such as Somalia and Korea. Nor is pride dependent on group size: members of large ethnic groups are not more proud of their country than are small minorities, in contrast to the arguments put forward by social psychologists and some political scientists. Overall, this chapter shows that national pride is a matter of power and politics, rather than the demographic makeup of the population.

I was not able to directly test whether causality flows in the opposite direction—that pride produces political representation rather than the other way around. But the small number of cases where I could follow groups whose political status changed across surveys seemed to support my interpretation of why power and pride go together. Another limitation of this chapter is that I could not empirically disentangle which kinds of exchanges with the national government motivate citizens to embrace a nationalist vision of the world. Are political representation and the sense of symbolic inclusion that it provides enough, or do individuals identify with the nation only if representation also improves access to public goods? To answer this question, a major data challenge would have to be overcome: to measure, for a large enough number of countries, how individuals feel represented by government on the symbolic level and the extent to which they have access to public goods provided by the state. Chapter 8 takes a modest step in this direction and shows, with survey data from Afghanistan, that public goods provision indeed fosters identification with the nation. But the survey doesn't determine if political representation alone has similar consequences.

Despite these limitations, the present findings make an important contribution to our understanding of nationalism. Nationalism scholars have mostly debated the origins of national identities: whether they represent recent inventions or transformations of much older, existing ethnic identities (Smith 1986); whether they emerged because the rise of mass printing and the spread of literacy made imagining large-scale communities possible (Anderson 1991); or whether industrialization demanded cultural homogenization by nation-building states (Gellner 1983). These are interesting questions if we are mainly concerned with how nations developed from a premodern world of empires and dynastic kingdoms. I have addressed some of them in previous work (Wimmer and Feinstein 2010).

Once nationalism has entered the historical arena and nation-states have replaced empires and dynastic states, a new set of questions arises, on which I have focused in this chapter: When do citizens adopt into the nationalist narratives crafted by state-building elites and their intellectual allies, who describe the nation as the very center of the moral universe, a unique historical achievement every citizen should be proud of? In which nation-states are these discourses falling on fertile ground, and in which ones do they not take root? Dozens of country studies have provided rich answers to these questions and have explored the consequences of national pride for voting, attitudes toward immigrants, support for the welfare state, and the like. Some comparative studies exist, as discussed earlier, that have searched for patterns across a couple dozen countries. This chapter assumed a more encompassing perspective by evaluating some of the most prominent arguments with a large dataset that covers almost the entire world. It also introduced a new theory of national identity based on the idea that collective identities are shaped by political alliances and the power configurations they produce.

7

Is Diversity Detrimental?

The last two chapters have each looked at one side of the nation-building coin: under which conditions different ethnic communities are integrated into the national power structure and how such political integration then fosters a common national identity. I now take a step to the side and focus on the role of language diversity in this two-sided process. To recall, Chapters 4 and 5 showed that diversity tends to hamper the extension of alliance networks across a country and thus leads to less encompassing coalitions, which in turn makes identifying with the nation less attractive, as Chapter 6 demonstrated.

In this chapter, I explore another, indirect way in which diversity might influence nation building: the governments of more diverse countries could be less able or willing to provide their citizens with public goods. Indeed, a booming research tradition in economics argues that diversity is detrimental to public goods provision. This in turn would make nation building more difficult, as the comparison of Somalia and Botswana as well as the statistical analysis of Chapter 5 have shown. In the following pages, however, I will argue that a diverse population does not impede governments from providing public goods. The statistical associations that economists have discovered are not causal: countries that provide fewer public goods don't do so *because* they are more diverse. Rather, as already argued in Chapter 5, *both* linguistic diversity *and* low public goods provision are influenced by a history of weak state centralization. Other than through these common historical origins, diversity and public goods provision are not related to each other. This chapter shows this in detail: once we include past levels of state centralization in the statistical picture, the association between diversity and public goods indeed disappears.

To understand how diversity relates to public goods provision, I will conclude, we have to assume a longer-term, historically informed perspective that allows disentangling and specifying their mutual relationships. This parallels other research that has shown that diversity in and of itself is not detrimental to peace (Fearon and Laitin 2003; Wimmer et al. 2009), public goods provision (Baldwin and Huber 2011; Glennerster et al. 2013), or democracy (Gerring et al. 2013). As we have seen in Chapters 4 and 5, however, it does hamper the prospects of political integration across ethnic divides by making it more difficult to knit encompassing networks of alliances. The next section outlines the detrimental diversity argument in more detail.

Detrimental Diversity

In politics, academia, and business, ethnic and racial diversity is generally embraced as a positive aspect of human life, with the notable exception of populist, anti-immigrant movements. Governments seek to attract talent from around the world to create a vibrant economy based on innovation; universities strive to create a faculty and student body that mirrors the ethnic and racial diversity of the population at large; business organizations believe that enhancing employee diversity will stimulate creativity—and help with minority costumers. On the other hand, however, social scientists find that ethnic and racial diversity is detrimental for social trust, economic development, peace, public goods provision, and more.

Easterly and Levine (1997) were the first to explore the possible downsides of diversity and calculated that ethnically diverse countries experience yearly growth rates of up to 2% lower than homogeneous states. Compounded over decades, this explains a large part of the "growth tragedy" afflicting many developing countries, especially Africa's diverse nations. Many subsequent studies have found a similar correlation between ethnolinguistic diversity and growth rates (Rodrik 1999; Alesina et al. 2003; Sala-i-Martin et al. 2004; Alesina and La Ferrara 2005; Montalvo and Reynal-Querol 2005). Economists and political scientists soon probed into other detrimental consequences of diversity, including distrust of strangers (Bjornskov 2004; Soroka et al. 2007; Knack and Keefer 1997; Glennerster et al. 2013), feeble welfare states (Alesina and Glaeser 2004; also see Desmet et al. 2010; for the most recent overview, see Gerring et al. 2015), and social isolation (Alesina and La Ferrara 2000; Putnam 2007).

According to a seminal study by Alesina and coauthors, highly diverse communities also provide fewer public goods (Alesina et al. 1999)—the focus of this chapter. They identify two reasons why this should be the case. First, individuals might not want to share public goods with people of a different ethnic background, and thus fewer such goods are delivered overall (for US cities, see Poterba 1997). I call this the "ethnic egotism" mechanism (for US-based evidence, see Trounstine ND). Second, members of different ethnic groups might prefer different public policies. For example, whites in the United States might prefer low taxes, while African Americans favor investing government resources in high-quality public schools. This in turn makes it more difficult to coordinate opinions and make decisions, resulting in a lack of public goods overall. I call this the diverse preference mechanism. Alesina and coauthors offered a variety of reasons why members of different groups might prefer different kinds of public goods. High levels of spatial segregation could lead to different needs for public infrastructure; speakers of different languages advocate their own as the official language of instruction; and so on (Alesina et al. 1999: 1251; see also Easterly and Levine 1997: 1214–1216).

In the meantime, a growing body of research has confirmed that the governments of more diverse communities indeed provide fewer public goods. This has been shown for US cities (Goldin and Katz 1999; Vigdor 2004; but see the conclusion from a more dynamic analysis in Hopkins 2011), Kenyan villages (Miguel and Gugerty 2005), and Indian villages (Banerjee et al. 2005),[1] as well as entire countries: using a global dataset, La Porta et al. (1999) show that in linguistically diverse countries more infants die during the first year of their life and more individuals remain illiterate, their measurements for public goods (similarly Gerring et al. 2015: Table A7; Ahlerup 2009; Mahzab et al. 2013).[2]

That diversity diminishes public goods provision is now largely taken for granted. Most recent research has focused on the diverse preference mechanism and moved on to explore how exactly it works. Baldwin and Huber (2011) showed on the basis of data from 42 countries that economic inequality along ethnic lines leads to different preferences for public goods and thus underprovision overall. Lieberman and McClendon (2011), on the basis of data for 18 African countries, demonstrated that members of different ethnic groups indeed prefer different public policies, especially if ethnicity is politicized and if groups are separated by wealth disparities (in line with Baldwin and Huber 2011). Habyarimana et al. (2007), however, don't find that individuals of the same ethnic background prefer the same kinds of public goods. Their experiments in a slum of Kampala show that individuals prefer to cooperate with coethnics and punish coethnic cheaters more, both of which facilitate public goods provision in homogeneous communities. Algan and coauthors (2011) also believe in the sanctioning mechanism. They find that fewer public goods are provided in the more diverse social housing complexes in France. They argue that this is because it is more difficult to sanction norm violations across ethnic divides and to coordinate demanding public services from state authorities.

Endogenizing Diversity

Before we explore further which mechanism is at work, however, I suggest revisiting the relationship between diversity and public goods provision itself. Existing research often takes ethnic diversity as a naturally given feature of the social world, similar to topography or the weather, rather than a product of history, as Alesina and La Ferrara (2005: 788–789) acknowledge.[3] No one therefore considers the possibility that ethnic diversity and public goods provision might be related to each other because *both* depend on a third factor: whether or not a strongly centralized state has emerged in previous centuries. Ethnic diversity is not an exogenous fact but is shaped by slow-moving political forces as much as other aspects of society are.

As argued in more detail in the previous chapters, strong states encouraged minorities to adopt the language and culture of the dominant groups, thus decreasing diversity over generations. Well-developed states also left a tradition of bureaucratic rule on which postwar governments could build in order to provide public goods to their citizens. If state centralization in the past leaves a legacy of both ethnic homogeneity and the capacity to provide public goods, the statistical association between them might be a good example of "correlation without causation." Ethnic diversity *seems* to make public goods provision more difficult, while in reality, both diversity and low public goods provision are products of previous centuries of state formation.

This argument is evaluated empirically in the following two sections. The first shows that the statistical association between public goods provision and ethnic diversity disappears once we include a variable measuring the extent to which a centralized state had developed before Western colonization. The second section demonstrates that highly centralized states were able to assimilate their population into the dominant language, producing linguistically more uniform societies by the 1960s. Going beyond the more rudimentary analysis of Chapter 5, I now take all other factors into account that researchers think could influence language diversity; and I improve the analysis by using two different measures of past state centralization.

The First Step: Explaining Public Goods Provision

MEASUREMENTS AND DATA

As in Chapter 5, I take adult literacy rates and railway length as measurements of public goods provision, using the same data sources as before. A third indicator is infant mortality per 1,000 live births, which political economists often rely upon to measure public goods provision. The data come from the World Development Indicators assembled by the World Bank. They are available from 1960 onward only. While it is obvious that climate, diseases, and the general standard of living also have an impact on how many newborns die, many researchers (La Porta et al. 1999; Gennaioli and Rainer 2007) believe that government-run immunization programs and basic health care infrastructure have a strong enough impact to make infant mortality a good measure of public goods delivery.[4] In any case, to make sure that results are not dependent on my choice of outcome variables, I will replicate La Porta et al.'s (1999) well-known study of public goods provision and linguistic diversity. Appendix E discusses the results of this exercise, using their dataset, variables, and statistical models, but adding precolonial state centralization to the equations.

Let me now introduce the independent variables for the main models. The detrimental diversity argument, as discussed above, foresees two basic mechanisms: ethnic egoism and preference heterogeneity. If the ethnic egoism mechanism were at work, overall public goods provision should be low where the ruling coalition is small because governing elites should restrict access to public goods to their coethnics. I again rely on the EPR dataset (Wimmer et al. 2009) to measure the population share of ethnic communities not represented in government. Note that I am here testing the opposite hypothesis than the one advocated throughout this book. I have argued that states without much capacity to provide public goods will be governed by a narrower coalition of elites. Now, I will evaluate whether political exclusion reduces the overall level of public goods provision—although the instrumental variable analysis of Chapter 5 has already shed some doubt on whether the causal arrow points in this direction. To further explore this possibility, I measure ethnopolitical exclusion in the first year of data available (1946 or the year after independence) and check whether more exclusionary regimes provide fewer public goods later on.

The second mechanism, according to the detrimental diversity argument, is that members of different ethnic groups prefer different public policies. By implication, more diverse populations should be provided with fewer public goods. To measure ethnolinguistic diversity, I again use the earliest available data, which were assembled by Soviet ethnographers in the 1950s and 1960s (data adopted from Fearon and Laitin 2003). Since most of the data on public goods provision concern years after 1960, an early measure of diversity makes it less likely that we have to consider reverse causation (diversity could result from low public goods provision, rather than causing it). Two other datasets on ethnolinguistic fractionalization produce substantially identical results, as further analyses in Appendix E demonstrate.

To measure inherited levels of state centralization, I again rely on the Human Relations Area Files to calculate the percentage of today's population that was ruled by an indigenous state before colonization. As discussed in Chapter 5, these data are available for only half of the countries of the world, excluding the Americas and Europe. We therefore will have to carefully assess why the statistical association between public goods provision and diversity disappears once we include the measurement of precolonial statehood in the equation: is it because the sample shrinks to Africa and Asia or because precolonial statehood is indeed an important factor to consider, as my argument has it?

We also need to take other characteristics of a country into account that might influence public goods provision. Recent work in political science has shown that democracies are more likely to provide public goods to their citizens because rulers have incentives to curry the favor of voters (see Golden and Min 2013: 75). As in Chapter 5, I use the combined autocracy and democracy score from the Polity IV project, which ranges from –10 for total autocracies to +10 for full democracies. Other strands in the literature (Ross 2012) suggest that oil-rich countries provide fewer public goods because their rulers are prone to siphoning off state resources into their own pockets rather than investing them in the common good. I add a measurement of oil production per capita (data from Wimmer and Min 2006). We obviously also need to take into account whether a country is rich or poor (using GDP per capita as a measurement). Rich countries will have the necessary means to build health clinics, educate the population, and construct railways. Some authors think that "artificial" states that were cobbled together without much continuity with historical states or provinces will have less integrated bureaucracies and are thus less efficient at providing public goods (Somalia would be a case in point; see Englebert 2000; Bockstette et al. 2002). To explore this argument, I measure the number of years with constant borders since 1816 (data are from Wimmer and Min 2006).

I also add the chronological year as a variable to capture possible time trends. There could be a global, general upward trend as citizens around the world increasingly expect their governments to provide them with public goods. Finally, public goods provision is also influenced by economic modernization. Individuals in industrialized economies demand public goods from the state. In agricultural societies, families or village communities still assume many state functions, for example by maintaining local roads or wells. I introduce a variable that measures the GDP share of agriculture (from the World Bank Development Indicator data suit). These data are unfortunately available only from 1960 onward. I will thus run all models with and without the share of agriculture variable. This will ensure that we don't arrive at the results because we drop all observations before 1960, as we have to do when considering this factor.

For each of the three dependent variables, one additional factor is considered. Literacy rates may vary with the size of the population. The per capita cost of teaching a person to read and write could be lower in large countries, thus leading to economies of scale. Or, quite the opposite, a very large population might discourage the government from teaching everybody to read and write. For railroad density, we need to take topography into account. It is more difficult to build railways in Nepal than in the Netherlands. The most effective variable turned out to be steepness of terrain, measured as the difference between the highest and lowest elevations in a country (these data are from Fearon and Laitin 2003). As mentioned earlier, climate and diseases also affect infant mortality. I add a measurement of the risk of being infected by fatal malaria (the data refer to 1990 and are from Sachs 2003).

MODELING STRATEGY AND RESULTS

To test the main hypothesis, I have to proceed step by step because the universe of country-years differs from one statistical model to the next, depending on which variables we include. As mentioned previously, we are forced to exclude many countries because information on precolonial state centralization is only meaningful for Asia and Africa and data on the GDP share of agriculture is missing before 1960. We want to make sure that changes in the results are because we considered an additional country characteristic and not because we changed the pool of countries or years under consideration.

In the first step, I run a model with all independent variables that are available for all countries and years, leaving out the GDP share of agriculture and precolonial state centralization.[5] A second model adds the GDP share of agriculture, which limits the data universe to years after 1960. In a second step, I reduce the sample to the African and Asian countries that do have data on the precolonial statehood variable without, however, adding this variable at this point. This is to ensure that the analysis of how diversity relates to public goods is not affected by changing the universe of cases. These models are again run both with and without the GDP share of agriculture variable, thus producing a set of two models. In the third step, the equations include the precolonial statehood variable but not ethnic fractionalization. This model will tell us whether centralized states in the past enhance public goods provision in the present when not considering that diversity might affect public goods as well. The last and analytically crucial step includes both fractionalization and precolonial statehood. I hope to show that the association between fractionalization and public goods provision is no longer statistically significant if we consider how previous levels of state formation affect both.

Tables 7.1–7.3 show the results, each table referring to a different measurement of public goods as the dependent variable. Before I proceed to the main analysis of how precolonial state centralization and diversity are related to public goods provision, a brief discussion of other influential factors is in order. As Tables 7.1–7.3 show, the most consistently significant control variables are the combined democracy/autocracy score, the oil production measurement, levels of economic development, the GDP share of agriculture, and the time trend. As expected, more democratic states have more literate populations (though not consistently across models), railway systems with longer tracks, and fewer newborns die during the first year, while oil-rich countries show the opposite characteristics. Economies based on agriculture are governed by states that provide fewer public goods, though there is no association with railroads. Over time, more public goods are being provided (again with the exception of railways). Richer countries deliver more public goods, again with the exception of railways, perhaps because some wealthy countries have ceased to build railways, as mentioned previously. Among the additional control variables specific to each outcome, malaria risk is a very powerful predictor of child mortality, while neither topography nor population size matters consistently for the building of railways or teaching the population how to read and write.

Moving to the main analysis, the ethnic egoism mechanism seems not to affect public goods provision. Governments that excluded large proportions of their populations from representation early on do not subsequently provide fewer public goods. The initial share of the excluded population variable is never significant in Tables 7.1–7.3. This is in line with the general argument of the book, according to which public goods provision leads to nation building, as shown in Chapter 5, rather than the other way around.

However, much seems to speak in favor of the preference heterogeneity argument, according to which the governments of diverse countries provide fewer public goods because there are too many conflicting ideas about what kinds of goods the state should provide. Both in the full sample (Models 1 and 2) and in the reduced sample of Asian and African countries (Models 3 and 4), linguistic heterogeneity is significantly associated with low public goods provision and with a quite large coefficient, thus reproducing the results of previous research (the one exception is Model 2 of Table 7.2).

The picture changes dramatically, however, as soon as we take into account that countries differ in their history of state formation. Where centralized precolonial states had emerged by the late 19th century, postcolonial governments built more railways (Table 7.2) and were better able to teach their citizens how to read and write (Table 7.1). A previous history of state formation, however, doesn't seem to affect infant mortality (Table 7.3). In substantial terms, increasing the share of the population that was governed by states in the precolonial period by 40% (one standard deviation) would increase the length of railway tracks by a third of a standard deviation and literacy rates by 6% (standardized coefficients based on Model 7 in Tables 7.1 and 7.2). The results for literacy and railways hold whether we disregard the ethnolinguistic diversity of the population (Models 5 and 6) or include it in the equation (Models 7 and 8). Most importantly, with *both* precolonial statehood and ethnolinguistic diversity in the equation (Models 7 and 8), diversity is no longer significantly associated with *any* of the three measurements of public goods provision. In other words, diversity does not impede states from providing public goods.

SOME ROBUSTNESS CHECKS

However, one might object, why does this analysis neglect the role of intervening colonial rule? Shouldn't it matter if the imperial powers destroyed, ossified, or in other ways transformed indigenous states? Going beyond the discussion in Chapter 5, we can evaluate whether different styles of colonial rule affect postcolonial public goods provision. Appendix Table E.1 shows a model that takes into account whether a territory has ever been under Ottoman, Portuguese, French, or British rule. The results are substantially identical to the ones presented in Tables 7.1–7.3. Styles of imperial rule, which differed across these four empires, don't seem to influence contemporary public goods provision in a consistent way. Neither does it matter much how long the colonial period lasted: a variable measuring the proportion of years since 1816 spent under imperial or colonial rule is not significantly associated with public goods provision (results not shown).

As an additional robustness check, Appendix Table E.2 offers a series of models that use the same data, variables, and statistical models as do La Porta et al. (1999). This is to ensure that we arrive at the same conclusions when operating within the data universe created by authors who pursued the opposite argument. I proceed in the same four steps as above but also add a model with average school achievement as a dependent variable in order to follow La Porta and coauthors' definition of public goods provision one by one. The results are generally consistent with those discussed above.

As a final robustness check, I used two different codings of linguistic diversity: a fractionalization index based on Roeder's (2007) list of ethnolinguistic groups and the often-used linguistic fractionalization index assembled by Alesina et al. (2003). As Appendix Table E.3 shows, the results are substantially very similar to those presented above. When infant mortality rates are the dependent variable (Model 6 in Appendix Table E.3), however, Alesina et al.'s linguistic fractionalization index remains weakly significant even when the model includes the precolonial statehood variable.[6]

TABLE 7.1. Generalized linear models of proportion adult literates

	Full model		With ethnic fractionalization		Without missing values on precolonial state centralization			
					With precolonial state centralization		With both	
	Without % agriculture	With % agriculture	Without % agriculture	With % agriculture	Without % agriculture	With % agriculture	Without % agriculture	With % agriculture
	1	2	3	4	5	6	7	8
Combined autocracy and democracy score, Polity IV	0.0063**	0.0056**	0.0074***	0.0037	0.0065**	0.0027	0.0068**	0.0027
	(0.003)	(0.003)	(0.003)	(0.003)	(0.003)	(0.003)	(0.003)	(0.003)
Oil production per capita, averaged Humphreys 2005, BP, IHS	−0.0840***	−0.0657***	−0.0257*	−0.0260**	−0.0266*	−0.0241**	−0.0255*	−0.0236**
	(0.015)	(0.013)	(0.014)	(0.011)	(0.014)	(0.010)	(0.014)	(0.010)
GDP per capita, Penn World Table (inter– and extrapolated, lagged)	0.2301***	0.1719***	0.0840**	0.0744**	0.0907***	0.0700**	0.0845**	0.0671**
	(0.036)	(0.033)	(0.036)	(0.031)	(0.033)	(0.029)	(0.033)	(0.029)
Number of years since 1816 with constant borders (incl. provincial), Wimmer and Min 2006	0.0024	0.0035**	0.0035*	0.0036	0.0016	0.0017	0.0019	0.0017
	(0.002)	(0.002)	(0.002)	(0.002)	(0.002)	(0.002)	(0.002)	(0.002)

Year	0.0172***	0.0326***	0.0328***	0.0330***	0.0362***	0.0361***	0.0363***	0.0360***
	(0.003)	(0.004)	(0.005)	(0.005)	(0.004)	(0.035)	(0.004)	(0.005)
Population size in thousands, Gleditsch[a]	0.0000	0.0000**	0.0000***	0.0000***	0.0000	0.0000	0.0000	0.0000
	(0.000)	(0.000)	(0.000)	(0.000)	(0.000)	(0.000)	(0.000)	(0.000)
Agriculture's share of the economy (% of GDP), World Bank		-0.0116**	-0.0125**	-0.0125**		-0.0-45**		-0.0143**
		(0.006)	(0.006)	(0.006)		(0.006)		(0.006)
Proportion of excluded population at first year of available data (indep. or 1946), EPR	-0.4155	-0.3051	-0.4086	-0.2306	-0.3854	-0.1615	-0.3049	-0.1377
	(0.308)	(0.290)	(0.338)	(0.311)	(0.383)	(0.345)	(0.378)	(0.347)
Linguistic fractionalization, Soviet Atlas, Fearon and Laitin 2003	-1.2186***	-0.8616***	-0.8448**	-0.6491*			-0.4765	-0.2162
	(0.320)	(0.306)	(0.365)	(0.343)			(0.425)	(0.382)
Proportion of population ruled by states before colonization, HRAF, Müller 1999					0.7817***	0.7011***	0.6124**	0.6348**
					(0.261)	(0.267)	(0.300)	(0.294)
Constant	-34.0030***	-64.5222***	-65.2555***	-65.4129***	-72.6296***	-71.9041***	-72.4180***	-71.5798***
	(5.996)	(8.449)	(8.942)	(9.957)	(8.261)	(8.898)	(8.228)	(8.851)
Observations	6,538	4,103	3,557	2,513	3,557	2,513	3,557	2,513
AIC	0.781	0.749	0.903	0.905	0.897	0.897	0.895	0.897

Note: Robust standard errors in parentheses.

[a]Expanded Population Data, from Webpage of Kristian Skrede Gleditsch, http://privatewww.essex.ac.uk/~ksg/exppcp.html.

*p < .1

**p < .05

***p < .01

TABLE 7.2. OLS regression on railway density

	Full model		Without missing values on precolonial state centralization					
			With ethnic fractionalization		With precolonial state centralization		With both	
	Without % agriculture	With % agriculture	Without % agriculture	With % agriculture	Without % agriculture	With % agriculture	Without % agriculture	With % agriculture
	1	2	3	4	5	6	7	8
Combined autocracy and democracy score, Polity IV	0.0555	0.0780*	0.0864***	0.0636**	0.0769**	0.0525*	0.0793**	0.0527*
	(0.049)	(0.041)	(0.031)	(0.028)	(0.029)	(0.026)	(0.030)	(0.027)
Oil production per capita, averaged Humphreys 2005, BP, IHS	−1.0553***	−1.0010***	−0.3859*	−0.5624*	−0.3955*	−0.5631*	−0.3873*	−0.5585*
	(0.210)	(0.193)	(0.216)	(0.321)	(0.228)	(0.327)	(0.218)	(0.323)
GDP per capita, Penn World Table (inter– and extrapolated, lagged)	2.3090***	1.9895***	0.8920	1.2455	0.9464	1.2452	0.8902	1.2233
	(0.532)	(0.426)	(0.588)	(0.851)	(0.626)	(0.879)	(0.587)	(0.859)
Number of years since 1816 with constant borders (incl. provincial), Wimmer and Min 2006	−0.1344***	−0.0862***	0.0002	−0.0016	−0.0207	−0.0222	−0.0175	−0.0219
	(0.043)	(0.032)	(0.022)	(0.023)	(0.023)	(0.024)	(0.024)	(0.024)
Year	−0.2634***	−0.0458	−0.0518	−0.0778	−0.0237	−0.0470	−0.0229	−0.0479
	(0.090)	(0.065)	(0.058)	(0.052)	(0.064)	(0.052)	(0.062)	(0.053)

	(1)	(2)	(3)	(4)	(5)	(6)	(7)	(8)
Difference between highest and lowest elevation (in m), Fearon and Laitin 2003	-0.0013* (0.001)	-0.0010 (0.001)	0.0005 (0.000)	0.0006* (0.000)	-0.0001 (0.000)	0.0000 (0.000)	0.0001 (0.000)	0.0001 (0.000)
Agriculture's share of the economy (% of GDP), World Bank	-0.1029 (0.088)			-0.0270 (0.062)		-0.0345 (0.062)		-0.0342 (0.062)
Proportion of excluded population at first year of available data (indep. or 1946), EPR	-5.1221 (5.465)	0.7239 (3.620)	-3.2361 (2.378)	-1.4481 (1.977)	-2.1922 (2.721)	0.0222 (2.141)	-1.6177 (2.504)	0.1301 (2.114)
Linguistic fractionalization, Soviet Atlas, Fearon and Laitin 2003	-15.4302* (8.253)	-9.7390 (6.068)	-9.1709** (4.375)	-6.8958** (3.394)			-4.9782 (4.224)	-1.3799 (3.062)
Proportion of population ruled by states before colonization, HRAF, Müller 1999					8.8506*** (2.404)	7.7875*** (2.653)	6.8673** (2.619)	7.2809*** (2.685)
Constant	554.7683*** (177.414)	114.4439 (129.892)	111.834 (113.901)	160.0065 (100.438)	50.2364 (124.911)	95.9503 (100.292)	51.3702 (122.765)	98.6135 (101.350)
Observations	6,458	4,088	3,492	2,513	3,492	2,513	3,492	2,513
R-squared	0.382	0.463	0.271	0.345	0.294	0.390	0.306	0.391

Note: Robust standard errors in parentheses.

*p < .1

**p < .05

***p < .01

TABLE 7.3. OLS regression on infant mortality rate

	Full model		With ethnic fractionalization		With precolonial state centralization		With both	
			Without missing values on precolonial state centralization					
	Without % agriculture	With % agriculture	Without % agriculture	With % agriculture	Without % agriculture	With % agriculture	Without % agriculture	With % agriculture
	1	2	3	4	5	6	7	8
Combined autocracy and democracy score, Polity IV	−0.2638***	−0.1896***	−0.2789***	−0.1889***	−0.2544***	−0.1628***	−0.2746***	−0.1668***
	(0.066)	(0.055)	(0.076)	(0.065)	(0.077)	(0.059)	(0.074)	(0.058)
Oil production per capita, averaged Humphreys 2005, BP, IHS	0.5400***	0.4795***	0.4938*	0.6050***	0.5018*	0.6078***	0.4971*	0.5931***
	(0.134)	(0.095)	(0.265)	(0.212)	(0.280)	(0.206)	(0.271)	(0.210)
GDP per capita, Penn World Table (inter– and extrapolated, lagged)	−2.0097***	−1.3817***	−2.1859***	−1.9144***	−2.3023***	−2.0152***	−2.2193***	−1.9070***
	(0.312)	(0.292)	(0.695)	(0.675)	(0.711)	(0.635)	(0.710)	(0.666)
Number of years since 1816 with constant borders (incl. provincial), Wimmer and Min 2006	−0.0100	−0.0127	0.0167	−0.0062	0.0375	0.0290	0.0287	0.0289
	(0.039)	(0.037)	(0.069)	(0.065)	(0.067)	(0.063)	(0.066)	(0.063)
Year	−1.3233***	−1.2228***	−1.7600***	−1.3827***	−1.7981***	−1.4415***	−1.7762***	−1.4292***
	(0.118)	(0.133)	(0.182)	(0.199)	(0.180)	(0.193)	(0.176)	(0.190)

Fatal malaria risk probability in 1994, Sachs 2003	40.5332***	26.6427***	34.5395***	24.5698**	39.6502***	23.5426**	33.2519***	19.4740*
	(6.519)	(6.351)	(9.279)	(9.576)	(10.517)	(11.220)	(10.088)	(10.684)
Agriculture's share of the economy (% of GDP), World Bank		0.7604***		0.7028***		0.7673***		0.7836***
		(0.140)		(0.167)		(0.194)		(0.192)
Proportion of excluded population at first year of available data (indep. or 1946), EPR	15.6947	9.5660	11.0582	5.9740	12.7886	4.3746	10.0638	2.7293
	(10.668)	(9.812)	(11.791)	(10.844)	(12.128)	(11.495)	(11.942)	(11.430)
Linguistic fractionalization, Soviet Atlas, Fearon and Laitin 2003	28.2957***	22.7812***	22.7072*	17.8383*			20.6322	13.1578
	(8.783)	(7.471)	(12.011)	(9.741)			(12.522)	(10.522)
Proportion of population ruled by states before colonization, HRAF, Müller 1999					-8.9551	-15.4265	-4.7174	-13.1039
					(10.247)	(9.456)	(10.330)	(9.713)
Observations	5,102	4,000	2,910	2,419	2,910	2,419	2,910	2,419
R-squared	0.689	0.745	0.564	0.617	0.556	0.621	0.565	0.625

Note: Robust standard errors in parentheses. Constant not shown

*p < .1
**p < .05
***p < .01

The Second Step: Understanding Ethnic Fractionalization

A crucial part of the argument developed in this chapter is that previous state centralization not only enhances the capacity to deliver public goods after World War II but also leaves behind a more homogeneous population. This was already shown, in a preliminary fashion, in Chapter 5. In this section, I explore the argument with more rigor. I will use two different measurements of historical levels of statehood and I will take all factors into account that according to other scholars could have an effect on linguistic diversity.

MEASUREMENTS, DATA, AND MODELING STRATEGY

The first measurement of state centralization is the same as used above: the proportion of the population governed by states before colonization, available for Africa and Asia. The second is the index of indigenous statehood between 1850 and 1900, which I already used for a different purpose in Chapter 5. It covers 133 countries. Since ethnic fractionalization is now the dependent variable, we have to consider what other characteristics of a country could influence its linguistic diversity. As briefly discussed in Chapter 5, Michalopoulos (2012) identified some climatic and geographic factors that encouraged different segments of the population, in the very remote past, to pursue different strategies of economic survival, which in turn led to a process of ethnic differentiation. I include the four variables, all from his dataset, that are consistently associated with linguistic diversity in his models: variability in suitability of a territory for agriculture, variability in average precipitation, average precipitation, and distance from the ocean.

As also discussed previously, past ethnic and nationalist wars could affect the diversity of a population today because ethnic cleansing and wars of secession produce more homogeneous societies. I again use a cumulative count of the number of ethnic or nationalist wars fought from 1816 to 1900 (data are from Wimmer and Min 2006). GDP per capita measures levels of economic development, which could be associated with ethnic diversity because diversity is bad for growth, as argued by the detrimental diversity school. Alternatively, citizens of rich countries are geographically more mobile, which enhances linguistic assimilation (à la Deutsch 1953).

A final argument was recently introduced by proponents of "ethno-symbolism," a prominent school of thinking about nationalism. Ethnic groups that look back on a very long history and that eventually become the majority of an independent nation-state, it is argued, will have had ample time to assimilate smaller ethnic communities in their vicinity, leading to a more homogeneous society. Conversely, majorities of more recent origin will live in a more diverse environment today. To test this hypothesis, Kaufmann (2015) assembled a dataset with the "foundation year" of state-owning ethnic majorities around the world. Finally, I add two variables that are associated with diversity in the statistical models of Kaufmann: the surface area of a country because larger countries can house a more diverse population; and the year when a country became independent, assuming that younger countries had less time to assimilate the population through the school system.

Because linguistic diversity is measured at only one point in time (in the early 1960s), the data now include only one observation per country.[7] I again proceed in a step-by-step fashion. The first model shows how other country characteristics—besides its history of state formation—are associated with diversity, using the full sample of countries. The next model does the same but considers only the countries of Africa and Asia for which we have data on precolonial levels of state centralization. The third model adds the precolonial state centralization variable to the equation. The fourth and fifth models proceed in the same fashion for the state antiquity variable. This procedure guarantees that we know whether results change because we added a new variable to the model or because this new variable changes the pool of countries under consideration.

RESULTS

Table 7.4 reports the results. Countries with a history of state centralization before the onset of colonialism are linguistically more homogeneous in the early 1960s than others (Model 3). This association is also substantially important: a 40% increase in the percentage of the population ruled by states in the precolonial period (roughly a standard deviation) decreases the chances that two randomly chosen individuals speak different languages by around 15%.

In Model 5, I use the index of state antiquity as an alternative measurement of state centralization. It is again strongly associated with linguistic diversity in 1960, and again with a substantial, though considerably weaker effect: decreasing levels of inherited state centralization by .23 (or one standard deviation; the index runs from 0 to 1) will produce a 6% lower chance that two randomly chosen individuals will speak a different language in the 1960s.

Few of the other country characteristics influence linguistic diversity. GDP per capita, the year of independence, and the variability of suitability for agriculture are significantly associated with diversity in at least three of the five models. The ethnonationalist wars of the 19th century do not seem to have shaped—through ethnic cleansings or boundary redrawing—the linguistic makeup of states in the early 1960s. Nor are countries linguistically more uniform if their dominant majorities look back on a long history or if they govern a large territory.

TABLE 7.4. Generalized linear models of linguistic fractionalization

	Baseline	Without countries lacking data on precolonial state centralization	With precolonial state centralization	Without countries lacking data on state antiquity	With state antiquity
	1	2	3	4	5
GDP per capita, Penn World Table (inter- and extrapolated)	-0.0455*** (0.013)	-0.0385 (0.030)	-0.0201 (0.026)	-0.0471*** (0.014)	-0.0453*** (0.014)
Dispersion of elevation across regions, Michalopoulos 2012	0.0598 (0.080)	-0.0902 (0.091)	0.1100 (0.123)	0.0424 (0.084)	0.0940 (0.093)
Dispersion of suitability for agriculture across regions, Michalopoulos 2012	0.9328** (0.422)	1.1390* (0.610)	0.9102 (0.639)	1.1132** (0.495)	1.2883*** (0.495)
Average monthly precipitation between 1961 and 1990 (in 1,000 mm), Michalopoulos 2012	0.0016 (0.002)	0.0034 (0.002)	0.0048* (0.003)	0.0017 (0.002)	0.0009 (0.002)
Distance from coast to country center, Michalopoulos 2012	0.2895 (0.306)	0.8367 (0.668)	1.0268** (0.511)	0.3336 (0.317)	0.2357 (0.315)
No. of ethnonationalist wars fought between 1816 and 1900, Wimmer and Min 2006	-0.0487 (0.137)	0.5852* (0.312)	0.6605* (0.354)	-0.0394 (0.137)	-0.0606 (0.137)
Year of ethnogenesis of majority group, Kaufmann 2015	0.0004* (0.000)	0.0004 (0.000)	0.0001 (0.000)	0.0004* (0.000)	0.0002 (0.000)
Surface area, Fearon and Laitin 2003	0.0000 (0.000)	-0.0000 (0.000)	-0.0000 (0.000)	0.0000 (0.000)	0.0000 (0.000)
Year of independence, Correlates of War Project	0.0061** (0.003)	0.0028 (0.005)	-0.0040 (0.005)	0.0054** (0.003)	0.0049* (0.003)
Proportion of population ruled by states before colonization, HRAF, Müller 1999			-1.6165*** (0.370)		
Cumulative index of state centralization since 1000 BC (5% discounted), Putterman 2006					-1.0139** (0.467)
Observations	143	74	74	134	134

Note: Robust standard errors in parentheses. Constant not shown.

*p < .1
**p < .05
***p < .01

As with the previous analysis in this chapter, we again have to ask if the colonial experience didn't transform the linguistic landscape in profound ways. Appendix Table E.4 tests this possibility in two ways. First, it could be that the longer colonial rule lasted, the more homogeneous a population is today because the colonizers imposed their own language as a lingua franca. However, the number of years that a country had been an imperial or colonial dependency since 1816 is not associated with linguistic diversity in 1960. Second, I explore whether styles of colonial rule matter by again comparing across different empires. In general, this does not seem to be the case as no consistent pattern emerges that would hold in both Model 2 and Model 4.

A comparison of models with and without these empire variables is instructive as well. The sizes of the coefficients and the standard errors of the two variables measuring levels of indigenous state centralization in the 19th century remain largely identical. This means, in plain English, that whether or not the Ottomans ruled a country, or the British or Romanov Russia, and whether a country was never colonized or had a long history of colonial domination did not alter the linguistic legacy left by precolonial states all that much. This lends some support to the conjecture made in Chapter 1: that colonial rule modified, but rarely radically changed, the linguistic landscape that indigenous states had already shaped.

CONCLUSION

This short chapter showed that a diverse population does not prevent a government from providing public goods, once we take into account that its capacity to do so is shaped by the previous history of state formation. Tanzania is different from Korea, among other things, because Korea looks back on a thousand years of state building while mainland Tanzania was not governed by a state before colonization. Providing public goods in Korea today is therefore easier than in Tanzania. In a second step, I showed that the formation of centralized states in the past also left its mark on the linguistic makeup of today's populations. Highly centralized states such as Korea were able to impose the language of the elites on their subjects, while the population of stateless societies such as mainland Tanzania continued to speak in many tongues. Therefore, the association between homogeneity and public goods provision that previous research has brought to light should not be interpreted in a causal way. Diversity is not detrimental to public goods provision because members of different ethnic groups can't agree on what goods the state should provide or because they don't want to share such goods with ethnic others. Rather, the lack of centralized states in the past left a legacy of *both* high diversity and a limited capacity of providing public goods in the present.

I conclude with a rather speculative remark on how this research could address questions relevant to policymakers. We cannot, of course, engineer the past to create a legacy of centralized states that would help contemporary governments provide public goods. But the association between the history of state formation and public goods provision represents a tendency, not a law. There is plenty of room for political leaders to improve public goods provision in formerly stateless societies such as Tanzania.

We can explore the possible role of political leadership by analyzing the discrepancy between observed and predicted values, that is, by looking at the countries that offer more public goods than expected, given their histories of state formation, their level of economic development, and all the other variables that went into the statistical models. With regard to at least two of the three public goods considered above, Japan, North Korea, South Korea, and Taiwan perform better than predicted, but so do Tunisia, Libya, Kuwait, and Bangladesh. Most of these countries were led over decades by strongmen (Kim Jong of North Korea, Gaddafi of Libya, the military dictators of South Korea, the emir of Kuwait, Tunisia's Ben Ali) or one-party regimes (the LDP in Japan) with a strong commitment to nation building. To be sure, this interpretation should not lead us to plead for autocratic rule. The analysis of which countries deviate from predicted values already considers how democratically or autocratically they are governed. In other words, the countries in the above list don't provide more public goods than expected *because* they are autocratic. Furthermore, in almost all of the models of Tables 7.1–7.3, democracy is positively associated with public goods provision, in line with previous scholarship.

In addition to showing a strong commitment to nation building, many of these governments were less plagued by corruption than the neo-patrimonial regimes of Africa and the Middle East, many of which appear on the list of countries that provide fewer public goods than one would expect. Also noteworthy is the political stability of many of these countries—at least until the recent wave of democratization in the Middle East.

All of the above leads me to conclude that a sustained political commitment to nation building might at least partially offset the disadvantages that a short history of statehood brings about. This is quite in line with Miguel's (2004) comparison of Kenya and Tanzania, whose government maintained over decades a strong commitment to nation building that proved advantageous, compared to Kenya, for providing public goods to the citizenry. My conclusion is also in line with Singh (2015), who has shown that in Indian states where political leaders had developed a strong and distinctive regional identity (or "subnationalism" in Singh's term), governments performed decisively better at providing public goods.

8

Policy Implications with Some Lessons Learned from Afghanistan

This concluding chapter continues the discussion of policy implications with which the previous ended. Quite obviously, this book did not evaluate different policies of nation building, but sought to identify the historical forces fostering political integration and national identification in the long run. It highlighted slowly developing, institutional factors that are hard to influence through short-term policies. This in itself already implies possible lessons for politicians and policymakers who would like to better understand the conditions under which nation building can succeed and to know what outsiders can and cannot do to help integrate fractured political arenas around the world. Other, more straightforward policy implications will be discussed in this chapter, some based on additional analysis of survey data from Afghanistan. I start with what we can learn from examining some global trends that influence the future prospects of nation building around the world.

Grounds for Optimism: A Global Trend toward Inclusion

Newspaper headlines are filled with stories of "failed states" such as Somalia, Afghanistan, Yemen, and Libya. They have become one of the top concerns of foreign policymakers around the globe, mostly because such states have often served as launching grounds for international terror organizations. How representative are these recent state failures for the world overall? Or to come

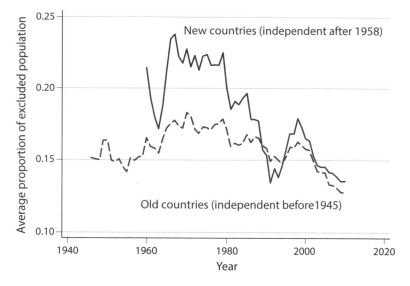

FIGURE 8.1. Average levels of ethnopolitical exclusion in old and new countries, 1945–2010

back to the operational definition of nation building used throughout the preceding chapters: Do governments around the world exclude a larger share of their populations from representation than previously, thus preparing the ground for future civil wars and the collapse of already weak states?

Figure 8.1 shows average levels of ethnopolitical exclusion in the world over the past decades, calculated across all countries. Exclusion is again measured as the population share of ethnic groups not represented in national level government. Why are there two lines in the graph? When considering global averages, we should distinguish between trends within countries and changes in the composition of the world's countries due to decolonization or the breakup of the Soviet Empire. I therefore graph one separate line for new countries that became independent from the late 1950s onward and another one for older countries that already existed in 1945 when the data series starts.

Both lines describe an encouraging trend toward less exclusion. It is a bumpy road, however, rather than a straight ride. For example, we see an upward peak toward more exclusion around 2000 because the successor states of the Soviet Union and Yugoslavia were more unequal than the countries that already existed. The general tendency, however, is clear: over a period of just four decades, average levels of exclusion declined, in newly independent countries, to half of their peak value during the mid-1960s.

In line with the theory offered here, the average capacity of states to provide public goods also increased during this period, the communicative arenas

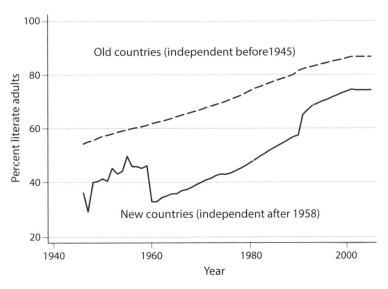

FIGURE 8.2. Average literacy rates in old and new countries, 1945–2010

of countries around the world have become less fragmented, and voluntary organizations have spread nearly everywhere, all of which contributed to improving the global prospects of nation building. Figure 8.2 gives an overview of how adult literacy rates have evolved since World War II. Again, I differentiate between old and new states. After the governments of both old and new countries massively invested in their public school systems, literacy rates improved markedly. While only a third of the population of new countries was able to read and write in the early 1940s, today almost three-quarters of the citizens of these countries are literate. Literacy rates in old countries rose steadily as well, starting from a much higher level.

New communication technologies, especially the spread of telephones in the aftermath of World War II, of cell phones from mid-1990s onward, and of the Internet during the same period, have made it easier to establish political ties across the territory of a country. Also contributing to this trend, the linguistic diversity of the average country has decreased over the past decades. Most likely, global economic growth has contributed to this development: it becomes more valuable for minorities to learn the majority language when the economy grows and the different regions of a country are more closely tied to each other (see Model 1 in Table 7.4); the expanding public school systems have certainly undermined minority languages as well.

One indicator of increasing linguistic homogeneity is language loss. While deplorable from a cultural diversity point of view, it may facilitate, as we have seen in previous chapters, building political alliances across the territory of a

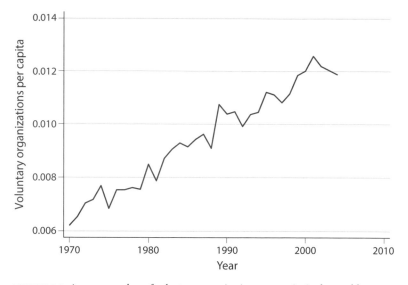

FIGURE 8.3. Average number of voluntary organizations per capita in the world, 1970–2005

country and thus nation building. As a matter of principle, sustained bilingualism (as in Switzerland) could provide the linguistic glue for national political integration and at the same time keep minority languages alive. In reality, however, many languages have been lost. According to a recent study, only 63% of the 7,480 languages in use in 1950 were still spoken by the younger generations in 2010, thus ensuring their survival. Twenty percent of these languages were no longer transmitted fully to the next generation and were in various states of disappearance; 17% were dead or very close to extinction (Simons and Lewis 2013). Using a different measure, linguists have estimated that 639 known languages are now extinct. Of these, a full 35% ceased to be spoken after 1960, illustrating how language loss has accelerated over time (Campbell et al. 2013).

We observe a similar global trend with regard to the number of voluntary organizations, the third factor that enhances the prospects of nation building. Figure 8.3 shows a clear tendency: from 1970 to 2005, the number of such organizations per capita roughly doubled, as a result of economic growth and the global rise of democracy (at least this is what Models 1 and 5 in Table 5.4 lead us to expect).

Overall, then, the growing capacity of states to provide basic public goods, the increasing linguistic homogeneity of countries around the world, and the global rise of civil society organizations have facilitated political integration across ethnic divides such that fewer and fewer ethnic communities remain without political representation in the national centers of power. Seen through the eyes of a bird that flies at very high altitude, the prospects for nation building are better than ever.

More Grounds for Optimism:
Moving off the Predicted Path

Seen from less distance, however, we might discover that many countries or even entire world regions maintain exclusionary regimes and thus eschew the optimistic trends reported above. After all, doesn't the theory introduced in previous chapters maintain that history is destiny? That countries such as Somalia that had not developed a centralized state before colonization are doomed to fail at nation building, whatever effort they might make to provide public goods or teach their populations to read and write in a lingua franca? Since we cannot retrospectively engineer centralized states to emerge in the 19th century, doesn't this book support a developmental pessimism according to which certain countries are forever caught in a vicious, self-reinforcing circle of failed nation building, conflict, and poverty?

The statistical analyses of the preceding chapters don't warrant such an overly deterministic and pessimistic view. They were based on average effects—calculated over thousands of observations—that do not allow us to precisely predict what will happen in a particular country. To put it differently, they represent probabilistic tendencies, rather than laws. Indigenous state centralization in the late 19th century makes contemporary nation building more likely but doesn't guarantee it. And conversely, contemporary nation building is less probable if no centralized state had emerged by the late 19th century, but it doesn't preclude it. As discussed in the previous chapter, there is therefore room for other factors that could overcome the handicap of a past without a state, or of weak organizational networks in the contemporary period, or of a state that lacks the capacity to provide public goods across the territory, or of linguistic diversity.

One way of exploring such other factors is to identify the countries whose configurations of power are not well predicted by the statistical models, a technique I already used in the previous chapter. I reran Models 1 and 10 from Table 5.3 and then calculated which countries are more or less inclusionary than the model predicts. The predictors used are literacy or railway density, the number of voluntary organizations per capita, and linguistic diversity. Countries that are more inclusionary than predicted are India, Mali, Senegal, Cameroon, Gambia, Zambia, Ghana, Burkina Faso, Malawi, Tanzania, Gabon, Haiti, and Mauritania. On the other hand, some countries exclude a larger share of the population from national-level representation than the model expects. This is the case for Syria, Jordan, Iraq, Sudan, Israel, Bolivia, Peru, Guinea, the Democratic Republic of the Congo, Angola, Brazil, and Estonia. How could we possibly interpret these two lists? We should not look for factors—such as colonial legacies, economic development, or globalization—that the analysis of Chapter 5 has already ruled out as possible explanations. Some other interpretations come to mind.

First, many of the more inclusionary countries developed an organizational infrastructure for building political alliances that was not based on voluntary organizations, the only variable in the models that refers to the organizational aspect of tie formation. These other infrastructures are, in other words, functionally equivalent to well-established civil society organizations (see the brief discussion in Chapter 1). Burkina Faso and Zambia are both known for their exceptionally strong trade unions with multi-ethnic memberships (on Zambia, see LeBas 2011; there are only a few such trade unions, however, and the associational density variable therefore doesn't capture their important role). The *marabou* networks of Senegal, briefly discussed in Chapter 1, may play a similar role (see Koter 2013). The Congress Party in India (and increasingly the Bharatiya Janata Party) also offers a political umbrella for myriad different, regionally and locally specific alliances between various professional, caste, and patronage groups.

Second, many more inclusionary countries were led over decades by strongmen (Senghor, the Gandhi dynasty, Nyerere, Kaunda, Nkrumah, Banda) through one-party regimes. These were committed not only to maintaining their iron grip on power but also to integrating the entire society into a web of alliances, patronage, and coercion. They often developed well-articulated and inclusionary nationalist ideologies (as in Ghana, India, Tanzania, and Malawi). Quite often, these one-party regimes built on already existing networks of civil society organizations that crossed ethnic divides (for Zambia, see LeBas 2011), rather than destroying them as did some other autocrats around the world (such as Saddam Hussein; see Wimmer 2002: chap. 6). With the exception of India, none of these countries was a model democracy, to say the least—quite in line with the statistical analysis of Chapter 5.

Conversely, many states that politically exclude a larger share of the population than predicted were ruled over long periods of time by political parties that embraced more narrowly defined nationalisms. Syria and Iraq were long dominated by Baath parties that embraced Arab nationalism, which by definition excluded Kurds and implicitly also Shii and Christians from full symbolic membership in the nation. The same holds true for Sudan's Arabist and Islamist ruling circles, in whose eyes the Christian southerners represented the infidel offspring of people who were once hunted and sold into slavery. Jordan's Hashemite monarchy privileges Bedouin tribal ancestry as a criterion to define the national community and excludes the vast numbers of Palestinians from its domains. Israel and Estonia have equally narrow, ethnonational definitions of the boundary of the people, defining non-Jewish or Russian citizens as unfit for participation in executive government. The same could be said about Bolivia's ruling elite who long held the descendants of the indigenous majority in contempt.

We should perhaps not overestimate the role of inclusionary ideologies, however. Without further research, it is unclear if such ideologies simply reflect an inclusive power structure or whether they actually caused it. Conversely, exclusionary ideologies might simply mirror and justify minority rule rather than contribute to its emergence. This cautionary interpretation is also supported by the fact that some ethnocracies (like contemporary Rwanda and Syria) officially deny the relevance or even the very existence of ethnic cleavages. They portray the nation as a harmonious community of all citizens, undivided by ethnic boundaries of any sort, to conceal the underlying political reality.

With less ambiguity, the above analysis shows that political integration can be achieved under difficult circumstances. Many of the countries that are more inclusionary than expected, such as Tanzania, Cameroon, Zambia, and Gambia, don't look back on much of a history of state formation predating the colonial period. Clearly, history is not destiny but a constraint. It leaves room for political craftsmanship and visionary leadership (Read and Shapiro 2014)—and of course for fortuitous political contexts, historical contingencies, and other important factors that cannot possibly be caught with the widely spun net of a quantitative analysis.

Further supporting such a probabilistic interpretation, I don't find consistent evidence for the idea of a conflict trap. Some scholars fear that failed nation building reduces economic growth, which in combination with the political exclusion of large minorities will lead to armed conflict, which might further undermine the prospects of nation building and economic growth, leaving countries trapped in poverty, violence, and political dysfunction (Collier and Sambanis 2016). The rather dire situations in Somalia and Afghanistan certainly illustrate what such a conflict trap could look like. But countries with a history of ethnic conflict don't exclude a larger share of their population from political representation, as additional analysis shows (see Appendix Table F.1; see also Models 1 and 2 in Table 5.1 for a similar finding). This is because sometimes an exclusionary regime is overthrown at the end of an armed conflict and replaced with a more equitable political order, as will be discussed in more detail below. Sometimes, however, a small elite and its ethnic constituency rises to power through an armed struggle. In other words, violence can lead two otherwise similar societies onto opposite tracks of nation building.

Democracy Promotion and Conflict Prevention?

So far I have discussed global trends for the prospects of nation building, which I found to be rather encouraging. Furthermore, skilled national leadership and an inclusive national ideology may overcome some of the existing obstacles and improve the prospect of building an integrated nation. But what can outside actors, such as Western governments or international organizations, do to help nation building in the Global South? First and foremost, Chapter 5 showed that democracy cannot be the primary tool to foster inclusive government. Rather, a foreign policy in the service of nation building would seek to build the capacity of states to provide public goods and help establish voluntary organizations that in the long run will encourage politicians to form alliances across ethnic divides. If the analyses offered in this book are correct, then such a two-sided policy would be much more effective than democracy export, the foreign policy doctrine under the Bush administration. It would also show better results, over the long run, than trying to "engineer" the specific rules of democratic elections in such a way that politicians would have to seek votes across ethnic divides (Reilly 2006).

The preceding analysis also doesn't encourage us to support a "peace at any price" approach. Preventing conflict is certainly a valuable goal in itself (Woocher 2009). Unfortunately, however, exclusionary regimes rarely disappear without a fight. Ethnocratic elites know that they will pay a high price for giving up their grip on the state and fear, often realistically, the revenge of those they have long suppressed. No prevention policy and no local "peace-building" initiative can overcome such obstacles. It is unlikely, to illustrate, that Saddam Hussein's tribalistic ethnocracy could have transformed gradually—under benevolent prodding by the "international community"—into a regime that would include Kurdish and Shiite elites in the ruling coalition. The same can be said about the situation in Syria under Assad, who at the time of writing is clinging to power at all military, humanitarian, and political costs. Similarly, Rhodesia under white rule showed little prospect, despite harsh international sanctions, to move toward a broad-based government with adequate representation of the black majority. Neighboring South Africa reminds us, however, that negotiated transitions away from ethnocracy are possible, if unfortunately rare.

Public Goods Provision and Nation Building: Lessons from Afghanistan

Advocating for building state capacity and political infrastructure raises the question of whether this can be done by outside actors themselves or whether outsiders should limit themselves to support local institutions (as argued by Wimmer and Schetter 2003). There is a small empirical literature on the subject. Sacks (2012) shows, using data from the Afrobarometer survey, that service provision by international aid agencies or NGOs does encourage citizens to accept the authority of the state. Outsiders can foster nation building, in other words, by providing the population with public goods (for a similar result based on experiments in India, see Dietrich and Winters 2015). I arrive at a more nuanced and less optimistic conclusion when analyzing data from Afghanistan. They are fine-grained enough to directly compare how public goods affect nation building when provided by the government or by foreigners.[1]

The data come from the Asia Foundation's Survey of the Afghan People, which was conducted every year from 2006 to 2015. These nationally representative surveys ask a range of questions about whether or not respondents have heard of any development projects being implemented in their area over the previous year. Between 2008 and 2012, respondents were also asked who they believed funded these projects, whether the Afghan national government or foreign sponsors or both. To see how public goods provision affects the legitimacy of national government as well as national identities, I analyze four survey questions.

The first asks whether respondents think that the national government is "doing a good job." I grouped the answers "very bad job" and "somewhat bad job" together, thus creating a dichotomous dependent variable (1 = bad, 0 = good) that can be explored with a logistic regression model.[2] The second question asks whether respondents remember if their community sought outside help to resolve a local dispute over the previous 12 months. Those who answered yes were then asked whom they had approached. I grouped those who sought help from a government institution (a ministry, the army, the police, a member of parliament, a provincial governor, etc.) into one category of respondents who trust the functioning of government. This question is obviously more removed from the issue of service provision than the question about government performance and therefore potentially more interesting. After all, it is somewhat obvious that people who have heard about a government-sponsored public goods project see their government in a more positive light. It is far less evident that they would also rely on government institutions, rather than religious or tribal leaders, to resolve their local disputes.

The third question refers to support for the Taliban and measures the extent to which respondents accept the state's claim to the monopoly of violence. Respondents were asked whether they have sympathy for the use of violence by armed opposition groups: none at all, a little, or a lot. The fourth question, even more removed from the issue of public goods provision, asks respondents whether they primarily identify as Afghan citizens, as members of their ethnic group, or as Muslims. This question allows us to explore the identity aspect of nation building, while the first three questions about the effectiveness of government, trust in its capacity to settle disputes, and the acceptance of its monopoly of violence relate to the political aspects of nation building. The identity question will be analyzed in a separate section.

DOES PUBLIC GOODS PROVISION BY FOREIGNERS ENHANCE THE LEGITIMACY OF THE STATE?

In order to evaluate how far public goods provision enhances nation building, we also need to consider the characteristics of individual respondents, including their experiences with corruption and the extent to which they feel personally safe. Both will likely influence how they will perceive the government and their membership in the Afghan nation. Furthermore, the province where an individual lives as well as her ethnic background may influence her perception of government as well as her national identity. Provinces might differ in terms of existing levels of service provision, the security situation, or regional structures of political brokerage. I add "province fixed effects" to the models to take care of the unique characteristics of each province. The same goes for ethnic groups, which may or may not be represented in national-level government, which in turn should influence attitudes towards government as well as national identities, as shown in Chapter 6. Finally, I also add year fixed effects because macro-political events such as elections may shape the perception of government as well as identities. In other words, the association between public goods provision and nation building will be net of the specific characteristics of the province where an individual lives, her ethnic background, and the year in which she was interviewed.

I unfortunately cannot measure the actual structures of political linkages between citizens and the state. These might influence whether or not government projects enhance the legitimacy of the state and foster a sense of national belonging, however. It may well be, for example, that such projects are more effective if they are brought to the villagers via intermediaries who are members of both local-level government institutions and traditional local institutions—for example, provincial council members who also take part in local *shuras*, police chiefs who also serve as the right-hand men of local warlords, locally prominent families that include a member of parliament, and so on. Given the complete absence of corresponding data, such mediating factors cannot be taken into account here.

The first three questions are explored in Table 8.1. In Models 1–3, I compare respondents who reported having heard about projects sponsored by the national government versus those who didn't report any projects close by; those who heard about projects sponsored by both the government and foreigners versus those without any projects to report; and those who knew about foreign-sponsored projects versus those who hadn't heard about any projects in their area. In Model 1, we see that projects funded by *any* sponsor, including international agencies, lead to more favorable views of the national government—in line with Audrey Sacks's African findings. We also discover, however, that foreign-sponsored projects don't increase satisfaction with government nearly as much—they are only half as effective as government-sponsored projects. Model 2 produces very similar findings with a different dependent variable: the extent to which individuals trust government organizations—rather than traditional councils, local warlords, or religious authorities—to solve their local disputes. Again, a government-sponsored project is roughly twice as effective in building trust in government institutions as a foreign-sponsored project.

In Model 3, I investigate whether Afghani respondents accept the state's monopoly of violence and reject the Taliban insurgency. Respondents who report about foreign-sponsored projects in their area are *more* likely to see the Taliban insurgency as justified, while there is no statistically significant association with government-sponsored projects. This striking finding calls into question the very idea of nation building from the outside (see also Darden and Mylonas 2012). Existing studies based on a different survey conducted in northeastern Afghanistan arrive at similar conclusions: development projects by outside actors do not help convince locals that the foreign troops fight for a good cause (Böhnke et al. 2015: 88). Furthermore, Afghanis don't seem to get used to foreign troops and nation builders, quite the opposite: from 2007 to 2013, the perception of foreign troops and aid agencies had decisively turned more negative, with large majorities agreeing by 2013 that both endanger local customs and Islamic values (Böhnke 2015: 45–46).

We might wonder, however, how to interpret the statistical associations reported in Table 8.1. Could it be that both national governments and foreign actors direct their projects at areas that are already more loyal to the national government and the foreign forces supporting it, as many have argued? Support for national government would therefore result in projects, rather than the other way around. The opposite might be true with regard to the Taliban question: hoping to win the "hearts and minds" of the locals, the American military might direct its infrastructure projects to places where support for the Taliban is high, rather than where it is low.

Every year, different individuals are surveyed, and we therefore cannot follow specific respondents over time to see if their attitudes toward government change once they start to receive a project or, conversely, when they stop receiving help from the outside. This would have allowed us to address the reverse causation problem in a direct way. All I can do is look for districts in which most respondents did not report a government-

TABLE 8.1. Unfavorable views of government, trust in government for dispute resolution, and support for the Taliban in Afghanistan

	DV: Dissatisfaction with government	DV: Dispute resolution through government	DV: Support for Taliban
	1	2	3
Government projects (reference: no projects)	−0.2754***	0.3072***	−0.0180
	(0.027)	(0.062)	(0.028)
Government and foreign projects (reference: no projects)	−0.2116***	0.1566***	−0.0873***
	(0.029)	(0.059)	(0.028)
Foreign projects (reference: no projects)	−0.1386***	0.1670***	0.0746***
	(0.028)	(0.057)	(0.027)
Government projects for roads and bridges (foreign projects = 0, mixed = 1, only gov. = 2)			
Government projects for drinking water (foreign projects = 0, mixed = 1, only gov. = 2)			
Government projects for irrigation (foreign projects = 0, mixed = 1, only gov. = 2)			
Government projects for education (foreign projects = 0, mixed = 1, only gov. = 2)			
Foreign projects for roads and bridges (0 = gov. or mixed projects, 1 = foreign)			
Foreign projects for drinking water (0 = gov. or mixed projects, 1 = foreign)			
Foreign projects for irrigation (0 = gov. or mixed projects, 1 = foreign)			
Foreign projects for education (0 = gov. or mixed projects, 1 = foreign)			
Individual–level variables for age, gender, civil status, education, household income, perceived corruption, perceived insecurity	Yes	Yes	Yes
Ethnic background fixed effects	Yes	Yes	Yes
Province fixed effects	Yes	Yes	Yes
Year fixed effects	Yes	Yes	Yes
Observations	32,026	20,241	24,780

Note: The dependent variable in Models 1 and 4–11 is the responses "very bad job" and "somewhat bad job" to the question of how the Afghan national government performs. The dependent variable in Model 2 is whether those respondents who sought outside help in resolving local disputes had approached any kind of government organization (including provincial, district, municipal governments) rather than nongovernmental (traditional, foreign, etc.) organizations. The dependent variable in Model 3 is sympathy for the use of violence by armed opposition

			Dependent variable: Dissatisfaction with government				
4	5	6	7	8	9	10	11
−0.0645*** (0.022)							
	−0.1004*** (0.024)						
		−0.0649** (0.033)					
			0.0472** (0.024)				
				0.1025*** (0.039)			
					0.1544*** (0.045)		
						0.1322** (0.063)	
							−0.0466 (0.047)
Yes	Yes	Yes	Yes	Yes	Yes	Yes	Yes
Yes	Yes	Yes	Yes	Yes	Yes	Yes	Yes
Yes	Yes	Yes	Yes	Yes	Yes	Yes	Yes
Yes	Yes	Yes	Yes	Yes	Yes	Yes	Yes
17,371	13,887	8,311	17,443	17,378	13,898	8,312	17,443

groups (0 = none, 1 = a little, 2 = a lot). Model 3 is an ordered logit regression. Robust standard errors in parentheses, all other models are logistic regressions. Constant not shown.

**$p < .05$

***$p < .01$

sponsored project in 2008 and 2009 (the first years in which respondents were asked to identify the sponsors of projects). The population of these districts should have held rather unfavorable views of the government during these two years if the reverse causation story were true. Even in these districts, the effects of subsequent projects from 2010 to 2012 are roughly the same as the ones reported in the table (despite a much smaller sample size; results not shown). The same holds true if I look only at districts that did not receive any *foreign* projects in 2008 and 2009 and that therefore should be hostile to the Taliban according to the reverse causation story. In the following years, foreign projects in these districts still increase support for the Taliban. Both tests support the view that public goods projects influence how legitimate the government appears in the eyes of citizens, rather than the other way around.

Models 4–11 in Table 8.1 evaluate the differences between government- and foreign-sponsored projects more directly. I also disaggregate the data by project sector. Now, I reduce the sample to individuals who report having heard about a project, thus leaving out individuals in areas without any development activities. We see that among the major infrastructure projects, specifically those that improve access to clean water, build or repair roads and bridges, and dig irrigation channels, government-sponsored projects improve how individuals see the Afghan government (Models 4–6), while foreign-sponsored projects have the opposite effect compared to government-sponsored or mixed projects (Models 8–10). Note also the interesting, if somewhat difficult to interpret, finding that individuals who report a government-sponsored education project see the Afghan government in a less, rather than more favorable light (Model 7). The overall conclusion from Table 8.1 is that foreign public goods projects might help increase the legitimacy of government, in line with Sacks's findings, but they do so much less effectively than if those same projects were implemented by national-level government.[3] Furthermore, foreign-sponsored projects alienate the population over time and increase support for the Taliban—thus losing "hearts and minds" rather than winning them.

NATIONAL IDENTIFICATION AND PUBLIC GOODS PROVISION

We now turn to the other side of the nation-building coin: the degree to which individuals identify with the nation rather than with their own ethnic or religious community. Table 8.2 evaluates answers to the question of whether respondents primarily identify as Afghans, as members of their ethnic community, or as Muslims. This question was asked in 2013 and 2014 only. Unfortunately, during these two years respondents were not asked about who spon-

TABLE 8.2. Logistic regression on primary identity of survey respondents in Afghanistan, 2013–2014

	1	2	3
	DV: Identifies with country first	DV: Identifies with ethnic group first	DV: Identifies as Muslim first
Any project (by any sponsor) in past 12	0.1709***	0.0040	−0.2075***
months (reference: no projects)	(0.034)	(0.051)	(0.038)
Individual–level variables for age, gender, civil status, education, household income, perceived corruption	Yes	Yes	Yes
Ethnic background fixed effects	Yes	Yes	Yes
Province fixed effects	Yes	Yes	Yes
Year fixed effects	Yes	Yes	Yes
Observations	17,994	17,988	17,994

Note: Robust standard errors in parentheses. Constant not shown.
***$p < .01$

sored local development efforts, only whether or not they had heard of any project. To interpret the data despite this limitation, let us assume that if projects encourage individuals to identify primarily as Afghans, this would be due to those sponsored by the government. This is perhaps a reasonable assumption since we have already seen that government-sponsored development activities enhance the legitimacy of the state more than those sponsored by foreigners. Furthermore, the government funds the majority of projects reported in the survey.[4]

The results are quite unequivocal: individuals who report about a public goods project in their area are more likely to see themselves first and foremost as Afghans and less likely to identify primarily as Muslim. There is no effect on ethnic identities. This statistical association could again be produced by reverse causation: the government could reward more nationalist and less religious villages with public goods. To explore this possibility, I again reduce the sample to districts whose population did not report any projects in the two years before the identity questions were asked. If the causal arrow pointed in the reverse direction, the inhabitants of these districts should be less nationalist and more religious and not change their identity once the government starts to become active in the area. However, the results (not shown) are roughly the same as those for the whole sample, despite a dramatically reduced number of observations. In line with the theory proposed in Chapter 6, then, this suggests that individuals are more inclined to embrace a national identity if provided with public goods by the state.

Concluding Remarks

I conclude by drawing together the various points of policy relevance made in this chapter and before. First, we should distinguish nation building from democratization. The former describes how a national government establishes ties of alliance and loyalty with a population of varied ethnic backgrounds. The latter refers to an institution that determines how citizens choose their rulers. As has become clear in earlier chapters, democratization is not a recipe for nation building, as many governments that have recently democratized have subsequently not become more inclusionary. Furthermore, quite a few democracies, including Belgium, the United States, and South Africa, have persisted over generations all the while excluding large ethno-racial minorities or even majorities from the polity. Promoting democracy might represent a worthwhile goal in and of itself; it also helps spread voluntary organizations and encourages governments to provide public goods, as we have seen, thus indirectly helping to build ties across ethnic divides. But it does not represent the golden road to nation building.

Second, I have argued that it often takes armed struggle to replace an exclusionary, minority-dominated government. Violence in the present, then, is sometimes the price to be paid for the sustainable peace that political inclusion and nation building offer. Nothing guarantees, however, that the new rulers of the land do not simply turn the tables and exclude the hitherto dominant groups from political representation in national government. The disempowerment of Sunni elites in Shii-dominated Iraq after the American invasion is an example, and many others from around the world could be cited. Insisting on power-sharing arrangements, despite all its well-documented flaws (Rothchild and Roeder 2005), might therefore still represent the best strategy for outside forces with some leverage in the local political arena (see also Wimmer 2013: chap. 6).

Third, the tectonic theory of nation building introduced in this book suggests that one cannot fix failed states or build nations within the time span of an American presidency or two. Nation building is a generational project because the facilitating conditions take time to emerge: states capable of providing public goods, an organizational infrastructure for building alliances across ethnic divides, and an integrated communicative space. Over the past two decades, global institutions such as the World Bank have focused on improving the institutional capacity and governance structures of developing countries. Other organizations, such as the German party foundations, have long encouraged the development of civil society organizations around the world. These are welcome correctives to the more erratic foreign policies that the elected governments of Western countries pursue in search of winning the next vote.

A consistent and long-term commitment to making government institutions more efficient at public goods delivery as well as strengthening civil society organizations represents the best international policy to help build nations around the world.

Fourth and related, public goods should be provided by national governments, if nation building is the long-term strategic goal. It is perhaps more economically efficient to outsource the task to private companies or to foreign NGOs. As we have seen in the Afghan study, however, public goods provision by outsiders doesn't help in building the legitimacy of a national government nearly as much as when the government itself is in charge. It might even alienate the population and drive it into the arms of armed opposition groups such as the Taliban.

Fifth, citizens start to identify more with the nation if their ethnic community is represented in central government, as shown in Chapter 6. Where access to government power is granted, national identities will develop and deepen. Conversely, no national identification will emerge without political representation. No propaganda machine and no however well-crafted nationalist ritual, anthem, or tomb of the unknown soldier can substitute for the sense of belonging that emerges when one sees one's own kind of people in the seat of government and when that government is committed to serving its people.

Finally, I have pointed to the possible role of political leadership and inclusive nationalist ideologies in bringing about an integrated political arena. While far from conclusive, the analysis offered a caveat against an overly deterministic interpretation of this book's main findings. Skilled leadership motivated by an inclusive notion of the nation that embraces citizens of all ethnic backgrounds can help build ties across ethnic divides even where the circumstances, inherited from the past, are not conducive to national political integration.

Overall, however, this book has embraced a more structuralist view of political development. It has emphasized historical forces beyond the making of any particular individual—even if these forces represent nothing else, from an ontological point of view, than the sedimented consequences of myriads of individual actions undertaken in the past. It has shown how large, macrohistorical factors shape the riverbeds within which the histories of different societies flow. It has offered a comparative explanation for why these riverbeds sometimes assume the shape of the Colorado River in the Grand Canyon, sometimes that of the meandering Amazon when it approaches the Atlantic. Dramatic changes in the course of these riverbeds are perhaps possible. I leave it to others to understand the rare instances in which the stream of events breaks out into a new and unforeseen direction.

APPENDIXES

Appendix A can be found online at http://press.princeton.edu/titles/11197. html. The two figures that make up the online appendix show, for each country, how the two main aspects of nation building have evolved over time: the population share of ethnic groups not represented in national government (measuring the political integration aspect of nation building) and the degree to which citizens are proud of their nation (referring to the identification aspect).

APPENDIX B

Supplement to Chapter 4

TABLE B.1. Statehood, nation building, and armed conflict

	DV: Proportion of excluded population		DV: Onset of secessionist conflict by included group	DV: Onset of secessionist conflict by excluded group	DV: Onset of non-secessionist conflict by included group	DV: Onset of non-secessionist conflict by excluded group
	1	2	3	4	5	6
Index of degree of state centralization between 1850 and 1900, Putterman 2006	−0.0207** (0.010)					
Cumulative index of state centralization since 1000 BC (5% discounted), Putterman 2006		−0.6285 (0.543)	6.4967*** (1.784)	2.0659** (1.037)	−1.7182 (1.653)	−0.1950 (0.909)
Proportion of excluded population (relative to ethnopolitically relevant population), EPR			0.3640 (0.329)	0.2817* (0.152)	0.5334 (0.336)	0.6480*** (0.129)
Number of groups represented in government, EPR			0.8563*** (0.143)	0.0196 (0.075)	0.2129 (0.207)	−0.0683 (0.082)
Linguistic fractionalization, Soviet Atlas, Fearon and Laitin 2003			−1.2064 (1.845)	2.1273** (0.962)	1.2927 (2.324)	1.7586* (0.958)
GDP per capita, Penn World Table (inter- and extrapolated)			−0.2272 (0.252)	−0.0114 (0.042)	−0.2512 (0.217)	−0.2322** (0.111)
Population size, averaged between Fearon and Laitin 2003, WDI, Penn World Table			−1.1909*** (0.388)	0.4977*** (0.181)	−0.4996 (0.307)	0.2482*** (0.096)
Mountainous terrain, logged, Fearon and Laitin 2003			0.1404 (0.388)	−0.0174 (0.185)	0.4796 (0.305)	0.0310 (0.175)

TABLE B.1. (*continued*)

	DV: Proportion of excluded population		DV: Onset of secessionist conflict by included groups	DV: Onset of secessionist conflict by excluded group	DV: Onset of non-secessionist conflict by included group	DV: Onset of non-secessionist conflict by excluded group
	1	2	3	4	5	6
Regime change during past 3 years, Polity IV			−12.3598***	0.0822	1.0095	0.0575
			(0.499)	(0.578)	(0.796)	(0.450)
Anocracy, lagged, Polity II			1.6219***	0.4506	−0.4125	0.5455
			(0.607)	(0.449)	(0.757)	(0.375)
Oil production per capita, averaged Humphreys 2005, BP, IHS			−0.1120	−0.0401	0.0384	0.0735***
			(0.377)	(0.187)	(0.024)	(0.021)
Ongoing war			2.2865	0.2826	−0.2259	−0.0358
			(2.634)	(1.284)	(1.806)	(0.935)
Time controls	Yes	Yes	Yes	Yes	Yes	Yes
Ethno-demographic controls	Yes	Yes	No	No	No	No
Peace years and natural cubic splines on peace years	No	No	Yes	Yes	Yes	Yes
Observations	6,650	6,526	6,315	6,315	6,315	6,315

Note: Robust standard errors in parentheses. Constant not shown. Models 1 and 2 are generalized linear models with a logistic link function and the specification of a binomial distribution of the dependent variable. Models 3–6 are from a single multinomial logit regression with the reference category being no conflict. For details of model specification and control variables, see Wimmer et al. 2009.

$*p < .1$
$**p < .05$
$***p < .01$

Supplement to Chapter 5

TABLE C.1. Descriptive statistics, time coverage, and data sources

	No of observations	Mean	Std. dev.	Min	Max	Years of data	Source
Proportion of population excluded	7,138	0.1576534	0.225158	0	0.98	1945–2005	Wimmer et al. 2009
Change in the size of the excluded population during the next five years	6,365	−0.0005764	0.1874977	−0.98	0.98	1945–2000	Wimmer et al. 2009
Number of ethnopolitically relevant groups	7,138	4.133091	6.410085	0	57	1945–2005	Wimmer et al. 2009
Size of largest pol. relevant ethnic group (in %)	7,138	0.5239445	0.3243058	0	0.988	1945–2005	Wimmer et al. 2009
Prop. of years under imperial rule since 1816	7,155	0.4749055	0.3144366	0	1	1945–2005	Wimmer and Min 2009
Former Spanish dependency	7,155	0.1677149	0.373639	0	1	1945–2005	Wimmer and Feinstein 2010
Former Hapsburg dependency	7,155	0.0600978	0.2376846	0	1	1945–2005	Wimmer and Feinstein 2010
Former Ottoman dependency	7,155	0.1185185	0.3232437	0	1	1945–2005	Wimmer and Feinstein 2010
Former Russian dependency	7,155	0.0377358	0.19057	0	1	1945–2005	Wimmer and Feinstein 2010
Former French dependency	7,155	0.1587701	0.3654871	0	1	1945–2005	Wimmer and Feinstein 2010
Former British dependency	7,155	0.2665269	0.4421738	0	1	1945–2005	Wimmer and Feinstein 2010
Former Portuguese dependency	7,155	0.0283718	0.1660442	0	1	1945–2005	Wimmer and Feinstein 2010
Former dependency of other empires	7,155	0.1861635	0.3892658	0	1	1945–2005	Wimmer and Feinstein 2010
Number of memberships in IGOs	7,151	48.02808	22.4178	0	134	1945–2005	Pevehouse et al. 2004
Democracy, lagged	7,041	0.3469678	0.4760392	0	1	1945–2005	Polity IV
Democratic transition during next five years	6,932	0.076457	0.2657471	0	1	1945–2005	Polity IV

Variable	N	Mean	SD	Min	Max	Years	Source
Democratic transition during the past ten years	6,532	0.0692441	0.2538871	0	1	1945–2005	Polity IV
Fully proportional systems	3,463	0.3638985	0.4811893	0	1	1946–2002	Gerring and Thacker 2008
Fully parliamentary systems	3,455	0.4836941	0.4998062	0	1	1946–2002	Gerring and Thacker 2008
% literates among the adult population	7,155	64.30083	30.41654	1.3	99	1945–2005	Wimmer and Feinstein 2010
% literates among the adult population in 1900	6,331	25.99416	29.33812	0	96	1900, fixed	Wimmer and Feinstein 2010
Number of associations per capita	4,628	0.0097242	0.0204929	0.0000214	0.1735801	1970–2005	Schofer and Longhofer 2011
Linguistic fractionalization	7,155	0.3812028	0.2843958	0.001	0.9250348	1960, fixed	Fearon and Laitin 2003
Length of railway tracks (km) per 1,000 km^2	7,155	19.27059	29.55708	0	153.6556	1945–2005	Wimmer and Feinstein 2010
Length of railway tracks in 1900	7,155	13.09411	26.75258	0	137.8248	1900, fixed	Wimmer and Feinstein 2010
Proportion of population governed by states before colonization	3,778	0.5321575	0.4131228	0	1	Pre–1900, fixed	Müller 1999
Proportion of excluded population at first year of data	7,155	0.1549871	0.2254832	0	0.98	Varying	Wimmer et al. 2009
Number of years since 1816 with constant borders	6,709	106.86	56.6638	0	190	1945–2005	Wimmer and Feinstein 2010
GDP per capita, Penn World Table (inter- and extrapolated, lagged)	6,950	5.968217	7.292209	0.0278672	110.3153	1946–2005	Penn World Table
Difference between highest and lowest elevation (in meters)	7,046	3214.903	2007.652	53	9002	Fixed	Fearon and Laitin 2003
No. of ethnonational wars fought between 1816 and first year of data	6,833	2.739843	3.184423	0	22	1945–2005	Wimmer and Min 2006
Political instability (change of political regime during past 3 years)	7,155	0.1220126	0.3273232	0	1	1945–2005	Polity IV

TABLE C.2. Correlation matrix (variables for Tables 5.1, 5.2, and 5.3 only)

	1	2	3	4	5	6	7	8	9	10	Observations
1. Proportion of excluded population	1										7,116
2. Proportion years under imperial rule since 1816	0.0343	1									7,116
3. Former Spanish dependency	-0.0234	**-0.4453**	1								7,116
4. Former Hapsburg dependency	-0.0615	0.0967	-0.0743	1							7,116
5. Former Ottoman dependency	0.0784	0.2569	-0.1709	-0.038	1						7,116
6. Former Russian dependency	-0.0308	0.2082	-0.0941	-0.0312	-0.0507	1					7,116
7. Former French dependency	0.08	0.1101	-0.1946	-0.0758	0.0768	-0.096	1				7,116
8. Former British dependency	0.0397	0.3215	-0.2597	-0.1011	0.0832	-0.1281	-0.2547	1			7,116
9. Former Portuguese dependency	0.0373	0.031	-0.0743	-0.0289	-0.0665	-0.0366	-0.0758	-0.0105	1		7,116
10. Former dependency of other empires	0.0399	0.1464	-0.007	-0.0753	-0.0217	-0.0954	0.0513	-0.0997	-0.0753	1	7,116
11. Number of memberships in IGOs	-0.1352	-0.2872	0.0495	-0.0019	-0.0933	-0.0485	-0.0468	-0.0814	-0.0059	-0.1093	7,116
12. Democracy, lagged	-0.2346	-0.1122	0.0552	0.0255	-0.1023	0.0657	-0.2746	0.035	-0.0668	-0.1218	7,116
13. % literates among adult pop.	-0.2981	-0.1072	0.145	0.1686	-0.0671	0.2389	-0.416	-0.1318	-0.1053	-0.0518	7,116
14. Length of railway tracks (km) per 1000 km²	-0.2658	-0.1043	-0.1354	0.3055	-0.0802	0.0462	-0.2229	-0.2263	-0.0942	-0.0518	7,116
15. Linguistic fractionalization	0.3449	0.0639	-0.1498	-0.0325	-0.231	-0.0107	0.1864	0.196	0.093	0.0008	7,116
16. Number of politically relevant ethnic groups	0.2105	0.2396	-0.1182	0.0013	-0.0574	-0.002	-0.0227	-0.0024	-0.0241	-0.0433	7,116
17. Largest size of pol. relevant ethnic group	0.0273	-0.1516	0.2234	0.097	0.0093	0.1904	-0.0533	-0.2639	-0.0675	-0.0507	7,116
18. Year	0.0029	0.0127	-0.0927	0.0279	-0.0175	0.1602	0.0425	0.0482	0.05	-0.0117	7,116
19. Number of associations per capita	-0.1925	-0.0611	-0.1001	-0.0188	-0.0821	0.0202	-0.1933	0.177	-0.0711	-0.0623	4,611
20. Prop. of pop. governed by states before colonization	-0.2022	0.0507	0.129	.	0.0956	.	-0.1132	-0.1716	-0.211	0.0205	2,507

	11	12	13	14	15	16	17	18	19	20	
11. Number of memberships in IGOs	1										7,116
12. Democracy, lagged	**0.4839**	1									7,116
13. % literates among adult pop.	**0.4621**	**0.5113**	1								7,116
14. Length of railway tracks (km) per 1000 km²	0.3055	0.3579	**0.5227**	1							7,116
15. Linguistic fractionalization	-0.0747	-0.2061	**-0.4014**	-0.3011	1						7,116
16. Number of politically relevant ethnic groups	-0.0525	-0.1183	-0.016	-0.1168	0.19	1					7,116
17. Largest size of pol. relevant ethnic group	0.022	0.0723	0.2032	0.0638	-0.1639	0.07	1				7,116
18. Year	**0.5443**	0.1689	0.2852	-0.0894	0.0949	C.0071	-0.0513	1			7,116
19. Number of associations per capita	0.3451	**0.4414**	0.3957	0.3213	-0.1253	-0.1299	-0.0038	0.0911	1		4,611
20. Prop. of pop. governed by states before colonization	-0.0659	0.1416	0.3298	0.3529	**-0.5033**	0.0792	0.3547	-0.0211	-0.0549	1	2,507

Note: Correlations above 0.4 in bold.

TABLE C.3. Country fixed effects version of Model 4 in Table 5.2 (fixed effects regression of proportion excluded population).

	Coef.	Std. err.	t	$P > \|t\|$	[95% CI]	
Democracy (lagged)	−0.017885	0.0048706	−3.67	.000	−0.0274329	−0.0083371
GDP per capita (lagged)	0.0007432	0.0004427	1.68	.093	−0.0001247	0.0016111
No. of groups	0.0130056	0.0006433	20.22	.000	0.0117446	0.0142666
Size of the largest group	0.8069203	0.0280106	28.81	.000	0.7520107	0.8618299
Natural cubic spline on calendar year 1	0.0004731	0.0002283	2.07	.038	0.0000257	0.0009206
Natural cubic spline on calendar year 2	−0.0007269	0.000257	−2.83	.005	−0.0012307	−0.0002231
Constant	−1.243277	0.4481065	−2.77	.006	−2.121707	−0.3648463

Notes: Group variable: country code; number of observations: 6,902; number of groups (countries): 154

TABLE C.4. Proportional system of representation and parliamentarism measured with the World Bank dataset (generalized linear models of proportion excluded population; replicates Model 5 in Table 5.2)

	Coef.	Robust std. err.	z	$P > \|z\|$	[95% CI]	
Proportional system	−0.0000654	0.0002122	−0.31	.758	−0.0004813	0.0003506
No. of groups	0.034444	0.0155476	2.22	.027	0.0039713	0.0649166
Democracy (lagged)	−0.8682988	0.2625135	−3.31	.001	−1.382816	−0.3537818
Natural cubic spline on calendar year 1	0.008753	0.0311605	0.28	.779	−0.0523204	0.0698264
Natural cubic spline on calendar year 2	−0.0011355	0.022851	−0.05	.960	−0.0459225	0.0436515
Constant	−19.18387	61.50296	−0.31	.755	−139.7275	101.3597

Note: No. of observations: 3,730; standard errors adjusted for 148 clusters in country code.

	Coef.	Robust std. err.	z	$P > \|z\|$	[95% CI]	
Parliamentary system	−0.21814	0.2619788	−0.83	.405	−0.731609	0.295329
No. of groups	0.032043	0.0159273	2.01	.044	0.000826	0.0632599
Size of the largest group	0.5893172	0.3790728	1.55	.120	−0.1536518	1.332286
Democracy (lagged)	−0.4979894	0.2462309	−2.02	.043	−0.980593	−0.0153858
Natural cubic spline on calendar year 1	−0.0145297	0.029571	0.49	.623	−0.0724877	0.0434283
Natural cubic spline on calendar year 2	0.0108239	0.0216516	0.50	.617	−0.0316126	0.0532603
Constant	27.07891	58.36285	0.46	.643	−87.31016	141.468

Note: No. of observations: 4,180; standard errors adjusted for 154 clusters in country code.

TABLE C.5. Parliamentary systems and proportional systems of representation measured with the IAEP dataset (generalized linear models of proportion excluded population; replicates Model 5 in Table 5.2)

	Coef.	Robust std. err.	z	$P>\|z\|$	[95% CI]	
Democracy (lagged)	−0.8144472	0.2520323	−3.23	.001	−1.308421	−0.320473
Proportional system	0.0100726	0.2669819	0.04	.970	−0.5132024	0.5333476
No. of groups	0.0354641	0.0244186	1.45	.146	−0.0123956	0.0833238
Size of the largest group	0.0347939	0.3452725	0.10	.920	−0.6419277	0.7115155
Natural cubic spline on calendar year 1	0.0277593	0.026667	1.04	.298	−0.024507	0.0800257
Natural cubic spline on calendar year 2	−0.0171608	0.0195853	−0.88	.381	−0.0555473	0.0212257
Constant	−56.50911	52.62305	−1.07	.283	−159.6484	46.63016

Note: No. of observations: 3,730; standard errors adjusted for 148 clusters in country code.

	Coef.	Robust std. err.	z	$P>\|z\|$	[95% CI]	
Democracy (lagged)	−0.8778607	0.2476084	−3.55	.000	−1.363164	−0.3925571
Parliamentary system	−0.1004006	0.6652717	−0.15	.880	−1.404309	1.203508
No. of groups	0.0339564	0.0152626	2.22	.026	0.0040423	0.0638705
Size of the largest group	0.2154869	0.3498683	0.62	.538	−0.4702423	0.9012161
Natural cubic spline on calendar year 1	0.0165063	0.0244007	0.68	.499	−0.0313182	0.0643308
Natural cubic spline on calendar year 2	−0.0088911	0.0182114	−0.49	.625	−0.0445848	0.0268025
Constant	−34.3559	48.15663	−0.71	.476	−128.7412	60.02937

Note: No. of observations: 4,035; standard errors adjusted for 154 clusters in country code.

TABLE C.6 Effects of parliamentary systems and proportional representation systems when restricting observations to democracies (generalized linear model of proportion excluded population; replicates Model 5 in Table 5.2)

	Coef.	Robust std. err.	z	$P>\|z\|$	[95% CI]	
Parliamentary system	−0.5856844	0.3751614	−1.56	.118	−1.320987	0.1496185
Proportional system	0.3511789	0.3949419	0.89	.374	−0.4228931	1.125251
No. of groups	0.1044723	0.0579691	1.80	.072	−0.0091451	0.2180898
Size of the largest group	0.0820008	0.4492789	0.18	.855	−0.7985698	0.9625713
Natural cubic spline on calendar year 1	0.0217465	0.0126619	1.72	.086	−0.0030704	0.0465634
Natural cubic spline on calendar year 2	−0.021846	0.0139411	−1.57	.117	−0.04917	0.005478
Constant	−45.39446	24.82527	−1.83	.067	−94.05111	3.262179

Note: No. of observations: 2,279; standard errors adjusted for 98 clusters in country code.

TABLE C.7. Ethnopolitical inclusion and ethnic nationalism (measured as refusal to live with a neighbor who speaks a different language; generalized linear model of the proportion of the excluded population)

	Coef.	Robust std. err.	z	$P>|z|$	[95% CI]	
Refusal	−0.0184419	0.0155537	−1.19	.236	−0.0489265	0.0120427
No. of groups	0.0289859	0.0100193	2.89	.004	0.0093484	0.0486234
Size of the largest group	0.2959445	0.5063778	0.58	.559	−0.6965378	1.288427
Constant	−1.925934	0.4603245	−4.18	.000	−2.828154	−1.023715

Note: No. of observations: 71

TABLE C.8. Ethnopolitical exclusion and ease of imagining the nation (generalized linear model of the proportion of the excluded population)

	Territorial stability	Ethno-national core	Country age	History of state formation
Number of years since 1816 with constant borders (incl. provincial), Wimmer and Min 2006	−0.0002 (0.002)			
Year of ethnogenesis of majority group, Kaufmann 2015		0.0004 (0.000)		
Years since independence, Correlates of War Project			−0.0022 (0.003)	
Cumulative index of state centralization since 1000 BC (5% discounted), Putterman 2006				−0.4748 (0.541)
Time and ethno–demographic controls	Yes	Yes	Yes	Yes
Observations	7,141	7,137	7,141	6,647

Note: Robust standard errors in parentheses.

TABLE C.9. OLS regression on "willingness to fight for country" (data from World Value Survey)

	Coef.	Std. err.	t	$P>|t|$	[95% CI]	
% literate adults	0.000183	0.0009362	0.20	.846	−0.0016846	0.0020506
GDP per capita (lagged)	−0.0085715	0.0032587	−2.63	.011	−0.0150725	−0.0020706
Democracy (lagged)	−0.0150502	0.0394823	−0.38	.704	−0.0938153	0.0637149
Share of global material capabilities	−0.3687816	1.155498	−0.32	.751	−2.673937	1.936374
Oil production per capita	0.0086757	0.0042826	2.03	.047	0.0001323	0.0172192
Population size	1.37e−07	1.53e−07	0.89	.374	−1.68e−07	4.42e−07
Linguistic fractionalization	−0.0121291	0.062872	−0.19	.848	−0.1375553	0.113297
Constant	0.809407	0.0846328	9.56	.000	0.6405692	0.9782449

Note: No. of observations: 77; R-squared: 0.2353; adjusted R-squared: 0.1577

Instrumental Variable Regressions for
Models 1 and 10 in Table 5.3

As mentioned in the main text, it is difficult to find instrumental variables that are entirely unrelated to nation building. The following analysis is therefore of a preliminary nature. For railway density, I found that the average suitability of a country's territory for agriculture (data from Michalopoulos 2012) is strongly related to railway density. In a desert, it doesn't make much sense to build a railway because no one lives there and there are no agricultural products to be shipped out. From a theoretical point of view, I cannot exclude the possibility that another, indirect causal pathway exists. It could lead from agricultural suitability to economic wealth, which could enhance ethnopolitical inclusion because distributional conflicts appear less as a zero-sum game in richer countries. Those in power might therefore be more willing to broaden their coalition. This concern is somewhat alleviated, however, since we already know from the previous analysis that GDP per capita is not associated with exclusion as soon as we control for other relevant variables (see Model 2 in Table 5.3).

For postwar literacy, the number of foreign Catholic priests or Protestant missionaries per 10,000 inhabitants, counted by Woodberry (2012) for 1923, will serve as an instrument. During that period, both Catholic and Protestant churches around the world tried to teach the populations of the Global South to read and write, most often as part of a colonial project (the data are limited to non-Western countries). As far as I can see, there are two possible causal links between the number of foreign priests and pastors in 1923 and the ethnopolitical configuration of power after World War II, both of which would make the measurement unsuitable as an instrument. It could be that missionaries were more likely to become active where the colonial government was weak, which could in turn influence postcolonial nation building. We have already seen from Table 5.1, however, that none of the measurements of the strength or nature of colonial rule is systematically related to ethnopolitical exclusion. The second possible pathway is that Protestant missionaries, as argued by Woodberry (2012), fostered civil society organizations, which in turn enhance nation building. This is why I include foreign Catholic priests in my measurement as well, for which Woodberry finds no such effect. If I instrument literacy with foreign Catholic priests alone, the results are substantially the same.

I instrument associations per capita with the number of ethnonationalist wars fought in a country between 1816 and the first year of data on ethnopolitical exclusion. Such wars tear apart the fabric of society, reduce the probability that new voluntary associations are founded, or even destroy existing ones (see Model 5 in Table 5.4). As we have already seen (Model 1 in Table 5.1), past ethnonationalist wars are not related to contemporary ethnopolitical exclusion because such wars can lead to more or less exclusionary regimes depending on who wins. Similarly, wars might enhance or destroy state capacity (which would indirectly affect ethnopolitical inclusion), depending on the nature of the fighting and the outcome. This certainly doesn't mean that no other causal pathway from a war-prone past to contemporary nation building could theoretically exist. The instrument for voluntary organizations is therefore perhaps the most problematic. The placebo tests (see below) should alleviate at least some of the concerns about whether this instrument meets the exclusion criterion and is related to the outcome through some other causal pathway.

Finally, to instrument linguistic heterogeneity I rely on the work and data of Michalopoulos (2012). Many of his instruments for linguistic heterogeneity, however, are also influencing levels of ethnopolitical exclusion indirectly through their effect on levels of state centralization in the 19th century (explored in Table 5.5). The variable I retained is the heterogeneity of the suitability for agriculture across regions. Iraq, with fertile areas along the shores of the Euphrates and Tigris and dry deserts beyond them, scores high on this measure. To my knowledge, there is no historical or theoretical argument linking diversity in agricultural conditions across regions *within* a country to nation building. As is discussed in the main text in connection with Table 5.5, there is also no plausible indirect pathway through the formation of precolonial states, which would in turn enhance nation building in the postcolonial era.

Since I found only one instrumental variable for each of the four independent variables, there is no statistical test to see whether the instruments are valid and meet the exclusion criterion, that is, are not related to the outcome through some other causal pathways. I therefore ran a series of "placebo" tests. For each instrumental variable, I check whether it is associated with ethnopolitical exclusion when values on the original variable are very high or low. This should not be the case if the instrument meets the exclusion criterion. For example, suitability for agriculture should *not* affect levels of ethnopolitical exclusion in countries without any railroads if the effect of agricultural suitability on exclusion is mediated only through railways. Conversely, if agricultural suitability is statistically associated with exclusion in countries without a single railroad, then the two variables must be linked through an alternative causal pathway that has nothing to do with railways. For each instrumental variable, I ran subsample analyses with approximately 10% of the highest and lowest observations on the instrumented variable. The results are encouraging and reported in Appendix Table C.10. None of the instruments is significantly associated with ethnopolitical exclusion in the 8 subsample regressions, thus

TABLE C.10. Placebo regressions on the proportion of the population excluded from executive government (generalized linear models)

	Sample: 17 countries with highest railroad density	Sample: 25 countries without any railroads	Sample: 26 countries with more than 90% literacy	Sample: 31 countries with less than a fifth literates	Sample: 15 countries with most associations per capita	Sample: 41 countries with fewest associations per capita	Sample: 14 linguistically most homogenous countries	Sample: 15 linguistically most heterogeneous countries
Average agricultural suitability across regions based on climate (Michalopoulos 2012)	0.8599 (1.520)	−0.5911 (0.554)						
No. of foreign Catholic priests and Protestant missionaries per 10,000 inhabitants in 1923 (Woodberry 2012)			0.1798 (0.182)	−0.8679 (0.737)				
No. of ethnonationalist wars fought between 1816 and first year in data (Wimmer and Min 2006)					0.8488 (1.041)	−0.3495 (0.237)		
Dispersion of suitability for agriculture across regions (Michalopoulos 2012)							−0.4055 (1.743)	−1.2400 (1.702)
Ethnodemographic controls and natural cubic splines on calendar year	Yes	Yes	Yes	Yes	Yes	Yes	Yes	Yes
Observations	715	732	525	456	444	712	743	684

Note: Robust standard errors in parentheses. Constant not shown.

TABLE C.11. Two-stage least square instrumental variable regressions on the proportion of the population excluded from executive government, first stage now shown

	Railways instrumented with average suitability for agriculture	Literacy rates instrumented with no. of priests and missionaries	Associations pc instrumented with no. of ethnonationalist wars	Associations pc instrumented with no. of ethnonationalist wars	Linguistic fractionalization instrumented with diversity of suitability for agriculture	Linguistic fractionalization instrumented with diversity of suitability for agriculture
Length of railway tracks (km) per 1,000 km^2, Wimmer & Feinstein	-0.0046*** (0.001)		-0.0010*** (0.000)		-0.0004*** (0.000)	
% literates among the adult population, Wimmer & Feinstein		-0.0025*** (0.006)		-0.0012*** (0.000)		-0.0002 (0.000)
Associations per capita, 1970–, Schofer & Longhofer	0.2427 (0.401)	-10.2898*** (1.4672)	-2.6186*** (0.766)	-2.9505*** (0.683)	-1.3166*** (0.160)	-1.4592*** (0.173)
Linguistic fractionalization, Soviet Atlas, Fearon & Laitin	0.1029*** (0.019)	0.1233*** (0.022)	0.1756*** (0.013)	0.1527*** (0.013)	0.5273*** (0.037)	0.5070*** (0.039)
Time controls	No	No	No	No	No	No
Ethno–demographic controls	Yes	Yes	Yes	Yes	Yes	Yes
F–statistic of first stage regression	396	377	372	385	590	491
Observations	4,417	2,597	4,614	4,614	4,417	4,417

Note: Standard errors in parentheses. Constant not shown.

***p < .01

making it less likely that they are related to exclusion through some other causal pathway than through the instrumented variable.

We are now ready to run the instrumental variable regressions.[1] I instrument only one independent variable per model because the statistical program doesn't allow for the simultaneous instrumentation of more than one variable. Appendix Table C.11 therefore shows the results of separate models in which railways or literacy is instrumented (Models 1 and 2), two models for instrumented organizational density (Model 3 with railways as a public goods variable and Model 4 with literacy), and two for linguistic heterogeneity (again one combined with railways and the other one with literacy). All instrumented variables are highly significant in the expected direction. In other words, it is quite unlikely that ethnopolitical exclusion reduces public goods provision, organizational density, and linguistic homogeneity, rather than the other way around.

All models passed the test for weak identification, which checks whether the instrumental variable is closely enough associated with the original variable to serve as an instrument. The F values are shown in a separate row in Appendix Table C.11. They refer to the first stage regression, where public goods, linguistic fractionalization, or organizational density is the dependent variable. The statistic (the Kleibergen-Paap Wald F statistic, to be precise) ranges between 372 and 722, thus well above the critical threshold of 16.38 (calculated by Stata following Stock-Yogo). In two models, I should note, some of the variables that were not instrumented are no longer statistically significant. This is the case for associational density in Model 1 as well as literacy in Model 6.

Supplement to Chapter 6

TABLE D.1. List of surveys used

EUROPEAN VALUES		Poland	1990	Sweden	1999
SURVEY WAVE 1		Portugal	1990	Turkey	2001
Belgium	1981	Romania	1993	Ukraine	1999
Canada	1982	Slovenia	1992	United Kingdom	1999
Denmark	1981	Spain	1990	EUROPEAN VALUES	
France	1981	Sweden	1990	SURVEY WAVE 4	
Germany	1981	United Kingdom	1990	Albania	2008
Iceland	1984	United States	1990	Armenia	2008
Ireland	1981	EUROPEAN VALUES		Austria	2008
Italy	1981	SURVEY WAVE 3		Azerbaijan	2008
Malta	1983	Austria	1999	Belarus	2008
Netherlands	1981	Belarus	2000	Belgium	2009
Norway	1982	Belgium	1999	Bosnia and Herze-	
Spain	1981	Bulgaria	1999	govina	2008
Sweden	1982	Croatia	1999	Bulgaria	2008
United Kingdom	1981	Czech Republic	1999	Croatia	2008
United States	1982	Denmark	1999	Czech Republic	2008
EUROPEAN VALUES		Estonia	1999	Denmark	2008
SURVEY WAVE 2		Finland	2000	Estonia	2008
Austria	1990	France	1999	Finland	2009
Belgium	1990	Germany	1999	France	2008
Bulgaria	1991	Greece	1999	Georgia	2008
Canada	1990	Hungary	1999	Germany	2008
Czechoslovakia	1991	Iceland	1999	Greece	2008
Denmark	1990	Ireland	1999	Hungary	2008
Estonia	1990	Italy	1999	Iceland	2009
Finland	1990	Latvia	1999	Ireland	2008
France	1990	Lithuania	1999	Italy	2009
Germany	1990	Luxembourg	1999	Kosovo	2008
Hungary	1991	Malta	1999	Latvia	2008
Iceland	1990	Netherlands	1999	Lithuania	2008
Ireland	1990	Poland	1999	Luxembourg	2008
Italy	1990	Portugal	1999	Macedonia	2009
Latvia	1990	Romania	1999	Malta	2008
Lithuania	1990	Russia	1999	Moldova	2008
Malta	1991	Slovakia	1999	Montenegro	2008
Netherlands	1990	Slovenia	1999	Netherlands	2008
Norway	1990	Spain	1999	Norway	2008

TABLE D.1. (*continued*)

Poland	2008	Canada	2004	Chile	1996
Portugal	2008	Chile	2003	Columbia	1996
Romania	2008	Czech Republic	2003	Costa Rica	1996
Russia	2008	Denmark	2003	Ecuador	1996
Slovakia	2008	Finland	2003	El Salvador	1996
Slovenia	2008	France	2003	Guatemala	1996
Spain	2008	Germany	2004	Honduras	1996
Sweden	2009	Hungary	2003	Mexico	1996
ASIABAROMETER		Ireland	2003	Nicaragua	1996
2006 WAVE		Israel	2004	Panama	1996
China	2006	Japan	2003	Paraguay	1996
Japan	2006	Latvia	2003	Peru	1996
South Korea	2006	Netherlands	2005	Spain	1996
Taiwan	2006	New Zealand	2003	Uruguay	1996
Vietnam	2006	Norway	2003	Venezuela	1996
ASIABAROMETER		Philippines	2003	LATINOBAROMETER	
2007 WAVE		Poland	2005	1997 WAVE	
Cambodia	2007	Portugal	2004	Argentina	1997
Indonesia	2007	Russia	2003	Bolivia	1997
Laos	2007	Slovakia	2004	Brazil	1997
Malaysia	2007	Slovenia	2003	Chile	1997
Myanmar	2007	South Africa	2003	Columbia	1997
Philippines	2007	South Korea	2003	Costa Rica	1997
Switzerland	2008	Spain	2003	Ecuador	1997
Thailand	2007	Sweden	2003	El Salvador	1997
Turkey	2009	Switzerland	2003	Guatemala	1997
Ukraine	2008	Taiwan	2003	Honduras	1997
United King-		United Kingdom	2003	Mexico	1997
dom	2008–2009	United States	2004	Nicaragua	1997
Yugoslavia	2008	Uruguay	2004	Panama	1997
AFROBAROMETER WAVE 1		Venezuela	2004	Paraguay	1997
Botswana	1999	LATINOBAROMETER		Peru	1997
Lesotho	2000	1995 WAVE		Spain	1997
Malawi	1999	Argentina	1995	Uruguay	1997
Mali	2001	Brazil	1995	Venezuela	1997
Namibia	1999	Chile	1995	LATINOBAROMETER	
Nigeria	2000	Mexico	1995	2000 WAVE	
South Africa	2000	Paraguay	1995	Argentina	2000
Tanzania	2001	Peru	1995	Bolivia	2000
Zambia	1999	Uruguay	1995	Brazil	2000
Zimbabwe	1999	Venezuela	1995	Chile	2000
ISSP NATIONAL		LATINOBAROMETER		Columbia	2000
IDENTITY WAVE 2		1996 WAVE		Costa Rica	2000
Australia	2003	Argentina	1996	Ecuador	2000
Austria	2004	Bolivia	1996	El Salvador	2000
Bulgaria	2003	Brazil	1996	Guatemala	2000

TABLE D.1. (*continued*)

Honduras	2000	Venezuela	2002	Brazil	2005
Mexico	2000	LATINOBAROMETER		Chile	2005
Nicaragua	2000	2003 WAVE		Columbia	2005
Panama	2000	Argentina	2003	Costa Rica	2005
Paraguay	2000	Bolivia	2003	Dominican Re-	
Peru	2000	Brazil	2003	public	2005
Uruguay	2000	Chile	2003	Ecuador	2005
Venezuela	2000	Columbia	2003	El Salvador	2005
LATINOBAROMETER		Costa Rica	2003	Guatemala	2005
2001 WAVE		Ecuador	2003	Honduras	2005
Argentina	2001	El Salvador	2003	Mexico	2005
Bolivia	2001	Guatemala	2003	Nicaragua	2005
Brazil	2001	Honduras	2003	Panama	2005
Chile	2001	Mexico	2003	Paraguay	2005
Columbia	2001	Nicaragua	2003	Peru	2005
Costa Rica	2001	Panama	2003	Uruguay	2005
Ecuador	2001	Paraguay	2003	Venezuela	2005
El Salvador	2001	Peru	2003	LATINOBAROMETER	
Guatemala	2001	Spain	2003	2006 WAVE	
Honduras	2001	Uruguay	2003	Argentina	2006
Mexico	2001	Venezuela	2003	Bolivia	2006
Nicaragua	2001	LATINOBAROMETER		Brazil	2006
Panama	2001	2004 WAVE		Chile	2006
Paraguay	2001	Argentina	2004	Columbia	2006
Peru	2001	Bolivia	2004	Costa Rica	2006
Spain	2001	Brazil	2004	Dominican Re-	
Uruguay	2001	Chile	2004	public	2006
Venezuela	2001	Columbia	2004	Ecuador	2006
LATINOBAROMETER		Costa Rica	2004	El Salvador	2006
2002 WAVE		Dominican Re-		Guatemala	2006
Argentina	2002	public	2004	Honduras	2006
Bolivia	2002	Ecuador	2004	Mexico	2006
Brazil	2002	El Salvador	2004	Nicaragua	2006
Chile	2002	Guatemala	2004	Panama	2006
Columbia	2002	Honduras	2004	Paraguay	2006
Costa Rica	2002	Mexico	2004	Peru	2006
Ecuador	2002	Nicaragua	2004	Spain	2006
El Salvador	2002	Panama	2004	Uruguay	2006
Guatemala	2002	Paraguay	2004	Venezuela	2006
Honduras	2002	Peru	2004	LATINOBAROMETER	
Mexico	2002	Spain	2004	2009 WAVE	
Nicaragua	2002	Uruguay	2004	Argentina	2009
Panama	2002	Venezuela	2004	Bolivia	2009
Paraguay	2002	LATINOBAROMETER		Brazil	2009
Peru	2002	2005 WAVE		Chile	2009
Spain	2002	Argentina	2005	Columbia	2009
Uruguay	2002	Bolivia	2005	Costa Rica	2009

TABLE D.1. (*continued*)

Dominican Re-		WORLD VALUES SURVEY		Ukraine	1996
public	2009	WAVE 3		United Kingdom	1998
Ecuador	2009	Albania	1998	United States	1995
El Salvador	2009	Argentina	1995	Uruguay	1996
Guatemala	2009	Armenia	1997	Venezuela	1996
Honduras	2009	Australia	1995	Yugoslavia	1996
Mexico	2009	Azerbaijan	1997	WORLD VALUES SURVEY	
Nicaragua	2009	Bangladesh	1996	WAVE 4	
Panama	2009	Belarus	1996	Albania	2002
Paraguay	2009	Bulgaria	1997	Algeria	2002
Peru	2009	Chile	1996	Argentina	1999
Spain	2009	China	1995	Bangladesh	2002
Uruguay	2009	Columbia	1997–1998	Bosnia and Herze-	
Venezuela	2009	Croatia	1996	govina	2001
WORLD VALUES		Dominican Re-		Canada	2000
SURVEY WAVE 1		public	1996	Chile	2000
Argentina	1984	El Salvador	1999	China	2001
Australia	1981	Estonia	1996	Egypt	2001
Finland	1981	Finland	1996	India	2001
Hungary	1982	Georgia	1996	Indonesia	2001
Japan	1981	Germany	1997	Iran	2000
Mexico	1981	Hungary	1998	Iraq	2004
South Africa	1982	India	1995	Israel	2001
South Korea	1982	Latvia	1996	Japan	2000
Sweden	1981	Lithuania	1997	Jordan	2001
United States	1981	Macedonia	1998	Kyrgyzstan	2003
WORLD VALUES		Mexico	1995–1996	Macedonia	2001
SURVEY WAVE 2		Moldova	1996	Mexico	2000
Argentina	1991	Montenegro	1996–1998	Moldova	2002
Belarus	1990	New Zealand	1998	Montenegro	2001
Brazil	1991	Nigeria	1995	Morocco	2001
Chile	1990	Norway	1996	Nigeria	2000
China	1990	Pakistan	1997	Pakistan	2001
Czecho-		Peru	1996	Peru	2001
slovakia	1990–1991	Philippines	1996	Philippines	2001
India	1990	Poland	1997	Saudi Arabia	2003
Japan	1990	Romania	1998	South Africa	2001
Mexico	1990	Russia	1995	South Korea	2001
Nigeria	1990	Slovakia	1998	Spain	2000
Poland	1989	Slovenia	1995	Sweden	1999
Russia	1990	South Africa	1996	Tanzania	2001
South Africa	1990	South Korea	1996	Turkey	2001
South Korea	1990	Spain	1995	Uganda	2001
Spain	1990	Sweden	1996	United States	1999
Switzerland	1990	Switzerland	1996	Venezuela	2000
Turkey	1990	Turkey	1996	Vietnam	2001

TABLE D.1. (*continued*)

Yugoslavia	2001	Poland	2005	Iraq	2013
Zimbabwe	2001	Romania	2005	Japan	2010
WORLD VALUES SURVEY		Russia	2006	Jordan	2014
WAVE 5		Rwanda	2007	Kazakhstan	2011
Argentina	2006	Slovenia	2005	Kuwait	2013
Australia	2005	South Africa	2006	Kyrgyzstan	2011
Brazil	2006	South Korea	2005	Lebanon	2013
Bulgaria	2005	Spain	2007	Libya	2013
Burkina Faso	2007	Sweden	2006	Malaysia	2011
Canada	2006	Switzerland	2007	Mexico	2012
Chile	2006	Taiwan	2006	Morocco	2011
China	2007	Thailand	2007	Netherlands	2012
Columbia	2005	Trinidad and To-		New Zealand	2011
Egypt	2008	bago	2006	Nigeria	2011
Ethiopia	2007	Turkey	2007	Pakistan	2012
Finland	2005	Ukraine	2006	Peru	2012
France	2006	United Kingdom	2005	Philippines	2012
Georgia	2009	United States	2006	Poland	2012
Germany	2006	Uruguay	2006	Romania	2012
Ghana	2007	Vietnam	2006	Russia	2011
Guatemala	2004	Yugoslavia	2005	Rwanda	2012
Hungary	2009	Zambia	2007	Slovenia	2011
India	2006	WORLD VALUES SURVEY		South Korea	2010
Indonesia	2006	WAVE 6		Spain	2011
Iran	2007	Algeria	2014	Sweden	2011
Iraq	2006	Armenia	2011	Taiwan	2012
Italy	2005	Australia	2012	Trinidad and To-	
Japan	2005	Azerbaijan	2011	bago	2010
Jordan	2007	Belarus	2011	Tunisia	2013
Malaysia	2006	Chile	2011	Turkey	2011
Mali	2007	China	2012	Ukraine	2011
Mexico	2005	Columbia	2012	United States	2011
Moldova	2006	Ecuador	2013	Uruguay	2011
Morocco	2007	Egypt	2012	Uzbekistan	2011
Netherlands	2006	Estonia	2011	Yemen	2013
New Zealand	2004	Germany	2013	Zimbabwe	2011
Norway	2007	Ghana	2011		

TABLE D.2. Summary statistics

	Number of observations	Mean	Standard deviation	Minimum	Maximum
Gender: 0 = missing, 1 = female, 2 = male	771,502	1.470381	0.5112429	0	2
Age in years: 0 = missing	771,049	41.03269	16.80329	0	108
Education: 0 = missing, 1 = primary or less, 2 = secondary, 3 = postsecondary	771,530	1.850169	0.7932022	0	3
Civil status: 0 = missing, 1 = not married, 2 = married	771,530	1.565358	0.5562626	0	2
Politics important: 0 = missing, 1 = not, 2 = yes	771,530	1.219854	0.6451267	0	2
Religion important: 0 = missing, 1 = not, 2 = yes	771,530	1.352786	0.5716487	0	2
Class: 0 = missing, 1 = lower or middle class, 2 = upper class	771,530	0.8760917	0.6405518	0	2
Group size as a proportion of total population, EPR	170,467	0.5705205	0.3135468	0.0004	0.979
Group representatives dominate regional/provincial government, EPR	170,467	0.0202385	0.1408156	0	1
Group representatives neither in central nor regional government, EPR	170,467	0.0947456	0.2928641	0	1
Group members political discriminated against, EPR	170,467	0.0157919	0.12467	0	1
Status loss, EPR	170,467	0.0930679	0.2905284	0	1
Number of ethnic conflicts in group history since 1946, EPR	170,467	0.0703773	0.3219461	0	4
Size of excluded population, EPR	768,244	0.1331004	0.1610572	0	0.89
Powersharing: 0 = no, 1 = yes, EPR	768,244	0.2617827	0.4396053	0	1
Number of ethnic armed conflicts in country history since 1946, UCDP	768,244	0.6232161	1.286968	0	8
Percentage share of global material capabilities, logged, Correlates of War Project	771,530	-1.035625	1.700875	-10.3783	2.988596
Military expenditures in 1000s of current USD, extended 2007-, logged, Correlates of War Project	771,530	7.357169	2.533796	-13.81551	13.22233
Number of years since 1816 with constant borders (incl. provincial), Wimmer and Min 2006	768,244	0.2261873	54.83072	-143	56
Years since foundation of first national organization (means centered), Wimmer and Min 2006	768,244	0.3243084	54.37251	-105	103
Former British dependency	768,244	0.1631916	0.3695407	0	1
Percentage Muslim population in 2010, PEW	768,244	24.1924	28.54804	0	99
No. of wars fought since 1816, Wimmer and Min 2006	771,530	5.883761	5.093534	0	34
Average combined autocracy/democracy score since 1816, Polity II	768,244	0.7181838	4.659064	-10	10
Proportional or mixed electoral system, extended from 2005-, IAEP	768,244	0.7828607	0.4122985	0	1
Federation or federal system, extended from 2005-, IAEP	768,244	0.6092114	0.4879274	0	1

TABLE D.3. Exploring candidate country–level control variables (DV: pride in country)

Model	Variable	Coef.	Individual–level variables
1	Index of global integration, extended 2012–, KOF	0.0008 (−0.001)	Yes
2	Population size, interpolated, logged, WDI	0.0736 (−0.057)	Yes
3	No. of wars fought since 1816, Wimmer and Min 2006	0.0411* (−0.024)	Yes
4	Percentage share of global material capabilities, logged, Correlates of War Project	−0.0881 (−0.059)	Yes
5	GDP per capita in constant USD, inter- and extrapolated, logged, WDI	0.0029 (−0.035)	Yes
6	Former British dependency, Wimmer and Feinstein 2010	0.2641*** (−0.038)	Yes
7	Number of years since 1816 with constant borders (incl. provincial), Wimmer and Min 2006	0.0024** (−0.001)	Yes
8	Years since foundation of first national organization (means centered), Wimmer and Feinstein 2010	0.0023** (−0.001)	Yes
9	Percentage Muslim population in 2010, PEW	0.0019*** (−0.001)	Yes
10	Percentage literate adults UNESCO, Wimmer and Feinstein 2010, interpolated and extended	−0.0005 (−0.003)	Yes
11	Military expenditures in 1000s of current USD, extended 2007–, logged, Correlates of War Project	−0.0099 (−0.008)	Yes
12	Axis power during World War II (1 = yes)	−(0.4033*** (−0.067)	Yes
13	Number of wars lost since 1816, Correlates of War Project	−0.02223 (0.019)	Yes
14	Proportional or mixed electoral system, extended from 2005–, IAEP	0.0619 (−0.068)	Yes
15	Federation or federal system, extended from 2005–, IAEP	−0.0868*** (−0.028)	Yes
16	Human Development Index, interpolated, UNDP	0.2923* (−0.17)	Yes
17	Religious fractionalization, Fearon and Laitin 2003	−0.2772** (−0.123)	Yes
18	Years since independence, Correlates of War Project	0.0023** (−0.001)	Yes
19	Former or current communist country	−0.2024*** (−0.058)	Yes
20	Former German dependency, Wimmer and Feinstein 2010	0.0972 (−0.077)	Yes
21	Average combined autocracy/democracy score since 1816, Polity II	−0.0151*** (−0.005)	Yes
22	Independence achieved through war (1 = yes)	0.0448 (−0.05)	Yes

TABLE D.3. (*continued*)

Model	Variable	Coef.	Individual–level variables
23	Linguistic fractionalization, Fearon and Laitin 2003	0.1883** (−0.089)	Yes
24	Combined autocracy (−10) to democracy (+10) score (interpolated), Polity II	0.003 (−0.004)	Yes
25	Gini index of inequality, interpolated, UNU Wider, WDI for some countries	−0.0011 (−0.002)	Yes
26	Landlocked country (1 = yes)	0.0248 (−0.055)	Yes

Note: Standard errors in parentheses. Constant not shown.
*$p < .1$
**$p < .05$
***$p < .01$

Matching Ethnic Categories from the Surveys to the EPR Dataset

We were able to connect the ethnic background information in the surveys with the ethnic categories listed in the EPR dataset for a total of 224 groups in 64 countries. This represents roughly a third of the 758 ethnic groups that the EPR lists for the entire world from 1946 to 2010. The 64 countries amount to a little less than half of the 157 countries covered by the EPR dataset. Out of the 1,569 ethnic categories that were listed in any of the surveys, 164 came from countries without EPR categories to match because EPR considers ethnicity not to be politically relevant there. Of the 1,405 remaining survey categories, we were able to match 671, or roughly 50%, with EPR categories.

Since the categories listed in EPR vary over time, we made sure we used the list of EPR categories for the survey year. We took advantage of the fact that many systems of ethnic categorization are segmentally nested, as Figure D.1 illustrates with the ethnic categories of the United States. Several lower-level categories combine on a higher level into a more encompassing category, which in turn might aggregate into an even broader category at a third level of differentiation, and so on.

This allows using many-to-one and one-to-many matching for the following situations. We matched many-to-one if the matched EPR category represented a higher-level category. For example, the Latinobarometer survey differentiates between Mestizos and whites in Nicaragua, while the EPR lists only "Nicaraguans (Mestizo)." On that higher level of categorical differentiation, white Nicaraguans would certainly identify with the "Nicaraguan" category.

TABLE D.4. Building a model with country-level control variables (DV: pride in country)

	1	2
Individual–level variables	Yes	Yes
No. of wars fought since 1816, Wimmer and Min 2006	0.0170	
	(0.017)	
Number of years since 1816 with constant borders (incl. provincial), Wimmer and Min 2006	0.0020**	0.0024**
	(0.001)	(0.001)
Years since foundation of first national organization (means centered), Wimmer and Feinstein 2010	0.0016	
	(0.001)	
Former British dependency, Wimmer and Feinstein 2010	0.3826***	0.2796***
	(0.096)	(0.048)
Percentage Muslim population in 2010, PEW	0.0018	
	(0.001)	
Axis power during World War II (1 = yes)	-0.2216**	-0.2312***
	(0.091)	(0.075)
Federation or federal system, extended from 2005–, IAEP	-0.0816***	-0.0864***
	(0.025)	(0.026)
Human Development Index, interpolated, UNDP	-0.4437	
	(0.382)	
Religious fractionalization, Fearon and Laitin 2003	-0.1374	
	(0.137)	
Years since independence, Correlates of War Project	0.0010	
	(0.001)	
Former or current communist country	0.0922	
	(0.120)	
Average combined autocracy/democracy score since 1816, Polity II	-0.0061	
	(0.007)	
Linguistic fractionalization, Fearon and Laitin 2003	0.0345	
	(0.106)	
Number of individuals	767,759	767,759
Number of countries	123	123

Note: Standard errors in parentheses. Constant not shown.

**$p < .05$

***$p < .01$

We therefore gave all respondents who identified as white or as Mestizo in the survey the power status of the EPR category Nicaraguans. In the Netherlands, to give another example, the EPR lists "post-colonial immigrants," while the ISS of 1995 has Creole, Surinamese/Sranan, and Metis, all of which were assigned the political status of the "post-colonial immigrants" category.

Conversely, we matched one-to-many if a higher-level category was listed in the survey data, while EPR contained a series of lower-level categories. This was the case, for example, for the various indigenous groups in Panama, of

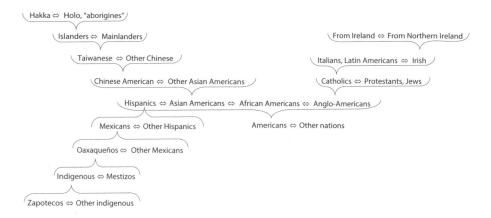

FIGURE D.1. Example of a nested system of ethnic classification

which the EPR lists Kuna Yala, Emberá-Drua, Kuna de Madungandi, Ngöbe-Buglé, and Kuna de Wargandi. The Latinobarometer survey of 2009, however, lists only the category "indigenous." If the EPR groups all had the same power status, that status was assigned to the higher-level survey category; if they differed, we assigned the power status of the most populous EPR category, which was the Kuna Yala in the Panamanian example.

I should also mention that in many cases, the ethnic background questions in the surveys were of poor quality, a problem especially with the WVS and the ISS. This was the case for 22 ethnic categories in the final dataset. We marked these with a dummy variable and ran the group-level analysis without these cases; the results remained substantially very similar.

Coding of Individual-Level Variables across Datasets

Age (continuous): Missing data coded as 0. In addition to the continuous variable, a dummy variable was included in each model with 1 indicating that age was missing and 0 indicating that it was not.

Education (categorical): 0 = missing, 1 = primary education or less, 2 = at least some secondary education, 3 = at least some postsecondary education.

Religiosity (categorical): 0 = missing, 1 = not religious, 2 = religious. Individuals are coded as religious if they attended religious services at least once a month or, if no information about religious attendance was available, if they identified as very practicing or practicing.

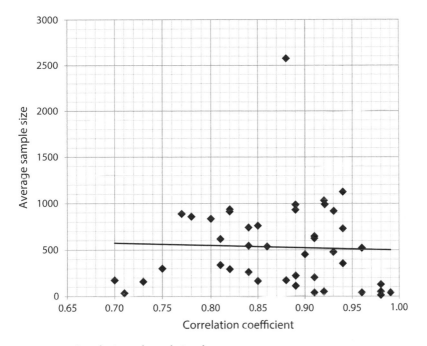

FIGURE D.2. Sample size and correlations between average responses across surveys.
Note: Average sample size of 43 status groups for which two different surveys were available, and the correlation coefficient between the responses in the two samples.

Marital status (categorical): 0 = missing, 1 = not married, 2 = married. People who are separated, widowed, or divorced are treated as not married, while people who are living with a partner but not legally married are treated as married.

Gender (categorical): 0 = missing, 1 = female, 2 = male.

Politics is important to respondent (categorical): 0 = missing, 1 = not important, 2 = important. Politics is coded as important if the respondent is somewhat or very interested in politics or, if that is missing, if the respondent often discusses politics or considers political circles important.

Subjective social class (categorical): 0 = missing, 1 = middle or below, 2 = upper. Repondents were coded as upper class if they indicated that they were upper or upper-middle class, or that they had living conditions better or much better than others, or if they described their standard of living as relatively high or high, or if they said social class was 8 or higher on a 10-point scale.

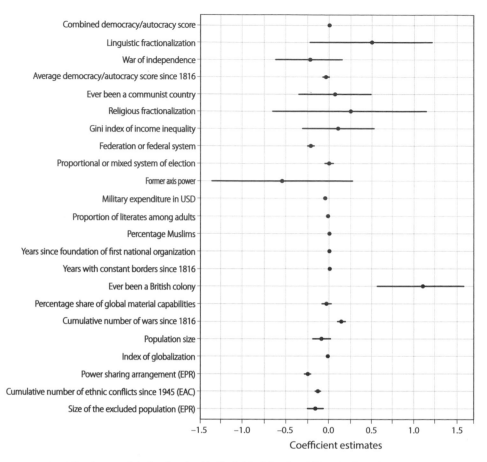

FIGURE D.3. A Boolean model of national pride (individual-level variables not shown)

A Boolean Model of Country-Level Variables (Implemented in STAN)

Figure D.3 relates to Model 2 of Table 6.2 in the main text. It uses a different estimation technique, based on a statistical program called STAN, and a different set of control variables chosen through a Boolean technique. Only country-level variables are shown in this figure.

Supplement to Chapter 7

TABLE E.1. Models 7, 8, and 9 of Tables 7.1–7.3 with controls for colonial rulers

	DV: Railway density		DV: Proportion adult literates		DV: Infant mortality	
	(1)	(2)	(3)	(4)	(5)	(6)
	With precolonial stateness	With % agriculture & precolonial stateness	With precolonial stateness	With % agriculture & precolonial stateness	With precolonial stateness	With % agriculture & precolonial stateness
Former Ottoman dependency, Wimmer and Feinstein 2010	-5.2229*	-3.8146	-0.1682	-0.1722	1.5793	4.3617
	(3.130)	(3.504)	(0.305)	(0.323)	(10.585)	(10.197)
Former French dependency, Wimmer and Feinstein 2010	-2.1077	-0.3549	-0.5722**	-0.7717***	-1.2355	5.1140
	(1.920)	(1.878)	(0.253)	(0.230)	(8.216)	(6.886)
Former British dependency, Wimmer and Feinstein 2010	-0.1541	1.4855	0.0001	0.0830	-6.7656	-4.8120
	(2.190)	(2.061)	(0.264)	(0.245)	(8.966)	(8.139)
Former Portuguese dependency, Wimmer and Feinstein 2010	0.9769	2.8493	-0.3286	-0.3054	9.4441	8.9769
	(1.916)	(1.877)	(0.224)	(0.256)	(13.776)	(16.161)
Combined autocracy and democracy score, Polity IV	0.0742**	0.0457*	0.0062**	0.0017	-0.2567***	-0.1422***
	(0.030)	(0.027)	(0.003)	(0.002)	(0.070)	(0.051)
Oil production per capita, averaged Humphreys 2005, BP, IHS	-0.3912*	-0.5710*	-0.0248*	-0.0208**	0.5293*	0.5993***
	(0.211)	(0.316)	(0.013)	(0.009)	(0.287)	(0.222)
GDP per capita, Penn World Table (inter– and extrapolated, lagged)	0.8702	1.2157	0.0787**	0.0511*	-2.2696***	-1.8245**
	(0.574)	(0.833)	(0.033)	(0.027)	(0.777)	(0.735)
Number of years since 1816 with constant borders (incl. provincial), Wimmer and Min 2006	-0.0239	-0.0237	0.0021	0.0016	0.0188	0.0261
	(0.022)	(0.023)	(0.002)	(0.002)	(0.071)	(0.066)
Year	-0.0248	-0.0525	0.0376***	0.0378***	-1.7732***	-1.4395***
	(0.061)	(0.055)	(0.004)	(0.005)	(0.177)	(0.187)
	(0.061)	(0.055)	(0.004)	(0.005)	(0.177)	(0.187)

	(1)	(2)	(3)	(4)	(5)	(6)
Agriculture's share of the economy (% of GDP), World Bank	−1.3242	−0.0513		−0.0172***		0.8264***
	(2.437)	(0.052)		(0.006)		(0.195)
Proportion of excluded pop. at first year of available data (indep. or 1946), EPR		0.7846	−0.3799	−0.2124	8.3312	1.5169
		(1.997)	(0.365)	(0.320)	(11.918)	(11.324)
Linguistic fractionalization, Soviet Atlas, Fearon and Laitin 2003	−8.0310	−3.4910	−0.5398	−0.2706	22.9198	16.7270
	(5.511)	(4.068)	(0.453)	(0.427)	(14.441)	(11.894)
Proportion of population ruled by states before colonization, HRAF, Müller 1999	6.0365**	7.4771***	0.6880**	0.5479*	−5.2226	−12.6313
	(2.781)	(2.776)	(0.308)	(0.295)	(10.628)	(10.701)
Difference between highest and lowest elevation (in m), Fearon and Laitin 2003	−0.0000	0.0001	0.0000	0.0000		
	(0.000)	(0.000)	(0.000)	(0.000)		
Population size in thousands, Gleditsch[a]					31.3109**	
					(12.333)	
Malaria prevalence in 1994, Sachs 2003						16.4382
						(13.366)
Constant	59.3236	109.1287	−74.6977***	−74.7161***	3,583.2219***	2,908.1966***
	(120.958)	(107.815)	(7.790)	(9.055)	(348.382)	(368.793)
Observations	3,489	2,513	3,554	2,513	2,910	2,419
R-squared	0.336	0.413	0.413	0.571	0.571	0.636

Note: Robust standard errors in parentheses.

[a] Expanded Population Data from Webpage of Kristian Skrede Gleditsch, http://privatewww.essex.ac.uk/~ksg/exppop.html.

*p < .1
**p < .05
***p < .01

TABLE E.2. Robustness tests with La Porta's dataset: OLS regressions on illiteracy, infant mortality, and school attainment

	Full models			Without countries lacking data on stateness		
	DV: Illiteracy	DV: Infant mortality	DV: School attainment	DV: Illiteracy	DV: Infant mortality	DV: School attainment
	1	2	3	4	5	6
Ethnolinguistic fractionalization	12.6838***	0.4052***	−0.1813	16.7753**	0.3510*	−0.0806
	(4.711)	(0.117)	(0.115)	(7.889)	(0.188)	(0.205)
Share of Muslim population in 1980	0.1491***	0.0038***	−0.0038***	0.2313***	0.0018	−0.0006
	(0.052)	(0.001)	(0.001)	(0.078)	(0.002)	(0.002)
Share of Catholic population in 1980	−0.0920	−0.0010	0.0009	−0.0743	0.0013	0.0071**
	(0.057)	(0.001)	(0.001)	(0.133)	(0.003)	(0.003)
Socialist legal tradition	−8.8806	0.0133	0.3984*	−4.8974	0.0228	
	(7.649)	(0.145)	(0.214)	(9.309)	(0.212)	
French legal tradition	7.1295**	0.2180***	−0.1980***	6.1851	0.1414	−0.2545**
	(3.299)	(0.081)	(0.075)	(4.596)	(0.111)	(0.110)
German legal tradition	−4.1745	0.0789	−0.2342*	7.0371	−0.9617***	0.0837
	(14.017)	(0.181)	(0.138)	(16.622)	(0.321)	(0.254)
Scandinavian legal tradition		−0.1895	−0.1307			
		(0.203)	(0.174)			
Absolute latitude	6.3882	−0.4276*	0.0302	−12.7089	0.2925	0.2038
	(12.402)	(0.258)	(0.239)	(22.390)	(0.514)	(0.533)
GDP per capita, logged	−12.2843***	−0.4724***	0.2936***	−13.4497***	−0.2828***	0.2938***
	(1.307)	(0.032)	(0.032)	(2.321)	(0.054)	(0.062)
Proportion of population ruled by states before colonization, HRAF, Müller 1999						
Constant	103.4466***	7.0409***	−0.5388**	109.3795***	5.9239***	−0.8626*
	(10.014)	(0.238)	(0.239)	(15.722)	(0.366)	(0.450)
Observations	116	151	102	63	66	46
R-squared	0.687	0.858	0.797	0.592	0.636	0.646

Note: Robust standard errors in parentheses.
*p < .1
**p < .05
***p < .01

The data of La Porta et al. are not varying over time but represent a cross-section. The authors include a series of controls that are supposed to be associated with both the size and quality of government—the dual focus of their article. The controls include the legal tradition of a country—with no clear theoretical expectation of how this should affect public goods provision—as

	With precolonial stateness, without ethnic fractionalization			With ethnic fractionalization and precolonial stateness		
DV: Illiteracy	DV: Infant mortality	DV: School attainment	DV: Illiteracy	DV: Infant mortality	DV: School attainment
7	8	9	10	11	12
			14.0599	0.2399	0.1388
			(9.029)	(0.216)	(0.219)
0.2332***	0.0016	−0.0003	0.2246***	0.0015	−0.0002
(0.075)	(0.002)	(0.002)	(0.079)	(0.002)	(0.002)
−0.0847	0.0015	0.0069**	−0.0734	0.0013	0.0071**
(0.132)	(0.003)	(0.003)	(0.134)	(0.003)	(0.003)
−6.1022	0.0019		−4.2755	0.0428	
(9.085)	(0.204)		(9.413)	(0.212)	
4.6874	0.0944	−0.2516**	6.2140	0.1437	−0.2532**
(4.373)	(0.104)	(0.104)	(4.622)	(0.111)	(0.105)
0.1450	−1.0306***	0.0232	6.9453	−0.9558***	0.0277
(16.442)	(0.306)	(0.241)	(16.716)	(0.321)	(0.243)
−23.1411	0.2853	−0.0847	−9.4505	0.4027	0.0418
(22.035)	(0.494)	(0.469)	(23.103)	(0.524)	(0.513)
−11.3298***	−0.2798***	0.3013***	−13.4854***	−0.2854***	0.3104***
(1.811)	(0.042)	(0.057)	(2.335)	(0.054)	(0.059)
−8.7395	−0.2634**	0.2399**	−3.8696	−0.1529	0.2758**
(5.322)	(0.125)	(0.110)	(6.144)	(0.147)	(0.125)
112.3100***	6.2327***	−1.0093***	112.2847***	6.0495***	−1.1863**
(11.066)	(0.257)	(0.353)	(16.470)	(0.385)	(0.453)
67	71	46	63	66	46
0.569	0.651	0.683	0.595	0.643	0.687

well as the religious composition of a country, the argument being that Muslim and Catholic populations are governed by more authoritarian governments less oriented toward the public good. As can be seen from Models 1–6 in Table E.2, ethnolinguistic fractionalization is associated with public goods provision except in the models on school attainment, reproducing La Porta's findings.

TABLE E.3. Models 1 and 7 of Tables 7.1–7.3 with four different codings of the diversity variable

	DV: Railway density		DV: Proportion adult literates	
	1	2	3	4
Proportion of population ruled by states before colonization, HRAF, Müller 1999		7.4566**		0.6504**
		(2.955)		(0.317)
Linguistic fractionalization, Alesina et al. 2003	−15.3354*	−6.0919	−1.3515***	−0.5232
	(8.287)	(5.122)	(0.342)	(0.445)
Ethnolinguistic fractionalization, Roeder 2001				
Observations	6,296	3,462	6,376	3,527
R–squared	0.231	0.174		

	DV: Railway density		DV: Proportion adult literates	
	13	14	15	16
Proportion of population ruled by states before colonization, HRAF, Müller 1999		10.2166***		0.9603***
		(3.211)		(0.310)
Religious fractionalization, Fearon and Laitin 2003	6.2913	3.6788	0.1746	0.7484
	(10.990)	(4.260)	(0.441)	(0.539)
Religious fractionalization, Alesina et al. 2003				
Observations	6,471	3,505	6,551	3,570
R–squared	0.211	0.151		

Note: Robust standard errors in parentheses. All models include the additional variables of Tables 7.1–7.3. Constant not shown. All models are OLS regressions except those on the proportion adult literates, which are generalized linear models.
*$p < .1$
**$p < .05$
***$p < .01$

This is true for both the full sample and the reduced sample with Asian and African countries for which we have information on levels of precolonial statehood. This variable, in turn, is also significantly associated with the provision of public goods except in models on illiteracy (Models 7–9). When both statehood and ethnolinguistic diversity are considered in the same models (Models 10–12), they generally both lose significance, except the precolonial statehood variable in the model on school attainment (Model 12). This is because both variables are highly correlated with each other (.67), as we expect given the endogenous relationship between historically inherited levels of statehood and contemporary ethnic diversity.

	DV: Infant mortality		DV: Railway density		DV: Proportion adult literates		DV: Infant mortality	
	5	6	7	8	9	10	11	12
		−5.3874		5.3286		0.7320**		−5.6602
		(10.821)		(3.382)		(0.340)		(11.415)
	23.9845***	25.5295*						
	(8.840)	(13.820)						
			23.6573***	−9.6596	−1.2543***	−0.4557	18.8586*	12.9604
			(8.812)	(6.212)	(0.392)	(0.491)	(9.653)	(16.094)
	4,976	2,873	6,354	3,505	6,369	3,505	5,108	2,916
	0.660	0.541	0.241	0.191			0.654	0.531

	DV: Infant mortality		DV: Railway density		DV: Proportion adult literates		DV: Infant mortality	
	17	18	19	20	21	22	23	24
		−11.0302		11.8411***		1.1640***		−11.8299
		(10.892)		(3.211)		(0.301)		(10.967)
	−13.1320	−23.4006						
	(9.483)	(15.882)						
			7.0010	10.6244**	0.5534	1.2467***	−11.5479	−19.4449
			(8.699)	(4.531)	(0.362)	(0.438)	(9.343)	(13.431)
	5,108	2,916	6,457	3,505	6,537	3,570	5,108	2,916
	0.649	0.536	0.213	0.204			0.649	0.537

TABLE E.4. Table 7.4 with additional controls for imperial background (generalized linear models of linguistic fractionalization)

	(1)	(2)	(3)	(4)
Proportion years under colonial or imperial rule since 1816, Wimmer & Feinstein		−0.3029 (0.674)		−0.3114 (0.450)
Former Spanish dependency		0.8396 (0.755)		−1.0566*** (0.402)
Former Ottoman dependency		−1.4196*** (0.472)		−0.5981 (0.388)
Former French dependency		0.3576 (0.339)		0.5865* (0.312)
Former British dependency		0.2414 (0.305)		0.4505* (0.256)
Former Portuguese dependency		0.3711 (0.420)		−0.0359 (0.703)
Former Hapsburg dependency		No obs.		−0.4299 (0.426)
Former Russian dependency		No obs.		0.4435 (0.355)
Former dependency of other empires		−0.2332 (0.299)		0.1347 (0.267)
GDP per capita, Penn World Table (inter– and extrapolated, lagged)	−0.0275 (0.024)	−0.0269 (0.021)	−0.0521*** (0.013)	−0.0490*** (0.014)
Dispersion in elevation across regions, Michalopoulos 2012	0.0564 (0.135)	0.0359 (0.151)	0.0444 (0.094)	0.1265 (0.096)
Dispersion of suitability for agriculture across regions, Michalopoulos 2012	0.8962 (0.616)	1.1579** (0.542)	1.2307** (0.489)	1.2430** (0.544)
Average monthly precipitation between 1961 and 1990 (in 1,000mm), Michalopoulos 2012	0.0049* (0.003)	0.0013 (0.002)	0.0003 (0.002)	0.0016 (0.002)
Distance from coast	0.8256* (0.479)	0.4938 (0.475)	0.3431 (0.300)	0.0516 (0.336)
No. of ethnonationalist wars fought between 1816 and 1900, Wimmer & Min	0.5152 (0.347)	0.6023 (0.386)	−0.1491 (0.124)	0.1053 (0.121)
Proportion of population ruled by states before colonization, HRAF, Müller	−1.5326*** (0.315)	−1.3967*** (0.285)		
Cumulative index of state centralization since 1000 BC (5% discounted), Putterman 2006			−1.2515*** (0.425)	−1.2583*** (0.460)
Constant	−0.6339 (0.671)	−0.2851 (0.577)	−0.5076 (0.440)	−0.6409 (0.568)
Observations	75	75	135	135

Note: Robust standard errors in parentheses.
*p < .1
**p < .05
***p < .01

Supplement to Chapter 8

TABLE F.1. A conflict trap? Past ethnic conflicts and ethnopolitical exclusion (generalized linear models of proportion excluded population)

	Coef.	Robust std. err.	z	P > |z|	[95% CI]	
Number of ethnic conflicts in country history since 1946, EPR	0.875074	0.1079635	0.81	.418	−0.1240971	0.2991119
Length of railway tracks (km) per 1,000 km², Wimmer and Feinstein 2010	−0.0240398	0.0067304	−3.57	.000	−0.0372312	−0.0108485
Total no. of associations per capita, 1970–2005, Schofer and Longhofer 2011	−13.40405	7.695087	−1.74	.082	−28.48615	1.678038
Linguistic fractionalization in 1960, Soviet Atlas, Fearon and Laitin 2003	1.184619	0.5614481	2.11	.035	0.0842006	2.285037
No. of groups, EPR	0.0423139	0.0157585	2.69	.007	0.0114279	0.0731999
Size of the largest group, EPR	0.9075417	0.4420308	2.05	.040	0.0411772	1.773906
Natural cubic spline on calendar year 1	−0.0126211	0.0166024	−0.76	.447	−0.0451612	0.019919
Natural cubic spline on calendar year 2	0.0019573	0.0135214	0.14	.885	−0.0245441	0.0284587
Constant	22.55917	32.73429	0.69	.491	−41.59886	86.7172

Note: No. of observations: 4,472; standard error adjusted for 141 clusters in country code.

NOTES

Preface

1. This was noted in the concluding chapter of *Ethnic Boundary Making* and critically highlighted in Mara Loveman's (2015b) review of the book.

Introduction

1. This measurement is not without its problems. It cannot distinguish whether power sharing at the center is enforced from the outside after the end of an ethnic war (as in Bosnia) or emerged through cooperation and alliance building without outside intervention (as in Switzerland). Obviously, Bosnia should not be seen as a case of successful nation building because the power-sharing arrangement between Serbian, Muslim, and Croatian elites would quickly fall apart without outside enforcement. To test whether this problem is systematic beyond the suggestive but exceptional Bosnian case, I relied on a dataset on civil wars that came to an end through negotiation (Hartzell and Hoddie 2003). Ten countries were governed, once their ethnic civil war had come to an end, through power-sharing arrangements with third-party enforcement, broadly comparable to the Bosnian case. The power configurations of these countries are indistinguishable from all others. Enforced power sharing therefore doesn't lead, overall, to more inclusionary arrangements such as in Bosnia. All the main analyses remain substantially identical if we exclude these ten countries during the years after the war settlements had been reached.

2. For literacy, for example, the standard deviation is 28%. Two-thirds of all literacy rates measured every year in every country of the world since 1945 don't differ more than 28% from the global mean of 65% of literate adults. Two-thirds of literacy rates, in other words, lie somewhere between 37% and 93%. We can now calculate how much lower the share of the excluded population is on average if we increase the literacy rate of an average country by 28%. Using standard deviations allows us to compare the magnitude of statistical associations across variables that are measured in different units (e.g., percentages, kilometers, or dollars) and that show more or less variation.

Chapter 1: A Relational Theory and Nested Methods

1. For other relational accounts of politics, see Gould 1995, 1996; Tilly 2006; Barkey 2008; Ikegami 2005; Levi Martin 2009.

2. A formal model of these exchange relationships has been introduced by Kroneberg and Wimmer 2012.

3. For an agent-based model that supports this rational-choice argument, see Laitin and van der Veen 2012.

4. For other explanations of linguistic homogeneity, see Nunn 2008; Michalopoulos 2012; Ahlerup and Olsson 2012; Kaufmann 2015.

5. This argument assumes that capable states are attempting to homogenize their populations in ethnic and linguistic terms. This is, obviously, a strong assumption since some states pursued a policy of maintaining, rather than eliminating, linguistic diversity.

6. See the classic study on Rhodesia's mining towns by Mitchell (1974). Sometimes, however, anti-assimilation movements emerged (Chai 1996).

7. For a more precise understanding of path dependency, see Mahoney 2000.

8. This criticism has resurged in reviews of Acemoglu and Robinson's book (Easterly 2012).

9. Other studies, according to this typology, are focusing on the typical (or representative) case, various cases with diverse values on the independent variable of interest, deviant cases that disconfirm a hypothesis, influential observations that are responsible for an overall association between variables, or cases that diverge on most variables but not on the core independent variable of interest (to rule out other possible causes).

10. According to Levy's (2008) typology, the approach pursued here is hypothesis testing—as distinct from ideographic case studies aimed at understanding a particular case, the hypothesis-generating case study, or the "illustrative" case study that probes the plausibility of an argument.

11. Cross-tabulating certainty and uniqueness, we arrive at two other kinds of causal inferences that process tracing allows: in a "smoking gun" test, the process does not need to be observed for the theory to be valid, but its presence excludes other possible explanations; the "straw in the wind" test looks at a process that is not necessary for the hypothesis to be true and that is not incompatible with other interpretations.

Chapter 2: Voluntary Organizations: Switzerland versus Belgium

1. For a review of how classical theories of nationalism dealt with the Swiss case, see Wimmer 2011.

2. The sole exception is a brief episode during the Napoleonic period, when a group of radicals tried to unify the Italian-speaking Ticino with a Napoleonic puppet state called the Cisalpine Republic (today's northern Italy). An outburst of Swiss patriotism throughout Italian-speaking Switzerland followed, and the separatists were quickly overwhelmed (Stojanovic 2003).

3. According to Stojanovic (personal communication), the share of French and Italian speakers among the councillors who served from 1848 to 2010 was 32%.

4. Ethnolinguistic differences, however, are often politicized in cantons with bilingual populations. An analysis of these developments is beyond the scope of this book.

5. To be sure, the rise of the socialist labor movement after the war also helped cement the existing, trans-ethnic coalition of elites (see du Bois 1983: 88–89).

Chapter 3: Public Goods: Botswana versus Somalia

1. I prefer the term "kingdom" over the colonial term "chieftaincy," and I will use "ethnic groups" rather than "tribes."

2. Many political anthropologists would not classify these kingdoms as early states, owing to their small populations and lack of a formal bureaucracy. This is also how the Human Relations Area Files (HRAF), a dataset based on classical ethnographies, represents the Tswana case. The HRAF will be used for the statistical analysis in Chapter 5. As Robinson and Parsons point out

(2006: 119ff.), this is probably a misclassification—which I do not correct in the HRAF data for the sake of consistency.

3. All kingdoms were dominated by Tswana speakers except for one with a ruling house of Ndebele origin, which adopted Tswana language and customs over time (Bennett 2002).

4. At the same time, the colonial administration curtailed the kings' earlier foray into commerce and trade by closing down royal trading companies around World War I (Murray and Parsons 1990: 161) and severely limiting the number of trading licenses to Africans in general (du Toit 1995: 27, 50).

5. In the first year of the initiative (1963), the committee recommended 14 continuing students for university education, many of whom later became high-ranking functionaries such as the long-serving chief of justice as well as the minister of finance and development planning. It also recommended 10 new bursaries for tertiary education. These students, who graduated in the late 1960s, formed the nucleus of the indigenous parts of the bureaucracy after independence.

6. All executive power came to lie in the hands of the president, who needs to consult only with the cabinet. Presidents can dissolve the national assembly, and bills can be approved by parliament only if recommended by the president. The parliament asks questions about policies, but the cabinet and the bureaucracy formulate these. District councils, set up in the last years of colonial rule, have no budgetary autonomy but get 80% of their funding from the center (on more recent decentralization efforts, see Tordoff 1988). Council civil servants are part of the national government service and thus depend on the ministry in the capital (Holm 1987).

7. For a critique of the Marxist thesis that the state was "captured" by cattle capitalists, see du Toit 1995: 10.

8. In Botswana, only 10% of government expenditures went to fund the military and police in the 1980s (Holm 1987: 25; in the United States, this figure is 28–38% for military expenses alone).

9. However, the reverse is true for the groups that became serfs of the Tswana elites: many more self-identify with the categories of Sarwa and Yeyi than their population estimate based on the ethnopolitical origins of ward heads. This is due to the fact, as Schapera explains (1952: 99), that as serfs these groups were rarely granted ward heads of their own—and his measurement of population size is therefore not suited for them.

10. Only in 1942 were three elementary schools opened, and in 1945 seven schools educated a total of 400 boys. The lack of taxes also prevented other projects such as drilling wells for the camel and sheep herds or building roads.

11. A year earlier, there had been only two Somali district commissioners and a handful of district officers on the police force.

12. Some modest efforts at providing public goods to the indigenous population should be mentioned: in the early 1930s, 150 wells were drilled to serve the nomadic population, while some of the irrigation schemes along the Shebelle River also benefited the local population outside the plantations.

13. Some projects aimed at providing public goods to the population at large, however. They included a £3 million budget, between 1950 and 1955, to invest in roads, public works for schools and clinics, and so on. A seven-year plan for agricultural development was unveiled in 1954. It included an extension for irrigation farming, clearing additional land, silos for the storage of grains, an agricultural bank for farmers, well drilling for the nomads, and incentives to diversify agricultural exports away from bananas and toward cotton and sugarcane. However, the economy remained dependent on banana exports, which in 1955 totaled five times the volume of 1937 (Laitin and Samatar 1987: 143).

14. It did not help much that most emerging civil society organizations were clan associations (for British Somalia, see Lewis 1999 [1961]: 280) rather than equivalents to the Swiss early

modern shooting clubs, choral societies, and literary associations that recruited members across cantonal and language boundaries.

15. This trend was reinforced when the government decided to conduct the secondary school system in English (Laitin and Samatar 1987: 75ff.).

16. While agricultural producers were taxed by offering them lower than world market prices, the nomads received internationally competitive prizes mainly because of the political clout and independence of Isaaq cattle traders, not because of a policy decision by the central government.

17. Other efforts should be noted: the regime tried to bring electricity to the hinterland by decentralizing the electricity grid; it also sent peace emissaries to clan groups in conflict and provided resources to help settle these conflicts, thus exerting more government control and authority in the hinterland than previously.

18. For a more nuanced assessment that emphasizes genuine but largely unsuccessful attempts by Barre to ban corruption through public shaming, see Lewis 1983: 157, 169, 175n47.

19. One of the reasons for this was that Barre's own clan of the Mareehaan, part of the Darood clan family, was relatively small and had not been a crucial player in clan alliance politics of the first 10 years of independence. Given the lack of established alliances, Barre made appointments based on merit rather than clan affiliation during the first months of his reign.

Chapter 4: Communicative Integration: China versus Russia

1. This counterfactual suggests that we cannot attribute the existence of cross-ethnic ties to the centralized nature of the empire or to the examination system alone.

2. The various warlord factions aligned broadly speaking into a northern and a southern, Kuomintang-dominated coalition, claiming to represent the national government. It is interesting to note that the southern coalition included provinces dominated by Mandarin speakers, such as Szechwan, Yunnan, and Kweichow, and represented a linguistically extraordinarily diverse set of populations.

3. The CCP had more sons of peasants among their leading ranks than did the Kuomintang, but otherwise the social backgrounds of their leaders were quite comparable (North 1952: 76–85).

4. Since the Communist takeover in China, it should be noted, the population has become considerably less polyglot, mostly due to the regime's efforts to promote a standardized, modern, "national" language. To that effect, it simplified the script and introduced a standard way of pronunciation (using a newly created phonological notation system) based on the Peking dialect. Northern Mandarin was thus elevated to the national language and taught in schools throughout the country. While the Communist regime initially hoped that Northern Mandarin would eventually replace all other languages, this policy was later abandoned (Guo 2004; see Rohsenow 2004).

5. Exceptions are the Sino-Tibetan language family (of which the Chinese languages form a part), the Afro-Asiatic family (to which Arabic belongs), the Dravidian family (of South Indian languages), Japanese, and three language families of Southeast Asia.

6. As Kappeler (2001: 262–264) shows, this policy of Russification was mostly limited to the west. In the Volga-Ural region, Cyrillic alphabets were developed for minority languages and native language schools established—quite the opposite policy compared to that of the European parts of the empire. The *inorodtsy* communities of Central Asia were largely left on their own during that period.

7. This was also true for the Jewish Bund and the Armenian Dashnak party, the Belorussian

Socialist Hromada, the Georgian Socialist Federalist Party Sakartvelo, and the Jewish SERP. All saw nonterritorial, cultural autonomy on an individual basis as a supplement to the federal, territorial autonomy of their people's homeland (Pipes 1997: 28).

8. An unsystematic but instructive list of states founded during the Russian Civil War can be found on this website: http://www.worldstatesmen.org/Russia_war.html.

9. For this analysis, I use an index of state antiquity, to be discussed in detail in the next chapter. It comes in two variants. The first measures whether a territory was governed, between 1850 and 1900, by a state above the local community level, whether local groups (rather than foreign empires) controlled it, and how much of today's territory that state actually governed. China and Russia score identically on that index, which is available for 141 countries. From the point of view of the theory outlined here, they are therefore most similar cases. In line with the theory, this measure is significantly associated with ethnopolitical inclusion after World War II (see Appendix Table B.1, Model 1). 19th century levels of statehood enhance nation building later on.

The second version of the state antiquity index takes the entire history of state formation over the past 2,000 years into account. The longevity of a state is thus added as a criterion. On this measure, China scores the maximum value of the entire dataset, while Russia gets only about half of that. Does this explain the divergent trajectories of nation building in China and Russia? Model 2 in Appendix Table B.1 tells us that this does not seem to be the case.

I do find, however, that secessionist conflicts are more likely in countries that look back on a long history of indigenous statehood (Models 3 and 4 in Appendix Table B.1; Models 5 and 6 refer to nonsecessionist conflicts; the model specification replicates Wimmer et al. 2009). If anything, then, China's longer history of statehood should have predisposed it to face more secessionist violence than Russia.

Chapter 5: Political Integration: Evidence from Countries around the World

1. More specifically, I refer here to a series of measures that indicate how far patronage politics influence everyday government operations: the World Bank measures of rule of law as well as government effectiveness, Transparency International's perceived corruption index, and the International Country Risk Guide's perceived quality of government measure. The correlations with the number of voluntary organizations are between .72 and .73.

2. Nonstate institutions such as religious schools historically had a large impact on literacy levels as well. This should be less of a problem, however, in postcolonial societies and more generally in the postwar world, after most states had taken over the task of schooling the population from religious organizations (Meyer et al. 1992).

3. Other interpretations of what railway density indicates certainly remain possible and plausible (see Wimmer and Feinstein 2010).

4. In the meantime, more fine-grained analyses both of institutional rules and of their interaction with ethnic demography have emerged (see Mozaffar et al. 2003; Birnir 2007). Such analysis is beyond the reach of this chapter.

5. I omitted the United States, Canada, Australia, and New Zealand from consideration here because in these British settler colonies the measurement does not make too much sense: most of these colonies were de facto governed autonomously by the European settlers, and yet the proportion of court cases ruled by "customary" courts is zero, suggesting that these territories were directly ruled by London.

6. An index of political globalization, as provided by the Konjunkturforschungsstelle of the ETH Zürich, produces substantially identical results (not shown).

7. Robust standard errors are clustered by country, following standard practice. Since the

dependent variable is a proportion and not overdispersed, the appropriate statistical model is a generalized linear regression with a logistic link function and the specification of a binomial distribution of the dependent variable. This takes into account that possible values are bound by 0 and 1. Since many countries do not exclude any citizen on the basis of ethnicity, there is a problem of excess zeros (about 30% of observations), which the above specification of the link function is supposed to handle effectively (McCullagh and Nelder 1989). To be on the safe side in terms of interpretation, I also ran models without countries where ethnicity was never relevant and where, therefore, ethnopolitical exclusion cannot possibly exceed zero. This is to make sure that the models do not depend on these zeros, which is not the case.

8. The main models were also tested using a polarization or a fractionalization index based on EPR's group lists, which generated substantially similar results.

9. As Appendix Table C.2 shows, there are no collinearity problems except in models that combine literacy or IGOs, or linguistic heterogeneity, or associational density with democracy. None of these correlations exceeds .55, however. I conducted collinearity tests on all models and removed the time trends from problematic models, which will be pointed out in the footnotes and the tables.

10. Democracy is also highly significant in a fixed effects model (see Appendix Table C.3), which focuses on changes over time within countries rather than on comparisons across countries.

11. This model is a logistic regression because the dependent variable is dichotomous: a nondemocratic regime transitions to democracy or not.

12. Some other theoretically interesting results are noteworthy. First, one could argue that nation building is easier when certain types of nationalist ideologies prevail. Civic nationalism, focused on the institutions of the state, might produce more tolerant attitudes toward domestic minorities than ethnic nationalism with its emphasis on shared descent and language. Data that allow distinguishing between civil and ethnic national identities are available for only two dozen countries. To arrive at a larger sample, I used a question in the World Values Survey (Waves 5 and 6) as a proxy. It asked whether respondents would mind having neighbors who speak a different language. For the 71 countries for which these data are available, I find no association between average responses and levels of ethnopolitical inclusion (see Appendix Table C.7).

Second and related, it is reasonable to think, perhaps with Benedict Anderson, that certain nations are easier to imagine than others, which in turn could facilitate nation building. Countries that have existed for a long time, or that look back on a long history of independent statehood, or that have existed in their current borders for many decades (including as imperial provinces before independence), or whose core ethnic group looks back on a long history are not, however, more successful at nation building (see Appendix Table C.8).

Third, ethnopolitical exclusion is also not associated, if we control for the political development variables shown in Table 5.3, with income inequality (such as GINI indices), various measures of government size (government share of GDP, tax share of GDP, absolute size of government or of tax revenues), various measures of quality of government (perception of corruption, quality of administration and services, anticorruption, and rule of law), some geographic variables (mountainous terrain, elevation differences), demography (population size, population density, geographic dispersal of population), some faster-paced political factors (previous regime change, number of military coups in the past), or economic variables (oil production per capita, the share of agriculture in GDP, economic globalization), as well as globalization (both as a composite measure and with regard to political globalization more specifically).

13. In Appendix Table C.9, nationalism is measured with a "willingness to fight for country" question (available for 71 countries). Results are similar if we use the question, "How proud are you of your country?" to measure nationalism (available for 123 countries; see Model 10 in Appendix Table D.3). Results for the mediation argument are also not fully encouraging: while lit-

eracy is indeed associated with more tolerance toward linguistic minorities (results not shown), the latter doesn't influence ethnopolitical inclusion (Appendix Table C.7).

14. A Sobel-Goodman mediation test shows that 6–10% of the nonsignificant effect of wars on ethnopolitical exclusion is mediated by railway density or literacy.

15. These two models do not include time controls because tests indicated that they created a collinearity problem.

16. Note that country fixed effects models take into account possible omitted variable problems except for common time trends across countries. These, however, are already controlled for by the cubic splines on chronological year, included in all previous models. Year fixed effect models generate substantially identical results (not shown).

17. Model 6 has no time controls because tests indicated that they created a collinearity problem.

18. Both measurements of historically achieved levels of statehood used in the previous sections are strongly associated with ethnopolitical inclusion. A Sobel-Goodman mediation test shows that a large portion of that statistical association is indeed channeled through the two public goods variables and linguistic heterogeneity, at least in tests with the state antiquity variable: about half of the effect is mediated through linguistic fractionalization and literacy, about one-fifth through railroads. These proportions are much smaller (about one-tenth) when using the precolonial statehood variable. All mediation tests are highly significant.

19. We could also use a measurement of the average temperature or of the contemporary prevalence of malaria (data from Sachs 2003), which is at least partly endogenous to state capacity, however. Results using both of these measures are substantially identical to those obtained with the absolute latitude variable.

20. The same results are obtained if we use population data for 1820 or 1870 from Maddison 2003, which are available for only 38 countries in Africa and Asia. See the findings of Bates (1983: 35) on Africa.

21. For technical reasons, this second variable could not be used in the previous instrumental variable regressions reported in Appendix Table C.11.

22. All instrumental variable regression models use a two-stage least squares estimator. Other model specifications (such as a GMM estimator) produce substantially identical results. For all instrumental variable models, the first stage is not shown. Unfortunately, both sets of models have relatively weak instruments (with a T-value of 7.3 and 10.3 for the Kleibergen-Paap rk Wald F statistic for Models 1 and 2, respectively, calculated through the Stata command ivreg2). All models pass the over- and underidentification tests, however.

23. Tilly (1990: chap. 7) himself cautioned that his theory would not apply to contemporary developing states but left it open whether it holds for earlier processes of state formation outside Europe.

24. I defined all former Soviet Union republics, including those of Transcaucasia and Central Asia, as Western countries. Unfortunately, the results change somewhat when altering this coding decision.

25. It could also be that the war variable is simply not measured well enough in the case of African and Asian countries for which historical records of precolonial wars are often sketchy (see the discussion in Wimmer and Min 2009).

Chapter 6: Identifying with the Nation: Evidence from a Global Survey

1. National pride is also associated with protectionism (Mayda and Rodrik 2005), negative sentiment toward the euro (Müller-Peters 1998), and negative attitudes toward immigrant populations (Wagner et al. 2012).

2. For an overview of other approaches to nationalism, see Smith 1998; for the social bases of early nationalist movements, see Hroch 2000 (1969).

3. This focus on transactions, rather than network structures as in much network research, follows up on Blau 1986 (1964).

4. See also, for 18 African countries, Franck and Rainer 2012; for Kenya, Burgess et al. 2015, Jablonski 2014; for large US cities, Nye et al. 2014.

5. For empirical evidence that is compatible with this view, see Knack and Keefer 1997; for the conflict-proneness of coalition regimes with many power-sharing partners, see Wimmer et al. 2009.

6. Note that possible power shifts resulting from armed conflict, such as the loss of political status for some groups or the emergence of coalition regimes from peace agreements, are captured by the third and fourth hypotheses.

7. I did not count the dismemberment of existing states such as Yugoslavia and the Soviet Union as cases of change. Countries in which ethnicity is not politically relevant (according to EPR coding rules, such as Germany and Burkina Faso) are treated as cases of stability.

8. The correlation coefficient between answers to the proud question and a dichotomous variable indicating whether a person identifies primarily with the nation, rather than with an ethnic group or both, is 0.08 based on about 92,000 observations.

9. Another issue is whether a single question can capture the multidimensional nature of national identities (Davidov 2009). Based on the 2003 ISS dataset and its rich catalogue of questions, the consensus seems to be that at least two different components need to be distinguished: On the one hand, a "constructive patriotism" component relates to a series of "proud" questions, such as "How proud are you of how democracy works in your country?" and "How proud are you of how minorities are treated in your country?" and so on. On the other hand, a "nationalist" (or "chauvinist") component is captured by questions that suggest the superiority of one's country vis-à-vis others.

There are reasons to believe that the generic "how proud are you of your nationality" question measures national pride in both its "nationalist" and "patriotic" aspects and thus serves the current purpose quite well. Bekhuis and coauthors (2014) have demonstrated that the single question "How proud are you of your country?" captures the underlying "national identification" dimension as well as do the multiple questions asked in the ISS data. They found that analyzing responses to that single question led to the same substantial conclusions as when using multiple questions.

10. A clarifying note on the time aspects of this coding is perhaps in order here. In the group-level EPR dataset, the political status variables are coded for periods that can last any number of years. During a period, the list of groups that are politically relevant in a country remains the same and the political status of all groups is identical. Conversely, whenever the list of politically relevant groups changes or any of those groups changes its political status, a new period commences. For statistical analysis, these group-periods are then expanded to create a dataset with years as units of observation. Declining political status is assigned to a group during all years of a period if that group held more power in the previous period. Since I matched survey with EPR years, a coding of lost power for a survey year means that members of that ethnic category had lost power sometime in the past.

11. This procedure is not ideal from a technical, statistical point of view. I therefore also use a fully Boolean approach to model selection, in which all possible combinations of variables are explored and the best-fitting combination retained. The results are broadly consistent and reported in the footnotes as well as in Appendix D.3.

12. There are missing data on these individual-level variables (4,752 for gender, 5,031 for age, 25,989 for education, 37,980 for religiosity, 24,573 for marriage status, 94,385 for politi-

cization, and 212,004 for class). Instead of losing these observations and dropping dozens of countries, I decided to amend the coding of the individual-level variables with a 0 indicating missing data and then create dummy variables for observations with missing data on each of these variables and add these to the model. Dropping observations instead does not change the main results.

13. As a rule of thumb, at least 5% of variation in the dependent variable should be situated at higher than the individual level of aggregation to justify a hierarchical model approach (Bacikowski 1981; Goldstein 2003). It turns out that in the dataset, 14% of variation in pride is due to differences between countries and 23% due to differences between ethnic groups within countries. These figures are quite high compared to those of other studies, and a hierarchical modeling approach is therefore in order.

14. Since we are only interested in the main associations between the independent variables and pride in the nation, rather than whether these associations vary across countries or ethnic groups, each control variable is entered into the model as a fixed rather than random effect.

An ordered logit is clearly preferable because the number of categories is small, and many categories are rarely or even never used (the "not proud at all" and "not very proud" categories) (see Gelman and Hill 2006: 123). Ordered logit regression is not affected by the problem of heteroscedasticity (because there are no error terms when the dependent variable is a probability), and we therefore cannot and should not specify robust standard errors.

15. As mentioned in a previous note, we also produced a country-level model following a Boolean approach to model selection available for multilevel models in the STAN program. The program runs thousands of models with all possible combinations of variables and then suggests which combination has the most explanatory power. The results of this robustness exercise are encouraging. The main variables of theoretical interest produce substantially identical results to those reported below (see Appendix Figure D.3). While STAN includes a very large number of nonsignificant control variables in the optimal country-level model, the ones that are significant in STAN are also relevant in Model 2 of Table 6.2 (with the exception of an additional war variable). I decided to use the Boolean approach for robustness purposes only because it turned out to be stunningly intense in terms of the computational power and time needed to digest such a big dataset.

16. The same is true for the STAN models (see Appendix Figure D.3).

17. Since we are not interested in the individual-level variables such as age or gender, I don't display them in Table 6.2. It suffices to note here that in line with previous research, I find that men as well as older, less educated, more politicized, and more religious persons are more proud of their nationality.

18. I also explored whether differences in income between ethnic groups might affect pride because either poorer or richer groups could identify less positively with the nation, as suggested, for example, by Hechter (1979). Using the geocoded version of EPR3, I found that the difference in GDP (measured through nighttime luminosity) between an ethnic group's territory and the national average does not affect levels of pride (results not shown).

19. In the STAN models, former Axis powers and countries with many years of constant borders are not significantly associated with pride, but former British territories and federalist countries are, as is the case in Model 2 of Appendix Table 6.2. A second difference is that the number of wars—whether ethnic or not—fought since 1816 is positive in the STAN model and also in a bivariate ordered logit model (Model 3 in Appendix Table D.3), but no longer retains significance once other variables are introduced into the model, as Appendix Table D.4 shows.

20. As a side note, I also find that the citizens of countries with proportional representation are not more proud of their nation, as Model 14 in Appendix Table D.3 shows. This stands in contrast to the findings of Elkins and Sides (2007).

21. The above results can also be found in the STAN models (see Appendix Figure D.3), except that the variable for former Axis powers fails to reach standard levels of significance, while its coefficient is again large and negative.

22. Similar results are obtained at the country level: the citizens of 14 countries that were surveyed before an ethnic conflict report to be proud at 3.53, while after conflict average pride levels in these countries drop to 3.47, a difference that is again not statistically significant.

Chapter 7: Is Diversity Detrimental?

1. The one dissenting finding concerns participation in community efforts to provide public goods in the villages of Sierra Leone (Glennerster et al. 2013). In a related study, Miguel (2004) finds that diversity affects local public goods provision only in Kenya, which lacks a history of nation-building efforts comparable to that of neighboring Tanzania.

2. They also find, however, that diversity sometimes has a positive impact on public goods provision at the subnational level in a sample of 34 countries (Gerring et al. 2015).

3. One recent working paper moves beyond these assumptions and tests whether diversity *results* from low public goods provision or a lack of economic growth (Ahlerup 2009).

4. To be sure, these are not pure public goods as originally defined by economists (Olson 1965). They are not completely "non-rival" because if everyone used the railway system at the same time, for example, most people would get nowhere. They are also not entirely "non-excludable": not everybody gets the same chance at an education (see Kramon and Posner 2016). But they are the kinds of outcomes that previous research on public goods provision by governments has focused upon.

5. I cluster robust standard errors at the country level to take the nonindependence of subsequent observations in the same country into account. Since railways and infant mortality are continuous outcomes, a standard OLS regression model will be adequate. Literacy rates represent proportions, bound by 0 and 1. The dependent variable is not overdispersed, and the appropriate statistical model is therefore a generalized linear model with a logistic link function and the specification of a binomial distribution of the dependent variable.

6. Appendix Table E.3 contains two additional sets of models with religious instead of linguistic fractionalization indices (data are from Fearon 2003; Alesina et al. 2003). Even without taking the previous history of state formation into account, countries with a religiously diverse population do not provide fewer public goods. This very much runs against the detrimental diversity argument because religions should be more closely associated with public policy preferences since they prescribe specific normative orientations. This is much less the case for languages (Brubaker 2013).

7. These are generalized linear models since 0 and 1 bound the outcome. Because the data are not overdispersed, the appropriate model specification is again a logistic link function with the specification of a binomial distribution of the dependent variable.

Chapter 8: Policy Implications with Some Lessons Learned from Afghanistan

1. Published work on Afghanistan focuses on the effects of development projects on the perception of provincial, rather than national, governments and doesn't distinguish between foreign- and domestically sponsored projects (Böhnke and Zürcher 2013; Böhnke et al. 2015).

2. An ordered logistic regression with the original answers as dependent variable produces substantially identical results.

3. According to my theory, this is because individuals expect such goods and services from

the state, to whom individuals develop ties of loyalty and support in return. An alternative mechanism would be, quite obviously, that foreign donors are less effective. They know less about the local society and therefore have to rely on brokers and contractors to implement projects, who in turn take advantage of the donors and perform less well than state agencies and their local contractors. I am unable to empirically test whether this alternative interpretation holds.

4. Approximately 20,000 of the 64,000 respondents report a project with at least some government involvement, while 14,000 report a project with at least some foreign involvement.

Appendix C: Supplement to Chapter 5

1. Some notes on model specification are in order. The models shown in Appendix Table C.11 don't include time controls because these produced collinearity problems. All models were implemented using the ivreg2 command in Stata with a two-stage least square estimator. Other model specifications (such as with GMM estimators) lead to substantially identical results. For all instrumental variable models, the first stage is not shown.

REFERENCES

Acemoglu, Daron, Simon Johnson, and James Robinson. 2001. "The colonial origins of comparative development: An empirical investigation," in *American Economic Review* 91: 1369–1401.

Acemoglu, Daron and James A. Robinson. 2006. *Economic Origins of Dictatorship and Democracy*. New York: Cambridge University Press.

———. 2012. *Why Nations Fail: The Origins of Power, Prosperity, and Poverty*. New York: Crown.

Ahlerup, Pelle. 2009. "The causal effects of ethnic diversity: An instrumental variable approach." University of Gothenburg Working Papers in Economics 386.

Ahlerup, Pelle and Gustav Hansson. 2011. "Nationalism and government effectiveness," in *Journal of Comparative Economics* 39: 431–451.

Ahlerup, Pelle and Ola Olsson. 2012. "The roots of ethnic diversity," in *Journal of Economic Growth* 17 (2): 17–102.

Albouy, David Y. 2012. "The colonial origins of comparative development: An empirical investigation: Comment," in *American Economic Review* 102: 3059–3076.

Alesina, Alberto, Reza Baqir, and William Easterly. 1999. "Public goods and ethnic divisions," in *Quarterly Journal of Economics* 114: 1243–1284.

Alesina, Alberto, Arnaud Devleeschauwer, William Easterly, Sergio Kurlat, and Romain Wacziarg. 2003. "Fractionalization," in *Journal of Economic Growth* 8 (2): 155–194.

Alesina, Alberto and Edward L. Glaeser. 2004. *Fighting Poverty in the US and Europe: A World of Difference*. Oxford: Oxford University Press.

Alesina, Alberto and Eliana La Ferrara. 2000. "Participation in heterogeneous communities," in *Quarterly Journal of Economics* 115 (3): 847–904.

———. 2005. "Ethnic diversity and economic performance," in *Journal of Economic Literature* 63: 762–800.

Alesina, Alberto, Stelios Michalopoulos, and Elias Papaioannou. 2016. "Ethnic inequality," in *Journal of Political Economy* 124 (2): 428–488.

Alesina, Alberto, Enrico Spolaore, and Romain Wacziarg. 2005. "Trade, growth and the size of countries," in Philippe Aghion and Steven N. Durlauf, eds., *Handbook of Economic Growth*, vol. 1B. Amsterdam: Elsevier. 1500–1542.

Algan, Yann, Camille Hémet, and David Laitin. 2011. "Diversity and public goods: A natural experiment with exogenous residential allocation." Institute for the Study of Labor Discussion Paper 6053.

Ali, Merima, Odd-Helge Fjeldstad, Boqian Jiang, and Abdulaziz B. Shifa. 2015. "Colonial legacy, state building and the salience of ethnicity in sub-Saharan Africa." Chr. Michelsen Institute Working Paper 2015:16.

Anderson, Benedict. 1991. *Imagined Communities: Reflections on the Origin and Spread of Nationalism*. London: Verso.

Andrey, Georges. 1986. "Auf der Suche nach dem neuen Staat (1798–1848)," in Ulrich Im Hof et al., eds., *Geschichte der Schweiz und der Schweizer*. Basel: Helbing & Lichtenhahn. 527–637.

Ariely, Gal. 2012. "Globalisation and the decline of national identity? An exploration across sixty-three countries," in *Nations and Nationalism* 18 (3): 461–481.

Arvelle, Joel. 1995. *Histoire de la franc maconnerie belge*. Braine-l'Alleud: J.-M. Collet.

Bacikowski, Robert S. 1981. "Statistical power with group mean as the unit of analysis," in *Journal of Educational Statistics* 6 (3): 267–285.

Back, Les. 1996. *New Ethnicities and Urban Culture: Racism and Multiculture in Young Lives*. London: Routledge.

Bagby, Wesley M. 1992. *The Eagle-Dragon Alliance: America's Relations with China in World War II*. Cranbury: Associated University Presses.

Baldassari, Delia and Mauro Diani. 2007. "The integrative power of civic networks," in *American Journal of Sociology* 113 (3): 735–780.

Baldwin, Kate and John D. Huber. 2011. "Economic versus cultural difference. Forms of ethnic diversity and public goods provision," in *American Political Science Review* 104 (4): 644–662.

Banerjee, Abhijit, Iyer Lakshimi, and Rohini Somanathan. 2005. "History, social divisions, and public goods in rural India," in *Journal of the European Economic Association* 3 (2–3): 639–647.

Barkey, Karen. 2008. *Empire of Difference: The Ottomans in Comparative Perspective*. Cambridge: Cambridge University Press.

Bates, Robert H. 1983. *Essays on the Political Economy of Rural Africa*. Cambridge: Cambridge University Press.

Beck, Thorsten, George Clarke, Alberto Groff, Philip Keefer, and Patrick Walsh. 2001. "New tools in comparative political economy: The Database of Political Institutions," in *World Bank Economic Review* 15 (1): 165–176.

Bekhuis, Hidde, Marces Lubbers, and Maykel Verkuyten. 2014. "How education moderates the relation between globalization and nationalist attitudes," in *International Journal of Public Opinion Research* 26 (4): 487–500.

Bendix, Regina. 1992. "National sentiment in the enactment and discourse of Swiss political ritual," in *American Ethnologist* 19: 768–790.

Bendix, Reinhard. 1964. *Nation-Building and Citizenship: Studies in Our Changing Social Order*. New York: John Wiley.

Bennett, Andrew. 2010. "Process tracing and causal inference," in Henry Brady and David Collier, eds., *Rethinking Social Inquiry*, 2nd ed. Lanham, MD: Rowman & Littlefield. 207–220.

Bennett, Bruce. 2002. "Some historical background on minorities in Botswana," in Isaac N. Mazonde, ed., *Identities in the Millennium: Perspectives from Botswana*. Gabarone: Lightbooks. 5–15.

Billiet, Jaak, Bart Maddens, and Roeland Beerten. 2003. "National identity and attitude toward foreigners in a multinational state: A replication," in *Political Psychology* 24 (2): 241–257.

Binsbergen, Wim van. 1991. "Minority language, ethnicity and state in two African situations: The Nkoya of Zambia and the Kalanga of Botswana," in R. Fardon and G. Furniss, eds., *African Languages, Development and the State*. London: Routledge. 142–188.

Birnir, Johanna Kristin. 2007. *Ethnicity and Electoral Politics*. Cambridge: Cambridge University Press.

Birnir, Johanna Kristin and David M. Waguespack. 2011. "Ethnic inclusion and economic growth," in *Party Politics* 17 (1): 243–260.

Bjornskov, Christian. 2004. "Determinants of generalized trust: A cross-country comparison," in *Public Choice* 130 (1–2): 1–21.

Blanton, Robert, David T. Mason, and Brian Athow. 2001. "Colonial style and post-colonial ethnic conflict in Africa," in *Journal of Peace Research* 38 (4): 473–491.

Blau, Peter. 1986 (1964). *Exchange and Power in Social Life*. New Brunswick, NJ: Transaction.

Bockstette, Valerie, Areendam Chanda, and Louis Putterman. 2002. "States and markets: The advantage of an early start," in *Journal of Economic Growth* 7: 347–369.

Böhnke, Jan R., J. Köhler, and Christoph Zürcher. 2015. *Assessing the Impact of Development Cooperation in North East Afghanistan 2007–2013*. Bonn: Federal Ministry for Economic Cooperation and Development.

Böhnke, Jan R. and Christoph Zürcher. 2013. "Aid, minds, and hearts: The impact of aid in conflict zones," in *Conflict Management and Peace Science* 30 (5): 411–432.

Boix, Carles. 2015. *Political Order and Inequality*. Cambridge: Cambridge University Press.

Boldrin, Michèle, David K. Levine, and Salvatore Modica. 2015. "A review of Acemoglu and Robinson's Why Nations Fail," in *Huffington Post*. http://www.huffingtonpost.com/david-k-levine/why-nations-fail_b_2007916.html.

Bollen, Kenneth and Juan Diez Medrano. 1998. "Who are Spaniards? Nationalism and identification in Spain," in *Social Forces* 77: 587–621.

Bratton, Michael and Nicolas van de Walle. 1994. "Neopatrimonial regimes and political transitions in Africa," in *World Politics* 46: 453–489.

Braudel, Fernand. 1995. *The Mediterranean and the Mediterranean World in the Age of Philip II*. Berkeley: University of California Press.

Brecke, Peter. 2012. *Conflict Catalog: Violent Conflicts 1400 A.D. to the Present in Different Regions of the World*. Utrecht: University of Utrecht Centre for Global Economic History.

Broockman, David E. 2013. "Black politicians are more intrinsically motivated to advance blacks' interests: A field experiment with manipulating political incentives," in *American Journal of Political Science* 57 (3): 521–536.

Brubaker, Rogers. 1999. "The Manichean myth: Rethinking the distinction between 'civic' and 'ethnic' nationalism," in Hans-Peter Kriesi, Klaus Armingeon, Hannes Siegrist, and Andreas Wimmer, eds., *Nation and National Identity: Collective Identities and National Consciousness at the End of the 20th Century*. Chur: Rüegger.

———. 2002. "To return to assimilation? Changing perspectives on immigration and its sequels in France, Germany, and the United States," in *Ethnic and Racial Studies* 24 (4): 531–548.

———. 2013. "Language, religion, and the politics of difference," in *Nations and Nationalism* 19 (1): 1–20.

Bulag, Uradyn E. 1998. *Nationalism and Hybridity in Mongolia*. Oxford: Oxford University Press.

Burgess, Robin, Remi Jedwab, Edward Miguel, Ameet Morjaria, and Gerard Padro i Miquel. 2015. "The value of democracy: Evidence from road building in Kenya," in *American Economic Review* 105 (6). 1817–1851.

Busekist, Adrian von. 1998. *La Belgique: Politique des langues et construction de l'Etat de 1780 à nos jours*. Paris: Duculot.

Campbell, Lyle, Raina Heato, Nala Lee, Eve Okra, Sean Simpson, Kaori Ueki, and John Van Way. 2013. "New knowledge: Findings from the Catalogue of Endangered Languages." Paper given at the Third International Conference on Language Documentation and Conservation, Honolulu.

Cantillon, Bea, Veerle De Maesschalck, Stijn Rottiers, and Gerlinde Verbist. 2013. "Social redistribution in federalized Belgium," in Marleen Brans et al., eds., *The Politics of Belgium: Institutions and Policy under Bipolar and Centrifugal Federalism*. London: Routledge. 172–194.

Carlson, Elizabeth. 2015. "Ethnic voting and accountability in Africa: A choice experiment in Uganda," in *World Politics* 67 (2): 353–385.

Carneiros, Robert L. 1970. "A theory of the state," in *Science* 21 (169): 733–738.

Carrico, Kevin. 2012. "Recentering China: The Cantonese in and beyond the Han," in Thomas S.

Mullaney et al., eds., *Critical Han Studies: The History, Representation, and Identity of China's Majority*. Berkeley: University of California Press. 23–44.

Cederman, Lars-Erik, Andreas Wimmer, and Brian Min. 2010. "Why do ethnic groups rebel? New data and analysis," in *World Politics* 62 (1): 87–119.

Chai, Sun-Ki. 1996. "A theory of ethnic group boundaries," in *Nations and Nationalism* 2 (2): 281–307.

Chandra, Kanchan. 2004. *Why Ethnic Parties Succeed: Patronage and Ethnic Head Counts in India*. Cambridge: Cambridge University Press.

Chandra, Kanchan and Steven Wilkinson. 2008. "Measuring the effect of 'ethnicity,'" in *Comparative Political Studies* 41 (4/5): 515–563.

Chang, Chung-Li. 1967 (1955). *The Chinese Gentry: Studies on Their Role in Nineteenth Century Chinese Society*. Seattle: University of Washington Press.

Chao, Kuo-chün. 1955. "How Communist power is organized in China," in *Foreign Affairs* 34: 148–153.

Chaoju, Tang and Vincent J. van Heuven. 2009. "Mutual intelligibility of Chinese dialects experimentally tested," in *Lingua* 119: 709–732.

Coenders, Marcel, Mérauve Gijsberts, and Peer Scheepers. 2004. "Chauvinism and patriotism in 22 countries," in Mérauve Gijsberts, Louk Hagendoorn, and Peer Scheepers, eds., *Nationalism and Exclusion of Migrants: Cross-national Comparisons*. Aldershot: Ashgate. 26–69.

Cohen, Ronald and John Middleton. 1970. *From Tribe to Nation in Africa: Studies in Incorporation Processes*. Scranton: Chandler.

Collier, Paul and Nicholas Sambanis. 2016. "Understanding civil war," in *Journal of Conflict Resolution* 46: 3–12.

Congleton, Roger D. 1995. "Ethnic clubs, ethnic conflict, and the rise of ethnic nationalism," in Albert Breton et al., eds., *Nationalism and Rationality*. Cambridge: Cambridge University Press. 71–97.

Connor, Walker. 1972. "Nation-building or nation-destroying?" in *World Politics* 24: 319–355.

Dardanelli, Paolo and Nenad Stojanovic. 2011. "The acid test? Competing theses on the nationality-democracy nexus and the case of Switzerland," in *Nations and Nationalism* 17: 357–376.

Darden, Keith. 2013. *Resisting Occupation: Mass Schooling and the Creation of Durable National Loyalties*. Cambridge: Cambridge University Press.

Darden, Keith and Harris Mylonas. 2012. "The Promethean dilemma: Third-party state-building in occupied territories," in *Ethnopolitics* 11 (1): 85–93.

Dardess, John W. 2002. *Blood and History in China: The Donglin Faction and Its Repression*. Honolulu: University of Hawai'i Press.

Davidov, Eldad. 2009. "Measurement equivalence of nationalism and constructive patriotism in the ISSP: 34 countries in a comparative perspective," in *Political Analysis* 17: 64–82.

de Capitani, François. 1986. "Beharren und Umsturz (1648–1815)," in Ulrich Im Hof et al., eds., *Geschichte der Schweiz und der Schweizer*. Basel: Helbing & Lichtenhahn. 97–175.

de Luca, Giacomo, Roland Hodler, Paul A. Raschky, and Michele Valsecchi. 2015. "Ethnic favoritism: An axiom of politics?" Center for Economic Studies & Ifo Institute Working Paper 5209.

Desmet, Klaus, Shlomo Weber, and Ignacio Rotuno-Ortin. 2010. "Linguistic diversity and redistribution," in *Journal of the European Economic Association* 7 (6): 1291–1318.

Deutsch, Karl W. 1953. *Nationalism and Social Communication: An Inquiry into the Foundations of Nationality*. Cambridge, MA: MIT Press.

———. 1966. *Nationalism and Social Communication: An Inquiry into the Foundation of Nationality*. Cambridge, MA: MIT Press.

Diamond, Jared. 1997. *Guns, Germs, and Steel: The Fates of Human Societies*. New York: Norton.

Diamond, Larry Jay. 1994. "Toward democratic consolidation," in *Journal of Democracy* 5 (3): 4–17.

———. 1995. *Promoting Democracy in the 1990s: Actors and Instruments, Issues and Imperatives.* Washington, DC: Carnegie Commission on Preventing Deadly Conflict.

Dietrich, Simone and Matthew S. Winters. 2015. "Foreign aid and government legitimacy," in *Journal of Experimental Political Science* 2: 164–171.

Dikötter, Frank. 1991. *The Construction of Racial Identities in China and Japan: Historical and Contemporary Perspectives.* Honolulu: University of Hawai'i Press.

Dobbins, James F. 2003–2004. "America's role in nation-building: From Germany to Iraq," in *Survival* 45 (4): 87–110.

Duara, Prasenjit. 1993. "De-constructing the Chinese nation," in *Australian Journal of Chinese Affairs* 30: 1–26.

du Bois, Pierre. 1983. "Mythe et realité du fossé pendant la Première Guerre mondiale," in Pierre du Bois, *Union et division des Suisses: Les relations entre Alémaniques, Romands et Tessinois aux XIXe et XXe siècles.* Lausanne: Editions de l'Aire. 65–91.

Dunning, Thad and Janhavi Nilekani. 2013. "Ethnic quotas and political mobilization: Caste, parties, and distribution in Indian village councils," in *American Political Science Review* 107 (1): 35–56.

du Toit, Pierre. 1995. *State Building and Democracy in Southern Africa: Botswana, Zimbabwe, and South Africa.* Washington, DC: USIP.

Easterly, William. 2012. "The roots of hardship: Despite massive amounts of aid, poor countries tend to stay poor. Maybe their institutions are the problem," in *Wall Street Journal*, March 24.

Easterly, William and Ross Levine. 1997. "Africa's growth tragedy: Policies and ethnic divisions," in *Quarterly Journal of Economics* 112: 1203–1250.

Elkins, Zachary and John Sides. 2007. "Can institutions build unity in multi-ethnic states?" in *American Political Science Review* 101 (4): 693–708.

Elliott, Mark. 2012. "Hushuo: The northern other and the naming of the Han Chinese," in Thomas S. Mullaney et al., eds., *Critical Han Studies: The History, Representation, and Identity of China's Majority.* Berkeley: University of California Press. 173–190.

Elman, Benjamin A. 2013. *Civil Examinations and Meritocracy in Late Imperial China.* Cambridge, MA: Harvard University Press.

Encausse, Carrère d'. 1980. *Decline of an Empire.* New York: Newsweek Books.

Englebert, Pierre. 2000. "Pre-colonial institutions, post-colonial states, and economic development in tropical Africa," in *Political Research Quarterly* 53 (1): 7–36.

Ertman, Thomas. 1997. *The Birth of the Leviathan: Building States and Regimes in Medieval and Early Modern Europe.* New York: Cambridge University Press.

———. 2000. "Liberalization, democratization, and the origins of 'pillarized' civil society in nineteenth-century Belgium and the Netherlands," in Nancy Bermeo and Philip Nord, eds., *Civil Society before Democracy: Lessons from Nineteenth-Century Europe.* Lanham, MD: Rowman & Littlefield. 155–180.

Fairbank, John King. 1987. *The Great Chinese Revolution, 1800–1985.* New York: Harper.

Fearon, James D. 1999. "Why ethnic politics and 'pork' tend to go together." Unpublished manuscript, Department of Political Science, Stanford University.

———. 2003. "Ethnic and cultural diversity by country," in *Journal of Economic Growth* 8 (2): 195–222.

Fearon, James D. and David D. Laitin. 2003. "Ethnicity, insurgency, and civil war," in *American Political Science Review* 97 (1): 1–16.

Fenske, James. 2014. "Ecology, trade, and states in pre-colonial Africa," in *Journal of the European Economic Association* 12: 612–640.

Fernandez, James W. 1966. "Folklore as an agent of nationalism," in Immanuel Wallerstein, *Social Change and the Colonial Situation*. New York: John Wiley. 585–591.

Flora, Peter, Stein Kuhnle, and Derek Urwin. 1999. *State Formation, Nation-Building and Mass Politics in Europe: The Theory of Stein Rokkan*. Oxford: Oxford University Press.

Flyvbjerg, Bent. 2006. "Five misunderstandings about case-study research," in *Qualitative Inquiry* 12 (2): 219–245.

Franck, Raphael and Ilia Rainer. 2012. "Does the leader's ethnicity matter? Ethnic favoritism, education and health in Sub-Saharan Africa," in *American Political Science Review* 106 (2): 294–325.

Fukuyama, Francis. 2004. "Nation-building 101," in *Atlantic Monthly* 293 (1): 159–162.

———. 2011. *The Origins of Political Order: From Prehuman Times to the French Revolution*. New York: Farrar, Straus and Giroux.

———. 2014. *Political Order and Political Decay: From the Industrial Revolution to the Globalization of Democracy*. New York: Farrar, Straus and Giroux.

Gadibolae, Mabunga Nlshwa. 1985. "Serfdom ('Bolata') in the Nata area, 1926–1960," in *Botswana Notes and Records* 17: 25–32.

Geertz, Clifford. 1963. "The integrative revolution: Primordial sentiments and civil politics in the new states," in Clifford Geertz, ed., *Old Societies and New States: The Quest for Modernity in Asia and Africa*. New York: Free Press. 105–157.

Gellner, Ernest. 1964. *Thought and Change*. London: Weidenfeld and Nicolson.

———. 1983. *Nations and Nationalism*. Ithaca, NY: Cornell University Press.

Gelman, Andrew and Jennifer Hill. 2006. *Data Analysis Using Regression and Multilevel/Hierarchical Models*. Cambridge: Cambridge University Press.

Gennaioli, Nicola and Ilia Rainer. 2007. "The modern impact of precolonial centralization in Africa," in *Journal of Economic Growth* 12: 185–234.

Geraci, Robert P. 2001. *Window on the East: National and Imperial Identities in Late Tsarist Russia*. Ithaca, NY: Cornell University Press.

Gerring, John and Strom Thacker. 2008. *A Centripetal Theory of Democratic Governance*. Cambridge: Cambridge University Press.

Gerring, John, Strom Thacker, Yuan Lu, and Wei Huang. 2015. "Does diversity impair human development? A multi-level test of the diversity debit hypothesis," in *World Development* 66 (2): 166–188.

Gerring, John, Dominic Zarecki, and Michael Hoffman. 2013. *Ethnic Diversity and Democracy*. Boston: Department of Political Science.

Gerring, John, Daniel Ziblatt, Johan van Gorp, and Julian Arévalo. 2011. "An institutional theory of direct and indirect rule," in *World Politics* 63 (3): 377–433.

Giesen, Berhard and Christoph Schneider, eds. 2004. *Tätertrauma: Nationale Erinnerung im öffentlichen Diskurs*. Konstanz: Konstanzer Universitätsverlag.

Glennerster, Rachel, Edward Miguel, and Alexander D. Rothenberg. 2013. "Collective action in diverse Sierra Leone communities," in *Economic Journal* 123 (568): 285–316.

Golden, Miriam and Brian Min. 2013. "Distributive politics around the world," in *Annual Review of Political Science* 16: 73–99.

Goldin, Clauda and Lawrence F. Katz. 1999. "The shaping of higher education: The formative years in the United States, 1890–1940," in *Journal of Economic Perspectives* 13: 37–62.

Goldstein, Harvey. 2003. *Multilevel Statistical Models*. London: Edward Arnold.

Good, Kenneth. 1992. "Interpreting the exceptionality of Botswana," in *Journal of Modern African Studies* 30 (1): 69–95.

Gorenburg, Dmitry. 2006. "Soviet nationalities policy and assimilation," in Blair Ruble et al., eds., *Rebounding Identities: The Politics of Identity in Russia and Ukraine*. Baltimore: Johns Hopkins University Press. 273–303.

Gould, Roger V. 1995. *Insurgent Identities: Class, Community, and Protest in Paris from 1848 to the Commune*. Chicago: University of Chicago Press.

———. 1996. "Patron-client ties, state centralization, and the Whiskey rebellion," in *American Journal of Sociology* 102 (2): 400–429.

Gould, Roger V. and Roberto M. Fernandez. 1989. "Structures of mediation: A formal approach to brokerage in transaction networks," in *Social Methodology* 19: 89–126.

Grant, Sandy. 1980. "'Reduced to almost nothing?' Chieftancy and a traditional town. The case of Linchwe II Kgafela and Mochudi," in *Botswana Notes and Records* 12: 89–100.

Grenoble, Lenore A. 2003. *Language Policy in the Soviet Union*. Dordrecht: Kluwer.

Grodeland, Ase B., William L. Miller, and Tatyana Y. Koshechkina. 2000. "The ethnic dimension to bureaucratic encounters in postcommunist Europe: Perceptions and experience," in *Nations and Nationalism* 6 (1): 43–66.

Grunder, Hans-Ulrich. 1998. "Alphabetisierung," in *Historisches Lexikon der Schweiz*. Bern: Swiss Academy of Humanities and Social Sciences.

Guo, Longsheng. 2004. "The relationship between Putonghua and Chinese dialects," in M. Zhou and H. Sun, eds., *Language Policy in the People's Republic of China: Theory and Practice since 1949*. Boston: Kluwer. 45–54.

Guy, R. Kent. 2010. *Qing Governors and Their Provinces: The Evolution of Territorial Administration in China, 1644–1796*. Seattle: University of Washington Press.

Habyarimana, James, Macartan Humphreys, Daniel N. Posner, and Jeremy M. Weinstein. 2007. "Why does ethnic diversity undermine public goods provision?" in *American Political Science Review* 101 (4): 709–725.

Hajda, L. A. and Mark Beissinger. 1990. *The Nationalities Factor in Soviet Politics and Society*. Boulder, CO: Westview.

Hale, Henry E. 2000. "The parade of sovereignties: Testing theories of secession in the Soviet setting," in *British Journal of Political Science* 30: 31–56.

———. 2013. "Explaining machine politics in Russia's regions: Economy, ethnicity, and legacy," in *Post-Soviet Affairs* 19 (3): 228–263.

Handley, Antoinette. 2017. "The origins of state capacity in Southern Africa's mining economies: Elites and institution-building in Botswana, Zambia and South Africa," in Miguel Centeno et al., eds., *States in the Developing World*. Cambridge: Cambridge University Press. 217–247.

Harries, Patrick. 1989. "Exclusion, classification and internal colonialism: The emergence of ethnicity among the Tsonga-speakers of South Africa," in Leroy Vail, ed., *The Creation of Tribalism in Southern Africa*. London: James Currey. 82–110.

Harris, Marvin. 1969. *The Rise of Anthropological Theory: A History of Theories of Culture*. London: Routledge & Kegan Paul.

Harrison, Henrietta. 2001. *China: Inventing the Nation*. London: Hodder Education.

Hartzell, Caroline and Matthew Hoddie. 2003. "Institutionalizing peace: Power sharing and post–civil war conflict management," in *American Journal of Political Science* 47 (2): 318–332.

Hechter, Michael. 2000. *Containing Nationalism*. Oxford: Oxford University Press.

Hechter, Michael and Margaret Levi. 1979. "The comparative analysis of ethnoregional movements," in *Ethnic and Racial Studies* 2 (3): 260–274.

Hendrix, Cullen S. 2010. "Measuring state capacity: Theoretical and empirical implications for the study of civil war," in *Journal of Peace Research* 47 (3): 273–285.

Herbst, Jeffrey. 2000. *States and Power in Africa: Comparative Lessons in Authority and Control*. Princeton, NJ: Princeton University Press.

Hermans, Theo, ed. 1992. *The Flemish Movement: A Documentary History (1780–1990)*. London: Athlone.

Hess, Robert. 1967. *Italian Colonialism in Somalia*. Chicago: University of Chicago Press.

Heuschling, Xavier. 1851. *Résumé du Recensement Général de la Population, de L'Agriculture et de L'Industrie de la Belgique, Exécuté á la Date du 15 Octobre 1846*. Bruxelles: Etablissement Géographique.

Hillmann, Henning. 2008. "Localism and the limits of political brokerage: Evidence from revolutionary Vermont," in *American Journal of Sociology* 114: 287–331.

Hilty, Carl. 1875. *Vorlesungen über die Politik der Eidgenossenschaft*. Bern: Max Fiala.

Hirsch, Francine. 2005. *Empire of Nations: Ethnographic Knowledge and the Making of the Soviet Union*. Ithaca, NY: Cornell University Press.

Ho, Ping-ti. 1962. *The Ladder of Success in Imperial China: Aspects of Social Mobility, 1368–1911*. New York: Columbia University Press.

Holm, John D. 1987. "Botswana: A paternalistic democracy," in *World Affairs* 150 (1): 21–30.

Holm, John D. and Patrick P. Molutsi. "State-society relations in Botswana: Beginning liberalization," *Governance and Politics in Africa* (1992): 75–96.

Hopkins, Daniel J. 2011. "The limited impacts of ethnic and racial diversity," in *American Politics Research* 39 (2): 344–379.

Horowitz, Donald L. 1985. *Ethnic Groups in Conflict*. Berkeley: University of California Press.

———. 1993. "Democracy in divided societies," in *Journal of Democracy* 4 (4): 18–38.

———. 2002. "Constitutional design: Proposals vs. process," in Andrew Reynolds, ed., *The Architecture of Democracy: Constitutional Design, Conflict Management, and Democracy*. Oxford: Oxford University Press. 15–36.

Hroch, Miroslav. 2000 (1969). *Social Preconditions of Patriotic Groups among the Smaller European Nations*. New York: Columbia University Press.

Hucker, C. 1966. *The Censorial System of Ming China*. Stanford, CA: Stanford University Press.

Humphreys, Macartan. 2005. "Natural resources, conflict, and conflict resolution: Uncovering the mechanisms," in *Journal of Conflict Resolution* 49 (4): 508–537.

Humphreys, Macartan and Alan M. Jacobs. 2015. "Mixing methods: A Bayesian approach," in *American Political Science Review* 109 (04): 653–673.

Huntington, Samuel. 1996. "Democracy for the long haul," in *Journal of Democracy* 7 (2): 3–13.

Ikegami, Eiko. 2005. *Bonds of Civility: Aesthetic Networks and the Political Origins of Japanese Culture*. Cambridge: Cambridge University Press.

Im Hof, Ulrich and Nicolai Bernard. 1983. "Les relations des communautés linguistiques au sein des associations nationales suisses avant la création de la nouvelle Confédération de 1848," in Pierre du Bois, ed., *Union et division des Suisses: Les relations entre Alémaniques, Romands et Tessinois aux XIXe et XXe siècles*. Lausanne: Editions de l'Aire. 9–24.

Im Hof, Ulrich and François de Capitani. 1983. *Die Helvetische Gesellschaft: Spätaufklärung und Vorrevolution in der Schweiz*. Frauenfeld: Huber.

Jablonski, Ryan S. 2014. "How aid targets votes: The impact of electoral incentives on foreign aid distribution," in *World Politics* 66 (2): 293–330.

Jones, David S. 1983. "Traditional authority and state administration in Botswana," in *Journal of Modern African Studies* 21 (1): 133–139.

Jones, Stephen F. 2005. *Socialism in Georgian Colors: The European Road to Social Democracy, 1883–1917*. Cambridge, MA: Harvard University Press.

Jost, Hans-Ulrich. 1986. "Bedrohung und Enge (1914–1945)," in Ulrich Im Hof et al., eds., *Geschichte der Schweiz und der Schweizer*. Basel: Helbing & Lichtenhahn. 731–748.

———. 1998. "Der helvetische Nationalismus: Nationale Identität, Patriotismus, Rassismus und Ausgrenzungen in der Schweiz des 20. Jahrhunderts," in Hans-Rudolf Wicker, ed., *Nationalismus, Multikulturalismus und Ethnizität*. Bern: Haupt. 65–78.

Kaiser, Robert J. 1994. *The Geography of Nationalism in Russia and the USSR*. Princeton, NJ: Princeton University Press.

Kappeler, Andreas. 2001. *The Russian Empire: A Multiethnic History*. London: Routledge.

Kaufmann, Chaim. 1996. "Possible and impossible solutions to ethnic civil wars," in *International Security* 20 (4): 136–175.

Kaufmann, Eric. 2015. "Land, history or modernization? Explaining ethnic fractionalization," in *Ethnic and Racial Studies* 38 (2): 193–210.

King, Gary and Margaret E. Roberts. 2014. "How robust standard errors expose methodological problems they don't fix, and what to do about it," in *Political Analysis* 23: 159–179.

Kiser, Edgar and Xiaoxi Tong. 1992. "Determinants of the amount and type of corruption in state fiscal bureaucracies: An analysis of late imperial China," in *Comparative Political Studies* 25 (3): 300–331.

Knack, Stephen and Philip Keefer. 1997. "Does social capital have an economic payoff? A cross-country investigation," in *Quarterly Journal of Economics* 112 (4): 1251–1288.

Kohn, Hans. 1944. *The Idea of Nationalism*. New York: Collier.

———. 1956. *Nationalism and Liberty: The Swiss Example*. London: Allen & Unwin.

Konrad, Kai A. and Salmai Qari. 2012. "The last refuge of a scoundrel? Patriotism and tax compliance," in *Economica* 79: 516–533.

Koter, Domonika. 2013. "King makers: Local leaders and ethnic politics in Africa," in *World Politics* 65 (2): 187–232.

Kramon, Eric and Daniel N. Posner. 2016. "Ethnic favoritism in primary education in Kenya," in *Quarterly Journal of Political Science* 11: 1–58.

Kriesi, Hanspeter. 1999. "Introduction: State formation and nation building in the Swiss case," in Hanspeter Kriesi, ed., *Nation and National Identity: The European Experience in Perspective*. Chur: Rüegger. 13–28.

Kroneberg, Clemens and Andreas Wimmer. 2012. "Struggling over the boundaries of belonging: A formal model of nation-building, ethnic closure, and populism," in *American Journal of Sociology* 118 (1): 176–230.

Kunovich, Robert M. 2009. "The sources and consequences of national identification," in *American Sociological Review* 74 (4): 573–593.

Kurzban, Robert, John Tooby, and Leda Cosmides. 2001. "Can race be erased? Coalitional computation and social categorization," in *Proceedings of the National Academy of Sciences USA* 98 (26): 15388–15392.

Kymlicka, Will. 2007. *Multicultural Odysseys: Navigating the New International Politics of Diversity*. Oxford: Oxford University Press.

Laitin, David and Said S. Samatar. 1987. *Somalia: Nation in Search of a State*. Boulder, CO: Westview.

Laitin, David. 1977. *Politics, Language, and Thought: The Somali Experience*. Chicago: University of Chicago Press.

Laitin, David and Maurits van der Veen. 2012. "Ethnicity and pork: A virtual test of causal mechanisms," in Kanchan Chandra, ed., *Constructivist Theories of Ethnic Politics*. Oxford: Oxford University Press. 277–312.

Lange, Matthew. 2005. "British colonial state legacies and development trajectories: A statistical analysis of direct and indirect rule," in Matthew Lange and Dietrich Rueschemeyer, eds., *States and Development: Historical Antecedents of Stagnation and Advance*. Basingstoke: Palgrave Macmillan. 117–140.

———. 2009. "Developmental crises: A comparative-historical analysis of state-building in colonial Botswana and Malaysia," in *Commonwealth and Comparative Politics* 47 (1): 1–27.

La Porta, Rafael, Florencio Lopez-de-Silanes, Andrei Shleifer, and Robert Vishny. 1999. "The quality of government," in *Journal of Law, Economics, and Organization* 15 (1): 222–279.

Latham, Michael E. 2000. *Modernization as Ideology: American Social Science and "Nation Building" in the Kennedy Era*. Chapel Hill: University of North Carolina Press.

LeBas, Adrienne. 2011. *From Protest to Parties: Party-Building and Democratization in Africa*. Oxford: Oxford University Press.

Leibold, James. 2012. "Searching for Han: Early twentieth-century narratives of Chinese origins and developments," in Thomas S. Mullaney et al., eds., *Critical Han Studies: The History, Representation, and Identity of China's Majority*. Berkeley: University of California Press. 210–233.

Lemarchand, René. 1964. *Political Awakening in the Congo*. Berkeley: University of California Press.

———. 1972. "Political clientelism and ethnicity in tropical Africa: Competing solidarities in nation-building," in *American Political Science Review* 66: 68–90.

Levi, Margaret. 1988. *Of Rule and Revenue*. Berkeley: University of California Press.

Levi Martin, John. 2009. *Social Structures*. Princeton, NJ: Princeton University Press.

Levine, Ari Daniel. 2011. "Public good and partisan gain: Political languages of faction in late imperial China and eighteenth-century England," in *Journal of World History* 23 (4): 841–882.

Levy, Jack S. 2008. "Case studies: Types, designs, and logics of inference," in *Conflict Management and Peace Science* 25: 1–18.

Lewis, Ioan M. 1983. *Nationalism and Self Determination in the Horn of Africa*. London: Ithaca Press.

———. 1988. *A Modern History of Somalia: Nation and State in the Horn of Africa*. Boulder, CO: Westview.

———. 1994. *Blood and Bone: The Call of Kinship in Somali Society*. Lawrenceville, NJ: Red Sea Press.

———. 1999 (1961). *A Pastoral Democracy: A Study of Pastoralism and Politics among the Northern Somali of the Horn of Africa*. Münster: LIT & James Currey.

Li, Cheng. 2005. *One Party, Two Factions: Chinese Bipartisanship in the Making?* Washington, DC: Carnegie Endowment for International Peace.

Lieberman, Evan S. 2005. "Nested analysis as a mixed-method strategy for comparative research," in *American Political Science Review* 99 (3): 435–452.

Lieberman, Evan S. and Gwyneth C. H. McClendon. 2011. "Endogenous ethnic preferences." Princeton, NJ: Department of Political Science.

Lieven, Dominic. 1981. "The Russian civil service under Nicholas II: Variations on the bureaucratic theme," in *Jahrbücher für Geschichte Osteuropas* 29 (3): 366–403.

Lijphart, Arend. 1977. *Democracy in Plural Societies: A Comparative Exploration*. New Haven, CT: Yale University Press.

———. 1994. *Electoral Systems and Party Systems: A Study of Twenty-Seven Democracies, 1945–1990*. Oxford: Oxford University Press.

———. 1999. *Patterns of Democracy: Government Forms and Performance in Thirty-Six Countries*. New Haven, CT: Yale University Press.

Lindemann, Stefan and Andreas Wimmer. 2017. "Repression and refuge: Why only some politically excluded ethnic groups rebel." Vol. 54. Göttingen: Max-Planck Institute for Religious and Ethnic Diversity.

Linz, Juan J. 1990. "The perils of presidentialism," in *Journal of Democracy* 1 (1): 51–60.

Lipset, Seymour Martin. 1960. *Political Man: The Social Bases of Politics*. Garden City, NY: Doubleday.

Loveman, Mara. 2015a. *National Colors: Racial Classification and the State in Latin America*. Oxford: Oxford University Press.

———. 2015b. "Review of *Ethnic Boundary Making: Institutions, Power, and Networks* by Andreas Wimmer," in *American Journal of Sociology* 120 (4): 1226–1229.

Loveman, Mara and Jeronimo Muniz. 2006. "How Puerto Rico became white: Boundary dynamics and inter-census racial classification," in *American Sociological Review* 72 (6): 915–939.

Maddison, Angus. 2003. *The World Economy: Historical Statistics*. Paris: OECD.

Mahoney, James. 2000. "Path dependency in historical sociology," in *Theory and Society* 29: 507–548.

———. 2010. *Colonialism and Postcolonial Development: Spanish America in Comparative Perspective*. Cambridge: Cambridge University Press.

———. 2012. "The logic of process tracing tests in the social sciences," in *Sociological Methods Research* 41 (4): 570–597.

Mahoney, James and Gary Goertz. 2004. "The possibility principle: Choosing negative cases in comparative research," in *American Political Science Review* 98 (4): 653–669.

Mahzab, Moogdho, Mohsina Atiq, and Nino Devrariani. 2013. "Comparative analysis of ethnic diversity measures on provisioning of basic public goods: Cross country assessment." Unpublished manuscript, Center for Development Economics, Williams College.

Makgala, Christian John. 2009. "History and perceptions of regionalism in Botswana, 1891–2005," in *Journal of Contemporary African Studies* 27 (2): 225–242.

Mann, Michael. 1993. *The Sources of Social Power*. Vol. 2, *The Rise of Classes and Nation States, 1760–1914*. Cambridge: Cambridge University Press.

Martin, Terry D. 2001. *An Affirmative Action Empire: Nations and Nationalism in the Soviet Union, 1923–1939*. Ithaca, NY: Cornell University Press.

Masella, Paolo. 2013. "National identity and ethnic diversity," in *Journal of Population Economics* 26: 437–454.

Maundeni, Zibani. 2002. "State culture and development in Botswana and Zimbabwe," in *Journal of Modern African Studies* 40 (1): 105–132.

Mayda, Anna Maria and Dani Rodrik. 2005. "Why are some people (and countries) more protectionist than others?" in *European Economic Review* 49 (6): 1393–1430.

Mazur, Kevin. 2015. *Ordering Violence: Identity Boundaries and Alliance Formation in the Syrian Uprising*. Princeton, NJ: Department of Politics, Princeton University.

McClendon, Gwyneth C. H. 2016. "Race and responsiveness: An experiment with South African politicians," in *Journal of Experimental Political Science* 3: 60–74.

McCullagh, P. and J. A. Nelder. 1989. *Generalized Linear Models*. London: Chapman and Hall.

McRae, Kenneth. 1983. *Conflict and Compromise in Multilingual Societies: Switzerland*. Waterloo: Wilfrid Laurier University Press.

Messerli, Alfred. 2002. *Lesen und Schreiben 1700 bis 1900*. Tübingen: Niemeyer.

Meuwly, Olivier. 2010. *Les partis politiques: Acteurs de l'histoire suisse*. Lausanne: Presses polytechniques et universitaires romandes.

Meyer, John, John Boli, George M. Thomas, and Francisco O. Ramirez. 1997. "World society and the nation-state," in *American Journal of Sociology* 103 (1): 144–181.

Meyer, John W., Francisco O. Ramirez, and Yasemin Nuhoglu Soysal. 1992. "World expansion of mass education, 1870–1980," in *Sociology of Education* 65 (2): 128–149.

Michalopoulos, Stelios. 2012. "The origins of ethnic diversity," in *American Economic Review* 102 (4): 1509–1539.

Miguel, Edward. 2004. "Tribe or nation? Nation building and public goods in Kenya versus Tanzania," in *World Politics* 56 (3): 327–362.

Miguel, Edward and Mary Kay Gugerty. 2005. "Ethnic diversity, social sanctions, and public goods in Kenya," in *Journal of Public Economics* 89 (11–12): 2325–2368.

Miller, Alexei. 2008. *The Romanov Empire and Nationalism: Essays in the Methodology of Historical Research*. Budapest: CEU Press.

Miller, David. 1995. *On Nationality*. Oxford: Oxford University Press.

Mitchell, J. Clyde. 1974. "Perceptions of ethnicity and ethnic behaviour: An empirical exploration," in Abner Cohen, ed., *Urban Ethnicity*. London: Tavistock. 1–35.

Montalvo, José G. and Marta Reynal-Querol. 2005. "Ethnic polarization, potential conflict and civil wars," in *American Economic Review* 95: 796–816.

Mozaffar, Shaheen, James R. Scarritt, and Glen Galaich. 2003. "Electoral institutions, ethnopolitical cleavages, and party systems in Africa's emerging democracies," in *American Political Science Review* 97 (3): 379–389.

Müller, Hans-Peter. 1999. *Atlas vorkolonialer Gesellschaften. Sozialstrukturen und kulturelles Erbe der Staaten Afrikas, Asiens und Melanesiens. Ein ethnologisches Kartenwerk für 95 Länder mit Texten, Datenbanken und Dokumentationen auf CD-ROM*. Berlin: Reimer.

Müller-Peters, Anke. 1998. "The significance of national pride and national identity to the attitude toward the single European currency: A Europe-wide comparison," in *Journal of Economic Psychology* 19 (6): 701–719.

Mummendey, Amelie and Michael Wenzel. 2007. "Social discrimination and tolerance in ingroup relations: Reactions to inter-group difference," in *Personality and Social Psychology Review* 3 (2): 158–174.

Murphy, Alexander. 1988. *The Regional Dynamics of Language Differentiation in Belgium: A Study in Cultural-Political Geography*. Chicago: University of Chicago Press.

Murray, Andrew and Neil Parsons. 1990. "The modern economic history of Botswana," in Zbigniew A. Konczacki et al., eds., *Studies in the Economic History of Southern Africa*. London: Frank Cass. 159–199.

Mylonas, Harris. 2012. *The Politics of Nation-Building: Making Co-nationals, Refugees, and Minorities*. Cambridge: Cambridge University Press.

Nathan, Noah L. 2016. "Local ethnic geography, expectations of favoritism, and voting in Urban Ghana," in *Comparative Political Studies* 49 (14): 1896–1929.

North, Douglass C., John Joseph Wallace, and Barry R. Weingast. 2009. *Violence and Social Orders: A Conceptual Framework for Interpreting Human History*. New York: Cambridge University Press.

North, Robert C. 1952. *Kuomintang and Chinese Communist Elites*. Stanford, CA: Stanford University Press.

Nunn, Nathan. 2008. "The long-term effects of Africa's slave trades," in *Quarterly Journal of Economics* 123 (1): 139–176.

Nyati-Ramahobo, Lydia. 2002. "Ethnic identity and nationhood in Botswana," in Isaac N. Mazonde, ed., *Identities in the Millennium: Perspectives from Botswana*. Gaborone: Lightbooks. 17–28.

———. 2006. "Language policy, cultural rights and the law in Botswana," in Martin Pütz et al., eds., *Along the Routes to Power: Explorations of Empowerment through Language*. Berlin: Mouton de Gruyter. 285–304.

Nye, John V. C., Ilia Rainer, and Thomas Stratmann. 2014. "Do black mayors improve black relative to white employment outcomes? Evidence from large US cities," in *Journal of Law, Economics, and Organization* 31 (2): 383–430.

Olson, Mancur. 1965. *The Logic of Collective Action: Public Goods and the Theory of Groups*. Cambridge, MA: Harvard University Press.

Olsson, Ola. 2007. "On the institutional legacy of mercantilist and imperialist colonialism." University of Göteborg Working Paper in Economics 247.

Osafo-Kwaako, Philip and James A. Robinson. 2013. "Political centralization in pre-colonial Africa," in *Journal of Comparative Economics* 41: 6–21.

Osler Hampson, Fen and David Mendeloff. 2007. "Intervention and the nation-building debate," in Chester A. Crocker et al., eds., *Leashing the Dogs of War: Conflict Management in a Divided World*. Washington, DC: USIP Press. 679–700.

Parson, Jack. 1981. "Cattle, class and the state in rural Botswana," in *Journal of Southern African Studies* 7 (2): 236–255.

Parsons, Neil. 1985. "The evolution of modern Botswana: Historical revisions," in Louis Picard, ed., *The Evolution of Modern Botswana*. London: Rex Collings. 26–40.

Peel, John D. Y. 1989. "The cultural work of Yoruba ethnogenesis," in Elizabeth Tonkin et al., eds., *History and Ethnicity*. London: Routledge & Kegan Paul. 964–982.

Perrie, Maureen. 1972. "The social composition and structure of the socialist-revolutionary party before 1917," in *Soviet Studies* 24 (2): 223–250.

Petersen, Roger D. 2002. *Understanding Ethnic Violence: Fear, Hatred, and Resentment in Twentieth-Century Eastern Europe*. Cambridge: Cambridge University Press.

Pevehouse, Jon C., Timothy Nordstrom, and Kevin Warnke. 2004. "The COW-2 International Organizations dataset version 2.0," in *Conflict Management and Peace Science* 21 (2): 101–119.

Pierson, Paul. 2003. "Big, slow-moving, and . . . invisible: Macrosocial processes in the study of comparative politics," in James Mahoney and Dietrich Rueschemeyer, eds., *Comparative Historical Analysis in the Social Sciences*. Cambridge: Cambridge University Press. 177–207.

Pipes, Richard. 1997. *The Formation of the Soviet Union: Communism and Nationalism, 1917–1923*. Cambridge, MA: Harvard University Press.

Pirenne, Henri. 1902. *Histoire de Belgique*. Vol. 6. Brussels: Lamertin.

Polachek, James. 1991. *The Inner Opium War*. Cambridge, MA: Harvard East Asian Monographs.

Polasky, Janet. 1981. "Liberalism and biculturalism," in Arend Lijphart, ed., *Conflict and Coexistence in Belgium: The Dynamics of a Culturally Divided Society*. Berkeley: University of California Press. 34–45.

Poterba, James M. 1997. "Demographic structure and the political economy of public education," in *Journal of Policy Analysis and Management* 16 (1): 48–66.

Pratto, Felicia, Jim Sidanius, and Shana Levin. 2006. "Social dominance theory and the dynamics of intergroup relations: Taking stock and looking forward," in *European Review of Social Psychology* 17: 271–320.

Putnam, Robert. 2007. "E pluribus unum: Diversity and community in the twenty-first century," in *Scandinavian Political Studies* 30 (2): 137–174.

Putterman, Louis. 2006. *Agricultural Transition Year Country Data Set*. Providence: Department of Economics, Brown University.

Putterman, Louis and David N. Weil. 2010. "Post-1500 population flows and the long-run determinants of economic growth and inequality," in *Quarterly Journal of Economics* 125: 1627–1682.

Qari, S., K. A. Konrad, and B. Geys. 2012. "Patriotism, taxation and international mobility," in *Public Choice* 151: 695–717.

Rae, Douglas W. and Michael Taylor. 1970. *The Analysis of Political Cleavages*. New Haven, CT: Yale University Press.

Ragin, Charles. 1989. *The Comparative Method: Moving beyond Qualitative and Quantitative Strategies*. Berkeley: University of California Press.

Ranger, Terence. 1966. "Traditional authorities and the rise of modern politics in Southern Rhodesia, 1898–1930," in Eric Stokes and Richard Brown, eds., *The Zambesian Past: Studies in Central African History*. Manchester: University of Manchester Press. 94–136.

Rasler, Karen and William R. Thompson. ND. "War making and the building of state capacity: Expanding the bivariate relationship." Bloomington: Indiana University.

Read, James H. and Ian Shapiro. 2014. "Transforming power relationships: Leadership, risk, and hope," in *American Political Science Review* 108 (1): 40–53.

Regan, Patrick and David Clark. 2011. *Institutions and Elections Project*. Binghamton, NY: Department of Political Science.

Reilly, Benjamin. 2006. *Democracy and Diversity: Political Engineering in the Asia-Pacific*. Oxford: Oxford University Press.

Reis, Jaime. 2005. "Economic growth, human capital formation and consumption in Western Europe before 1800," in Robert C. Allen et al., eds., *Living Standards in the Past*. Oxford: Oxford University Press. 195–225.

Rigby, T. H. 1972. "The Soviet Politburo: A comparative profile, 1951–71," in *Soviet Studies* 24 (1): 3–23.

Robinson, Amanda Lea. 2014. "National versus ethnic identification in Africa: Modernization, colonial legacy, and the origins of territorial nationalism," in *World Politics* 66 (4): 709–746.

Robinson, James A. and Q. Neil Parsons. 2006. "State formation and governance in Botswana," in *Journal of African Economies* 15 (1): 100–140.

Rodrik, Dani. 1999. "Where did all the growth go? External shocks, social conflict, and growth collapses," in *Journal of Economic Growth* 4 (4): 385–412.

Rodrik, Dani, Arvind Subramanian, and Francesco Trebbi. 2004. "Institutions rule: The primacy of institutions over geography and integration in economic development," in *Journal of Economic Growth* 9: 131–165.

Roeder, Philip G. 2001. "Ethnolinguistic Fractionalization (ELF) Indices, 1961 and 1985." http//:weber.ucsd.edu\~proeder\elf.htm.

———. 2005. "Power dividing as an alternative to ethnic power sharing," in Philip G. Roeder and Donald Rothchild, eds., *Sustainable Peace: Power and Democracy after Civil War*. Ithaca, NY: Cornell University Press. 51–82.

———. 2007. *Where Nation-States Come From: Institutional Change in the Age of Nationalism*. Princeton, NJ: Princeton University Press.

Roessler, Philip G. 2011. "The enemy from within: Personal rule, coups, and civil wars in Africa," in *World Politics* 63 (2): 300–346.

Rohsenow, J. S. 2004. "Fifty years of script and written language reform in the P.R.C.," in M. Zhou and H. Sun, eds., *Language Policy in the People's Republic of China: Theory and Practice since 1949*. Boston: Kluwer. 21–43.

Ross, Michael. 2012. *The Oil Curse: How Petroleum Wealth Shapes the Development of Nations*. Princeton, NJ: Princeton University Press.

Rothchild, Donald. 1986. "Hegemonial exchange: An alternative model for managing conflict in Middle Africa," in Dennis Thompson and Dov Ronen, eds., *Ethnicity, Politics, and Development*. Boulder, CO: Lynne Rienner. 65–104.

Rothchild, Donald and Philip G. Roeder. 2005. "Power sharing as an impediment to peace and democracy," in Philip G. Roeder and Donald Rothchild, eds., *Sustainable Peace: Power and Democracy after Civil Wars*. Ithaca, NY: Cornell University Press. 29–50.

Ruffieux, Roland. 1986. "Die Schweiz des Freisinns (1848–1914)," in Ulrich Im Hof et al., eds., *Geschichte der Schweiz und der Schweizer*. Basel: Helbing & Lichtenhahn. 639–730.

Sachs, Jeffrey D. 2003. "Institutions don't rule: Direct effects of geography on per capita income." NBER Working Paper 9490.

Sacks, Audrey. 2012. *Can Donors and Non-state Actors Undermine Citizens' Legitimating Beliefs*. Washington, DC: World Bank.

Saideman, Stephen M., David J. Lanoue, Michael Campenni, and Samuel Stanton. 2002. "Democratization, political institutions, and ethnic conflict: A pooled time-series analysis, 1985–1998," in *Comparative Political Studies* 35 (1): 103–129.

Sala-i-Martin, Xavier, Gernot Doppelhoffer, and Ronald I. Miller. 2004. "Determinants of long-term growth: A Bayesian averaging of classical estimates (BACE) approach," in *American Economic Review* 94 (4): 813–835.

Samatar, Abdi Ismail. 1999. *An African Miracle: State and Class Leadership and Colonial Legacy in Botswana Development*. Portsmouth: Heinemann.

Sambanis, Nicholas. 2000. "Partition as a solution to ethnic war: An empirical critique of the theoretical literature," in *World Politics* 52: 437–483.

Sambanis, Nicholas and Jonah Schulhofer-Wohl. 2009. "What's in a line? Is partition a solution to civil war?" in *International Security* 34 (2): 82–118.

Sambanis, Nicholas and Moses Shayo. 2013. "Social identification and ethnic conflict," in *American Political Science Review* 107: 294–325.

Sambanis, Nicholas, Stergios Skaperdas, and William Wohlforth. 2015. "Nation-building through war: Military victory and social identification after the Franco-Prussian war," in *American Political Science Review* 109 (2): 279–296.

Scarritt, James R. and Shaheen Mozaffar. 1999. "The specification of ethnic cleavages and ethnopolitical groups for the analysis of democratic competition in contemporary Africa," in *Nationalism and Ethnic Politics* 5 (1): 82–117.

Schapera, Isaac. 1938. *A Handbook of Tswana Law and Custom: Compiled for the Bechuanaland Protectorate Administration*. Oxford: Oxford University Press.

———. 1952. *The Ethnic Composition of Tswana Tribes*. London: London School of Economics and Political Science.

Schapiro, Leonard. 1961. "The role of Jews in the Russian revolutionary movement," in *Slavonic and East European Review* 40 (94): 148–167.

Schofer, Evan and Wesley Longhofer. 2011. "The structural sources of association," in *American Journal of Sociology* 117 (2): 539–585.

Schryver, Reginald de. 1981. "The Belgian revolution and the emergence of Belgium's biculturalism," in Arend Lijphart, ed., *Conflict and Coexistence in Belgium: The Dynamics of a Culturally Divided Society*. Berkeley: University of California Press. 13–33.

Scott, James C. 1972. "Patron-client politics and politician change in Southeast Asia," in *American Political Science Review* 66 (1): 91–113.

Seawright, Jason and John Gerring. 2008. "Case selection techniques in case study research," in *Political Research Quarterly* 61 (2): 294–308.

Selolwane, Onalenna Doo. 2004. *Ethnic Structure, Inequality and Governance of the Public Sector in Botswana*. Geneva: UNRISD Project on Ethnic Structure, Inequality and Governance in the Public Sector

Selway, Joel Sawat. 2010. "Cross-cuttingness, cleavage structures and civil war onset." *British Journal of Political Science* 41: 111–138.

Senghaas, Dieter. 1982. *Von Europa lernen: Entwicklungsgeschichtliche Betrachtungen*. Frankfurt: Suhrkamp.

Sewell, William H. 1996. "Three temporalities: Toward an eventful sociology," in Terence J. McDonald, ed., *The Historic Turn in the Human Sciences*. Ann Arbor: University of Michigan Press. 245–280.

Shachar, Ayelet. 2009. *The Birthright Lottery: Citizenship and Global Inequality*. Cambridge, MA: Harvard University Press.

Shayo, Moses. 2009. "A model of social identity with an application to political economy: Nation, class and redistribution," in *American Political Science Review* 103: 147–174.

Shils, Edward. 1972. "The integration of society," in Edward Shils, *The Constitution of Society*. Chicago: University of Chicago Press. 3–52.

Sidanius, Jim and Felicia Pratto. 1999. *Social Dominance: An Intergroup Theory of Social Hierarchy and Oppression*. Cambridge: Cambridge University Press.

Siegenthaler, Hansjörg. 1993. "Supranationalität, Nationalismus und regionale Autonomie: Erfahrungen des schweizerischen Bundesstaates—Perspektiven der Europäischen Gemeinschaft," in Heinrich August Winkler and Hartmut Kaelble, *Nationalismus–Nationalitäten–Supranationalität*. Stuttgart: Klett-Cotta. 309–333.

Simons, Gary F. and M. Paul Lewis. 2013. "The world's languages in crisis: A 20-year update," in Elena Mihas et al., eds., *Responses to Language Endangerment: In Honor of Mickey Noonan*. Amsterdam: John Benjamins. 3–19.

Singh, Prerna. 2015. *How Solidarity Works for Welfare: Subnationalism and Social Development in India*. Cambridge: Cambridge University Press.

Siu, Helen. 1993. "Cultural identity and the politics of difference in South China," in *Daedalus* 122: 19–28.

Slater, Daniel. 2010. *Ordering Power: Contentious Politics and Authoritarian Leviathans in Southeast Asia*. Cambridge: Cambridge University Press.

Smith, Anthony D. 1986. *The Ethnic Origins of Nations*. Oxford: Blackwell.

———. 1996. "Culture, community and territory: The politics of ethnicity and nationalism," in *International Affairs* 72 (3): 445–458.

———. 1998. *Nationalism and Modernism: A Critical Survey of Recent Theories of Nations and Nationalism*. London: Routledge & Kegan Paul.

Smith, Jackie and Dawn West. 2012. *Transnational Social Movement Organization Dataset, 1953–2003*. Ann Arbor, MI: Inter-university Consortium for Political and Social Research.

Smith, Jeremy. 2013. *Red Nations: The Nationalities Experience in and after the USSR*. Cambridge: Cambridge University Press.

Smith, Tom W. and Seokho Kim. 2006. "National pride in comparative perspective: 1995/6 and 2003/4," in *International Journal of Public Opinion Research* 19 (1): 127–136.

Soroka, Stuart, Richard Johnston, and Keith Banting. 2007. "Ethnicity, social capital, and the welfare state," in Fiona Kay and Richard Johnston, eds., *Diversity, Social Capital and the Welfare State*. Vancouver: University of British Columbia Press. 95–132.

Staerklé, Christian, Jim Sidanius, Eva G. T. Green, and Ludwin E. Molina. 2010. "Ethnic minority-majority asymmetry in national attitudes around the world: A multilevel analysis," in *Political Psychology* 31 (4): 491–519.

Stinchcombe, Arthur L. 1968. *Constructing Social Theories*. Thousand Oaks, CA: Pine Forge.

Stojanovic, Nenad. 2003. "Swiss nation-state and its patriotism: A critique of Will Kymlicka's account of multination states," in *Polis* 11: 45–94.

Subrahmanyam, Sanjay. 1997. "Connected histories: Notes towards a reconfiguration of early modern Eurasia," in *Modern Asian Studies* 31 (3): 735–762.

Subtelny, Orest. 2009. *Ukraine: A History*. 4th ed. Toronto: University of Toronto Press.

Tajfel, Henri. 1981. *Human Groups and Social Categories: Studies in the Social Psychology*. Cambridge: Cambridge University Press.

Tamir, Yael. 1995. *Liberal Nationalism*. Princeton, NJ: Princeton University Press.

Taylor, Ian. 2002. "Botswana's 'developmental state' and the politics of legitimacy." Paper given at the Towards a New Political Economy of Development conference, University of Sheffield, July 4–6.

Tefft, S. K. 1999. "Perspectives on panethnogenesis: The case of the Montagnards," in *Sociological Spectrum* 19 (4): 387–400.

Thelen, Kathleen and James Mahoney. 2015. "Comparative-historical analysis in contemporary political science," in James Mahoney and Kathleen Thelen, eds., *Advances in Comparative-Historical Analysis*. Cambridge: Cambridge University Press. 3–38.

Tilly, Charles. 1975. "Western state-making and theories of political transformation," in Charles Tilly, ed., *The Formation of National States in Western Europe*. Princeton, NJ: Princeton University Press. 601–638.

———. 1990. *Coercion, Capital and European States: AD 990–1990*. Oxford: Blackwell.

———. 2000. "Processes and mechanisms of democratization," in *Sociological Theory* 18 (1): 1–16.

———. 2005. *Trust and Rule*. Cambridge: Cambridge University Press.

———. 2006. *Identities, Boundaries, and Social Ties*. Boulder, CO: Paradigm Press.

Tordoff, William. 1988. "Local administration in Botswana," in *Public Administration and Development* 8: 183–202.

Trounstine, Jessica. ND. "One for you, two for me: Support for public goods investment in diverse communities." Unpublished manuscript, University of California, Merced.

UNESCO. 1957. *World Illiteracy at Mid-century: A Statistical Study*. Paris: UNESCO.

Van Evera, Stephen. 1997. *Guide to Methods for Students of Political Science*. Ithaca, NY: Cornell University Press.

Varshney, Ashutosh. 2003. *Ethnic Conflict and Civil Life*. New Haven, CT: Yale University Press.

Vigdor, Jacob L. 2004. "Community composition and collective action: Analyzing initial mail response to the 2000 census," in *Review of Economics and Statistics* 86 (1): 303–312.

Vogt, Manuel. 2016. "Colonialism, elite networks, and the origins of ethnic power sharing in multiethnic states." Unpublished manuscript, ETH Zurich.

Vries, C. W. de and J. de Vries. 1949. *Texts Concerning Early Labour Legislation I (1791–1848)*. Leiden: Brill.

Vu, Tuong. 2009. "Studying the state through state formation," in *World Politics* 62 (1): 148–175.

Wagner, Ulrich, Julia C. Becker, Oliver Christ, Thomas F. Pettigrew, and Peter Schmidt. 2012. "A longitudinal test of the relation between German nationalism, patriotism, and outgroup derogation," in *European Sociological Review* 28 (3): 319–332.

Wakeman, Frederic. 1972. "The price of autonomy: Intellectuals in Ming and Ch'ing politics," in *Daedalus* 101 (2): 35–70.

Wang, Yuan-kang. 2001. "Toward a synthesis of the theories of peripheral nationalism: A comparative study of China's Xinjiang and Guangdong," in *Asian Ethnicity* 2 (2): 177–195.

Weber, Eugen. 1979. *Peasants into Frenchmen: The Modernisation of Rural France, 1870–1914*. London: Chatto and Windus.

Weber, Max. 1968 (1922). *Economy and Society: An Outline of Interpretive Sociology*. New York: Bedminster Press.

Wei, Shang. 2015. "Writing and speech: Rethinking the issue of vernaculars in early modern China," in Benjamin A. Elman, ed., *Rethinking East Asian Languages, Vernaculars, and Literacies, 1000–1919*. Leiden: Brill. 254–301.

Weilenmann, Hermann. 1925. *Die vielsprachige Schweiz: Eine Lösung des Nationalitätenproblems*. Basel: Im Rhein-Verlag.

Wenzel, Michael, Amelie Mummendey, and Sven Waldzus. 2007. "Superordinate identities and intergroup conflict: The ingroup projection model," in *European Review of Social Psychology* 18: 331–372.

Werbner, Richard. 2002. "Cosmopolitan ethnicity, entrepreneurship and the nation: Minority elites in Botswana," in *Journal of Southern African Studies* 28 (4): 731–753.

———. 2004. *Reasonable Radicals and Citizenship in Botswana: The Public Anthropology of Kalanga Elites*. Bloomington: Indiana University Press.

Willerton, John P. 1992. *Patronage and Politics in the USSR*. Cambridge: Cambridge University Press.

Wilmsen, Edwin N. 2002. "Mutable identities: Moving beyond ethnicity in Botswana," in *Journal of Southern African Studies* 28 (4): 825–841.

Wimmer, Andreas. 1995. *Transformationen. Sozialer Wandel im indianischen Mittelamerika*. Berlin: Reimer.

Wimmer, Andreas. 2002. *Nationalist Exclusion and Ethnic Conflicts: Shadows of Modernity*. Cambridge: Cambridge University Press.

Wimmer, Andreas. 2008. "The making and unmaking of ethnic boundaries: A multi-level process theory," in *American Journal of Sociology* 113 (4): 970–1022.

Wimmer, Andreas. 2011. "A Swiss anomaly? A relational account of national boundary making," in *Nations and Nationalism* 17 (4): 718–737.

———. 2013. *Waves of War: Nationalism, State-Formation, and Ethnic Exclusion in the Modern World*. Cambridge: Cambridge University Press.

———. 2014. *Ethnic Boundary Making: Institutions, Networks, Power*. New York: Oxford University Press.

———. 2015. "Race centrism: A critique and a research agenda," in *Ethnic and Racial Studies* 38 (13): 2186–2205.

Wimmer, Andreas, Lars-Erik Cederman, and Brian Min. 2009. "Ethnic politics and armed conflict: A configurational analysis of a new global dataset," in *American Sociological Review* 74 (2): 316–337.

Wimmer, Andreas and Yuval Feinstein. 2010. "The rise of the nation-state across the world, 1816 to 2001," in *American Sociological Review* 75 (5): 764–790.

Wimmer, Andreas and Nina Glick Schiller. 2002. "Methodological nationalism and beyond: Nation state formation, migration and the social sciences," in *Global Networks* 2 (4): 301–334.

Wimmer, Andreas and Brian Min. 2006. "From empire to nation-state: Explaining wars in the modern world, 1816–2001," in *American Sociological Review* 71 (6): 867–897.

———. 2009. "The location and purpose of wars around the world: A new global dataset, 1816–2001," in *International Interactions* 35 (4): 390–417.

Wimmer, Andreas and Conrad Schetter. 2003. "Putting state-formation first: Some recommendations for reconstruction and peace-making in Afghanistan," in *Journal of International Development* 15: 1–15.

Winant, Howard. 2001. *The World Is a Ghetto: Race and Democracy since World War II*. London: Basic Books.

Witte, Els, Jan Craeybeckx, and Alain Meynen. 2009. *The Political History of Belgium from 1830 Onwards*. Brussels: Academic & Scientific Publishers.

Wolf, Eric. 1982. *Europe and the People without History*. Berkeley: University of California Press.

Woodberry, Robert D. 2012. "The missionary roots of liberal democracy," in *American Political Science Review* 106 (2): 244–274.

Woocher, Lawrence. 2009. *Preventing Violent Conflict: Assessing Progress, Meeting Challenges*. Washington, DC: United States Institute of Peace.

Xigui, Qiu. 2000. *Chinese Writing*. Berkeley: Chinese Popular Culture Project.

Young, Crawford. 1965. *Politics in the Congo: Decolonization and Independence*. Princeton, NJ: Princeton University Press.

———. 1994. *The African Colonial State in Comparative Perspective*. New Haven, CT: Yale University Press.

Zimmer, Oliver. 2003. *A Contested Nation: History, Memory and Nationalism in Switzerland, 1761–1891*. Cambridge: Cambridge University Press.

INDEX

NOTE: Page numbers followed by *f* indicate a figure. Those followed by a *t* indicate a table.

A NOTE ON THE TYPE

This book has been composed in Adobe Text and Gotham.
Adobe Text, designed by Robert Slimbach for Adobe,
bridges the gap between fifteenth- and sixteenth-century
calligraphic and eighteenth-century Modern styles.
Gotham, inspired by New York street signs, was designed
by Tobias Frere-Jones for Hoefler & Co.